"Imagine a book that seeks to rehabilitate theology's tenuous connection to the church's worship, mission and discipleship. Put the idea into the hands (and heart) of a master theologian who is an artist, playwright and vision-caster operating in the interface of Scriptural canon and shifting culture. The result is the picture/play book you are about to enjoy. Imagine (no) more!"

Gregg R. Allison, Southern Baptist Theological Seminary

"Vanhoozer has a reputation for unveiling the big picture for us, but here he devotes his considerable critical powers to a series of small ones. For fans of his earlier work, there are characteristic delights and a few surprises—not least the interspersed sermons that answer the question, 'Yes, but will it preach?' Vanhoozer's playfulness, recursions, puns and layered allusions all pay off exceptionally well in these miniature studies. And readers who have heard that Vanhoozer's theology deserves attention but have wondered where to begin studying are well advised to start with these rich and accessible essays."

Fred Sanders, Torrey Honors Institute, Biola University

"Kevin Vanhoozer writes of the church's worship and wisdom with enormous discernment and love. Deeply revealing and fascinating!"

Cornelius Plantinga Jr., author of *Reading for Preaching*

"I have always loved *Pictures at an Exhibition*, both the music and the art, and now that Vanhoozer has structured his theology book according to its promenade and galleries, I will remember his descriptions and clarifications that much better. He is a meticulous explainer, so his work in this book is very unambiguous as he reckons with many issues such as the role of a pastor in interpreting a text, the affective relation of doctrine and worship, and debates about cognitive enhancement. Then there is the added presentation of his artistic sermons. Don't miss this display!"

Marva J. Dawn, theologian, author, speaker

Pictures at a

THEOLOGICAL
EXHIBITION

Scenes of the Church's Worship,
Witness and Wisdom

KEVIN J. VANHOOZER

IVP Academic

An imprint of InterVarsity Press
Downers Grove, Illinois

InterVarsity Press
P.O. Box 1400, Downers Grove, IL 60515-1426
ivpress.com
email@ivpress.com

InterVarsity Press® is the book-publishing division of InterVarsity Christian Fellowship/USA®, a movement of
students and faculty active on campus at hundreds of universities, colleges and schools of nursing in the United
States of America, and a member movement of the International Fellowship of Evangelical Students. For
information about local and regional activities, visit intervarsity.org.

Scripture quotations, unless otherwise noted, are from The Holy Bible, English Standard Version, copyright © 2001
by Crossway Bibles, a division of Good News Publishers. Used by permission. All rights reserved.

Cover design: Cindy Kiple
Interior design: Beth McGill
Images: art gallery: archideaphoto/iStockphoto
     baptism: hept27/iStockphoto
     choir singing: Deposit Photos/Glow Images
     church service: Christopher Futcher/iStockphoto
     Cripplegate church: A service in Old Cripplegate Church, English School, private collection/Bridgeman Images
     group worship: Deposit Photos/Glow Images
     Martin Luther preaching: Martin Luther preaching, German School, Private Collection / The Stapleton
       Collection / Bridgeman Images
     Martin-Scholfield Choris: Martin-Scholfield Choir, Lake County Discovery Museum /UIG / Bridgeman Images
     old Catholic church: Deposit Photos/Glow Images
     worship concert: dvan/iStockphoto

ISBN 978-0-8308-3959-9 (print)
ISBN 978-0-8308-9379-9 (digital)

Printed in the United States of America ∞

Library of Congress Cataloging-in-Publication Data

Names: Vanhoozer, Kevin J., author.
Title: Pictures at a theological exhibition : scenes of the church's worship,
   witness, and wisdom / Kevin J. Vanhoozer.
Description: Downers Grove : InterVarsity Press, 2016. | Includes index.
Identifiers: LCCN 2015050916 (print) | LCCN 2016001992 (ebook) | ISBN
   9780830839599 (pbk. : alk. paper) | ISBN 9780830893799 (eBook)
Subjects: LCSH: Church. | Public worship. | Theology.
Classification: LCC BV600.3 .V35 2016 (print) | LCC BV600.3 (ebook) | DDC
   230--dc23
LC record available at http://lccn.loc.gov/2015050916

P	23	22	21	20	19	18	17	16	15	14	13	12	11	10	9	8	7	6	5	4	3	2	1
Y	35	34	33	32	31	30	29	28	27	26	25	24	23	22	21	20	19	18	17	16			

To my faculty colleagues at

Trinity Evangelical Divinity School

CONTENTS

PREFACE

Theology exists to serve the church. Its vocation is to help people think, imagine and understand how all areas of life relate to the God of the gospel made known in the Scriptures. Theology ministers understanding by setting forth the biblically attested meaning of the words and deeds of the triune God, inviting all those with eyes and ears to understand to participate in what the Father, Son and Spirit are doing in the world to make all things new. Theology thus helps disciples fulfill their vocation to be "little Christs": saints who know how to embody the mind of Christ everywhere, at all times and to everyone.

Theology exists to serve the church, but the sobering reality is that many churches are not particularly inclined to accept theology's help. Indeed, some churches avoid all deliberation about doctrine like the plague. After all, doctrine divides, and in any case who is in a position to know which doctrinal position is correct? These churches would rather keep the conversation going than arrive at a conclusion. At the other end of the spectrum are churches in which the doctrinal watchword is not *relative* but *absolute*. The challenge here is to relate frozen doctrinal formulations to a changing cultural climate. The way forward is to cultivate minds and hearts characterized not only by evangelical fidelity but also by convictional civility, hermeneutical humility and Christian charity.

Despite both its skeptical detractors and its too-certain supporters, theology at its best is the worshipful, witnessing and wise art and science of faithful understanding, and its sole purpose is to edify the church's worship, witness and wisdom. Theology's special remit is to love the truth of Jesus Christ with mind, heart, soul and strength in order to make straight the way of life in Christ. The chief way that theologians respond to their mandate is to reflect on what God has said and done provisionally in the history of Israel and definitively in the history of Jesus Christ. Theology, then, is an exercise in creative fidelity (or faithful creativity), where new ways of articulating understanding are accountable both to the magisterial authority of prior canonical texts and to the ministerial authority of catholic interpretive traditions.

In a previous collection of essays, *First Theology* (also published by Inter-Varsity Press), I attempted to navigate my way through the postmodern challenges confronting the academy, especially in the humanities. The humanities share with biblical studies and theology an interest in hermeneutics: how to understand textual meaning and interpretation. The various chapters of *First Theology* represented my best efforts to explain how God, Scripture and hermeneutics—in their humanity and divinity—come together in the pattern of theological authority and comprise a three-stranded prolegomenal cord. This collection is different (I had to resist the urge to title it *Second Theology*). The focus here is not on theories of interpretation debated in the academy but on the practice of biblical interpretation that makes up the life of the church. Each of the essays (only three of which have been previously published) begins with a real-life issue on the borderlands of church, society and academy and then searches for understanding—a way for the community of faith to live this understanding out. With the exception of the introduction, chapter 5 and chapter 11, all these essays were originally delivered orally, and though I have revised them (and added footnotes), I have tried to preserve their less formal tone.

In this book I attempt to "stand in the breach" (Ezek 22:30) between theology and the life of the church, theory and practice, knowledge and obedience—not simply to occupy space but to fill it by creating connections. The overall concern is to rehabilitate a biblically invigorated imagination as a means and mode of doing theology—or rather, as a key to healing the breach between knowing, feeling and doing as well as the distance between Scripture and the church's contemporary situation. When captive to Christ, the imagination is the capacity to envision all of reality as related to God the Father in the Son through the Spirit. And to the extent that the vision of a God-so-loved-world orients all of life, it is a capacity that is as practical as it is theological.

We can go further. If what disciplines the imagination is first and foremost verbal rather than visual, then we can say that theological imagination is a mode of faith, a way of believing *without* seeing (Jn 20:29) and, as such, comes not from fanciful speculation but rather from the hearing of the biblical word (Rom 10:17). Having said that, this book is not primarily a theoretical reflection on the nature of imagination. There are some theoretical reflections (and some attempts at definition), but ultimately the vision must be caught, not simply taught. To that end, many of the chapters show the biblically grounded, theologically formed evangelical imagination at work, exhibited in concrete scenes of Christian life, where contemporary culture confronts the church with new problems and opportunities.

Theological understanding of the Bible involves learning to think not simply about but *along* the biblical texts, making sense not only of various propositions but also of the various scenes—the things that happen or are said—that comprise the drama of redemption and give those propositions their sense. This imaginative theological appropriation of Scripture encourages church members to indwell these texts in new contexts: the story of Israel and the early church is our story too. The truth that doctrine spells out also demands to be done: to be staged in city gates and suburban tracts by actors who embody the meaning of the divine play. This too is evangelism, and discipleship. Theology exists to preserve the integrity of the church's worship, witness and wisdom alike.

This book can be read in three ways. The essays in this collection are, first and foremost, portraits of the theologian at ministerial work. The pictures in the three galleries tend to be close-ups rather than landscapes: studies of particular pastoral scenes rather than grand theoretical systems. As I explain in my introductory comments to each chapter, most of these essays began as oral presentations to various Christian groups in England, Scotland and North America. Some are formal academic lectures, some are informal addresses and five are sermons. Together, they serve as examples of theology on the ground: small-scale snapshots of one theologian trying to minister understanding, vignettes of how to think about and, more importantly, *do* theology in a way that brings Christian doctrine to bear on specific situations and particular problems. Divided they may have originally stood, but united they display not so much a finished systematic theology as examples of what we could call *applied systematics*.

The book is, second, a sidelong glance at my attempt to rehabilitate doctrine for the church: a life and research project of *theodramatic systematics*. For some time now people have asked me to provide a more convenient account—by which they mean less than five hundred pages, with practical illustrations—of my approach to theology. This book partially responds to that request by focusing on particular "scenes" (i.e., the approach in action) rather than redoing the large-scale landscape picture I have painted elsewhere.[1]

Third, one may read this book as a sustained, though largely indirect, plea for incorporating the *imagination* into the work of theology as *sapiential systematics*. Indeed, it is best viewed as an exercise in vision-casting, a prolonged attempt to change the current picture of what it means to be biblical, which has held modern theologians and churches captive for too long. The culprit in question is the picture of theology as a system of doctrines that demand to be thought and professed but not necessarily embodied and practiced. Those who view theology in these terms sentence it to an abstract absoluteness that fails to connect with the rough and tumble of the church's twenty-first century life. By way of contrast, I have tried to soften the dichotomy between belief and behavior, dogmatics and moral theology, by working a kind of paradigm revolution.

In particular, I have sought to reorient theology away from the model of theoretical knowledge toward one of practical wisdom. Doctrine is vital for the church's health (*salus*) precisely because the understanding that faith gets from doctrine is eminently practical. In particular, I argue that we need to recover a biblically rooted, theologically formed imagination for the sake of the church's worship, witness and wisdom. If this picture of theology as a function of analytic reason has indeed held the evangelical church captive, then this book, inasmuch as it highlights the imagination as a cognitive capacity, can be seen as an exercise in "evangelical liberation theology." To be sure, analytic reason has its place in theological method, but it is strictly second place. The biblical pictures that generate and govern theological

---

[1]Most notably, in *The Drama of Doctrine: A Canonical-Linguistic Approach to Christian Theology* (Louisville, KY: Westminster John Knox, 2005) and *Faith Speaking Understanding: Performing the Drama of Doctrine* (Louisville, KY: Westminster John Knox, 2014).

understanding must be clarified, not discarded. We need both the clarity of crisp concepts and the intricacy of lush metaphors in order to get sound, life-giving doctrine.[2]

As a final prefatory image, it may help to think of this book as a playbook for understanding, a guidebook for helping pastors run plays. The point is to get doctrine into the lives of people, individuals and communities, and onto the field of contemporary culture, not least by waking the sleeping giant, the evangelical imagination, thereby giving long-dormant church bodies the Word-and-Spirit kiss of life.

I dedicate this book to my faculty colleagues at Trinity Evangelical Divinity School in the year of its Jubilee—2014 marked the fiftieth anniversary of the school's relocation to Deerfield and restart under Kenneth Kantzer. These essays trespass on the territory of—or, to state it more positively, *integrate*—several academic departments in the seminary, and for that reason will doubtless occasion the usual disciplinary discontent. Done in the right spirit, though, criticism too counts as a means of edification and even ministry, especially when it leads to greater understanding, either of oneself or of God. I am therefore grateful to my TEDS colleagues for some twenty years of partnership in higher theological education, that all-important work of training pastor-theologians who can rightly handle the word of truth and thus minister evangelical understanding to everyone, everywhere, at all times.

---

[2]Elsewhere I advocate a "theological arc" that moves from naïve to illumined understanding of the Bible, with conceptual analysis as a necessary middle stage. See my "Love's Wisdom: The Authority of Scripture's Form and Content for Faith's Understanding and Theological Judgment," *Journal of Reformed Theology* 5 (2011): 247-75.

ACKNOWLEDGMENTS

The author and publisher gratefully acknowledge permission to reprint the following material:

"Worship at the Well: From Dogmatics to Doxology (and Back Again)," *Trinity Journal* 23 (Spring 2002): 3-16.

"Praising God in Song: Beauty and the Arts," in Stanley Hauerwas and Sam Wells, eds., *The Blackwell Companion to Christian Ethics* (Oxford: Blackwell, 2004), 110-22.

"Enhancement in the Cathedral: Wisdom from Theology," in John Kilner, ed., *Why the Church Needs Bioethics: A Guide to Wise Engagement with Life's Challenges* (Grand Rapids: Zondervan, 2011), 105-24.

THE DISCARDED IMAGINATION

Metaphors by Which a Holy Nation Lives

A picture held us captive.
And we could not get outside it.

LUDWIG WITTGENSTEIN

THE CAPTIVE EVANGELICAL IMAGINATION

Most Christians living in the Western world in the twenty-first century would probably resist the idea that they are being held captive by a picture. Pictures don't hold us in their power; we hold them, in our gaze. In context, Wittgenstein's oft-cited statement is referring to a conception of language that had held him and other modern philosophers in its power; namely, the idea that the meaning of a word is the fact to which it refers. Wittgenstein calls this the "picture theory" of language. He devoted most of his later philosophy to the task of dismantling this notion, suggesting instead that people do many things with words besides picturing states of affairs.

Several theologians, including evangelicals, took up Wittgenstein's cause, believing that it had important implications for the way we understand biblical authority. A modern picture of how language works, they argued, may have distorted our appreciation of the Bible. I jumped on that bandwagon too, claiming that God is doing many things in the Bible besides representing states of affairs—promising, commanding and consoling, to name a few. This book moves in a different, though related direction, arguing that "we"—by which I mean contemporary evangelicals—may be captive to a (modern) picture of the imagination as a factory for producing images of things that are not there, rather than a cognitive faculty for conceiving what we cannot see, despite having physical eyes (Mk 8:18).

The following statement is a typical expression of this modern prejudice: "There is an imagination; it is a faculty or a power; specifically it is a faculty for internal representations; these representations are image-like; therefore they share a certain character with external images; in particular, like material images, they represent absent objects as present; they do so by means of resemblance."[1] The imagination is reliable, then, when it creates mental representations of the things we experience with our senses. Representing things that are absent, however, or perhaps never were there, sounds suspiciously like lying. And this is what many philosophers have concluded: the imagination is not to be trusted because the images it manufactures do not correspond to the facts. This is comparable to Plato banishing poets from his Republic. Creative writing has nothing to offer when it comes to contemplating the Good, Plato thought, because its images are far removed from what is most real.[2] By way of contrast, Jesus came proclaiming the kingdom of God poetically, with metaphorical narratives (parables).

Of the making of images there is no end—especially today. Human beings are inveterate image-mongers, quick to produce (and then admire) representations of things in a variety of media, from sand (think castles) to celluloid to computer-generated imagery. The French sociologist Jacques Ellul, a Protestant, worries that the visual has virtually eclipsed the verbal in contemporary society, so much so that he can speak of (and title his book) *The Humiliation of the Word*.[3] Indeed, Ellul even speaks of the church being invaded by images, more evidence of the devaluation of the written and proclaimed Word. The problem, he believes, is that the image cannot bear the weight of glory: images are limited to representing the material world, and cannot penetrate beyond the surface of reality to the meaning at its depths. A society (or church) fixated on images will thus be unable to get a fix on truth.

---

[1]Eva T. H. Brann, *The World of the Imagination: Sum and Substance* (Lanham, MD: Rowman & Littlefield Publishers, 1991), 5.
[2]Plato, *The Republic*, Book X.
[3]Jacques Ellul, *The Humiliation of the Word* (Grand Rapids: Eerdmans, 1985).

Furthermore, certain segments of the church have succumbed to cultural conditioning. Pictures of success disseminated by business schools and television shows have not trickled but flooded into our collective unconscious. The use of technology to promote efficiency and growth has led to what George Ritzer calls the "McDonaldization" of society (and, we might add, the church), where one can find the same praise choruses serving up the same religious experience to seeker-sensitive consumer-worshipers from one end of the country to the other.[4] Another sociologist, Christian Smith, has discovered that America's teenagers profess a theology—"Moralistic Therapeutic Deism"—that affirms the existence of a God who wants everyone to be nice and to feel happy (and who thus bears a suspicious resemblance to Oprah Winfrey).[5] All this plays right into the hands of so-called "masters of suspicion" like Freud and Feuerbach, who argue that God is simply a projection of what humans most value.[6]

This concern over projections has led large swaths of evangelicals, on the other hand, to condemn all imaginings—including novels—as vain, if not idolatrous.[7] After all, the Ten Commandments prohibit making images of God. The etymology of the term does not help either. The Latin *imaginatio* means "the making of images" and the Greek equivalent, *phantasie*, conjures up pictures of dungeons and dragons: the realm of fantasy, not reality. The King James Version only reinforces the prejudice: though there is no Hebrew or Greek term for imagination, the English term is used pejoratively in passages like Genesis 6:5: "And God saw that the wickedness of man was great in the earth, and that every imagination of the thoughts of his heart was only evil continually" (KJV). This may also have something to do with why so many evangelical Christians have no time for reading fiction. Shouldn't we be thinking about "whatever is true" (Phil 4:8) instead of things that never existed? Isn't the has-been (history) more important than the might-be (poetry)?

It is precisely this picture of the imagination as a purveyor of false images that holds us captive. Yet, ironically, this picture of the imagination is itself a

---

[4]George Ritzer, *The McDonaldization of Society* (Thousand Oaks, CA: Pine Forge Press, 2000).
[5]Christian Smith, *Soul Searching: The Religious and Spiritual Lives of American Teenagers* (Oxford: Oxford University Press, 2005).
[6]See esp. Ludwig Feuerbach, *The Essence of Christianity*, trans. George Eliot (Buffalo, NY: Prometheus Books, 1989).
[7]See Barton Swaim, "Novel Ideas," *Touchstone* (November/December 2009): 13-14.

false image, or at best a half truth. The irony has a tragic edge: though the church has a low view of the imagination as a theological resource, many Christians are suffering from malnourished imaginations, captive to culturally conditioned pictures of the good life. It is difficult in the extreme to connect these pictures of the good life with biblical pictures of discipleship. A further difficulty is that many Christians want to live for God's glory but have trouble relating what they read in Scripture and hear in church to everyday life. We want to believe the Bible—we do believe it, and we are prepared to defend doctrinal truth—but we find ourselves unable to see our world in biblical terms. There is a fatal disconnect between the world we live in and the world of the biblical text that we confess as truth. In sum, we too often do not know what authentic Christian discipleship should look like in the present situation. The story of Israel and the early church seems all too remote from our lives in the post/industrial West. Modern or postmodern, we are all orphans in the fog, unable to establish meaningful connections between our belief system and our daily behavior, our faith and our life. If faith's influence is waning, then it is largely because of a failure of the evangelical imagination to connect the biblical and cultural dots. It is simply not clear how the biblical story of what God has done and is doing in Christ relates to the modern world of climate change, stock market fluctuations and mass immigration. These are the hard realities that demand our attention and keep us humble.

It was not always so. Contrast imagination-starved post/moderns with their premodern medieval forbears. Today's universities are so focused on teaching marketable skills and training students for careers that there is little room in the curriculum to discuss big questions pertaining to the meaning of life. This stands in sharp contrast to C. S. Lewis's description of the medieval situation, in which everyone shared a worldview that was as wide as it was deep: "We see how everything links up with everything else; at one, not in flat equality, but in a hierarchical ladder."[8] In his book *The Discarded Image*, Lewis describes the medieval model of the universe as "essentially bookish" and "systematic." These are precisely the features of the evangelical imagination that this book is trying to recover, inasmuch as the evangelical imagination, as we shall see, is both "bookish" (i.e., biblical) and "systematic"

---

[8]C. S. Lewis, *The Discarded Image: An Introduction to Medieval and Renaissance Literature* (Cambridge: Cambridge University Press, 1964), 12.

(i.e., comprehensive) in its persistent effort to view every particular person, thing and event in light of the "big evangelical picture," namely, God in Christ reconciling the world to himself (2 Cor 5:19).[9]

For many denizens of the modern era, however, the "world" is something solely natural. The pre-Socratic philosophers invented the idea of Nature as a way of thinking about the great variety of phenomena under heaven. According to Lewis, however, the medieval poets believed that Nature was not everything, but was God's creature: "It is precisely this limitation and subordination of Nature which sets her free for her triumphant poetical career."[10] It is precisely because Nature did not need to carry the weight of providing the ultimate context for meaning that that she acquires meaningfulness herself. On the medieval model, to look up is to look in, toward the heavens, the source of the divine being in which earthly things participate and the place where the music of the spheres is crystal clear and the light of God shines brightest. By way of contrast, modern men and women feel that they are looking out when they look up at the sky, away from themselves and their true home.

My concern is not to commend the medieval model of the universe as superior in every respect to modern astronomy, but rather to call attention to the power of models to hold thought captive, as well as to exhort us to search for a model that is as comprehensive and satisfying for our age as the medieval model was for theirs. The prevailing model at present is arguably Darwinian in spirit, a story of complexity progressively emerging from chaos over vast periods of time.[11] What Richard Dawkins terms "Darwin's big idea" is that all forms of life—human and nonhuman, individual and social—may ultimately be explained in terms of genes adapting over time in ways that better guarantee their survival. On this model, "higher" properties like love and rationality emerge from lower ones.[12] The Darwinian picture may be nearly as comprehensive as the medieval, but it is nowhere

---

[9] Another way of describing the "big evangelical picture" would be to speak of "the biblical meta-narrative" or, simply and succinctly, what is "in Christ."

[10] Lewis, *The Discarded Image*, 39.

[11] See, for example, Arthur Peacocke, *A Naturalistic Faith for the Twenty-First Century* (Minneapolis: Fortress, 2009) and Philip Clayton, *Mind and Emergence: From Quantum to Consciousness* (Oxford: Oxford University Press, 2006).

[12] On the theme of "emergence" in science and religion, see Philip D. Clayton, *Adventures in the Spirit: God, World, Divine Action* (Minneapolis: Fortress, 2008), part two.

near as satisfying or as conducive to answering the question of life's meaning. Those who subscribe to it are in danger of losing the means to specify what, if anything, is distinct to humanity, and thus to becoming what Lewis called "men without chests" (i.e., hearts).[13]

What we lack in the physicist's or biologist's account of complexity emerging from chaos is a satisfactory account of *fittingness*. The glory of the medieval world picture was the underlying conviction that there was a place before God for everything and that everything glorified God in its proper place. Moreover, every particular thing had *meaning* because it fit into something larger and greater than itself. What premoderns had but post/moderns lack is precisely this sense of belonging, where each particular thing comes into its own precisely through its relationship to God. It was for this reason, Lewis notes, that medieval poets, unlike their post/modern counterparts, did not have to use language for the purpose of socially constructing reality.[14] There was no need to create meaning or to invent exciting new features for things; it was enough to bear witness to the richness already inherent in them. One need not gloss God's good creation if it is already suffused with his glory. Medieval poets did not want to be "original," but simply to do justice to the subject matter itself. Why make up new stories, Lewis asks, "when the world teems with so many noble deeds, wholesome examples, pitiful tragedies, stranger adventures, and merry jests which have never yet been set forth quite so well as they deserve?"[15]

A picture of the poetic imagination springing from individual genius holds moderns captive. We tend to concentrate on the poet, her experiences and her creativity. Moderns looking for meaning celebrate the poet's imaginative constructions. Modern evangelicals are more likely to denounce these same creations as empty images. Yet both are captive to the modern idea of the imagination as the faculty for creating pictures. The medieval view is altogether different: what is central in poetry is not the poet's experience, creativity or genius but the thing to which the poem points. Modern worshipers of personality celebrate the poet, but in the medieval model the poets are merely ministers of the things—real presences—that truly matter.

---

[13]C. S. Lewis, *The Abolition of Man* (New York: Macmillan, 1947), 34.
[14]Lewis, *The Discarded Image*, 202-15.
[15]Ibid., 211.

THE EVANGELICAL IMAGINATION SET FREE: REFRESHING THE "EYES OF THE HEART"

God is real, and the gospel is an account of what really happened in history, in and to Jesus Christ. Christian theology is but a noisy gong or clanging cymbal if it does not speak of reality—of *what is* "in Christ." Is it possible, however, for the imagination to minister reality? As with all trick questions, we had better first define our terms.

By "reality" I mean those things that exist independently of our speaking and thinking about them: all those things that have the potential to make a difference to our existence, those things upon which we ultimately rely, not only in our efforts to survive physically but also in our quest for human flourishing—the pursuit of truth, goodness and beauty. Today, however, like immunity in the reality television show *Survivor*, reality is "up for grabs." One of the purposes of this book, therefore, is to expand and enrich our understanding of reality, in part by retrieving an earlier, Christian understanding. I believe this is a pressing need, for at present even professing Christians find themselves in imaginative thrall to the power of modern cultural and Darwinian pictures of the "real" world. To be sure, these pictures may have an element of the truth. Yet, insofar as they purport to tell the whole truth, they invariably fall prey to reductionism—the temptation to be like God, all-knowing (Gen 3:5). For example, the prevailing naturalist picture (that reality is ultimately physical) explains away the things in which we used to believe by translating them into materialist terms: love is nothing but biochemistry; altruism is nothing but a genetic trick for prolonging the life of species rather than individuals; God is nothing but the projection of the corporate will to power (Nietzsche). This is a demythologized, detheologized and disenchanted view of the world, where reality is always matter but never meaning.

How can the imagination help? What is the imagination? Like music, one is hard pressed to define the imagination in words. This book is not a theoretical monograph on the nature of the imagination, but an attempt both to *say* and *show* why and how the imagination matters for theology, and for the life of the church. I am more concerned with the practice—the church's faithful use—than the theory of imagination. Nevertheless, the cause of understanding is seldom served without at least some provisional definitions, and these will be provided in due course in subsequent chapters. At present the following four points will have to suffice.

First, the imagination is not merely a faculty for making pictures but, more importantly, a faculty for making or discovering connections and meaningful forms. Analytic reason takes things apart; the synthetic imagination puts things together. The imagination with which this book is concerned is not irrational but a mode of rationality. Specifically, it is the cognitive capacity—an ability of the mind—that enables us to synthesize disparate things. Think of the imagination as a "formative" power: the ability to create or perceive meaningful wholes and coherent forms (including, as we shall see, *literary* forms). The imagination is thus a vital aid in discerning fittingness—the way parts "belong to" a whole. Without the synthesizing work of the imagination, we would not be able to discover complex patterns. We need the imagination in order to perceive meaningfulness. In particular, the church needs a biblically informed imagination in order to perceive how, in the fullness of time, all things have been "gathered up" into Christ (Eph 1:10, NRSV).

Second, the imagination is not merely cognitive. It engages the mind, will and emotions alike. It is therefore an integrative faculty that addresses human beings in their entirety. It is precisely for this reason that some posit a connection between the imagination and what the Bible calls the "heart" (*lēb* in Hebrew). That pictures take us captive is part of the rationale behind Proverbs 4:23: "Keep your heart with all vigilance, for from it flow the springs of life." 1 Chronicles 29:18 speaks of the "thoughts" of the heart, and the apostle Paul speaks of "having the eyes of your hearts enlightened" (Eph 1:18). As a pictorial representation of our cardiovascular system, Paul's phrase is hardly adequate. Yet is there a better way to speak of the new vision that accompanies the renewing of one's inner being upon conversion? The Bible regularly speaks of the heart as the locus of volition, emotion and belief or unbelief (Ps 14:1).[16] The phrase "eyes of the heart" eloquently communicates the way beliefs, desires, thoughts and feelings work together to define our humanity.[17]

---

[16]So George Caird: "In biblical terminology the *heart* is not the seat of the emotions, but stands for the whole inner self, without any tripartite division of will, intellect, and feelings" (*Paul's Letters from Prison* [Oxford: Oxford University Press, 1976], 45).

[17]For an extended discussion of this claim, see Alison Searle, *"The Eyes of Your Heart": Literary and Theological Trajectories of Imagining Biblically* (Milton Keynes and Colorado Springs: Paternoster,

James K. A. Smith makes a similar connection between the heart and our humanity, arguing that the primary purpose of Christian education is not informing the mind but transforming the imagination and forming good habits. "Because our hearts are oriented primarily by desire, by what we love, and because those desires are shaped and molded by the habit-forming practices in which we participate, it is the ritual and practices of the mall—the liturgies of mall and market—that shape our imaginations and how we orient ourselves to the world."[18] What Smith calls "liturgies" are those everyday habits that shape our character and desires. Smith believes that Christian education has put too much stock in belief-centered worldviews rather than the constellation of practices and routines "that inculcates a particular vision of the good life by inscribing or infusing that vision into the heart . . . by means of material, embodied practices."[19]

While Smith has clearly identified an important issue (the education of desire), his account trades on too sharp a dichotomy between thinking and desiring. As we have seen, the Bible has no qualms about speaking of the "thoughts [Greek *dianoia*] of the heart" (Lk 1:51; cf. Heb 4:12). While I agree with Smith that we need to recover the imagination for the sake of forming disciples, and while he and I both prioritize the importance of embodied actors and actions (i.e., practices), I am less willing to distinguish thinking from imagining so sharply, or to prioritize the latter over the former.[20] Although I agree that "what we love is a specific vision of the good life, an implicit picture of what we think human flourishing looks like," I think this picture, like the imagination itself, is fundamentally cognitive, not noncognitive, as Smith maintains.[21]

This brings us to my third preliminary point. If I continue to insist that the imagination is not less than cognitive, it is primarily because the imagi-

---

2008), 33-40 and Garrett Green, *Imagining God: Theology and the Religious Imagination* (Grand Rapids: Eerdmans, 1989), 108-13.

[18]James K. A. Smith, *Desiring the Kingdom: Worship, Worldview, and Cultural Formation* (Grand Rapids: Baker, 2009), 25.

[19]Ibid., 26.

[20]See Smith's incipient philosophical anthropology in part one of his book, which defines human beings as "desiring, imaginative animals." Ibid., 60.

[21]See, for example, ibid., 52-53. I shall return to this point below in my discussion of the "social imaginary." Nothing less than biblical authority as it relates to the life of the church is at stake in my debate with Smith over the cognitive status of the imagination.

nation is as *verbal* as it is visual.[22] Indeed, it is precisely the picture of the imagination as primarily visual—a picture-making faculty—that has held us captive. On the contrary: in the beginning of the imagination is the *word*, not the image. Christians of all people should be able to affirm this. Genesis depicts God's creativity in terms of his Word that brings things into existence—including the human creatures whose special remit is to *image* God. Furthermore, the most gripping images in Scripture for imagining theological realities are made of words. Jesus' parables, to cite but one example, teach us what "the kingdom of God is like" (Mt 13:31) by telling stories.[23]

Perhaps it is not necessary to decide whether words or pictures are more central in imagining. Suffice it to say that in its verbal dimension imagination involves much more than painting word-pictures. It is not simply that the Bible uses figures of speech. The literary forms of biblical discourse themselves are essential to their communicative function. The biblical texts do not simply convey information to fill the head or use images to warm the heart. Rather, they display in manifold ways the world as suffused by the presence and activity of the triune God, and they invite us to live into it. Scripture communicates the reality of God not simply by informing us what God has done, but also by enabling us to perceive the world in ways that transcend our empirical senses by inviting us to grasp in diverse ways the meaningful whole summed up "in Christ." For this crucial task, words—the imagination in its verbal aspect—are essential. "Faith comes from hearing" (Rom 10:17).[24] Theology can be defined as the attempt to imagine God's imaginings after him.

Finally, the imagination is a way of looking at things together, a *seeing as* in the mind's (and heart's) eye. As such, it is an essential ingredient in theology's vocation: to seek faith's understanding. To understand is to grasp how things fit together, and faith is the conviction of how things not seen (Heb

---

[22]By "cognitive" I simply mean what pertains to mental rather than bodily action. In the words of Alan R. White: "To imagine something is to *think of* it as possibly being so" (*The Language of Imagination* [Oxford: Basil Blackwell, 1990], 184; emphasis original).

[23]Jesus' parables are "metaphoric narratives," that is, metaphors writ large or extended. See Paul Ricoeur, "Biblical Hermeneutics," *Semeia* 4 (1975): 29-148 and Nicholas Perrin, *Jesus and the Language of the Kingdom: Symbol and Metaphor in New Testament Interpretation* (Minneapolis: Fortress, 1976). We will return to metaphor below.

[24]For further development of this point, see my *The Drama of Doctrine: A Canonical-Linguistic Approach to Christian Theology* (Louisville, KY: Westminster John Knox, 2005), 278-81 and my "Love's Wisdom: The Authority of Scripture's Form and Content for Faith's Understanding and Theological Judgment," *Journal of Reformed Theology* 5 (2011): 247-75.

11:1) fit together in Christ. Faith is unable to form the conception, much less the conviction, of these things not seen apart from the imagination: "Seeing so-and-so *as* such-and-such combines seeing and thinking."[25] Augustine speaks of the "eyes of faith," which comes close to what I mean by the believing imagination.[26] Theology is faith imagining, seeing everything that was, is and is to come as related to what God the Father has done in his Son through the Spirit. Faith is the enduring ability to imagine God, the world and ourselves in the light of the biblical story of salvation. Hence my key claims: (1) Only the imagination—the ability to grasp meaningful patterns or conceive unified wholes out of apparently unrelated elements—enables us to "see" God and the kingdom of God at work in the world. (2) It is faith that enables this imagination—and faith comes by *hearing*, and hearing from the word of Christ (Rom 10:17).

It is Word, biblical discourse, that sets the evangelical imagination free to see, judge and act in faith: to inhabit the world as created and redeemed, made through and for Christ (Col 1:16). Scripture forms the imagination of the disciples, which enables them both to see and inhabit the world as the place where Jesus came and will come again. Though we did not directly perceive the resurrection, we can think about and come to know the risen Christ. *The evangelical imagination is the word-and-Spirit means of dwelling in the world, understood not merely as nature but also as grace.* If there is no grace, then our faith is futile and death is the last word. But grace is real, and tangibly so: the incarnate Jesus was "full of grace and truth" (Jn 1:14) and the resurrected Jesus was no apparition: "See my hands and my feet, that it is I myself. Touch me, and see. For a spirit does not have flesh and bones as you see that I have" (Lk 24:39).

The evangelical imagination is not a flight of fancy but a freedom under the discipline and authority of the biblical Word. All other imaginings of human possibilities ultimately prove vain: fanciful, futile and foolish. The evangelical imagination alone opens up the real possibility of living in a way that corresponds to reality—to what was in the beginning, is now and ever shall be "in Christ."

---

[25]White, *The Language of Imagination*, 190 (emphasis mine).

[26]Augustine, *The City of God*, trans. Henry Bettenson (New York: Penguin Books, 1984), 14, 563, 725.

METAPHORS BY WHICH A HOLY NATION LIVES:
MUSSORGSKY'S PICTURES AND THE CHRISTIAN WALK

Among figures of speech, metaphors are the prime exhibit of the imagination's verbal dimension, and the Bible is replete with them.[27] Metaphor has traditionally been thought of as "deviant" naming, where words are "carried beyond" (Greek *meta* "beyond" + *phero* "to bear") their normal (literal) meanings (e.g., "forgive us our linguistic trespasses"). Philosophers habitually dismissed metaphor as a mere ornament of discourse, a noncognitive decoration expendable with no loss of meaning. That was then. Thanks to the work of a number of thinkers from the mid-1970s onwards, we have now come to see just how indispensable metaphor is: "Metaphor is not simply an ornamental aspect of language, but a fundamental scheme by which people conceptualize the world and their own activities."[28]

Metaphors help us to explain the unfamiliar in terms of the familiar and, as such, are important tools in scientific theorizing and theology alike. To say "chess is war" is to think about the game of chess in terms drawn from another realm of experience altogether. One approaches the game differently when the governing metaphor is *war* rather than, say, *picnic*. Our thinking about everyday life employs metaphors too. Imagine what a difference it would make to approach each day with the thought, "Life is war." According to George Lakoff and Mark Johnson, we all live by such governing metaphors: they structure what we do and how we do it.[29] They also orient our passions.

Consider Shakespeare's Romeo, who describes his beloved standing at a window by saying "Juliet is the sun."[30] No competent interpreter thinks that Romeo is calling Juliet a combustible ball of gas (of which ninety percent is hydrogen) that produces 400 septillion trillion watts of power. On the other hand, Romeo is not simply frothing at the mouth: he is saying something about someone in some way. In particular, he is seeing Juliet as the sun. He

---

[27]See, for example, J. Ellsworth Kalas, *The Parables of Paul: The Master of the Metaphor* (Nashville, TN: Abingdon, 2015) and Ian Paul, "Metaphor," in Kevin J. Vanhoozer, ed., *Dictionary for Theological Interpretation of the Bible* (Grand Rapids: Baker, 2005), 507-10.

[28]Raymond W. Gibbs Jr., "Metaphor and Thought: The State of the Art," in Raymond W. Gibbs Jr., ed., *The Cambridge Handbook of Metaphor and Thought* (Cambridge: Cambridge University Press, 2008), 3.

[29]See George Lakoff and Mark Johnson, *Metaphors We Live By* (Chicago: University of Chicago Press, 1980).

[30]Shakespeare, *Romeo and Juliet*, act 2, scene 2.

is applying certain concepts associated with the sun to say something about Juliet. This is metaphorical speaking: to use concepts from one source (domain) to describe something else (the target domain). Romeo's metaphorical description—his verbal picture, if you will—commits him, and us, "to a *way of thinking of* Juliet."[31] This is a crucial point, especially for theologians who have to speak of God without creating physical images. A metaphor like "The Lord is my shepherd" is a verbal picture that displays, in words, what it is talking about.

Jesus taught in parables because he wanted to display the kingdom of God in words. The parables are extended metaphors: images "thrown together" (Greek *parabolē*) or imaginatively associated in a short story. Not "Life is war" but "The kingdom of God is the Good Samaritan's loving action towards a hapless victim" (Lk 10:30-37). According to Richard Hays, New Testament ethics is a matter of having one's moral vision and judgment formed or instructed by just such imaginative stories, of "discerning analogies between our world and the world of the New Testament writers."[32] Being biblical necessarily involves engaging in "metaphor-making, placing our community's life imaginatively within the world articulated by the texts."[33] Hays goes so far as to suggest that a local church is not simply a living "letter" but a living *metaphor* for Christ, "written not with ink but with the Spirit of the living God, not on tablets of stone but on tablets of human hearts" (2 Cor 3:3). This is only fitting, for as there are multiple metaphors in the New Testament for the church, so the contemporary church is itself a moving picture or parable of the kingdom of God.

Metaphors with staying power, such as the church as "the body of Christ" (1 Cor 12:27), become models that structure our experience and allow us to achieve coherence. It follows that metaphors and other products of the verbal imagination perform a key function in facilitating understanding, that grasp of the whole and of our place in it.[34] The search for meaning in life is closely connected to the search for metaphors to live by. Metaphors are the raw material of the visions we live by.

---

[31]Josef Stern, *Metaphor in Context* (Cambridge, MA: MIT Press, 2000), 282; emphasis original.
[32]Richard B. Hays, *The Moral Vision of the New Testament: A Contemporary Introduction to New Testament Ethics* (San Francisco: Harper, 1996), 298.
[33]Ibid., 299.
[34]Lakoff and Johnson conclude their book with a chapter on understanding.

Like any other community, the church needs metaphors to live by. "Where there is no vision, the people perish" (Prov 29:18, KJV). Many of the pictures people have of the present-day church are less than flattering. Some think of it as a monolithic, corrupt institution that exists only to sustain itself—an image unfortunately encouraged by televangelists who prey without ceasing, always earning but never helping others come to the knowledge of the truth. On the other end of the spectrum are those who want to reinvent the church, including some who are claiming its newfound "emergence." Sociologists have noted a trend toward postdenominational and even postcongregational (i.e., churchless) Christianity. If there is a contemporary picture, it is a confusing one, raising the question: What is the church, and what is it for? We need to return to the New Testament and let its images for the church continue to nourish our imaginations.[35] With this thought we arrive at the heart of the current project: a consideration of theological pictures of the church, especially the biblical metaphor of the church as "holy nation" (1 Pet 2:9).

The title of this book is a grappling hook that imaginatively associates these essays with Modest Mussorgsky's famous 1874 composition *Pictures at an Exhibition*, a suite in ten movements originally composed for the piano but made popular by Maurice Ravel's orchestration. What does a nineteenth-century musical composition have to do with a collection of theological essays on the church? Let me count the ways.

We begin, however, with a bit of background. Mussorgsky was a friend of the artist and architect Viktor Hartmann, with whom he shared a passion for the cause of a distinctly Russian art. After Hartmann died suddenly at the age of thirty-nine, his friends organized an exhibition of over four hundred of his works in tribute. This inspired Mussorgsky to make his own tribute: he composed *Pictures at an Exhibition* in a scant six weeks. In it, Mussorgsky creates a musical version of ten of Hartmann's artworks, "drawing" in sound selected scenes from Hartmann's travels and observations of everyday Russian life: children playing, women gossiping, a few landscapes. The celebrated "Promenade" movement, with its melody that recalls Russian folk songs, represents the viewer as he or she walks through

---

[35]See Paul S. Minear, *Images of the Church in the New Testament* (Louisville, KY: Westminster John Knox, 2005).

the exhibit from one picture to the next, creating a narrative structure that unifies the work as a whole.

Music historians and musicologists have written entire books on Mussorgsky's unique composition:

> There is no other instrumental work like this one with its social messages from nineteenth-century Russia, its saturation in folk music and culture, and its innovative harmonic language. . . . These little pieces do not simply turn Hartmann's illustrations and designs into music, they bring them to life, creating little scenes out of them which, in turn, may carry messages about Russian culture and society.[36]

Mussorgsky was blazing a new trail, moving away from the form of the sonata toward the expression of more personal and nationalist concerns, as he makes clear in a letter: "I feel a certain regeneration; everything Russian seems suddenly near to me."[37] Mussorgsky belonged to that group of intellectuals in the mid-nineteenth century that resisted the "westernization" of Russian culture.[38]

The way the essays of this book parallel Mussorgsky's composition should now be clear. The church, as a "holy nation," should also resist westernization to the extent that it conflicts with the culture, as it were, of the kingdom of God. As Mussorgsky's rendering of Hartmann's pictures aided the cause of Russian national culture, so pictures of the people of God (ordinary Christian "folk") in the biblical exhibition are there to edify the church, not least by depicting scenes from the life of a holy nation. We who comprise the church need to remember where we have come from, who we are and where we are going. The Bible compares the Christian life to a walk: we are all pilgrim communities "on the way." Interestingly, the "Promenade" theme linking one picture/movement to another becomes smaller and smaller as Mussorgsky's piece progresses, thereby displaying, in Mussorgsky's words, how the viewer/listener "has been drawn into the pictures."[39]

---

[36]Michael Russ, *Mussorgsky: Pictures at an Exhibition* (Cambridge: Cambridge University Press, 1992), ix-x.

[37]Letter dated 1859, cited in ibid., 7.

[38]Mussorgsky was also a proponent of "programme" music over against "absolute" music. He believed that music did not exist in a pure form for itself but rather to communicate the truth and feel of life. The Bible does this too, communicating the truth and feel of *new life* in Christ. He was also Populist, and he wrote music against the Nihilists "who simply saw man as a product of biology without a spiritual nature" Russ Mussorgsky, 8).

[39]Ibid., 34.

Likewise, the purpose of these essays is to aid Christians in their own promenade as they seek to walk with other disciples, living by inspired metaphors that draw the people of God into the pictures of the biblical exhibition of the grace and truth of God made flesh in Jesus Christ.

SCENES OF CONGREGATIONAL LIFE: THE ECCLESIAL IMAGINARY

Every summer for several years First Presbyterian Church of Libertyville, Illinois has staged an annual display called the "Living Bible." It is always a noteworthy event, involving hundreds of church members, costumes, even livestock. The idea is to stage twelve key scenes from the Bible in chronological order to create a three-dimensional tableau of salvation history that wraps around the church building. Because it is a family show, Adam and Eve wear flesh-colored leotards. By common consent, the most powerful scene is the one that occupies center-stage, on the church's front porch. Seated at a long table are thirteen men, all dressed in robes or tunics, talking animatedly. Then, as if by an invisible cue, they suddenly freeze, creating a striking replica of Leonardo da Vinci's "The Last Supper," an effect that often takes away the audience's collective breath.

Impressive as it is, this is not the kind of picture I am concerned with in this book. The "Living Bible" is a wonderful evangelistic community event, but dressing up like Jesus' apostles is not the best way to train disciples. Being biblical requires more than replicating the past. Theology's search for understanding necessitates more than recreating static copies of biblical persons and events. The pictures I am concerned with in the present context are moving pictures—not still life but action scenes, pictures of people on the move, doing things, embodying the mind of Christ, enacting faith, hope and love.

To understand Christian faith is to grasp not only what happened in the past but also where we are in world history and what we are to do vis-à-vis the kingdom of God. To understand is to know what to say and do in order to go on following Jesus Christ in new contexts. Theology exists to train disciples to walk Christianly in the twenty-first century. My working hypothesis in this book is that we will receive guidance and greater understanding by letting biblical pictures, metaphors and dramatic scenes discipline (i.e., disciple) our imagination. In this regard, George Eliot's *Scenes of Clerical Life* is most instructive.

As a nineteen-year-old evangelical, George Eliot (Marian Evans) wrote a letter expressing her disdain for fiction. There is so much in the world to learn, she observes. "Have I, then, any time to spend on things that never existed?"[40] Some years later, Eliot lost her early faith and wrote her first novel. Published in 1858, *Scenes of Clerical Life* is comprised of three loosely connected tales, all focusing on country parsons in nineteenth-century England and their struggles to breathe life into moribund creeds while simultaneously dealing with their own personal problems. The first tale, "The Sad Fortunes of the Reverend Amos Barton," vividly recreates the impoverished life of an uninspiring preacher who is unable to cast an effective vision for the simple townsfolk of his parish, yet who evokes their compassion when tragedy strikes his family. Eliot wanted to depict the clergy in their human rather than theological aspect. Amos Barton becomes a Christ figure not because he is a successful minister but because he suffers.

Eliot is vision casting in these scenes. Her intent is to teach indirectly what she called the "doctrine of sympathy," a substitute for the evangelical faith she had lost. Her stories about the Christian clergy are in fact vehicles for communicating the "religion of Humanity"—an attempt to commend the power of compassionate love without the supernatural trappings of theism.[41] Eliot learned to delight in the religious feeling she associated with the evangelicalism of her youth, but she could not accept the doctrinal framework that accompanied it. Her scenes are thus depictions of humans (clergymen) acting religiously, not because the Holy Spirit indwells them (Eliot is agnostic about that), but rather because they come to experience, as humans, a genuine sympathy for others.

Eliot is an example of an author using the literary imagination to inculcate humanist values. This move, typical of religious liberalism, is alive and well. Leo Tolstoy believed that the purpose of fiction was to cultivate moral sympathy, to foster the feeling of universal brotherhood.[42] More recently, the ethicist Martha Nussbaum has written a manifesto on the importance of the literary imagination for public life. According to Nussbaum, we

---

[40]George Eliot, Letter to Miss Lewis, March 16, 1839, in *Life of George Eliot, As Related in Her Letters and Journals*, ed. J. W. Cross (New York: Thomas P. Crowell & Co., 1884), 27.

[41]David Lodge, "Introduction," in George Eliot, *Scenes of Clerical Life* (New York and London: Penguin, 1973), 8.

[42]See Tolstoy's *What Is Art?* trans. Richard Pevear (London: Penguin, 1996).

need poets and novelists because "in today's political life we lack the capacity to see one another as fully human."[43] She is particularly concerned with using the imagination to understand the situation of people different from ourselves. Interestingly, Nussbaum believes that the imagination bridges reason and emotion: it is a mode of both reasoning and feeling. It is not a cure-all, however. Nussbaum knows that stories alone are often powerless in the face of the refusal to imagine others with empathy and compassion, and that some stories only reinforce prejudice and hatred. This is not a defect of imaginative literature, however, but of the human heart. To refuse to imagine is akin to refusing hospitality to "the stranger in your midst" (Lev 19:33-34). Nussbaum's solution—to reform institutions so that they more perfectly embody the vision of compassionate justice—betrays her humanistic idealism. It is far more realistic to place our hope in the one who literally embodied the compassion of God: the Lord Jesus Christ.

The imagination cannot save us. To follow Tolstoy and Nussbaum gets us no further than Moralistic Therapeutic Deism, namely, the vision of the universal Fatherhood of God and brotherhood of man. While it is useful to employ the imagination, as Eliot and Nussbaum do, to cultivate moral sympathy, I am after bigger game. I want the church to recover the power of the *biblical* imagination. The challenge is to read Scripture, the "living and active" word of God (Heb 4:12), so that it fuels, forms and reforms our imaginations, cultivating not merely empathy with our fellow human creatures but, more importantly, the fear of the Lord we owe our Creator and, ultimately, saving faith. The goal is to see the triune God at work in the world, making all things new, and to foster a desire to participate in the renewal of all things in Christ through the Spirit. The "brotherhood of man" seems a puny thing next to this bracing eschatological vision of a new heavens and a new earth (Rev 21:1).

Theology is never more biblical, or of more service to the church, than when it provides directions for performing scenes of congregational life that enable Christians to bring to light the bright new world of the biblical text in the midst of other "nations" that abide in darker worlds generated and governed by other texts. Scripture lights and Christians walk the way of

---

[43]Martha C. Nussbaum, *Poetic Justice: The Literary Imagination and Public Life* (Boston: Beacon Press, 1995), xiii.

imaginative faith, not empirical sight. The saints who make up the church embody the evangelical imagination, living together to demonstrate the truth of what God the Father was doing in the Son through the Spirit: renewing all things and reconciling the world to himself. Christians display what Karl Barth called the "strange new world of the Bible" when they are able to imagine—"give concrete forms to"—their new life in Christ in the midst of the old world that is passing away.[44] It takes a robust biblical imagination to see the old world passing away, yet it is precisely the story of Jesus Christ that liberates us from the tyranny of the present. Thanks to the biblical imagination—the sum total of the metaphors and stories by which a holy nation lives (what Calvin called "the spectacles of faith"[45])—the church is able to discern not only the whole out of fragmented parts ("in Christ"), but also to see what is "already/not yet" the case ("in Christ").

The Bible's stories and other literary genres form and inform our minds, wills and emotions. This is one means of enlightening what Paul calls the "eyes of your hearts" (Eph 1:18). Theology falls short of its remit if it only conveys information, without the means to process and even feel it as well. Today, we are awash with information but lack the means of putting it together into a meaningful whole. Elsewhere I have argued that it is helpful to think of the whole summed up in Christ (Eph 1:10) as an ongoing drama of redemption.[46] God has the primary speaking and acting part, yet he accords his human images the dignity of dramatic participation, inviting us to play our parts and, in so doing, to grow into them even more. Reconciling the world in Christ is God's act, yet there remains something important for the church to say and do. Theology's task is to help the church understand the play and learn her part: to live out her worship, witness and wisdom to God's glory. Above all, the church embodies her love and knowledge of the grace of God in Christ in everything she does. Pastors and theologians are workers in dramatic fittingness, and their task is to help individuals and local churches understand,

---

[44]George MacDonald defines the imagination as "that faculty which gives form to thought," in *A Dish of Orts* (London: Sampson Low Marston & Company, 1893), 2. See also Kerry Dearborn, *Baptized Imagination: The Theology of George MacDonald* (Burlington, VT: Ashgate, 2006).

[45]John Calvin, *Institutes of the Christian Religion*, trans. Ford Lewis Battles (Philadelphia: Westminster Press, 1960), I.vi.1.

[46]For a more extended treatment of this idea, see my books *The Drama of Doctrine*, esp. parts 3 and 4, and *Faith Speaking Understanding*.

both theoretically and practically, their place in the drama of redemption. *The church sorely needs good habits of theological imagination: the ability to relate everything she says and does to what God has said and done in Jesus Christ.*

There is an important but often overlooked connection between the imagination and theology, understood as faith seeking understanding. What imagination and understanding have in common is the intent to make sense of something complex by grasping the relation of parts to the whole. A metaphor is a way of conceiving the whole; "root metaphors" are ways of conceiving the world as a whole, for example, as a machine, organism or book.[47] The pictures, metaphors and visions we live by are as important as our theories and perhaps even our confessions: "As a person imagines, so will she or he perceive, understand, love, and act."[48] Doctrines, too, enable us to imagine rightly because they tell us how to think about the shape and meaning of the whole: God, the world and human history. In saying what is "in Christ," doctrines provide not simply propositional information but also imaginative direction for seeing, judging, feeling and acting in ways that accord with the drama of redemption that lies at the heart of the Scriptures.

The Roman Catholic philosopher Charles Taylor affirms a similar connection between understanding and imagination in his account of modern secularity. What exactly was it that led George Eliot to abandon her evangelical faith and become a modern liberal? According to Taylor, it was not a single scientific discovery or a particularly devastating logical argument as much as it was a tectonic shift in those assumptions we take for granted that frame our everyday beliefs and practices. It was the result of a change in root metaphor: modern men and women came to see the world no longer as a gift (a created order) but as a given (a wholly natural order). The result was a disenchanted view of the world as a closed system of material nature. Secularization is thus an "immanentization"—a flattening process whereby meaning and value are sought without appealing to transcendence (something beyond this material world). Taylor locates this revolutionary change

---

[47]The notion of a "root metaphor" comes from Stephen Pepper's *World Hypotheses* (Berkeley: University of California Press, 1942), chapter 5.

[48]Sang Hyun Lee, *The Philosophical Theology of Jonathan Edwards* (Princeton, NJ: Princeton University Press, 2000), 133.

in what he calls the "social imaginary," which is not a set of ideas but rather "what enables, through making sense of, the practices of a society."[49]

Taylor's "social imaginary" is another name for the metaphors by which we live. The pictures that hold us captive today are all variations on the secular social imaginary. Any doctrine—whether philosophical, political, scientific or theological—that does not fit into the prevailing social imaginary may be technically true, but it will struggle to communicate its goodness and beauty. Conversely, doctrines that correspond to the prevailing social imaginary are experienced not merely as plausible but also desirable.

The Psalmist says that we are to "taste and see that the Lord is good" (Ps 34:8). It is of the utmost importance for reclaiming the imagination for theology to recall that C. S. Lewis associates tasting with the kind of experience we have by indwelling stories.[50] Taylor agrees: "the way ordinary people 'imagine' their social surrounds . . . is often not expressed in theoretical terms, but is carried in images, stories, and legends."[51] It is this social imaginary that allows us to make sense of, and find our way around, the everyday world. It is the glue that holds understanding and practice together, the storied understanding that is implicit in our everyday practices. Consider, for example, the practice of proposing marriage. The man on bended knee, the offering of the ring, the posing of the question—these are all activities that conform to and continue society's understanding of adult male-female relationships, families, romantic love and so on. A picture holds us captive. The modern secular imaginary understands marriage differently: it is less a covenant between a man and a woman before God than a human contractual agreement between two consenting adults, spouse one and spouse two. A new picture now holds us captive.

According to Taylor, a social imaginary is conveyed not by explicit propositions (what Kierkegaard calls "direct" communication) but by cultural practices ("indirect" communication). Call it the "hidden curriculum" of

[49]Charles Taylor, *Modern Social Imaginaries* (Durham, NC and London: Duke University Press, 2004), 2. See also his *A Secular Age* (Cambridge, MA: Harvard University Press, 2007), esp. chap. 4. For a helpful exposition and response to Taylor's work, see James K. A. Smith, *How (Not) to Be Secular: Reading Charles Taylor* (Grand Rapids: Eerdmans, 2014).

[50]For more on Lewis and the imagination, see my "In Bright Shadow: C. S. Lewis on the Imagination for Theology and Discipleship," in *The Romantic Rationalist: God, Life, and the Imagination in the Work of C. S. Lewis*, ed. John Piper and David Mathis (Wheaton, IL: Crossway, 2014), 81-104.

[51]Taylor, *Modern Social Imaginaries*, 23.

contemporary culture. Although contemporary Christians profess "the faith once proclaimed," too many take part in cultural practices that, at least implicitly, preach a very different gospel. David Wells has chronicled the way in which the evangelical church has adopted marketing and other practices of "foreign nations."[52] Wells is right to sound a warning cry and to call the church back to *sola Scriptura* rather than *sola cultura*, yet I wonder whether it is enough simply to reaffirm core Protestant beliefs. If the fundamental problem is the inability to connect what we confess with the cultural practices in which we engage, then the solution is not to simply believe harder. We must address the problem at its source: the captive imagination.

The gospel sets the captive imagination free. The gospel—the good news that Jesus Christ has conquered sin and death and has become exalted, Lord over all things visible and invisible—casts everything else in a new light: new creation light. The church walks in this light as it learns and lives theology, making sure that its worship, witness and wisdom correspond to the new reality revealed in Jesus Christ. The church lives out its theology throughout the week, but especially on Sunday, at worship: "What we do together in acknowledging God 'schools' us in ways of seeing the world and of being in it."[53] Worship trains the evangelical imagination for workday witness and wisdom.

The following essays are written in aid of recovering the *ecclesial imaginary*: not a set of ideas, but the metaphors that enable, through making sense of, the practices of the church—a *Christian* social imaginary. Call it the *theodramatic* imagination: a biblically generated and canonically governed vision of the triune God at work in his people to renew the whole world. If the church is to fulfill her vocation as a holy nation, she must pit this evangelical imagination against its secular counterpart. The church is a people set apart, both in its theological understanding of the whole (the plan of salvation centered in the cross of Christ) and the practices that embody and enact that understanding (e.g., baptism and the Lord's Supper). There is a difference, for example, between preaching and marketing the gospel. The latter is captive to a secular picture of how to change hearts and minds;

---

[52]See especially David F. Wells, *The Courage to Be Protestant: Truth-Lovers, Marketers, and Emergents in the Postmodern World* (Grand Rapids: Eerdmans, 2008).

[53]Don E. Saliers, *Worship and Spirituality*, 2nd ed. (Akron, OH: OSL Publications, 1996), 2.

the former is committed to the biblical understanding and practice of the ministry of Word and Spirit. The difference is ultimately one of imagination. At the heart of the theodramatic imagination is the conviction of things unseen, namely, God speaking and acting in Word and Spirit. To see the world and ourselves with theodramatic imagination is not to live in a fantasyland but in evangelical reality: the reality of a world where God's Word has entered and is presently active, and to which it will return again.

PICTURES AT A PETRINE EXHIBITION: THREE FAMILY PORTRAITS

The claim that being biblical involves the theodramatic imagination is hardly original to me. The Bible is replete with metaphors and stories that help us envision the reality of God's coming kingdom. 1 Peter 2:9, for example, presents us with three pictures of the church, comprising as it were a family album: "But you are a chosen race, a royal priesthood, a holy nation."[54] There is Petrine precedent for the exhibit that follows. Indeed, the tripartite structure of the present book takes its cue from Peter's metaphors for the church's corporate life (worship), vocation (witness) and the way she comports herself among those outside her own community (wisdom). Peter too believes that the church must engage in practices that communicate faith's understanding of the drama of redemption, both what God has done (grace) and what his people must do in response (gratitude). In each case Peter draws on prior imagery taken from the Old Testament. It takes cognitive effort—imagination—to grasp the connection between a single ethnic group with its own land (Israel) and a multiethnic group with no geographical boundaries (the church).

"A chosen race." "But you . . ." (1 Pet 2:9). The church is a contrast society, chosen and set apart by God for a special purpose. Peter opens his epistle by addressing "those who are elect exiles" (1 Pet 1:1). These two terms highlight the two most distinctive experiences of ancient Israel: God chose Israel, and Israel suffered exile. Peter is writing to Christians in the northern part of Asia Minor (part of present-day Turkey) who were suffering for their faith, but he is writing to them in terms that initially seem more suited to ancient Israel. This is Peter's way of helping his readers see themselves as caught up

---

[54]M. Eugene Boring comments: "This passage presents one of the most dense constellations of ecclesiological imagery in the New Testament" (*1 Peter* [Nashville, TN: Abingdon, 1999], 98).

in the ongoing drama of redemption that began with God's promise to Abraham and culminated in Christ's cross and resurrection. The control story at the heart of the ecclesial imaginary is the unified narrative of God forming a people for himself.

The image of "a chosen race" depicts the people of God gathered and set apart by God's call. Peter wants his readers to see themselves in terms of Exodus 19, where God gathered the people of Israel together and called them his own: "If you will indeed obey my voice and keep my covenant, you shall be my treasured possession among all peoples . . . and you shall be to me a kingdom of priests and a holy nation" (Ex 19:5-6). Israel was to express her part of the covenant relation by keeping the law God gives in Exodus 20. Ancient Israel was a distinct race, a particular ethnicity. In the early church some Christians saw themselves as a "third race," distinct from both Jews and Gentiles. The truth is that the church is made up of many peoples: Jews and Gentiles alike.

To be God's chosen people entails responsibility as well as privilege. Election implies vocation: Israel has a distinct calling, something to do as God's people. God told Abraham that through his seed, all nations would be blessed. The church participates in the realization of this Abrahamic covenant through the "ministry of reconciliation" (2 Cor 5:18), which consists in bearing witness to the reconciliation God has accomplished in Christ by performing works of love and forgiving those who offend us. When we imagine what it looks like to be a chosen race, then, we should not conjure up images of an office pool winning a lottery. God chooses people not simply to enjoy the good life but also to share it; we're called both to enjoy God and to serve others. Moreover, we are called to serve God not only as individuals, but also as part of a whole people of God, a new race. The vocation of the church is to act as one unified people without suppressing legitimate diversity. There is "one Lord, one faith, one baptism" (Eph 4:5), but more than one way of enacting discipleship.

"*A royal priesthood.*" In ancient Israel, the tribe of Levi was specially chosen for the priestly task. Yet God tells Moses that all the people of Israel will be "a kingdom of priests and a holy nation" (Ex 19:6). Since Jesus Christ, our high priest, offered himself as the sacrifice for our sin once for all time (Heb 10:12), we no longer need to offer sacrifices to stay right with God. If we're not literal priests then, what exactly is Peter saying? He is addressing our imagination, that is, our whole being, and suggesting that each member of the church enjoys a special right of access to God. To be a kingdom of priests means two things. First, we all have access to God through Jesus Christ. Second, we should all be making "spiritual sacrifices" (1 Pet 2:5), offering prayer and praise, yes, but also offering our bodies as "living sacrifices" (Rom 12:1). Our common practices—praying and praising, giving and forgiving, baptism and the Lord's Supper, and so on—embody our understanding of the nature and function of the church.

The church is the whole gathered assembly, not just the clergy. The Greek term for "people" is *laos*, from which we get our term *laity*. But *you*—you in the plural, you there in the pews—you are a royal priesthood. Being a member of Christ's royal priesthood does not require a seminary degree. There are no professional Christians. On the contrary, everyone in the church belongs to the royal priesthood. This is important. It means that God sets apart not only full-time ministers but all church members to serve him (here too a picture often holds us captive—the picture of ordained ministers existing on a higher spiritual plane than laypeople). The church is a kingdom of priests, not an audience of pew-potatoes.

"A holy nation." The church is holy because God has set it apart for a special task: "That you may proclaim the excellencies of him who called you out of darkness into his marvelous light" (1 Pet 2:9). God has called the church together to celebrate, talk about and live in the light of the gospel of Jesus Christ. But why does Peter refer to this people of light as a "nation" (*ethnos*)? What is the intended effect of this particular image? How are we to live by this particular metaphorical light?

Nationalism is nothing new, of course. As in the past, the global situation today is thick with conflicts between and even within nations. Why do the nations rage (Ps 2:1)? It is often hard to know where the real conflict is: race, ethnicity, religion and politics blur together like angry emotions. We may not know *why* the nations rage, but it is incontrovertible *that* they do. An enraged world is in desperate need of reconciliation.

Enter the church. The church is a nation, but not a racial or an ethnic group. This is the crucial difference between Israel and the church—though we should not exaggerate it. God made provision in the Sinai covenant for "strangers and sojourners" to be admitted to Israel (Ex 12:47-49). When the church falls into racist thinking and habits, it fails in its vocation as holy nation. It is to the church's shame that the eleven o'clock Sunday worship service has been called "the most segregated hour in America."

We will only understand what Peter means by "holy nation" to the extent that we are able to see the church as a continuation of Israel's history.[55] Israel was to live differently among the other nations in order to be a light (Is 49:6). Specifically, Israel was to live as befits a nation with God as her king, even in exile. Similarly, the church is a holy nation of "elect exiles" (1 Pet 1:1) charged with demonstrating the reality of God's reign on earth as it is in heaven. The apostle Paul agrees, urging the church at Philippi to lead lives in a manner that befits citizens of the gospel (Phil 1:27). The politics of God's rule are to be on conspicuous display in the church's common life. God's kingdom is already "being actualized and made visible, transforming the political, social, economic, and cultural life of God's people on earth according to the divine pattern revealed in the gospel."[56]

The church is a holy nation that marches to the beat of a different social imaginary. Its worship, witness and wisdom are distinct inasmuch as each takes its bearing from what God was doing in Jesus Christ. The church lives among the nations "but with its own distinct political raison d'être, authority, calling, and practice."[57] In this respect the church resembles the London neighborhood in the 1949 film *Passport to Pimlico*. Set just after World War II, the film begins with a shopkeeper sifting through the rubble of his bombed-out store and discovering an ancient document, a treaty that purportedly makes Pimlico, a small borough of London, a realm of the defunct French kingdom of Burgundy. In the wake of the war, the English authorities imposed strict rationing restrictions. One could buy only so much coffee, sugar and so forth because of post-war shortages. The shopkeepers of Pimlico shrewdly decide to declare themselves an independent nation in order to free themselves from these rationing restrictions. When other Londoners find out that they can buy unlimited quantities of sugar and coffee

---

[55]This is not to say "replacement." There are both continuities and discontinuities between Israel and the church. See Chad O. Brand, ed., *Perspectives on Israel and the Church: Four Views* (Nashville, TN: B&H Publishing Group, 2015).

[56]Douglas Harink, *1 & 2 Peter* (Grand Rapids: Brazos, 2009), 32.

[57]Ibid., 71.

in Pimlico, they arrive in flocks. The British authorities are not amused: they erect a fence around Pimlico and require people entering or leaving to show their passports (hence the film's title). Pimlico is a "holy" nation as it were: a nation in the midst of another nation, yet set apart at the same time.

As a holy nation, the church celebrates the coming kingdom of God in the midst of the world. What sets the church apart has nothing to do with DNA or geography, but the work of God. It is because it shares in the fellowship of the triune God that the church, like Pimlico, is a place of abundant living, rather than meager rations. Christians do not need special papers to enter the church, but faith. Baptism is our passport. Our status—whether we are people of God or not—depends entirely on whether or not we are "in Christ."

The church is no bounded territory, like the Burgundian kingdom of Pimlico. It is the kingdom of God, scattered among the nations of the world. It is over this people, this holy nation, that God reigns. God's rule holds sway in hearts and minds molded by the love of God poured out on the cross by the Son, which is in turn poured out in our hearts by the Spirit, not least through the words of Scripture. What is the church? It is God at work in his people, renewing and reconciling the world to himself. Such is the church's high and holy calling as a holy nation.

OVERVIEW OF CONTENTS

The final picture in Mussorgsky's *Pictures at an Exhibition* is Hartmann's design (never built) for the Great Gate of Kiev that he submitted as part of an architectural competition. Kiev was the birthplace of Christianity in Russia. Vladimir of Kiev became a Christian in 988 AD and ordered a mass baptism of his people in the local river, which may be why Mussorgsky incorporates a well-known hymn ("As You Are Baptized in Christ") in his musical rendering. It is fitting that this suite emphasizing nationalism concludes with a reference to a city. The Bible, too, ends with a picture of a great city: the new Jerusalem, the city of God come down from heaven (Rev 21:2). The church is not merely the entry gate but a real foretaste of heaven. For Paul, the church is itself a living temple, the place where God's glorious presence particularly resides (2 Cor 6:16). And in the book of Revelation, the new Jerusalem has no temple, for God's dwelling place is his people (Rev 21:22).

Holy nation, temple of God, city of God. These are just some of the biblical pictures of the church that the following chapters attempt to set to the music of theology. Theology is prophetic vision casting that seeks to take every imagination captive to the Word of God—to what God is doing in Christ.

My working hypothesis throughout this book is that the church needs a biblically formed, reformed and transformed imagination in order to live out a vital faith. Even to view itself as a holy nation takes imagination. The chapters that follow are organized like an art exhibit. The reader proceeds through a foyer and then through three galleries. Each gallery contains various biblical exhibits: essays that depict various scenes of the church's worship, witness and wisdom. Each part of the book also includes a sermon—an exercise in faithfully imagining biblical truth. The sermon, along with baptism and the Lord's Supper, is one of the most distinctive and quintessential "scenes" informed by theology. The sermons included here represent the story of my working life. Each had its provenance in an institution where I have taught: a Christian liberal arts college (Wheaton), a graduate school of theology (Wheaton College Graduate School), the Faculty of Divinity in a secular university (New College, University of Edinburgh) and a seminary (Trinity Evangelical Divinity School). These sermons provide evidence that it is possible to do theology for the church in the context of the academy.

The promenade begins in the foyer, where I discuss certain introductory matters or "prolegomena"—suggestions for imagining biblical authority and evangelicalism—including the importance of the imagination. The first gallery focuses on the church as a royal priesthood and examines scenes of the church's worship. The second gallery looks at the church as a school of prophets and focuses on Christian witness. The third and final gallery visits scenes that dramatically test the church's wisdom.

Why just these three galleries? They more or less correspond to the three offices that characterized Israel's life as a holy nation: prophet, priest and king. Of course, these three offices also apply to the work of Christ.[58] The church participates in a secondary and derivative way in Christ's work. The church worships (a kingdom of priests, offering up sacrifices of praise and bodily life), proclaims truth (a chosen race of prophets, bearing witness to

---

[58]See Calvin's discussion of the work of Christ in terms of the *munus triplex*, in the *Institutes* II.15.1-6.

the word of God) and walks in the way of wisdom (a temple of kings who represent the holy nation).

These biblical exhibits are dramatic scenes, not static pictures. The apostle Paul states that God has "exhibited" him and the other apostles "because we have become a spectacle [*theatron*] to the world" (1 Cor 4:9). God calls the church to be a public demonstration of the gospel, a corporate display of faith seeking and, more importantly, *doing* understanding. The book concludes as the company of the gospel leave the exhibit—hopefully edified, the eyes of their hearts refreshed.

VIEWING NOTES: FIVE UNIFYING THEMES

Though these pictures of the theologian at ministerial work arose in different contexts for various occasions, they display a number of common themes. Like the New Testament itself, this book exhibits both unity and diversity. Not every theme is equally apparent in every chapter, but there are unmistakable family resemblances in the way each seeks to minister theology.

First, there is a common concern for the well-being and edification of the church, as well as a high view of the church's task and the pastor's vocation. All of the essays are thoroughly theological from start to finish, for the church is a creature of the Word and owes its nature and purpose to God's triune mission to the world. Accordingly, these essays work hard to discern how the church is truly a peculiar people "of God."

Second, these essays are all concerned with what it means for the church to be biblical and for theology to be a species of biblical reasoning. By this I mean not simply reasoning *about* but, more importantly, *with* and *by means of* the Bible. It is a matter not simply of extracting content from the Bible but of letting the (literary) forms of the Bible guide the way we think. Being biblical means not merely thinking the contents but also the forms of God's thoughts after him. Only in this way can our minds be conformed to the divine genius of Scripture. For example, the Bible displays a narrative unity that requires us not to read simply for the "moral" or "lesson" of a story but to view the various stories as related by a metanarrative plot that concerns what God has promised to do to restore a fallen creation.

Third, these essays assume that the unity of the Bible is a function of the divine drama of redemption that it recounts, and of which it is an ingredient.

The focus is on the speech and acts of God (Greek *theo* + *drao* = God doing) that effect creation and salvation, revelation and redemption. This is historical drama: through his mighty acts, the triune God really is building a people and renewing creation. This is the mission in which the church is summoned to participate.

These three themes give rise to the fourth: a concern to rehabilitate what I am calling the evangelical imagination, which is the capacity to conceive—or rather, to think, see and feel—our lives and the life of the church as caught up in the great thing God is doing through the death, resurrection and ascension of Jesus Christ and the coming of the Holy Spirit. The church needs to inhabit the big biblical picture—theodrama, for short—as we live day by day, minute by minute as would-be followers of Jesus who desire above all to have our thoughts and lives correspond to the gospel. To do this, we have to keep the gospel story ever in mind, together with its Old Testament presuppositions and New Testament implications, and we have to view the story of our own lives in light of the story of Jesus. That requires a sanctified imagination set apart for the purpose of making these connections.

Finally, these essays share a common goal: that doctrinal theology be eminently practical, ministering understanding and vision to head, heart and hand. The understanding that faith seeks is not merely theoretical but also theatrical. Theology is less an intellectual achievement to admire from afar than an embodied interpretation staged by the believing community. We are to "put on" Christ (Rom 13:14; Gal 3:27), both as a costume, clothed in righteousness (Eph 6:14) and humility (1 Pet 5:5), and as a production, as Paul writes, "be imitators of me, as I am of Christ," (1 Cor 11:1). This is perhaps the ultimate vocation of theology: to help dress and direct the church, helping believers get into their God-given roles and equipping them to play their parts actively. Theology ultimately exists to serve and preserve the integrity of the church's exhibit to the world (1 Cor 4:9).

BEFORE THE PROMENADE

(Prolegomena)

one

WHAT ARE THEOLOGIANS FOR?

*Why Doctors of the Church Should
Prescribe Christian Doctrine*

This essay was originally presented as the inaugural lecture of the MA in Systematic Theology degree at Trinity Evangelical Divinity School in April 2013. The next day I delivered the same lecture to the Student Theological Society at Moody Bible Institute. I am grateful both to my department for the invitation to kick off the theology symposium series and to the students at Moody who wanted an evening lecture not for extra credit but just for the love of learning. It seemed appropriate for both groups to ask a rather fundamental question— not the philosopher's "Why is there something rather than nothing?" but rather "Why am I (a theologian) here?" I was inspired by a little essay by Wendell Berry entitled "What Are People For?"[1] A good part of my essay is taken up with examining more pictures of what a theologian is and more metaphors by which to imagine a theologian's ministry. I also examine some pictures of what doctrine is and what the church should do with it. The subtitle of the essay hints at the metaphor I prefer: theologians are doctors attending the body of Christ, administering doctrinal prescriptions intended either to cure the body or, like vitamins, to build it up.

INTRODUCTION: WORKING THE FARM, LIVING THE LIFE

Wendell Berry, the reaping prophet from Kentucky, wrote a three-page essay in 1985 about doctrine—agricultural doctrine. In particular, his topic

---

[1]Wendell Berry, "What Are People For?" in *What Are People For? Essays by Wendell Berry* (New York: Farrar, Straus and Giroux, 1990), 123-25.

was "the governing agricultural doctrine in government offices, universities, and corporations . . . that 'there are too many people on the farm.'"[2] Economists and others who hold this doctrine were saying that small farmers deserved to fail because they were among the "least efficient producers."[3] Berry points out that in the rush toward greater mechanization, efficiency and convenience we have overlooked one question, a question that also serves as the title of his essay: "What are people for?" Apparently not for manual labor—at least not according to the prevailing agricultural doctrine. Nevertheless, says Berry, in the country there is still work to be done: there is land to work.

To ask what people are for is to raise questions about ontology and teleology concerning human nature (being) and purpose (function). These are perennial questions, but Berry thinks they are especially urgent today as technology gives us more time for leisure. My question is more specific: What are *theologians* for? Who are they and what kind of work do they do? I will argue that theologians, like farmers, are here to cultivate something: not the land, but humanity. To paraphrase our Lord: theologians are called to be *farmers* of men and women: "The harvest is plentiful, but the laborers are few" (Lk 10:2). Theology is not an agribusiness profession for an elite class of persons, however. *All* Christians are to work the farm, since all people of faith need to grow in understanding. We need workers because growth is not automatic. We cannot cultivate humanity in the ways that count by using shortcuts like human growth hormone.

What work can theologians do that other cultivators of humanity cannot? Let me approach the answer indirectly via the work of two philosophers. Martin Heidegger asked an even more fundamental question than Wendell Berry—"What *are* people?"—and answered "beings-in-time." Only human beings are aware of the passing of time and thus of the angst of human existence. Many centuries earlier, the Roman philosopher Seneca had said something similar, and wrote his essay "On the Shortness of Life" probably about the same time that Jesus was giving his life up (49 AD).[4] Heidegger

[2]Ibid., 123.

[3]Berry wryly notes, "No agricultural economist has yet perceived that there are too many agricultural economists," ibid., 123.

[4]Seneca, *On the Shortness of Life: Life Is Long if You Know How to Use It*, trans. C. D. N. Costa (London: Penguin, 2005), 1-33.

and Seneca remind us that the condition from which humans suffer most, and which theology ultimately addresses, is nothing less than mortality itself.

Seneca opens his essay with a quotation from Hippocrates, the father of medicine: "*Ars longa, vita brevis*" ("Art is long, life is short"). The art in question is not music or painting but medicine: Hippocrates uses the Greek term *technē*, and the quote is from the opening statement of a medical text. The gist is that it takes a long time to acquire and perfect practical knowledge or skill, and we have only a short time to do so.[5] What is true for the study of medicine is even more true of mortal being. One of the characters in Douglas Adams's *The Hitchhiker's Guide to the Galaxy* put it well: "'This must be Thursday,' said Arthur to himself, sinking low over his beer. 'I never could get the hang of Thursdays.'"[6] We can generalize Arthur's bewilderment. Some of us never get the hang of any day of the week. Beyond information and knowledge, we need wisdom for the "craft of life." If Seneca is right, then our fundamental problem today, as it was in Jesus' day, is how to learn to live well despite the shortness of time. To live well means devoting oneself to what is most worthy—in Christian terms, what is most deserving of being worshiped—and this leads us straight to the need for theology, the craft of "living well to God."[7]

According to Seneca, the real challenge of being human is not only the shortness of time but also our tendency to waste it, largely by being preoccupied with peripheral matters. "Of all people only those are at leisure who make time for philosophy, only those are really alive."[8] Seneca believed that philosophers learn not only from their own individual experience but also from consulting the wisdom of the past. Fast-forward two thousand years: according to Dallas Willard, not even philosophers or universities have the time to pose the big questions anymore.[9] Big questions are time-consuming, and time is short. So why spend what little time we have on theology?

---

[5]Chaucer's variation is "The lyf so short, the craft so long to lerne" (from *The Parliament of Fowls*, in *The Riverside Chaucer*, 3rd ed. [Oxford: Oxford University Press, 2008], 385).

[6]Douglas Adams, *The Hitchhiker's Guide to the Galaxy* (New York: Del Rey, 2009), 22.

[7]Compare Williams Ames's definition of theology as "the doctrine or teaching of living to God" (*The Marrow of Theology* [Grand Rapids: Baker, 1997], 77).

[8]Seneca, *On the Shortness of Life*, 23.

[9]See the introduction in Dallas Willard, ed., *A Place for Truth: Leading Thinkers Explore Life's Hardest Questions* (Downers Grove, IL: InterVarsity Press, 2010), 15-22.

WHY SHEPHERDS AND SHEEP ARE LEAVING THE FARM
(OR, WHATEVER HAPPENED TO CHRISTIAN DOCTRINE?)

Theologians don't get much respect these days, whether in the academy, society or the church. Why are people saying awful things about theology? No doubt the reasons are complex, but a major factor is the demise of doctrine. If doctrine were a stock, it may well have bottomed out.

You may have heard the typical objections: it's unspiritual, irrelevant, divisive, boring. What can we say to these accusations except, "Guilty as charged"? Here is what I want to say: while doctrine *can* be dry, dull and debilitating to life and love, it need not be so. Moreover, there is no alternative to doctrine; we all believe *something*. For example, we invariably teach our children the difference between right and wrong. Doctrine is simply something that is taught. Every culture is founded on some set of teachings about what is true and good. In other words, doctrine is inevitable. As our gestures and accents give us away as people who have been raised, say, in the American Midwest, so much of what we believe betrays something about our upbringing. Being born in a particular time and place leads not only to enculturation but also to indoctrination. It is a truth seldom acknowledged: we have always already been indoctrinated. To believe anything is to hold to some doctrine.[10] Even those who believe in nothing hold to a doctrine (nihilism). Doctrine is here to stay. The only question is whether it is Christian or non-Christian, healthy or toxic.

Despite the inevitability of doctrine, there has been a conspicuous decline of interest in specifically Christian doctrine in many present-day churches. Sociologist Alan Wolfe speaks of "the strange disappearance of doctrine in the church" in his book *The Transformation of American Religion*: "Talk of hell, damnation, and even sin has been replaced by a nonjudgmental language of understanding and empathy. Gone are the arguments over doctrine and theology; if most believers cannot for the life of them recall what makes Luther different from Calvin, there is no need for [disagreement and schism]."[11] Feeling intimate with God (spirituality)

---

[10]Note, too, that the beliefs and values of a number of American presidents are typically described as doctrines (e.g., the Monroe Doctrine, that European expansion in the Americas would be met with resistance).

[11]Alan Wolfe, *The Transformation of American Religion: How We Actually Live Our Faith* (New York: Free Press, 2003), 3.

matters more than right doctrine (orthodoxy). Doctrine is an endangered species in conservative and liberal churches alike: "Evangelical churches lack doctrine because they want to attract new members. Mainline churches lack doctrine because they want to hold on to those declining numbers of members they have."[12]

Christian Smith, a sociologist at Notre Dame, discovered that while the majority of American teenagers are still religious believers who are active in their churches, they are also "incredibly inarticulate about their faith, their religious beliefs and practices, and its meaning or place in their lives."[13] That doesn't mean they don't have faith or hold to certain doctrines. On the contrary, Smith says they have a kind of theology—"Moralistic Therapeutic Deism" or MTD for short (an apt acronym for a socially transmitted disease!)—and a faith, though it is not associated with any particular church.[14] If those who hold this faith could articulate it as a creed, it might go something like this: "I believe in a creator God who orders and watches over life on earth. I believe that God wants people to be good and act nicely to one another (the moralistic tenet). I believe that the central goal of life is to be happy and feel good about myself (the therapeutic tenet). I believe that God is not involved in my life except when I need him to solve a problem. I believe that good people go to heaven, and that almost everyone is good (or at least nice). Glory be to God (and me). As it is now, may perhaps ever be (who knows?), virtual world without end. Amen." This too is doctrine, but alas: it expresses an unbiblical, non-Trinitarian faith.

A recent blog post listed the top ten reasons why our children are leaving the church of their youth. At least half of the reasons have to do with the poor diet of doctrine they've been fed. They have been given cultural fast food in a misguided attempt to sound cool and relevant, and consequently are suffering from intellectual and spiritual malnutrition. We've exchanged their theological birthright (catechism) for a mess of cultural pottage (choruses). "We've traded a historic, objective, faithful gospel based on God's

---

[12]Ibid., 87.

[13]Christian Smith with Melinda Lundquist Denton, *Soul Searching: The Religious and Spiritual Lives of American Teenagers* (Oxford: Oxford University Press, 2005), 131.

[14]Ibid., 162-63.

graciousness toward us for a modern, subjective, pragmatic gospel based upon achieving our goal by following life strategies. Rather than being faithful to the foolish simplicity of the gospel of the cross we've set our goal on being 'successful' in growing crowds with this gospel of glory. This new gospel saves no one. . . . Our kids leave because we have failed to deliver to them the faith 'delivered once for all' to the church."[15]

Not everyone is leaving. St. John's Anglican Cathedral in Brisbane, Australia, is holding on to its own young people and attracting others. The pastor chalks it up to the fact that they have replaced doctrine with *narrative*. The Bible is a story, not raw material for constructing systematic theology. Narrative theology invites people to fit their own life stories into something meaningful and compelling, not a fixed system but a dynamic story.

Is the system really the villain in the story of theology, and narrative its knight in shining armor? More pointedly: Is doctrine the problem to which narrative is the solution? Is "story" really the whole story? I resist the forced (false) choice between articulating intellectual convictions and participating in a story. This is too simplistic an either-or and ultimately gives rise to a debilitating dichotomy between theory and practice. I have argued at length elsewhere that doctrine gives direction to individuals and communities for fitting participation in what God is doing in the world to renew creation—directions for embodying and enacting the drama of redemption that culminates in Jesus Christ, God's story made flesh.[16] Doctrine is not inimical to story but a form of story appreciation. Like music appreciation, the point of theological teaching is to enable effective and affective participation in the activity. Here too, a picture has held us captive—in this case, a picture of doctrine as a closed, fixed and lifeless system of ideas. For many in the sea of twenty-first century Christianity, doctrine is dead in the water. The problem is not with doctrine itself but with its picture in contemporary society, which has unnecessarily marginalized and diminished it. Stated positively, Christian doctrine is a vital necessity not merely for doing church, but also for human flourishing.

---

[15]marc5solas.wordpress.com/2013/02/08/top-10-reasons-our-kids-leave-church/.

[16]Vanhoozer, *The Drama of Doctrine: A Canonical-Linguistic Approach to Christian Theology* (Louisville, KY: Westminster John Knox, 2005) and *Faith Speaking Understanding: Performing the Drama of Doctrine* (Louisville, KY: Westminster John Knox, 2014).

"THEOLOGIAN": A COMPACT PORTRAIT GALLERY

As a theologian, my mission is to speak well of God and to practice what I preach. It is a dangerous business. Idolatry and blasphemy are constant occupational hazards. It is ever so tempting to create God in my own image or in the image of my favorite ideology, political party, or special interest group. And it is ever so easy to say things that miss the divine mark and fall short of the glory of God. The last words of the first letter of John must therefore be the theologian's first and lasting thought: "Little children, keep yourself from idols" (1 Jn 5:21). Speaking well of God is also challenging because it often involves preserving certain tensions. For example, God is not merely love, he is loving *and* just; God is one God in three persons. Theology is something of a high-wire act. It is a bracing enterprise, for, as G. K. Chesterton says in *Orthodoxy*, "an inch is everything when you are balancing."[17] Moreover, balancing is hard work—which is perhaps why heretics are quick to seek relief by relaxing the tension (e.g., the Arian heresy that the Son is not fully God).

What theologians are not. It is important to be clear on what theologians should *not* be.

Theologians are not entertainers. They may be tightrope walkers, but they're not here simply to help pass the time. They may play the fool in the course of bearing countercultural witness, but fools for Christ mean serious business.

Theologians are not underwriters of the status quo. Their critics often portray them in this way, and sadly we can think all too readily of examples of people who invoke God's name in support of some ideology or another, such as National Socialism in Nazi Germany. Theologians should not deploy doctrine in the service of any institutional or national power interest. Luther was right to insist that a Christian theologian is a theologian of the cross, and this means suffering for bearing true witness.

Theologians are not overlords of the academy. Before the modern era theology was often referred to as the "queen of the sciences."[18] Revelation was thought to trump reason, but eventually the other academic disciplines

---

[17]G. K. Chesterton, *Orthodoxy* (New York: Dodd, Mead & Co., 1959), 184.

[18]Though Thomas Aquinas asked whether sacred doctrine is "nobler" than other sciences, he never used the exact phrase that is often attributed to him. See his *Summa Theologiae* I, Q. 1, Art. 5.

began to resent theologians lording it over them. What has Jerusalem to do with astronomy and molecular biology? As one who has compared theologians to theatrical directors, I want to say for the record that theologians are not drama queens. If theologians were chess pieces, they would not be queens but bishops—of course!

Theologians are not pretenders in the academy. Many secularists and skeptics claim that the university is no place for theology. Richard Dawkins's complaint, written as a letter to the editor of a London newspaper, is typical: "What has theology ever said that is of the smallest use to anybody? . . . If all the achievements of theologians were wiped out tomorrow, would anyone notice the smallest difference? Even the bad achievements of scientists, the bombs, and sonar-guided whaling vessels, work! The achievements of theologians don't do anything, don't affect anything and don't mean anything. What makes anyone think that 'theology' is a subject at all?"[19] Dawkins poses a fair question, which I have paraphrased as "What are theologians for?" I want to begin answering this question by examining six metaphors that state positively what theologians do.

Portrait of the theologian: six metaphorical models. Metaphors assert both *is* and *is not*, and each of the following six models captures some aspect of the theologian's vocation, though my own preference is for the last three.

Philosopher. Theologians are like philosophers to the extent that both seek wisdom and understanding. At their best, both pose big questions about the nature of reality and the meaning of the whole. It is precisely this feature that, according to Cardinal Newman, makes the theologians a precious resource in the university. Precisely because they are on guard against making idols, theologians also serve as a guard against disciplinary reductionism—the besetting temptation of the academic. Reductionism is the lust of the theoretical eye, the desire to be able to explain all relevant phenomena by means of one's own conceptual devices—to know as God knows. When theologians speak well of God, however, they remind every academic discipline of its own incompleteness. Theologians are more relevant than ever in an age that has lost wisdom in a sea of knowledge and knowledge in a sea of information. The problem is that we know more and more about

---

[19]Richard Dawkins, Letter to *The Independent*, March 20, 1993.

smaller and smaller bits of reality. Stanley Hauerwas complains that we are awash in specialist knowledge but have lost the ability to flourish: "Too often university curriculums make it impossible for anyone . . . to make sense of the world in which we find ourselves."[20] The absence of theology from the university only exacerbates the tendency to be swallowed up by specialist knowledge.

The weakness of viewing theology as a species of philosophy is the danger of unchecked speculation—of conceiving the whole of reality apart from the concrete activity of God's self-communication in history. While there may be some things we can know about God by contemplating the concept of "perfect being," there is always the danger that we may foist our own, culturally conditioned notions of perfection onto God. Metaphysician, heal thyself.

Poet. Friedrich Schleiermacher defines doctrines as "accounts of the Christian religious affections set forth in speech."[21] In this regard, theologians are like poets who search for the right words with which to articulate subjective experience. While I agree that theology, like poetry, is a form of word craft, theology cannot be poetry without remainder or else the only thing to which it would be accountable is its own subjectivity. Again, I am assuming that the proper subject matter of Christian theology is the triune God in self-communicative activity.[22]

Sociologist. More recently some have seen theologians as those whose task is to set forth in speech not the experience of an individual but a group: namely, the church as a believing community with its own grammar and vocabulary. On this view, the theologian articulates the "grammar" of Christian faith and life—what John Franke and Stanley Grenz call the "mosaic of community belief."[23] This image rightly highlights the theologian's role in formulating the church's corporate identity and mission, but wrongly locates the norms in the church's own practices, thus making it difficult to challenge the status quo with a prophetic "thus saith the Lord."

---

[20]Hauerwas goes on, "Too often university curriculums make it impossible for anyone . . . to make sense of the world in which we find ourselves" (*The State of the University: Academic Knowledges and the Knowledge of God* [Oxford: Blackwell, 2007], 2).

[21]*The Christian Faith* (Edinburgh: T&T Clark, 1928), §15.

[22]For a book-length elaboration of this claim, see my *Remythologizing Theology: Divine Action, Passion, and Authorship* (Cambridge: Cambridge University Press, 2010).

[23]Stanley J. Grenz and John R. Franke, *Beyond Foundationalism: Shaping Theology in a Postmodern Context* (Louisville, KY: Westminster John Knox, 2001), 16.

These first three images of the theologian at work roughly correspond to George Lindbeck's threefold typology of cognitive-propositional, experiential-expressivist and cultural-linguistic theology.[24] We turn now to three more images that represent my own pilgrim's progress, as it were, through the land of theology.

Hermeneutician. If Scripture is the "soul of theology,"[25] then hermeneutics—the study of "how we read, understand, and handle texts, especially those written in another time"[26]—becomes central to the task. I spent a decade and more exploring the model of the theologian as hermeneutician. Hermeneutics goes further than exegesis in explaining not only what the text meant to its original readers but also what it means to us today. The strength of this image is its focus on the text. Its weakness, however, is that it may be too beholden to secular theories of meaning and interpretation. This weakness led me to the next image, which intentionally seeks to conform theological method to theological matter.

Dramaturg. If Scripture does more than state universal truth—if it is essentially a transcript and medium of God's Word and God's acts—then it follows that the essence of Christianity is dramatic. In *The Drama of Doctrine* I explored the possibility that doctrine resembles theatrical direction for understanding a play and for right participation in it. The play in question is the economy of salvation: what the Father is doing in Jesus through the Spirit. The theologian is like a dramaturg who researches the meaning of a play and advises the director (pastor) and company (congregation) on the best way to perform the play in our present cultural space and time. What dramaturgy adds to hermeneutics is the idea that our most important interpretations are our *lived performances.* Christianity, after all, is a way. Theology here becomes a matter of giving theatrical direction for walking across the stage of the world, acting out the good news that is in Jesus Christ. The Bible is thus a transcript of past actions and a script that helps orient the church to its present and future.

Doctor. The word *script* has a pharmaceutical as well as a theatrical meaning. It is shorthand for "prescription"—a direction for taking medicine.

---

[24]George Lindbeck, *The Nature of Doctrine: Religion and Theology in a Postliberal Age* (Louisville, KY: Westminster John Knox, 1984), 84-90.

[25]*Dogmatic Constitution on Divine Revelation: Dei Verbum, Solemnly Promulgated by His Holiness Pope Paul VI on November 18, 1965,* §24 (Boston: St. Paul Books & Media, 1965).

[26]Anthony Thiselton, *Hermeneutics: An Introduction* (Grand Rapids: Eerdmans, 2009), 1.

One immediate benefit of this medicinal model is that there is plenty of biblical warrant for it. Not only does Jesus heal dramatically, but he also refers to himself as a physician (Mk 2:17; Lk 5:31-32; Mt 9:12-13; Lk 4:23). In addition, the author of the biggest single textual block in the New Testament, the two-volume work Luke-Acts, was written according to tradition by Luke, the "beloved physician" mentioned by Paul in Colossians 4:14, who was most likely also Paul's traveling companion. We need to turn to tradition, however, in order to get the fullest picture of the theologian as a "doctor" of the church.[27]

DOCTORS OF THE CHURCH

Roman Catholic. In early Christianity, teachers who were exceptionally wise in communicating the meaning of Jesus Christ came to be called "Fathers" of the church. Of these, some were singled out with the additional title "doctor of the Church." At first it was only an informal rubric, but the Roman Catholic Church eventually recognized them in an official way.[28] There are three requirements for this distinguished rank: holiness of life, importance and orthodoxy of writings, and official church recognition.

Pope Benedict XVI wrote a book—*Doctors of the Church*[29]—about all thirty-two Doctors of the Church, including St. Cyril of Alexandria ("Doctor of the Incarnation"), St. Leo the Great ("Doctor of the Unity of the Church"), St. Thomas Aquinas (the "Angelic Doctor"), St. John of the Cross ("Doctor of Mystical Theology) and, of course, St. Augustine ("Doctor of Grace," also known as "Doctor of Doctors"). In his introduction to the book, the late Francis Cardinal George articulates a mission statement for the church and theology alike: "The mission of the Church in every age is to introduce the world to Christ, its savior. The Church cannot accomplish her mission without learned men and women who are saints of God. These are the Doctors of the Church."[30] Of special interest is the christological remit:

---

[27]Merrill Kitchen and Paul Kitchen, "Health Issues and Medical Care in 1st Century Palestine," *Luke's Journal of Christian Medicine and Dentistry* 18 no. 1 (April 2013): 4-6.

[28]Although there are no women priests in the Catholic church, there are two doctors: Catherine of Siena (1348–1380) and Teresa of Avila (1515–1582).

[29]Pope Benedict XVI, *Doctors of the Church* (Rome: Libreria Editrice Vaticana, 2011)—material drawn from cathecheses given by Pope Benedict during his weekly general audiences.

[30]Ibid., 11.

"They help us to answer the questions about Jesus Christ: who He is, what He taught, what He wants us to do, how to be more like Him."[31]

Reformed. Protestants too speak of doctors of the church. The early Reformers saw "doctors" of the church as a distinct class of ministers who "serve the institutional church in its God-given task of interpreting Holy Scripture."[32] The *Ecclesiastical Ordinances* that governed Calvin's Geneva open with this statement: "There are four orders of offices that our Lord instituted for the government of his church"—and then goes on to list them: pastors, doctors/teachers, elders and deacons.[33] Calvin writes elsewhere: "[Doctors] are not put in charge of discipline, or administering the sacraments, or warnings and exhortations, but only of Scriptural interpretation— to keep doctrine whole and pure among believers."[34] Johannes Wolleb, a seventeenth-century Swiss Reformed theologian, describes the difference this way: "[Pastors] are chiefly intent upon moving their auditors, [doctors] upon teaching them."

There was some dispute over the interpretation of Ephesians 4:11, which pertains to gifts the ascended Christ gives the church: "And he gave the apostles, the prophets, the evangelists, the shepherds and teachers [*poimenas kai didaskalous*]."[35] Does "shepherds and teachers" designate one distinct office or two?[36] Scott Manetsch notes that in Calvin's Geneva the mandate of the doctors of the church "extended beyond the local congregation to the larger church . . . and included the responsibility to teach future pastors and protect the church from doctrinal error."[37] Doctors of

---

[31]Christopher Rengers, *The Thirty-Three Doctors of the Church* (Rockford, IL: Tan Books and Publishers, 2000), xxv.

[32]Bruce McCormack, "The End of Reformed Theology? The Voice of Karl Barth in the Doctrinal Chaos of the Present," in Wallace M. Alston and Michael Welker, eds., *Reformed Theology: Identity and Ecumenicity*, vol. 1 (Grand Rapids: Eerdmans, 2003), 59. The assumption is that a historic confession is the measure of "correctness." McCormack worries that the "doctor of the church" is being replaced by Free Church theologians who are not accountable to one of the particular historic Protestant confessional communities (46).

[33]Scott Manetsch, *Calvin's Company of Pastors: Pastoral Care and the Emerging Reformed Church, 1536–1609* (Oxford: Oxford University Press, 2013), 323.

[34]Calvin, *Institutes of the Christian Religion*, trans. Ford Lewis Battles (Philadelphia: Westminster Press, 1960), IV.iii.4.

[35]Cf. 1 Cor 12:28-29.

[36]There is also the question of whether Paul is referring to an "ordinary" or an "extraordinary" office (i.e., one that ended with the apostolic age).

[37]Manetsch, *Calvin's Company of Pastors*, 28. Manetsch notes that Calvin sometimes treats the role of pastor and doctor as a single office (323). Heinrich Heppe mentions both "pastors" and

the church are charged with the preservation of the purity of doctrine, its diffusion among the young and the training of future ministers. In his commentary on Ephesians 4:11, Calvin himself comments: "I have no objection to [pastors] receiving the name of doctors, if we realize that there is another kind of doctor, who superintends both the education of pastors and the instruction of the whole church."[38]

The Church of Scotland under John Knox adopted Calvin's distinction. (This is of particular interest to me because for eight years I practiced "doctrinal medicine": I taught theology at the University of Edinburgh to candidates for ministry in the Church of Scotland.) According to Knox, the doctor's special task is "to interpret scripture and confute errors (including those who taught theology in schools and universities)." Chapter five in *The Church's Second Book of Discipline* (1578) specifies the doctor's role: they are to "assist the Pastor in the government of the kirk" but not "to minister the sacraments or celebrate marriage." Instead, "[The doctor's] office is to open up the mind of the Spirit of God in the scriptures simply . . . to the end that the faithful may be instructed, and sound doctrine taught." The doctor "is different from the pastor. . . . For the doctor is given the word of knowledge, to open up, by simple teaching, the mysteries of the faith; to the pastor, the gift of wisdom, to apply the same."[39]

Evangelical. To what extent, I wonder, does the dichotomy of doctrine and life that bedevils the evangelical church today owe its existence to these exaggerated differences between pastors and theologians? Calvin read Ephesians 4:11 as referring to pastors and teachers as two different things—like the American tourist who exclaimed to her husband, "Look, honey. They buried two people in the same grave!" because the tombstone read, "Here lies a pastor and theologian." It is possible, after all, to read Paul as using two terms to designate the same office. As Jerome says in his commentary on Ephesians 4:11: "No one ought to assume to himself the

---

"doctors of the church" under the teaching office of the church (*Reformed Dogmatics* [Grand Rapids: Baker, 1978], 679-80).

[38]John Calvin, *Galatians, Ephesians, Philippians and Colossians*, Calvin's New Testament Commentaries, vol. 11, ed. T. F. Torrance and D. W. Torrance (Grand Rapids: Eerdmans, 1965), 179. See also Randall C. Zachman's comments on this passage in *John Calvin as Teacher, Pastor, and Theologian: The Shape of His Writings and Thought* (Grand Rapids: Baker, 2006), 62.

[39]See J. H. Good, "What Was the Old Reformed View of Doctors in the Church?," *The Reformed Church Monthly*, vol. 3 (1870): 424-30.

name of pastor unless he is able to teach them whom he feeds."[40] I propose that we evangelicals settle what the Reformed never did, and urge shepherds to think of themselves as doctors too. What the church needs now are pastor-theologians.

WHY DOCTRINE MATTERS: WHAT IT IS AND WHAT IT DOES

Introducing the "Doctoral" epistles. Doctrine (Latin *doctrina*) means teaching or instruction about confession and conduct alike. In light of the aforementioned pairing in Ephesians 4:11 ("shepherds and teachers"), it is surely no coincidence that Paul's Pastoral epistles (1 and 2 Timothy and Titus) are replete with references to doctrine (Greek *didaskalia*), for doctrine at its best exercises pastoral functions: correcting error, deepening understanding, fostering wisdom, funding endurance and encouraging godliness.

The term *didaskalia* occurs twenty-one times in the New Testament, and fifteen of those instances are in the Pastoral Epistles. This statistic emboldens me to suggest that we call 1 and 2 Timothy and Titus Paul's *Doctoral* epistles. To be sure, *didaskalia* is neither intrinsically Christian nor necessarily beneficial. As we have seen, there are many kinds of indoctrination, and some are damaging and disastrous. False teaching abounds, which suggests another aspect of the theologian's purpose: to distinguish true from false teaching. Paul uses a particularly interesting qualifier to make this point. 1 Timothy 1:10 is the first of four places where Paul mentions "sound doctrine" (*hygiainousē didaskalia*; see also 2 Tim 4:3; Tit 1:9; 2:1).[41]

"Sound" doctrine. Sound doctrine matters because it is vital to the life of the church. The Greek for "sound" (*hygiainō*) is the word from which we derive the English word hygienic, which refers to the conditions or practices conducive to maintaining health. Paul is speaking of doctrine in medical terms, and at least one commentator thinks that its use "may show the influence of the physician Luke."[42] Another commentator argues that Paul is following ancient philosophers who often depicted their opponents' posi-

---

[40]Ronald E. Heine, *The Commentaries of Origen and Jerome on St Paul's Epistle to the Ephesians* (Oxford: Oxford University Press, 2002), 175.

[41]He also speaks of "sound words" (1 Tim 6:3), the "pattern of sound words" (2 Tim 1:13), the importance of being "sound in faith" (Tit 1:13; 2:2) and a model of "sound speech" (Tit 2:8).

[42]George Knight, *The Pastoral Epistles*, New International Greek Commentary (Grand Rapids: Eerdmans, 1999), 89.

tions as "sick."[43] To affirm doctrine as "sound" is to make a health-claim, not a truth-claim. Sound doctrine is "healthy" or "health-giving," and thus stands in contrast to doctrine that is toxic or noxious—teaching that is inimical to the community's well-being. The context supports this understanding. We might have expected Paul to pit sound doctrine against, say, a christological heresy, but instead he contrasts sound doctrine not with ideas but particular practices: striking one's parents, lying, practicing homosexuality and kidnapping (1 Tim 1:10).

Doctrine for Paul is sound because it is conducive to healthy—godly, salvific, salutary—habits of life. Moreover, Paul's criterion of the good life is the good news: the gospel of Jesus Christ. Doctrine is sound when it opposes ungodly practices and when it is "in accordance with the gospel of the glory of the blessed God" (1 Tim 1:11). Why should the gospel be the standard of healthy living? Because we know what humans are for and what is ultimately good for humanity only when we come to understand that human beings were made for fellowship with God. Doctrine is good for us—health-giving—because it informs us about our identity and destiny. Doctrine is sound because it tells us what the Father has done in the Son through the Spirit, thereby teaching us both who we are and how much God loves us. Sound doctrine corresponds to and advances the unfolding of "the plan [*oikonomia*] of the mystery hidden for ages" (Eph 3:9) and revealed in Jesus Christ. To put it in a formula, *the hygienic is the economic* (and vice versa).

What doctrine is. A theologian is a doctor of the church who administers health-promoting doses of doctrine to the body of Christ. With this medical imagery in mind, let us return to the question of what theologians are for by examining what they do with doctrine: the immediate product of their labors.

Subscription. To avoid hypocrisy, theologians have to believe and do what they teach. They must *subscribe* to apostolic teaching with genuine conviction. They must make a whole person commitment to the truth of the gospel. In Calvin's words, "In a pastor there is demanded not only learning, but such zeal for pure doctrine as never to depart from it."[44]

---

[43]Abraham J. Malherbe, "Medical Imagery in the Pastoral Epistles," in Abraham Malherbe, *Paul and the Popular Philosophers* (Minneapolis: Fortress, 1989), 121-36.

[44]John Calvin, *Commentaries on the Epistles to Timothy, Titus, and Philemon* (Edinburgh: Calvin Translation Society, 1856), 295.

Proscription. Doctors of the church must also *proscribe* false teaching, the "doctrines of demons" (1 Tim 4:1). This is what Tertullian does in his *Prescription Against Heretics* (he's actually *proscribing*), where in chapter two he compares heresies to fever. Both weaken and, at the limit, destroy life, especially in those who are already weak in body or in faith respectively, though Tertullian notes that because they lead to eternal death, heresies bear "the heat of a stronger fire."[45] The point is that doctors of the church must be able to diagnose fevers and other debilitating illnesses in the body of Christ before they can wreak havoc. Calvin says, "The pastor ought to have two voices: one, for gathering the sheep; and another, for warding off and driving away wolves and thieves."[46]

Description. The "sure word" of the gospel (i.e., the apostolic testimony) is the touchstone for "sound doctrine" (Tit 1:9). If evil is nonbeing, and if Satan is the father of lies, and if the essence of foolishness is its orientation towards nothingness, then surely the remedy for false teaching—*un*sound doctrine—is a good dose of reality. The doctor of the church, I submit, is first and foremost a *minister of reality.* This thought brings us closer to answering our opening question, "What are theologians for?"

Aristotle famously defined truth in his *Metaphysics*: "To say of what is that it is, and of what is not that it is not, is true."[47] One reason why doctrine is sound—spiritual health-producing, conducive to *shalom*—is because it states the truth. Sound doctrine says of what is, *that* it is. Better, doctrine says of what is in Christ, that it is. This vocation—describing what is—lies at the heart of the theologian's ministry of reality.

The gospel is a sure word because it is a reliable indicator of reality. It makes known the nature and purpose, the source and destiny, of the whole created order. In describing what the Father has done, is doing and will do in Christ through the Spirit to make all things new, theologians minister an understanding of the whole—the whole of history and the whole universe. After all, Christ is the one by whom all things in heaven and on earth, visible and invisible were created (Col 1:15). "All things were created through him

---

[45]Tertullian, *Prescription Against Heretics*, in Alexander Roberts and James Donaldson, eds., *The Ante-Nicene Fathers*, vol. 3 *Latin Christianity* (Buffalo, NY: Christian Literature Publishing Company, 1887), 243.
[46]Calvin, *Commentaries on the Epistles to Timothy, Titus, and Philemon*, 296.
[47]Aristotle, *Metaphysics* 1011b25.

and for him" (Col 1:16); "in him all things hold together" (Col 1:17). To describe what is in Christ is thus to relate every part to a single and singular whole. To grasp the part-whole relationship is the signature move of understanding. Understanding is distinctly *theology* when it is able to think persons, events and things in relation to what is in Christ. We can be even more expansive. The purpose of theology—and thus what theologians are for—is to describe what was, is and is to come "in Christ."

We can here take only a small sampling of "all the treasures of wisdom and knowledge" (Col 2:3) in Christ. To begin with, there is true *deity* in Christ. The Son is the "exegesis" of the Father (Jn 1:18). His life in the flesh bore "the exact imprint of [God's] nature" (Heb 1:3). Christ is the Word of God made flesh, the definitive content of everything that Law and the Prophets were trying to say. What is in Christ is the fulfillment of God's promise and the climax of the covenant with Israel. What is in Christ is nothing less than the steadfast love and covenant faithfulness of God—his *hesed* and *'emet* (cf. Jn 1:14, "full of grace and truth"). What is in Christ is the authoritative display of all the divine perfections, including "the power of God and the wisdom of God" (1 Cor 1:24). What theologians describe when they say what is in Christ, then, is first and foremost the essence of God. If it is knowledge of God that you seek, then you had best look to Jesus Christ.

Secondly, in describing what is in Christ we are also describing true *humanity*. Men and women have been created in God's own image, but we have also defaced it. Only Jesus is the perfect image of God (2 Cor 4:4; Col 1:15). The Son of Man is the second Adam, the exemplary covenant servant, the template of the loving and obedient child. If it is knowledge of yourself that you seek, of your nature and destiny, then you had best look to Jesus Christ.

The third thing we find in Christ is the *relationship* the Son establishes between God and his people: "In Christ God was reconciling the world to himself" (2 Cor 5:19). What theologians are ultimately for is the joyful publication of the redemption that is in Christ: "Therefore, if anyone is in Christ, he is a new creation" (2 Cor 5:17). In Christ is salvation, the salve for our souls.[48] It is the wonderful vocation of the theologian—both privilege and

---

[48]See Marcus Peter Johnson, *One with Christ: An Evangelical Theology of Salvation* (Wheaton, IL: Crossway, 2013).

responsibility—to announce the good news of this new, reconciled creation for which old, alienated creation has been groaning. If it is the hope of redemption that you seek, then you had best look to Jesus Christ, and him only.

Much, much more could, and should, be said about this third aspect of what is in Christ.[49] What is in Christ is but the first fruits of what will be in Christ, who will eventually fill all in all (Eph 1:23). What we find in Christ is the life, light and love of God. We also find the reconciled people of God: Israel and the church, Jew and Greek. And if we look hard enough, we see ourselves in Christ, adopted into the family of God. Christ is in us and we are in Christ; union and communion. When theologians say what is and is to come in Christ Jesus, they make known the point of the Scriptures and fulfill their vocation as "stewards of the mysteries of God" (1 Cor 4:1). Systematic theology is always, everywhere and at all times Trinitarian to the extent that what is in Christ—true deity, true humanity, the created order, redemption, the new creation—is a joint work of Father, Son and Spirit.

Prescription. Many of Paul's epistles display a common pattern of imperatives following indicatives. There is good reason for this structure. Theologians must not only describe but also direct disciples to conform to what is in Christ. Doctors of the church offer prescriptions: directions for the people of God to follow for the sake of their salvation and spiritual health. Indeed, this is the whole of our Christian task: to correspond to what is in Christ, to align our daily speech and action to what is really real—like Jesus, doing the will of the Father on earth as it is in heaven. To be, or not to be, in Christ: that is the most basic existential question. The most important thing doctors of the church can prescribe is *being in Christ*: "For you have died, and your life is hidden with Christ in God" (Col 3:3). To act out our life with Christ has nothing to do with pretending. Faith in Christ is no placebo. On the contrary, being in Christ is the only thing in heaven or on earth that has the power to preserve and transform us. To follow doctrinal prescriptions is not to make-believe but rather, by faith, to lay hold of what is ultimately real: what is in Christ.

---

[49]A critic may here object, "What about sin and hell? How can we describe these doctrines in terms of what is in Christ?" The sad fact is that theologians must on occasion also speak of what *is not* in Christ. We do so with a heavy heart, and with some awkwardness. Following Augustine, who spoke of evil as nonbeing, we may here need to speak of nonbeing-in-Christ, something that by definition is an improper kind of existence, inasmuch as it is an existence without the promise of life.

What doctors do with doctrine to grow healthy disciples: six summary theses. "Do no harm." Hippocrates got this far. Doctors of the church, however, are under the orders of a greater physician, one who does not simply avoid doing harm but who does positive good. Jesus makes well. Theologians promote well-being by teaching sound doctrine and by prescribing the body of Christ, so that others can taste and see what is in Christ. We are now in a position to say what theologians are for: to dispense doctrine and thereby make disciples of all nations. Here are six summary theses on how doctrine builds up the body of Christ.

Doctrine tells us who God is and what God is doing in Christ. There are other discourses that purport to be about God, but Christian theology is the attempt to say what is in Christ. What the world needs now, as it needs in every age, is to understand the good news that God has communicated his own light, life and love in the person and work of Jesus Christ for the purpose of interpersonal communion with men and women created in his image for fellowship and friendship with God. This is the special task of Christian theology: to help the church grasp the full significance of the good news of reconciliation in Christ.

Doctrine tells us who and what we are in Jesus Christ. Doctors of the church prescribe doctrine to preserve the integrity of Christian identity. We are not like the other nations—we are a holy nation and a royal priesthood (1 Pet 2:9), a people of the new covenant. Our destiny is to become Christlike. Thus theologians say what people *are* (and are for).

Doctrine restores sinners to their senses. Doctors of the church prescribe doctrine in order to minister reality—the only reliable tonic to the toxins of worldliness, meaninglessness and hopelessness. It is a slap in the face to those in an existential stupor. Doctors of the church prescribe doctrine to awaken those who are sleepwalking their way through life to what is really going on. Doctrine fills out the true story of the world, directing the eyes of faith to the bright contours of the splendor of God, who has sent his light into the world in the person of his Son and into our hearts in the person of the Spirit (2 Cor 4:6).

Doctrine provides a fiduciary intellectual framework for understanding God, the world and ourselves. Doctors of the church prescribe doctrine to dissipate the mists of confusion about the meaning of life. In this regard, doctors of the church are ophthalmologists who specialize in correcting world vision.

Doctrine instructs the head, orients the heart and guides the hand. Doctors of the church prescribe doctrine so that our faith, hope and love will go with the grain of the gospel and correspond to the historical and eschatological reality of what is in Jesus Christ.

Doctrine directs the church in the way of wisdom, godliness and human flourishing. Doctors of the church prescribe doctrine to clarify the church's mission. Indicative statements of what is in Christ implicitly contain the imperatival whisper, "Go and do likewise" (i.e., be conformed to Christ). In this regard, statements of doctrine are also tacit mission statements, indicating not simply what people are for, but in particular what the people of God are for (to be a holy nation).

Systematic theology is a ministry of understanding. What theology provides are helps to understanding the length, breadth, height and depth of the gospel. It is both the attempt to set forth in speech what is in Christ (to formulate doctrine), and the attempt to set forth in people what is in Christ (to make disciples). C. S. Lewis puts it best: "Every Christian is to become a little Christ. The whole purpose of becoming a Christian is simply nothing else."[50] What are theologians for? Farming. Theologians are farmers of men and women, and the particular crop they are to grow is the next generation of disciples. What are theologians for? For helping sons and daughters of God grow up into mature adulthood, even the measure of the stature of the fullness of Christ (Eph 4:13-15).

Where Doctrine Belongs: In the Body of Christ

Medicine that remains in the bottle is of no use to anyone. Its healing power is released only when the body ingests and absorbs it. Though doctrine is a health-giving tonic, some Christians refuse to take their medicine, preferring instead to swill the sickly sweet fast food of popular culture. It is thanks largely to the doctoral work of pastor-theologians that doctrine—heavenly medicine from above—gets into the bloodstream of the body of Christ. The pastor, as minister of the Word and teacher of doctrine, is the

---

[50]*Mere Christianity* (New York: Touchstone, 1996), 154.

church's primary care physician. The problem is that many pastors have stopped doctoring.

The purveyor of doctrine: pastor as doctor. What are theologians for? To train shepherd-doctors (Eph 4:11) or, even better, to become one: a pastor-theologian. I have been arguing that the prime constituency the theologian serves is not the academy but the church. The pastor-theologian should be evangelicalism's default doctor of the church.[51] After all, it falls to local pastors both to diagnose what ails the body of Christ and then to administer a good dose of christological reality (the Word of God) via sermon and sacrament (since baptism and the Lord's Supper are visible words).

Theologians serve the church by helping pastors to understand and proclaim the full measure of the truth, goodness and beauty of what is in Christ. A good grasp of theology is one of the best means of sermon preparation. Sermons are intrinsically theological. They must do more than entertain or communicate the how-to therapeutic wisdom of the day. In the hands of a competent pastor-theologian, the sermon is lifesaving surgery on the body of Christ. The proclamation of God's Word—the scalpel of the Spirit—cuts to the cultural quick, exposing the joints and marrow, the idols and ideologies that risk infecting the church body.[52] If the life is in the blood, teaching the Word of God is the transfusion of Christ's blood into the bloodstream of the church. Doctrine is for growing healthy disciples who exhibit in their own bodies individually and corporately the life that is in Christ.

The domain of doctrine: church as operating theater. We can connect the dramatic and medical models of doing theology by viewing the church as an operating theater, and the world as God's theater of operations.

The church is the proper domain of doctrine, the operating theater in which pastor-doctors wield the scalpel of the Spirit to mend Christian hearts and minds. Recall that the risen Christ gives pastor-doctors as gifts to the church "to equip the saints for the work of ministry, for building up the body of Christ" (Eph 4:11-12).

---

[51]See further Kevin J. Vanhoozer and Owen Strachan, *The Pastor as Public Theologian: Reclaiming a Lost Vision* (Grand Rapids: Baker, 2015) and Todd Wilson and Gerald Hiestand, *The Pastor Theologian: Resurrecting an Ancient Vision* (Grand Rapids: Zondervan, 2015).

[52]Paul warns Timothy that some will stop listening to the truth and "wander off into myths" (2 Tim 4:4). Good preaching exposes idolatry—our tendency to find the unworthy worthwhile.

We build up the body of Christ in order to equip it to do its proper work—its mission in and for the world, which is our theater of operations. What should a healthy body do? When all the bodily systems are functioning as they were designed to function, the body of Christ, like Jesus himself, becomes a living parable of the kingdom of God. The local church does not simply occupy space. It is a particular place where God's love and truth are discovered, celebrated and demonstrated (acted out in worship, witness and wisdom). Doctrine is never more sound or health-giving than when it encourages disciples to exhibit the reality of the kingdom by living out our being-in-Christ in every corner of the world's stage—on earth as it is in heaven (Eph 2:6).

Conclusion: The Real Work of Theology

Seneca worried about people wasting their lives because they make no time for philosophy. I agree with his diagnosis, but not his remedy. Neither ancient, modern or postmodern philosophy has a compelling answer to the problem of mortality—but theology does. Thus we can answer Richard Dawkins's impertinent question as to whether theologians have ever done anything that is the smallest use to anybody. They have. Theologians have found, if not the cure, then at least the prescription for dealing with cancer, or any other mortal illness. Knowing Christ and the power of his resurrection (Phil 3:10) is the ultimate cure, not only for death but for the despair that prowls by death's door (1 Pet 5:8). In the final analysis, to describe what is in Christ is to proclaim victory to the oppressed, and eternal life to the dying. The gospel is the good news that Christ defeats even death, together with everything else that threatens abundant life.

Heidegger believed that human existence could be authentic only if we resolutely face our mortality. Being-there for Heidegger thus translates into being-toward-death. Theologians have a different view of authenticity. They know how to deal with the shortness of life: by "redeeming the time" (Eph 5:16), that is, responding wisely, even defiantly, to mortality by describing, and demonstrating in community, union and communion with Christ. Call it being-toward-resurrection. "O cancer, where is thy victory? O cancer, where is thy sting?" (cf. 1 Cor 15:54).

What are theologians for? The answer should be clear. The real work of theology is indeed doctoring and farming: growing healthy disciples. Theologians grow healthy disciples who know how to live out the created order made new in Christ. Theology is all about eschatologically-enhanced farming: reaping the first fruits of eternal life in the power of the Spirit. Theologians are for cultivating growth and ministering health to the body of Christ. It turns out that theology, far from being a waste of time, is the only way to redeem time: by cultivating godliness, the lived knowledge of God. Bodies that take the prescription of evangelical theology strive to conform their speech, thought and actions to the mind and heart of Jesus Christ, the source and standard of all truth, goodness and beauty. The real work of theology is the work of *getting real*.

two

TRUE PICTURES

What Every Pastor Should Know About Biblical Truth and Interpretation

This essay was originally presented as a lecture to the annual theology conference of the Evangelical Free Church of America, held at Trinity Evangelical Divinity School in January 2015. I am grateful to Greg Strand for the invitation to give a keynote address on a topic of both urgent and perennial significance. It is appropriate, before we begin our tour of the theological galleries, to pose the question of the truth: are the biblical pictures of Israel and the church's worship, witness and wisdom true? What does it mean for a metaphor to be true? The question "What does it mean to be biblical?" has been a key concern of mine for years, since it lies at the heart of debates about theological method, authority and interpretation. That concern is evident here, too, and I am quick to raise the question as it concerns Scripture's truth. We must first ask what the Bible means—and what kind of picture it paints— before we can rule on its truth or falsehood. We need to attend to the Bible's picture of what truth is. That is what I try to do here: to call attention to the Bible's own vision of what it means to call God's Word true. (Those wanting a fuller treatment of the issue should consult my chapter "Augustinian Inerrancy" in Five Views on Biblical Inerrancy.*)[1] What I say in the introduction of this book about pictures holding the church captive pertains to its picture of truth too. I am convinced that some of the disagreements about inerrancy*

---

[1]"Augustinian Inerrancy: Literary Meaning, Literal Truth, and Literate Interpretation in the Economy of Biblical Discourse," in *Five Views on Biblical Inerrancy*, ed. J. Merrick and Stephen M. Garrett (Grand Rapids: Zondervan, 2013), 199-235.

derive from a poorly drawn picture of truth as what literalistically corre-
sponds to some state of affairs, an error that I dub "cronkitis"(a chronic and
obstructive literary disease). The way forward is not to abandon our con-
fession that Scripture is wholly true and trustworthy, but to correct our picture
of truth. When we do, we will see that the Bible contains true pictures—of
God, ourselves and the world—that prove reliable guides to the way of Jesus
Christ: pictures to live by, and on which to stake our lives.

INTRODUCTION: "THE LITERAL TRUTH OF EVERY WORD"

It's a great pleasure to be here speaking about one of my favorite subjects—
what it means to be biblical—to one of my favorite people groups: evangelical pastors. You've come back to seminary and, as we're in school, it's only
appropriate that we begin with a pop quiz. It consists of a single true/false
question, which effectively makes it pass/fail. Here it is: "Evangelical Christians believe that every word of the Bible is literally true." This is how journalists typically describe evangelical belief concerning the Bible: "The literal
truth of every word." "Truth" pertains to inerrancy and "literal" to hermeneutics, so this question is in the crosshairs of the topic I have been asked to
address this morning: the relationship of inerrancy to hermeneutics.

Let's return to the statement on your pop quiz: true or false? Surely those
who hold a high view of Scripture as verbally inspired can affirm that every
word is literally true. The fact of the matter is that individual words are
neither true nor false. Words by themselves make no claims about the way
things are. Take the word *loincloth*. True or false? The question is absurd:
everything depends on what else you say about it.

Is it not pedantic or overly academic to interpret my question in so hair-
splitting a manner? Yes, it is—but I'm trying to make a point. Evangelicals best
honor the truth of Scripture by reading literally, not literalistically, and much
of what I want to say is intended to help us distinguish between these two
senses of truth. The problem is that the modern media has tricked even evangelicals into thinking that inerrancy means reading literalistically. Once one
forges a conceptual link between inerrancy and literalistic interpretation, it
becomes easy to discredit the former by debunking silly examples of the latter.

Many in our congregations, having heard journalists define inerrancy, may
think they have to believe "the literal truth of every word" in order to hold a

high view of biblical inspiration and authority. In so doing, they inadvertently identify literal truth with journalistic truth, the kind of factual truth that we expect of newspaper reporters. After all, isn't the gospel "good *news*"?

"The most trusted man in America." Let's examine journalistic truth in more detail by looking at one of its most respected recent exemplars. Walter Cronkite was working for a Kansas City radio station (KCMO) at the ripe old age of twenty-one when one day his boss's wife called to report that three firemen had jumped to their deaths while battling a blaze at city hall. His boss wanted Cronkite to interrupt the regularly scheduled program, but Cronkite, trained as a newspaper reporter to uphold high standards of accuracy, wanted to check with the fire department first. "You don't have to check on it," his boss insisted, "My wife called and told me." "I do have to check on it," replied Cronkite. The frustrated boss took the microphone and reported the incident himself. It so happened that the fire had been minor. There were no deaths—but Cronkite was fired anyway.

Cronkite went on to become the anchor of *The CBS Evening News* from 1962–1981, and his reputation for checking facts led to his being named "the most trusted man in America" in a 1972 opinion poll. The "father of television news"[2] was the nation's authoritative storyteller for years, upholding in the new medium the high standards of clarity, accuracy and objectivity that had made newspapers the "fourth estate," even as he dealt with some of the most traumatic events of the twentieth century, including the assassination of JFK and the landing of the first man on the moon.

Cronkite's famous sign-off ("And that's the way it is") summed up his journalistic philosophy. He once declared, "Facts are sacred."[3] Journalistic truth involves the discipline of assembling and verifying facts. The discipline of verification and dictums like "Accuracy is the foundation upon which everything else is built" are what separates journalism from other modes of communication. It would appear that belief in "the literal truth of every word" of the Bible commits us to journalistic truth. The reality, however, is that we need to do more investigative digging if we are to get to the bottom of this story.

---

[2]Douglas Brinkley, *Cronkite* (New York: HarperCollins, 2012), 659.
[3]Brinkley, *Cronkite*, 665. From an interview with Robert Vaughan, "Cruising with Cronkite," *Motor Boating & Sailing*, November 1976.

We begin with some background. A 2010 Pew Global Survey of Evangelical Protestant leaders from 166 countries found widespread agreement that the Bible is the Word of God. However, these same leaders were almost evenly split between those who thought the Bible should be read literally, word for word (50%), and those who thought that not everything in the Bible should be taken literally (48%).[4] This disagreement perfectly illustrates my point. There is confusion over what it means to read literally, perhaps because the term has been skewed in a modern journalistic direction.[5] In particular, note the prominence of the term *literally* in both of the above options. Because the term is never defined, I am reluctant to choose either option. To complicate matters further, the word *literally* has become one of the most misused words in the English language,[6] sometimes as a throwaway intensifier replacement for *figuratively*! *Literally* now means *not literally*, as in "Vanhoozer's lecture was literally electrifying." What does *literally* literally mean? Conservative evangelicals need to know. Wheaton, we have a problem!

A hyperliteral caricature of biblical truth holds us captive. The way forward, I submit, is to distinguish "literal" from "literalistic" truth: a supple literalism from a wooden literalism. We need to learn to associate *literal* with *limber*, not *lumber*. The literal sense is a function of the author's communicative intent. Because the Bible is clear, we do not need an advanced degree in hermeneutics to read for the literal sense, though we do need to learn to read well—as the text was intended to be read, as the unified story of God's plan of salvation and *shalom*. I call literal interpretation "well-versed" and

---

[4]www.pewforum.org/2011/06/22/global-survey-of-evangelical-protestant-leaders/. A June 2014 Gallup poll similarly found that 28% of Americans believe the Bible to be "the actual word of God and is to be taken literally, word for word" while 47% agreed with the statement "The Bible is the inspired Word of God but not everything in it should be taken literally." See www.gallup .com/poll/170834/three-four-bible-word-god.aspx.

[5]What I call "skewing" has been described by Hans Frei as a "great hermeneutical reversal." Frei believed that a sea change took place in the eighteenth century whereby literal meaning became a function of ostensive reference, that is, pointing out something in the world that was empirically verifiable. The Bible's literal meaning and truth were taken hostage to what moderns thought they could recover about "what actually happened." What used to be a purely textual function—literality—became a function of an extratextual reality. See the story in Hans Frei, *The Eclipse of Biblical Narrative: A Study in Eighteenth and Nineteenth Century Hermeneutics* (New Haven, CT: Yale University Press, 1974).

[6]See Christopher Muther, "Literally the Most Misused Word," *The Boston Globe*, July 19, 2011, www .boston.com/lifestyle/articles/2011/07/19/literally_the_most_misused_word/.

literalistic interpretation "poorly-versed." What the church needs now is "well-versed" inerrancy.[7]

Pictures of inerrancy. David Dockery helpfully distinguishes several types of inerrancy.[8] Each relies on a particular concept or picture of how language can be true. *Absolute inerrancy* minimizes the human aspects of Scripture, and comes close to a mechanical dictation view of inspiration. The assumption is because that the Bible is God's Word, and because God is omniscient (all-knowing), the Bible will be inerrant (all-correct). For example, James Orr defines inerrancy as "hard and fast literality in minute matters of historical, geographical, and scientific detail."[9] This mentality often leads its proponents to force the biblical authors to sing in chronological harmony, as when Harold Lindsell suggests, in order to smooth out the differences between the accounts in Matthew and Luke, that Peter denied Jesus a total of six times. However, we may query the implied picture of truth as meticulous correspondence. The assumption that the Gospels were intended as accurate chronological reports "is wrong insofar as it imposes a modern scientific frame of mind on the text."[10] I respond to absolute inerrancy the way Goldilocks did when she tried Papa Bear's big armchair: "Too hard!" I'm not comfortable sitting in the seat of the absolute inerrantist. The Bible does not read as a storehouse of factual information. I strongly suspect that many of the issues inerrancy's critics have with it arise because of this unnecessarily literalistic understanding of truth and the interpretive contortions that inevitably result—what I call "poorly versed inerrancy." It would be wrong to call "absolute" inerrancy the highest view of truth— unless of course we're thinking of the "high places" in ancient Israel (places of idolatry). To insist that biblical truth must be absolute is a little like insisting that God cannot have a body— and we know what the story of Jesus does with that assumption.

Partially in response to the above, some progressive evangelicals hold to *limited inerrancy*, restricting the domain of Scripture's truth to matters of faith and salvation only. Inspiration keeps the authors from making mistakes

---

[7]See further my "Augustinian Inerrancy: Literary Meaning, Literal Truth, and Literate Interpretation in the Economy of Biblical Discourse."
[8]David Dockery, "Variations on Inerrancy," *SBC Today* (May 1986): 10-11.
[9]James Orr, *Revelation and Inspiration* (Grand Rapids; Baker, 1969), 199.
[10]So Jitse M. van der Meer, "Infallibility and Inerrancy in the Canadian and American Reformed Churches," *Reformed Academic* (April 3, 2013): 9.

in areas related to salvation, but inspiration is not a blank check that pays for all historical or scientific truth claims. If absolute inerrancy is too hard, limited inerrancy is too soft, in that it fails to provide the needed support for gospel proclamation.

Finally, *critical inerrancy* is the position that the Bible is true in all that it affirms when taken on its own terms, not ours. We could also call this "well-versed" inerrancy. To be "well-versed" is to be a competent workman, a skilled reader who rightly handles the word of truth (2 Tim 2:15). Well-versed inerrancy is neither too hard nor too soft but "just right." It is not literalistic but *literate*, as in the ability not simply to read but to read well. Critical inerrancy is simply literate, well-versed inerrancy. Like discerning connoisseurs of art, well-versed readers of Scripture know that authors can communicate truth in a variety of forms, just as painters can render the world in a variety of genres and styles. It is this version of inerrancy, I believe, that the 1978 Chicago Statement on Biblical Inerrancy sets forth.[11]

THE NATURE OF SCRIPTURE: THESES ON INSPIRED DISCOURSE

Let me turn briefly to the nature of Scripture to unpack the suggestion that Scripture itself is a canonical art gallery—an assemblage of true pictures that, together, comprise a divinely authorized biblical exhibition of the "collected works of the triune God"—scenes of God creating, sustaining and redeeming.

Though ultimately authored by God, the Bible is not a word from outer space. It was not dropped from heaven but written by human beings. Nor is the Bible a buried time capsule from the ancient Near Eastern past. On the contrary, it is the living and active Word of God (Heb 4:12).

The Bible is like every other book inasmuch as it shows the telltale signs of its location in human language, history and culture. Some self-professing evangelicals say that a "fully human" Bible means an "errant" Bible, since "to err is human."[12] But this is faulty reasoning. Jesus was truly and fully human—"tempted as we are, yet without sin" (Heb 4:15; see also 2 Cor 5:21; 1 Jn 3:5). It is fallacious to insist that anything human must have errors.

---

[11]The Chicago Statement can be accessed at http://www.bible-researcher.com/chicago1.html.

[12]See, for example, Peter Enns, *Inspiration and Incarnation: Evangelicals and the Problem of the Old Testament* (Grand Rapids: Baker, 2005) and Kenton L. Sparks, *God's Word in Human Words: An Evangelical Appropriation of Critical Biblical Scholarship* (Grand Rapids: Baker Academic, 2008).

"Completely apart from the inspiration of God, humans can write long stretches of text without erring or making mistakes if they do thorough research and check their material carefully."[13]

Whereas other books *may* not err, the Bible *cannot* err because, unlike every other book, God is its ultimate author.[14] The Bible is not only human but holy, set apart for a divine purpose. God commissions just these texts to play a vital and authoritative role in the plan of salvation whereby the triune Lord communicates his light (knowledge), life (redemption) and love (fellowship). Specifically, the Father initiates, the Son effectuates and the Spirit consummates the discourse that Holy Scripture preserves in writing. Scripture is a means of God's self-presentation, a collection of diverse forms of discourse that, taken together, are ingredients in the extraordinary ministry of God's Word by which the risen Christ announces the gospel, administers his new creational kingdom and imparts his light and life to readers made right-minded and right-hearted—fit for communion with God— through the illumination of the Holy Spirit.

"Verbal" inspiration guards against the idea that God authorizes only the authors, or their thoughts, rather than their actual writings. "Plenary" inspiration guards against the idea that only certain books or passages are authored and authorized by God. Inerrancy rests on this insight into the nature of the text: the Bible is true and trustworthy because its ultimate Author is true and trustworthy. What is literally true in Scripture is not the individual Hebrew and Greek words but rather *what is said by means of them.* B. B. Warfield was right: what Scripture says, God says.[15]

Again, isolated words are neither true nor false, but they have the potential to be so. Speakers actualize that potential when they put words to use. Discourse is "language in use": something someone says to someone about something at some time in some way for some purpose. It is now well known that speakers and authors do many different kinds of things with words. Not

---

[13]Craig L. Blomberg, *Can We Still Believe the Bible? An Evangelical Engagement with Contemporary Questions* (Grand Rapids: Brazos Press, 2014), 122.

[14]The Bible is also unlike other books because (1) it has God (Jesus Christ) as its ultimate content, (2) it has God (the Holy Spirit) as its ultimate interpreter and (3) it has the church for its ultimate interpretive community.

[15]See B. B. Warfield, "'It Says:' 'Scripture Says:' 'God says:'" in *Inspiration and Authority of the Bible* (Phillipsburg, NJ: Presbyterian & Reformed, 1970), 299-348.

everything we say is a journalistic truth claim. Sometimes we use words as tools with which to explain the world in great detail; sometimes we use words to express our undying love; sometimes we use words that are familiar in one domain to describe something that cannot be seen with the naked eye (think of Jesus' parables of the kingdom).

While God personally stands behind everything he says, not everything in Scripture is intended primarily as a truth claim. In addition to telling history, God also assures his people about the future. There are psalms intended to celebrate the created order and the faithfulness of God who upholds it. Still other parts of Scripture are written to warn, encourage and comfort—unlike what one finds in most journalistic reporting. Above all, however, the Bible is unlike every other book in that its ultimate aim is to present Jesus Christ.

On the road to Emmaus the risen Christ explained to his disciples that the Law and the Prophets were intended to point to him and his work (Lk 24:13-35). He later declared, "All authority in heaven and on earth has been given to me" (Matt 28:18). We may draw two inferences: (1) because he *lives*, Christ continues to speak in and through Scripture by means of his appointed spokespeople; (2) because he *rules*, everything he says is authoritative. As the one through whom and for whom all things were created (Col 1:16), Jesus' voice has an intrinsic right to be heard and heeded. Scripture is both the cradle where the incarnate Christ lies and the scepter by which the ascended Christ now rules the church.[16] J. I. Packer describes Scripture as "God the Father preaching God the Son in the power of God the Holy Ghost."[17] The application of this inspired sermon is Christlikeness. The Holy Spirit uses Scripture to conform the people of God to the image of God made flesh in Jesus Christ. The purpose of Scripture is both to inform us about Christ and to form Christ in us. All kinds of Scripture—law, prophecy, wisdom and so forth—are "profitable for teaching . . . and for training in righteousness" (2 Tim 3:16)—for forming Christ in us.[18] Scripture renews our minds, reorients our hearts and revitalizes our imaginations.

---

[16]Luther refers to Scripture as a cradle in "Preface to the Old Testament," in *Martin Luther's Basic Theological Writing*, ed. Timothy Lull (Minneapolis: Fortress, 1989), 119. Calvin refers to Scripture as Christ's scepter in the *Institutes* IV.2.4.

[17]Packer, *God Has Spoken: Revelation and the Bible* (Grand Rapids: Baker, 1979), 97.

[18]"The Scriptures attest that God wishes to enter into communication with humanity, taking on multiple forms of mediation" (Pontifical Biblical Commission, *The Inspiration and Truth of Sacred Scripture* [Collegeville, MN: Liturgical Press, 2014], 118).

We can sum up this all-too-brief section on the nature and function of Scripture—its ontology and teleology—with five theses:

1. Scripture is not a word from outer space or a time capsule from the past, but a living and active Word of God for the church today.

2. The Bible is both like and unlike every other book: it is both a human, contextualized discourse and a holy discourse ultimately authored by God and intended to be read in canonical context.

3. The Bible is not a dictionary of holy words but a written discourse: something someone says to someone about something in some way for some purpose.

4. God does a variety of things with the human discourse that makes up Scripture, but above all he prepares the way for Jesus Christ, the climax of a long, covenantal story.

5. God uses the Bible both to present Christ and to form Christ in us.

WHAT EVERY PASTOR SHOULD KNOW: THESES ON INERRANCY AND INTERPRETATION

We turn now from a consideration of the nature of Scripture to theses on its interpretation and truth. The first set of theses guards against deceptive misunderstandings, the second provides definitions and the third offers some directions pastors can follow to facilitate better understanding.

Deceptions to avoid.

1. *Do not confuse inerrancy with "perfect book" theology.* Yes, the "law of the Lord is perfect" (Ps 19:7), but we must take care not to impose *our* standards of perfection on Scripture, in the same way that we must take care not to impose our standards of perfections on God, as "perfect being" theology is wont to do. That way leads to idolatry for the simple reason that we are too quick to assume that God conforms to *our* ideas of perfection.

2. *Do not confuse literal with literalistic interpretation.* One symptom of "perfect book" theology is what I call "cronkitis": an affliction that causes people to measure all truth by the standards of modern journalism. Inspiration and inerrancy do not mean that every biblical text has to be interpreted as making factual truth claims. As Craig Blomberg puts it, "To insist that there was an actual Good Samaritan would impose a standard of truth alien to a

parable's purpose."[19] Cronkitis gives rise to an overly literalistic reading of passages where other levels of meaning may be intended. The main problem with cronkitis is that it hinders biblical literacy. The Song of Songs is a good case in point. The author uses metaphors, similes, and other figures of speech to express the beauty of his Beloved. A literalistic artistic rendering runs roughshod over the imagery, and the result is a monstrosity. A "nose like a tower of Lebanon," "eyes like doves" and "hair like a flock of goats"—think about what kind of monster would result if this imagery were interpreted literalistically.[20]

3. *Do not mistake inerrancy for a decoding device of holy enigmas or a panacea for resolving interpretive disagreement.* Inerrancy is not a blunt instrument, nor does it take years to master. It is more like a car: driving lessons are recommended, but just about anyone can get a license. The mystery hidden for ages has indeed been revealed in Scripture (Col 1:26), but it is not enough to have the message. We have to be able to make sense of what it says. The broadcasts from German U-boats during World War II conveyed true information—indeed, life and death information. They conveyed not only weather reports but, more importantly, the location of both German and Allied ships. The British cryptologists trying to break the Enigma code knew that the information was true, but it was of no practical use until they could decode it. Inerrancy assures us that whatever Scripture reveals is true, but inerrancy alone does not tell us what God is saying in Scripture. Inerrancy is not a decoding key that allows evangelicals to lord it over other interpreters, nor can one appeal to inerrancy to resolve interpretive disputes. Truth is one thing; meaning another.

Definitions to ponder. Saying what inerrancy is not or what one cannot do with inerrancy gets us only so far. While it is important to avoid common mistakes, it is even more important to be able to say something positive about the truth of the Bible. What does it mean to confess that the canon displays "true pictures"? We need to define at least four key terms in order to rightly appreciate biblical inerrancy.

---

[19]Blomberg, *Can We Still Believe the Bible?*, 149.

[20]Avoiding literalistic interpretation becomes even more urgent when the language in question is predicated on God. See Mark Sheridan, *Language for God in Patristic Tradition: Wrestling with Biblical Anthropomorphism* (Downers Grove, IL: IVP Academic, 2015) and Brian C. Howell, *In the Eyes of God: A Contextual Approach to Biblical Anthropomorphic Metaphors* (Eugene, OR: Pickwick, 2013).

1. *Infallibility.* As Jesus was truly human yet incapable of sinning (i.e., "impeccable"), so biblical discourse is genuinely human yet incapable of failing to accomplish its purpose (i.e., "infallible"). It is not that the humanity of Jesus or the words of Scripture are themselves divine, but rather that a divine person is the agent or subject who animates and employs them: "For as the rain and the snow come down from heaven and do not return there but water the earth, making it bring forth and sprout . . . so shall my word be that goes out from my mouth; it shall not return to me empty, but it shall accomplish that which I purpose, and shall succeed in the thing for which I sent it" (Is 55:10-11).[21]

2. *Inerrancy.* Inerrancy is a subset of infallibility. When God sends us statements, they will be free from error. God does not lie (Heb 6:18; 2 Tim 2:13); neither is God ignorant (Heb 4:13). This—truth—is the kind of success at which assertions aim. Paul Feinberg's oft-cited definition remains valuable: "Inerrancy means that when all facts are known, the Scriptures . . . properly interpreted will be shown to be wholly true in everything that they affirm, whether that has to do with doctrine or morality or with the social, physical, or life sciences."[22]

Feinberg does not say "in everything that they *say*" but "in everything that they *affirm.*" It is a subtle but substantial difference. The biblical authors *say* "the sun rose," but that's simply a conventional way of speaking where the words correspond to the phenomenon or appearance of things, not to their reality. We'll come back to Feinberg's other loaded phrase: "properly interpreted." What *that* means is the $64,000 question.

David Dockery's definition of inerrancy is similar: "When all the facts are known, the Bible (in its original writings) properly interpreted, in light of which culture and communication means had developed by the time of its composition, will be shown to be completely true (and therefore not false) in all that it affirms, to the degree of precision intended by the author, in all matters relating to God and his creation."[23]

---

[21]Note that I am defining infallibility in a somewhat idiosyncratic way. In the North American discussion, infallibility is often associated with limited inerrancy: true in matters of faith and practice only.

[22]Paul D. Feinberg, "The Meaning of Inerrancy," in Norman L. Geisler, ed., *Inerrancy* (Grand Rapids: Zondervan, 1980), 294.

[23]David S. Dockery, *Christian Scripture: An Evangelical Perspective on Inspiration, Authority and Interpretation* (Nashville, TN: Broadman & Holman, 1995), 64.

My own proposed definition builds on the two previous ones. *Inerrancy means that the biblical authors speak the truth in all things they affirm (insofar as they make affirmations) and will eventually be seen to have spoken truly (when right-hearted and right-minded readers read rightly).* There are two things to notice. "When they make affirmations" suggests that the authors are not always stating how things are. "Right reading" suggests that you cannot really do justice to the Bible's literal truth without also talking about interpretation. Inerrancy and hermeneutics are joined at the exegetical hip.

Literal interpretation is all about following the way the words go (that is, understanding what authors are doing with their words). Literal interpretation acknowledges figures of speech and literary genres for what they are. The literal meaning of a metaphor is the metaphorical meaning. Historical narrative should be read as historical narrative, apocalyptic as apocalyptic, parable as parable, and so on. In contrast, literalistic interpretation stubbornly refuses to follow the way the words go, insisting for example that we read Jesus' parables as if they were historical narrative, or that we read all biblical narratives as though they were journalistic reporting.

Evangelicals usually have no trouble recognizing metaphors (no one says that inerrancy requires us to believe that trees have hands on the basis of Is 55:12). However, we're less adept when it comes to recognizing literary forms, especially those that are no longer in use. The danger of illiterate, poorly versed interpretation is that, in making a mistake about the kind of book we're reading, we risk going wrong not just in one verse, but everywhere. The moral is clear: literal truth requires literal interpretation, which in turn requires literary knowledge and sensitivity—in a word, *literacy*.

A final point about the term *inerrancy*. It is a negative construction, like *im*-possible (*not* possible). Why not keep things simple, and positive, and affirm the "truthfulness" of Scripture? The Bible is authoritative because it is God's true word. Yes—but, to steal a line, what is truth?

3. *Truth.* The words of Scripture are the words of the Word, the one who sits on the great white throne and says, "Write this down, for these words are trustworthy and true" (Rev 21:5). Here especially, we have to attend to what Scripture itself says rather than impose our ideas of what we think perfect truth should be. Here are some verses about truth that a well-versed inerrancy will ponder: "Let God be proved true" (Rom 3:4, NRSV), "Your

word is truth" (Jn 17:17) and "Heaven and earth will pass away, but my words will not pass away" (Mt 24:35).

What *is* truth? The Bible associates truth with what can be relied on. God's Word is true because both God and what he says are wholly reliable. Scripture is the utterly reliable personal Word of the triune God. Everything God says—promises, warnings, commands, and yes, statements—can be counted on to accomplish the purpose for which they were spoken. Indeed, through the biblical narrative God proves himself true by time and time again keeping his word. Truth in Scripture is thus closely connected with God's covenant faithfulness. Truth according to Scripture is a covenantal correspondence, a faithful fit, between God's Words and God's deeds.

The metaphorical statements in the Bible—that God is a shepherd, that the cross is a victory, that the church is a holy nation—are also true. They are true verbal pictures, true indications of the way things are. Truth concerns "aboutness." When we speak about things, our speech is true if what we say corresponds to reality. It is important to remember, however, that we can speak about reality in many ways, just as painters (or cartographers, as we will see below) can represent the world in a variety of genres and styles.

True words are words that can be counted on because they communicate what *is*. This is not to say that the Bible provides encyclopedic knowledge on every topic that it touches. Other texts do this too: travel books, TV listings, the *Guinness Book of World Records,* and so on. Only the Bible tells us what *is* in Jesus Christ. Jesus *is* the truth (Jn 14:6) because he communicates what God is, what humanity is and what the gospel is.

True words communicate reality (what is), and this is why they are reliable. J. I. Packer is right: "Authority belongs to truth and truth only.... I can make no sense—no reverent sense, anyway—of the idea, sometimes met, that God speaks his truth to us in and through false statements by biblical writers."[24]

4. *Error.* The Chicago Statement on Biblical Inerrancy clearly states that there are no errors in Scripture. Augustine, Roman Catholics and Protestants have historically agreed.[25] Conspicuous by its absence, however, is any

---

[24]J. I. Packer, *Truth and Power: The Place of Scripture in the Christian Life* (Wheaton, IL: Harold Shaw Publishers, 1996), 46.
[25]Augustine did not understand inerrancy in quite the same way some evangelicals today do, not least because of his penchant for figural interpretation.

consensus on the definition of error. Confusion over what counts as an error frequently clouds discussions about inerrancy and hermeneutics. In math, of course, it is easy enough to recognize an error (e.g., 2+2=5). The situation is not as simple with discourse. "What someone says about something in some way for some purpose" counts as an error only if the words purport to say what *is,* then fail to do so. If we follow the way *these* words go, they will lead us astray. Errant discourse is dangerous because the errors that infect discourse makes what one says unreliable and untrustworthy— a toxic communication.

Sir Christopher Ricks once gave a lecture called "Mistakes in Literature and Whether They Matter." He used as an example the episode in *Lord of the Flies* when Piggy's spectacles are used to start a fire.[26] Apparently William Golding got his optics backwards: Piggy is shortsighted, so the glasses he would have been prescribed could not possibly have been used to magnify the sun's light. Ricks calls this an "external" mistake, a contradiction between what happens in the book and what we know to be the case. "Internal" mistakes, in contrast, are those where the writer claims two incompatible things within the same work. Here Ricks cites Gustave Flaubert's *Madame Bovary* as an example, because at times the narrator says his heroine's eyes are brown but at other times he says they are blue.

What kind and degree of consistency should we expect from the biblical texts? The challenge is to refrain from imposing *our* standards of correctness or incorrectness on the biblical texts. To think that inerrancy requires modern standards of exactness is like insisting that everyone in the world use the metric system of measurement, or that all painters should strive to make their works as realistic as possible, as if photographs were truer to reality than Impressionist paintings. Blomberg observes, "We live in a scientific world that values high degrees of precision . . . hence by default we frequently impose modern standards of accuracy on ancient texts in hopelessly anachronistic fashion."[27] The Chicago Statement neatly sidesteps this temptation: "We . . . deny that inerrancy is negated by Biblical phenomena such as a lack

---

[26]I am taking this example from Julian Barnes's novel, *Flaubert's Parrot* (New York: Vintage, 1990), 76. See also Christopher Ricks's response to being featured (and debunked) as a character in Barnes's postmodern novel (Christopher Ricks, *Essays in Appreciation* [Oxford: Oxford University Press, 1996], 308-9).

[27]Blomberg, *Can We Still Believe the Bible?*, 126.

of modern technical precision, irregularities of grammar or spelling, observational descriptions of nature, the reporting of falsehoods, the use of hyperbole and round numbers, the topical arrangements of material, variant selections of material in parallel accounts, or the use of free citations."[28]

We must read the Bible on its own terms, not ours. "Perfect book" theology goes astray when it assumes that the Bible has to conform to our modern notions about truth. To be biblical means being willing to conform our understanding about truth to Scripture's. A well-versed inerrancy refuses to impose our modern standards of error on the biblical texts.[29] This refusal should provide adequate inoculation against the cronkitis that too often mars our biblical interpretation. For example, it should protect readers from thinking that verses like Psalm 93:1 are errors: "Yes, the world is established; it shall never be moved." Once upon a time this verse served as a proof text for a geocentric picture of the universe. We now know better. As the ESV note helpfully reminds us "The psalmist is not concerned with the kind of motion that physics studies."[30]

John Frame's analysis is well versed. Inerrancy means that Scripture is true, not that it is maximally precise. Frame defines "error" as the failure to make good on one's claim. Everything thus depends on what *kind* of claim is being made.[31] Because the Bible is written in everyday language for everyday readers, it does not claim to be maximally precise. It is as precise as it needs to be to do that for which it was sent. Inerrancy means that Scripture's aim is unerring (it can't miss) but it is incumbent on us to make sure we know what kind of discourse—what kind and degree of precision—it is aiming for. Thus we need to turn from defining inerrancy to developing morals for right interpretation.

Directions to follow: six morals for interpretation.

1. *Inerrancy is not a quick fix for pervasive interpretive pluralism, nor is it a way to determine in advance what kind of truth we will discover in Scripture.*

---

[28]Article XIII.

[29]For more on the importance of resisting modern scientific understandings of error, see van der Meer, "Infallibility and Inerrancy," and J. P. Holding and Nick Peters, *Defining Inerrancy: Affirming a Defensible Faith for a New Generation* (Clarcona, FL: Tekton E-Bricks, 2014).

[30]This recalls another saying: "The Bible tells us not how the heavens go but how to go to heaven."

[31]See the discussion in John Frame, *The Doctrine of the Word of God* (Phillipsburg, NJ: P&R Publishing, 2010), 172-74.

Inerrancy is not a full-blown hermeneutic. People who agree on inerrancy will continue to disagree about what the Bible actually says, at least on some things (e.g., women's ordination or predestination). Instead, inerrancy is a call to a long hermeneutical obedience—to interpret in the same direction the words are going. To understand is to *stand under*, to have faith that the divine author is utterly reliable, speaking truth in different ways, and that following the way his words go will lead us to the one who is the Word, Jesus Christ: the way to human flourishing, the truth of God and humanity, and the one in whom we find eternal life.

2. *Inerrancy applies to the authorial discourse of Scripture, not to our interpretations of it.* God's Word is utterly trustworthy and wholly reliable. Its interpreters? Not so much. Inerrancy does not extend to our interpretations. The best interpreter is therefore a humble interpreter, open to correction by the text and willing to listen to other interpreters, especially the "great cloud of interpreters" (Heb 12:1) who have preceded us in church history.

3. *Inerrancy does not entail a literalistic hermeneutic, but we must believe that the literal meaning, when rightly interpreted, is true.* The Bible is wholly true in all that it affirms *when rightly interpreted by right-minded and right-hearted readers.* This condition—"when rightly interpreted"—is a doozy. Indeed, "perfect book" theologians may insist that only "perfect interpreters" can read rightly. This raises the question whether the ideal reader must be a "historically omniscient perfect exegete"—one who can follow the way the words were meant to go in their original context. This sets the interpretive bar at an unrealistic height. Pastors cannot afford to wait to preach the Old Testament until they have mastered every ancient Near Eastern context, nor is it realistic to think that most laypeople will be able to make their way through the jungle of scholarly disagreement. To equate "right-minded" with scholarly is a mistake. Biblical interpreters must first and foremost be humble exegetes who rely not only on scholarly aids, but on the illumination of the Spirit. The Spirit does not bestow historical omniscience, but renewed minds and contrite hearts that are open rather than resistant to the truth.

Right interpretation requires *virtuous* readers, not perfect ones, and this is primarily a matter of saintly dispositions, not scholarly acquisitions. Humility is a prime interpretive virtue. It is a matter of readers' readiness to have their own opinions corrected by the text and, at times, by new scholarship. At the same time, interpretive humility must be tempered by the conviction that the Bible is God's true Word and by the mandate to preach the gospel. After all, God's purpose in speaking is communication. Inerrancy—the conviction that God's Word communicates truth—should give preachers boldness, even as hermeneutics, and the fact that we are fallible and fallen interpreters, should give us pause. Interpretive omniscience, then, is beyond our grasp, but not so interpretive virtue. The combination of inerrancy and hermeneutics makes for preachers who are both bold and humble. The best way to get this balance right is to become a person of interpretive virtue—one who prays, pays attention to and performs the text by doing what it says.

4. *The truth of the Bible does not depend on our interpretation, but determining this truth depends on a prior determining of its meaning.* The determination of truth presupposes meaning. We can affirm the Bible's truth, but we cannot say what that truth is until we discover what the biblical authors have said. It is something of an empty victory to know that the Bible is true if we do not also know what it means. Meaning is therefore prior to an appreciation of the truth. We cannot say "true" or "false" until we are clear about what has been said.[32] This is why the better definitions of inerrancy typically add some such phrase as "when properly interpreted." Similarly, literary form is prior to meaning-content. We will not know what a sentence means until we first determine what kind of a sentence it is. We should affirm the inerrancy of the Song of Songs, for example, but first we have to determine what kind of literature it is before judging its particular sentences true or false.

5. *The diverse forms of biblical literature are like maps in a canonical atlas that draw the world in different ways.* We will be able to follow what the Bible says only if we understand what kind of literature we are reading. A description requires one kind of response, a prescription quite another. It is one thing to make sense of straightforward statements, and something altogether different to read satire. There are many kinds of literature in the Bible, and we must be take care not come to the Bible with a ready-made concept of "perfect book" already in hand.

---

[32]As philosopher of language William P. Alston puts it: "It is only after the proposition has been assigned that the question of truth value can be raised" (*A Realist Conception of Truth* [Ithaca, NY: Cornell University Press, 1996], 260).

Maps—and cartography in general—are a good illustration of this point. Consider maps of city subways. The London Underground (the Tube) is a convenient way of traversing that great city. Now consider the standard Tube map, originally designed by Harry Beck in his spare time in 1931. City officials were initially skeptical of Beck's map, but when they tentatively introduced it to the public it was an immediate hit. Why? Because earlier maps, although in one sense "truer" to reality in their representation of the distance between stations, were also harder to use, since the centrally located stations were bunched close together and the out-of-town stations were almost off the map. Beck's genius was to realize that passengers were less interested in geographic accuracy than in how to get from one station to another, and where to change trains. So he adopted a cartographic convention of evenly spaced stations, with hash marks representing stations and circles representing stations where one could transfer from one line to another.

Is Beck's map true or false? Everything depends on what it claims. Does it claim that the central line, represented on the map by the red line, is literally red? No, it does not. Does it claim that the intervals between stations on the map correspond to the actual distance between them, so that the distance between Bond Street and Oxford Circus is one inch? Of course not! The "fit" between what the map shows and the way the London Underground actually is can only be determined once we understand the cartographer's intentions and the map's conventions.

Here is the crucial point: a map communicates something about the way the world is. It gives us a *true picture*. However, no one map captures everything that is true about the world. There are many kinds of maps, and each kind communicates a different type of information. Road maps highlight streets, freeways and interstates. They are useful for driving, but not for finding buried treasure. Weather maps give information about precipitation zones. A surveyor's plat shows where properties begin and end. Economic maps highlight the natural resources in a given region. Topographic maps use contour lines to describe the elevation of an area, and are invaluable for hiking.

I trust the point is clear. There is no one right way to map the world, no universal all-purpose map. There is more than one kind of fit: cartographic correspondence is a many-splendored thing. So, too, is canonical correspondence. The whole Bible is true, but there is no one-size-fits-all correspondence between what Scripture says and what is. No one kind of biblical literature is more true than another. On the contrary, there are many kinds of literary "maps" (genres) in Scripture, each of which communicates something about God, the world or human beings in its own distinct way. The Psalms and Paul's epistles both speak of God, but not in the same way. Yet each form of biblical discourse infallibly accomplishes the communicative and covenantal purpose for which God has sent it—whether to state facts, issue warnings, tell stories and histories, proffer wisdom or provide consolation. It therefore behooves us to become familiar with Scripture's various genres since, like maps, each form of biblical discourse has its own key, legend and scale—its own literary conventions for communicating and rendering reality. Each and every book in the Bible is wholly reliable, but we have to know how to read it: prophecy as prophecy, wisdom as wisdom, apocalyptic as apocalyptic and so on.[33] You can only follow a map if you know how to read it—and once you get oriented. The canon is a unique compass that keeps the church oriented to "true North": for all Scripture ultimately points to Jesus (Lk 24:27). This brings us to our final moral for interpretation.

6. *Inerrancy does not mean that all biblical narratives must pass the Cronkite test.* There are different ways, styles and genres of writing history. The problem with cronkitis is that it only skims the textual surface, as if the only relevant question to ask of a narrative was, "Did it actually happen?" To read only for the event is like listening to music only for the melody. However, as music is much more than a good tune, so narrative is much more than a report of who did what when.

History is first cousin to story. Both can tell a story in more than one way. No doubt Walter Cronkite would have had much to say about the furor over the recently released film *Selma*. Several fact-checkers dispute director Ava DuVernay's portrayal of President Lyndon Johnson as an opponent rather than ally of Martin Luther King Jr.[34] Some argue that it is unfair to hold

---

[33]Blomberg observes that inerrantists need to think more about what it means to say that non-historical genres like Proverbs or the Song of Songs are wholly truthful in all that they affirm. (Blomberg, *Can We Still Believe the Bible?*, 128.)

[34]The *New York Times* ran a front page story on the matter (see Jennifer Shuessler, "Depiction of Lyndon B. Johnson in 'Selma' Raises Hackles," Dec. 31, 2014).

filmmakers to the same standards as professional historians. Others complain that the film's critics are "trying to hold movies to a truth we can't hold history to."[35] In film, time and action must be compressed. The question is whether minor alterations in the way events are represented for the sake of good storytelling should count as mistakes. Hovering over the controversy is the question of genre. Is *Selma* closer to history or fiction? It would appear that *Selma* is neither a strict documentary nor even a docudrama but a drama: a historical drama, but a drama nevertheless. If this is correct, then viewers must temper their expectations of the film's historical accuracy accordingly.

What kind of literature is Genesis 1–3? Emotions run even higher when the story in question is not that of Martin Luther King Jr., or even Martin Luther, but Adam and Eve. Is the creation account a "docudrama"? Is it something that Richard Attenborough could narrate on BBC's long-running television show *Nature*? Here, too, the question concerns literary genre. While it is clear that Genesis 1–3 is about origins—of both the universe and the species—is it also meant to give scientific answers to questions about origins? I believe it is a logical and interpretive mistake to assume that biblical inerrancy requires a literal six-day creation interpretation of Genesis 1. To be sure, Genesis 1 communicates the truth about creation: what is in dispute is *what kind of true picture it is*. I'm hesitant to say that it is a chronologically accurate picture, not because I do not believe that God could create the universe with a microsecond snap of the fingers, but because I think the main interest of the text lies elsewhere. There are implications for science—the universe did not bring itself into being—but the opening chapters of Genesis do not read like a science textbook.

The title of Ziony Zevit's book *What Really Happened in the Garden of Eden?* signals his interest in "issues of truth, objectivity, and facticity beyond surface appearances."[36] It also signals his skepticism of the Bible's testimony, and a prideful confidence in the powers of his own ratiocination.

---

[35]Jeanine Basinger, former chairwomen of film studies at Wesleyan University, as cited in Cara Buckley, "When Films and Facts Collide in Questions," *New York Times*, January 21, 2015, www .nytimes.com/2015/01/22/movies/selma-questions-are-nothing-new-for-historical-films.html, accessed September 2, 2015.

[36]Ziony Zevit, *What Really Happened in the Garden of Eden?* (New Haven, CT: Yale University Press, 2013), xiii.

We are not in a position to lord it over the author of Genesis. We are far better off trusting the maker of heaven and earth when it comes to understanding creation. We may not know exactly what happened, but the truth that God created the heavens and the earth cannot be negated by modern science.

A final example. Is the book of Jonah essentially a fish story? To get preoccupied with the question of whether a great fish can swallow and then expectorate a man is to miss the main point. Jonah is not about a great fish. It is actually about Israel's ethnocentrism, which the author satirically subverts by depicting Jonah as a kind of antihero. A prophet by vocation, Jonah is in fact far from displaying the heart of God. Jonah has more compassion for a shade plant than for all the inhabitants of Assyria (Jon 4:6-11). I have no problem believing that a great fish swallowed Jonah, by the way. But to fixate only on "what actually happened"—the historical "melody"—is to miss the rich and challenging theological harmonies and rhythms that make the book of Jonah prophetic. Jonah stands as a perennial warning to those who think the gospel is for them and not others.

CONCLUSION: CHEAP VERSUS COSTLY INERRANCY (AND HERMENEUTICS)

Let me sum up my remarks by distinguishing cheap from costly inerrancy. Cheap inerrancy is the profession of biblical truth without the practice. It is one thing to have a high view of Scripture (and I hope you do). But it is quite another to follow the way the words go. We have to do more than say "It's true"; we have to say what it means, then do what it says. For example, "If we say we have fellowship with him while we walk in darkness, we lie and do not practice the truth" (1 Jn 1:6).

A second form of cheap inerrancy involves the profession of biblical truth accompanied by an *illiterate* interpretive practice. We cheapen inerrancy when we appeal to it in illegitimate ways—as an exegetical shortcut, for example. Professing inerrancy is no guarantee that your interpretations are correct. The truth of Scripture is one thing. The truth of one's interpretation of Scripture is quite another.

To profess and practice inerrancy rightly will cost us. Yet if the truth of God's Word is not worth our best interpretive efforts, what is? Let us therefore joyfully and energetically be the best advocates of inerrancy we can be, both in theory and in practice. Let us strive to become biblically literate, virtuous interpreters—right-hearted and right-minded readers who desire above all to hear and do God's Word. Let us be willing to endure ongoing interpretive difficulties rather than reach too hastily for facile answers.

I began by suggesting that inerrancy is problematic if we think in terms of modern journalistic truth. We must not forget, however, that at the heart of Scripture is the gospel: good *news*. The prophets and apostles write Scripture in large part to give a good report, to announce a stupendous development: namely, that the one true God, the maker of heaven and earth, has spoken and acted in the history of Israel and Jesus Christ. Men appointed by God and inspired by the Spirit have published a trustworthy account of these things (1 Pet 1:12).

The truth of Scripture *is* therefore journalistic, in two ways. First, it's journalistic because it is both like and unlike modern news reporting. Unlike reporters from, say, the *New York Times*, the biblical authors are inspired eyewitnesses who report the news not from a neutral stance of objectivity but from the stance of faith. But—and this is crucial—their faith perspective makes their report *more* true, not less, because it offers not thin but *thick* descriptions of the events that make up the history of redemption. We see *more* of the truth when we understand that God created the universe.

Despite his professionalism, Walter Cronkite would have provided only a thin account of Jesus' death: *that* he was crucified ("and that's the way it was"). This is where inerrancy can help enrich our interpretation by encouraging us to read the Old and New Testaments as a unified, true story. Thanks to the testimony of the prophets and apostles, readers understand the meaning and significance of Jesus' death on a cross as it comes into view as the climax of a long story involving a garden, an elect people, temples, prophets, priests, kings, exiles and so forth. Inerrancy is the confidence that the Bible gives us reliable accounts of God's unified plan of salvation and its meaning—call it "*theological* reportage."

There is another way that Scripture's truth is journalistic. If we think about our daily newspaper—I'm assuming some of us are still familiar with this endangered species—we'll see that, like the Bible, it too is made up of many kinds of discourse.

Obviously there is factual reporting. The morning headlines trumpet the important events of the day. But there is also wisdom literature in the newspaper—well, at least advice from Dear Abby, often about relationships: for example, how to deal with your inflexible father. There are letters to the editor, comics, economic data and editorials. Contemporary readers easily switch interpretive gears. We know the difference between reporting and an op-ed piece. Christians need to gain the same degree of familiarity with the books of the Bible that they have with the different sections of the newspaper.

The bulk of the Bible is narrative—eyewitness theological reportage—and it was given to us to reveal God and proclaim good news. It is prophetic and apostolic testimony to what was heard, seen and touched (1 Jn 1:1). Yes, it is told from the perspective of people of faith, but it is precisely this perspective that allows the biblical authors to tell the true story of the world. If faith corresponds to open eyes and open minds, why trust the eyewitness testimony of those who are blind to the presence and activity of God?

It is not enough to have a high view of Scripture. The doctrine of inerrancy is but a noisy gong and the canon a clanging cymbal if we don't know how to follow the Bible's words to the true pictures of God and the gospel. This is why inerrancy and hermeneutics ultimately matter—because discipleship is largely a matter of following the way the words go, in both senses of "following": understanding and obedience. To follow these words so that we grasp the Bible's true pictures of God and the gospel is to grasp the truth about reality. The world we think we know with our senses and our science will pass away, but God's Word will endure forever.

And that's the way it is, was and will be, world without end. Amen.

THREE WAYS OF SINGING *SOLA*

Scripture as Light, Compass and Script

A Sermon on Psalm 119:103-5,
Luke 24:25-27 and Colossians 3:15-17

I preached the following sermon on two occasions: in October 2007 to the North Shore Chinese Christian Church in Deerfield, Illinois, and in October 2010 as part of a Wheaton College Graduate School chapel series on the five Reformation solas. I am grateful to Pastor Dan Ying for the invitation to speak at his church, and to all those who supported the Graduate School chapel program. I do not always preach topical sermons, but the request in both cases was for a message that made Scripture itself central. The three texts I chose to weave together resemble a lectionary reading insofar as they include readings from the Old Testament, New Testament and Gospels, though as far as I know no lectionary puts them together. Whereas chapter one explored the model of the theologian as doctor and doctrine as medicinal prescription, this sermon features three more biblical pictures—three metaphors for describing God's Word. These three metaphors invite us to think about what Karl Barth called "the strange new world of the Bible" in terms of familiar old-world images: a lamp, an atlas and a play script. It is thus fitting that I include this sermon here, at the beginning of our promenade through the biblical exhibit of pictures of the work of theology and the people of God.

INTRODUCTION: THREE WAYS OF SWILLING INK

The driving question of much of my work over the past thirty years—"What does it mean to be biblical?"—assumes that being biblical matters. That it *does* matter may well be the big idea of the Protestant Reformation, expressed by its slogan *sola Scriptura*: the claim that Scripture alone is the written Word of God and hence the supreme authority for Christian faith, life and thought: "And we also thank God constantly for this, that when you received the word of God, which you heard from us, you accepted it not as the word of men but as what it really is, the word of God" (1 Thess 2:13). Biblical authority is grounded in divine authorship, that God speaks in and through the discourse of the Bible's human authors (2 Tim 3:16; Heb 1:1; 2 Pet 1:21). That God speaks is the distinguishing mark of the one true God from dumb idols. False gods can neither speak nor act. By contrast, the God of Israel acts *by* speaking: he creates the world, makes promises, establishes covenants, commands, warns, judges, comforts, makes known and so on. God also commissions prophets and apostles to be means of his self-communication to Israel and the church. The canonical Scriptures are the divinely elected medium of God's self-presentation and the means by which he imparts his life through the illumination of the Holy Spirit.[1]

It is important to distinguish *sola* from "solo" *Scriptura*. The Bible is not our only resource, either in life or theology. There are other things we need to know. It is, however, the supreme and singularly authoritative source and resource for knowing God and hearing the gospel. "Scripture alone" is neither a curse on extrabiblical knowledge nor a declaration of independence from modern learning. Rather, it is the confession that we do not need more words from God in order to come to saving faith in Jesus Christ. Scripture alone is a sufficient and authoritative guide to what is "in Christ."

What else, then, remains to be said? Quite a lot, it turns out. It is not enough to profess *sola Scriptura*; it has to be *done*. *Sola Scriptura* ultimately names not a theory but a *practice* of biblical authority. However, though the Bible occupies a prominent place in churches and homes, the texts that Christians often live by are from the culture: texts that promise health-giving success if they adopt their therapeutic techniques, marketing strategies, financial plans and so forth. These books effectively become a "canon outside the canon." David Wells has been playing the weeping prophet of

---

[1] See further my "Holy Scripture: Word of God; Word of Christ; Sword of the Spirit," in R. Michael Allen and Scott R. Swain, eds., *Christian Dogmatics: Reformed Theology for the Church Catholic* (Grand Rapids: Zondervan, forthcoming).

evangelicalism for years, lamenting our tendency to exchange our birthright, *sola Scriptura*, for a mess of pottage: *sola cultura*.[2]

It is not enough to have a high view of Scripture or even to read the Bible regularly. To practice biblical authority—to be biblical in one's life and thought—one must read it *formatively*, that is, in such a way that it shapes our view of truth, our values and our interactions with others—the way we live. Eugene Peterson's metaphor for this deep, participatory reading is "ingesting": to practice *sola Scriptura* is to "eat" this book. Peterson takes his metaphor from Scripture itself. "And I took the little scroll from the hand of the angel and ate it" (Rev 10:9).[3] Ezekiel and Jeremiah were also biblivores: "Eat this scroll" (Ezek 3:1; Jer 15:16). To eat the words of God is to assimilate them thoroughly. Peterson's comment on John's experience as the author of Revelation is apt: "The book he ate was metabolized into the book he wrote."[4] To practice biblical authority involves more than giving it lip service. It is rather to eat, pray and love the songs, stories, laws and other parts of Scripture.

The diversity of forms of biblical literature suggests that there may be more than one way to ingest the Bible. The philosopher J. L. Austin believed in the wisdom of analyzing the way we use words. In his essay "Three Ways of Spilling Ink," he attempted to get a better conceptual handle on the notion of responsibility by examining the various ways people make excuses.[5] He discovered that people use different words either to assume or to evade responsibility for doing something. One can spill ink "accidentally," "intentionally" or "deliberately." Austin's premise was that language has something to teach us. In similar fashion, I believe that the language of the Bible has something to teach us. I believe that we can gain a precious insight into what it means to be biblical by examining some of the key pictures the Bible suggests for itself. In this sermon I will examine three ways of eating the book— of swilling biblical ink.

Each of the passages we read this morning suggests a way of thinking about the practice of biblical authority. Before we consider them, it is worth

---

[2]David F. Wells, *The Courage to Be Protestant: Truth-Lovers, Marketers, and Emergents in the Post-modern World* (Grand Rapids: Eerdmans, 2008), 4.
[3]Eugene H. Peterson, *Eat This Book: A Conversation in the Art of Spiritual Reading* (Grand Rapids: Eerdmans, 2006).
[4]Ibid., 9.
[5]J. L. Austin, *Philosophical Papers*, 3rd ed. (Oxford: Oxford University Press, 1979), 272-87.

remembering that Scripture is not an end in itself but a means to Jesus Christ. *Sola Scriptura* serves *solus Christus*. If the Bible is "above all earthly powers," it's because it is the commissioned testimony of the one who rules over all. The written Word serves the living Word, the one who is the way, the truth and the life (Jn 14:6). We will see that Scripture lights the way, orients us to the truth and indwells us with the life of Jesus Christ. Let's turn, then, to our first way of singing *sola*.

"A LAMP TO LIGHT OUR WAY" (PSALM 119:103-5)

It is fitting that we begin with a Psalm, and with Psalm 119 in particular. Psalm 1 represents the whole Psalter's celebration of God's *torah*, or instruction given at Sinai. We need this instruction in order to walk (*hālak*) righteously. The book of Psalms is a curriculum unto itself for learning how to sing *sola*.

Psalm 119 uses eight different terms for the Word of God, including "statutes," "commands" and "precepts." Yes, it is law-heavy. Perhaps this is why Bonhoeffer was told in seminary that it was the most boring of the Psalms! What is striking, however, is the way the Psalm moves from *Torah* to the joy that mediating on *Torah* brings. Sinking our teeth into God's Word brings both satisfaction and wisdom. "How sweet are your words to my taste . . . through your precepts I get understanding" (Ps 119:103-4). This was Bonhoeffer's experience, too. Despite what he had been taught, when he was in a Nazi prison he found that Psalm 119 was the heartiest psalm of all, and he relished the times when he could meditate on it.[6]

The light of reason is dim when it comes to illuminating the God of the gospel. Scripture, by contrast, is the light of revelation. "Your word is a lamp to my feet and a light to my path" (Ps 119:105). The Word of God shows us the way to walk. If we ignore the light that streams from God's Word, we will soon lose our way. In Calvin's words, "The metaphor . . . implies . . . that unless the Word of God enlighten men's path, the whole of their life is enveloped in darkness and obscurity, so that they cannot do anything else than miserably wander from the right way."[7] By contrast, he who attends to the

---

[6]*Dietrich Bonhoeffer: Meditating on the Word*, ed. David McI. Gracie (Lanham, MD: Rowman & Littlefield, 2008), 13-14. See especially "Meditation on Psalm 119," 93-134.

[7]John Calvin, *Commentary on the Book of Psalms*, vol. IV (Edinburgh: Calvin Translation Society, 1847), 479.

Law of God will find "an unerring light."[8] The Bible is a reliable guide to knowing God and cultivating godliness.

The Bible is a light unto our academic path as well. St. Bonaventure's thirteenth-century treatise, *On the Reduction of the Arts to Theology*, ought to be required reading for every Christian student of the liberal arts. Its thesis is that all forms of human knowledge—and the human mind itself—serve one overarching purpose: to lead us back to God ("reduction" is from the Latin *re* + *ducere*, "to lead back"). Bonaventure's reduction takes its cue from James 1:17: "Every good gift and every perfect gift is from above, coming down from the Father of lights." Bonaventure calls what we know through the senses and reason the "inferior" and "interior" lights respectively. Scripture, however, is the "superior" light, because it alone yields saving truth.[9] Bonaventure also relates the six branches of knowledge that made up the medieval university to the six days of creation.[10] The Bible, he says, corresponds to the first day of creation, when God made light. Hence all the secular arts and sciences are seen for what they are only in the light of Scripture. Bonaventure's conclusion: the light given on the first day (Scripture) is needed to walk rightly the rest of the week.

We find a similar image in the New Testament. Like Genesis, the prologue to the Fourth Gospel begins with "In the beginning God" (Jn 1:1) and here too there is a mention of light—only now the light is identified with Jesus. "The true light, which gives light to everyone, was coming into the world" (Jn 1:9). Jesus claimed to be the light of the world (Jn 8:12; 9:5), and Peter indeed saw Jesus' light at his transfiguration, when Jesus' face "shone [Greek *lampō*] like the sun" and even his clothes "became white as light [*phōs*]" (Mt 17:2). Peter refers back to this experience in his second epistle as proof that he and the disciples were not following "cleverly devised myths" (2 Pet 1:16). Peter was with Jesus when he heard the divine voice attesting Jesus as the beloved Son. Peter infers from his experience of Jesus' transfiguration that "we have the word of prophecy made more sure, to which you do well to pay attention as to a lamp shining in a dark place" (2 Pet 1:19). God is light (1 Jn 1:5), Jesus

---

[8]Ibid., 480.

[9]*On the Reduction of the Arts to Theology*, Works of St. Bonaventure, vol. 1, trans. Zachary Hayes (St. Bonaventure, NY: Franciscan Institute of St. Bonaventure University, 1996), 37.

[10]Ibid., 40.

is light (Jn 8:12), and the Spirit is the one who shines the light of the gospel of Christ in our hearts (2 Cor 4:6). Scripture is the lamp through which the Spirit shines the light of the gospel. Thus Scripture too participates in the economy of divine light, casting away the darkness and indicating the way to walk as children of light (Eph 5:8; 1 Thess 5:5).[11]

"A Compass to Find Our Way" (Luke 24:25-27)

Luke 24:27 suggests a second way of singing *sola*. The risen Jesus explains to the two disciples on the road to Emmaus that the things that happened to him in Jerusalem—his suffering and death on a cross—were all part of God's plan: "And beginning with Moses and all the Prophets, he interpreted to them in all the Scriptures the things concerning himself" (Lk 24:27). While Psalm 119 highlights the Law, Jesus' reference is all-encompassing. All the writings in the Bible—law, prophecies, histories, psalms, apocalyptic and so on—ultimately point to Christ.

Jesus makes this point to disciples who are literally "on the way," travelling from one place to the next. But although they are on the road, they are also disoriented. They do not know how to process what happened to Jesus. His death had dashed their hopes that he was the one to redeem Israel (Lk 24:21). They are lost in Emmaus. They are on the road, but they are not yet part of the "Way" (Acts 9:2).

To live as a disciple of Jesus Christ is to walk his way after him. We have already seen how the Bible, in all its literary diversity, is a lamp that illumines our daily walk. The Law is a kind of map that charts out the way to live according to God's will.[12] The wisdom literature of the Bible offers a different kind of map that concerns human beings in the grand scheme of things. The Bible is like an atlas. It is made up of many types of literary maps, and only *these* maps are reliable guides for disciples looking to follow the way of Jesus Christ. Together, the various maps that make up Scripture comprise a ca-

---

[11]For more on the economy of light, see my "The Spirit of Light After the Age of Enlightenment: Renewing/Reforming Pneumatic Hermeneutics via the Economy of Illumination," in Jeffrey Barbeau and Beth Felker Jones, eds., *Spirit of God: Christian Renewal in the Community of Faith* (Downers Grove, IL: IVP Academic, 2015), 149-67.

[12]In chapter two we referred to maps to describe the ways the Bible corresponds to reality. The cartographic metaphor works out a bit differently in the present context. The focus here is on the way the various forms of Scripture help orient the reader to Jesus Christ.

nonical atlas. Scripture may be "alone," but the one canon is composed of many different kinds of biblical texts, each of which provides a distinct kind of guidance.

The ancient Israelites had biblical maps. They had the Law, which they used to determine where and how they should walk. But the tragedy of Israel's history was that, though they had the biblical maps, they did not know how to follow them correctly. Listen to Jesus' rebuke of their map-reading skills in John 5:39: "You diligently study the Scriptures because you think by them you possess eternal life. These are the Scriptures that testify about me, yet you refuse to come to me to have life." There is a lesson here for us. We are not saved simply because we have a high view of the Bible. I daresay the Pharisees had just as high a view of the Bible as contemporary evangelicals. But what good is a high view of the map if you are disinclined to follow it? Or if you are disoriented, unsure of how the map relates to the real world and where you stand in relation to the map?

In order to read a map rightly, we have to understand its legend and scale. But in order actually to use a map, to get from here to there, we have to relate the map to reality. We have to get our bearings—get *oriented*. Unless we can determine our position relative to other things, we will remain lost. If the map is to give us actual guidance, we have to know where true north is.

This is precisely what we see Jesus doing for the disciples on the road to Emmaus. Jesus orients them by helping them see how the various maps fit together, and in which direction they point. The Bible's orienting function is unique: wherever we happen to be and whatever we happen to be doing, it points us in the same direction—to the Christian's north star, Jesus Christ. He is the beginning, middle and end of all God's ways. The Scriptures are not a random collection of sacred writings. Taken together they comprise a canonical compass. To be a Christian is to know how to follow the biblical maps in such a way that both your attention and walk are consistently fixed on Jesus Christ. This, then, is the second way of singing *sola*—letting Scripture orient you consistently to the truth.

"A Script to Guide Our Way" (Colossians 3:15-17)

Scripture lights our way, orients us to the truth, and finally indwells our life together in Christ. "Let the word of Christ dwell in you richly" (Col 3:16).

This is the same word that Paul identifies as "the word of the truth, the gospel, which . . . is bearing fruit" (Col 1:5-6). Paul spends the first two chapters of Colossians explaining the supremacy of Christ and encouraging the Colossians to act out their union with Christ. Christ's story is also the Christian's: "And you, who were dead . . . God made alive together with him" (Col 2:13). Those who are one with Christ have died to the old way of doing things: "For you have died, and your life is hidden with Christ in God" (Col 3:3). Paul goes on to describe the new life that should characterize those who are walking the way of truth in Christ. The peace of Christ rules and the word of Christ dwells in the hearts of those who belong to the community of the faithful (Col 3:15-16).

In speaking of the "word of Christ" Paul could mean the word that Christ speaks or the word about Christ (or both). As we saw in Luke 24, all the Scriptures are ultimately about Christ. We may therefore take "word of Christ" broadly to refer to the whole of biblical discourse, or narrowly to the gospel in particular. The point to remember is that those who are in Christ must constantly have his story in mind as they seek to walk in the newness of his risen life.

How do words dwell in us? In graduate school we tend to focus on the head. We have ways of finding out what you've got there (or not)—final exams. One way to test whether you have internalized our teaching is to see if you can repeat it back, apply it or otherwise demonstrate that you have understood it. One of the chief ways words indwell us is through memorization—we speak of learning something "by heart." To have the Word of Christ indwell us is to remember the story of redemption, which culminates in Christ.

Paul does not explain the mechanism of the Word's dwelling, though it is clear that he wants his hearers to be not mere hearers but doers of the word (Jas 1:23-25). The "word of Christ" is a true word about *what is* in Christ and, as such, Paul expects his readers to conform to this reality. One way to conform to the reality indicated by this word is to walk in the way indicated. For example, Psalm 37:31 says of the righteous one that "The law of his God is in his heart; his steps do not slip." Eugene Peterson helpfully translates this verse as follows: "Let the Word of Christ—the Message—have the run of the house. Give it plenty of room in your lives" (*The Message*).

The word is in our hearts, directing us how to live. What kind of word is this? We obey orders and, to be sure, some of God's Word is law. We follow instructions and, sure enough, some of God's Word consists of wise sayings. We sing songs and, of course, a good portion of God's Word is psalms and hymns. Let me suggest, however, that there is another kind of indwelling word that better captures what Paul is getting at here: the script. The "word of Christ" is like a play script—a Passion play—that disciples have to know by heart in order to be part of it. It is not that the Bible offers a detailed blueprint for how to act in each and every situation; rather, the Bible is the transcript of how God has acted in a way that transforms all of our situations. The script we are to follow is the cross-and-resurrection pattern of Jesus' life. The Bible is like a script in that disciples are to act out what is in Christ.[13]

The word of Christ dwells in us richly as the script of our lives. Being biblical means living by the story of the Bible—the gospel—rather than other narratives (for example, the rags to riches story). When Paul says "Let the word of Christ dwell richly *in you*," he is probably referring both to each person individually and to the church corporately. Paul uses the same verb for dwelling (*enoikeō*) in 2 Corinthians 6:16 in connection with God inhabiting the church as his temple or dwelling-place (Lev 26:11). If Paul intends the corporate sense, this rich indwelling "would occur when they came together, listened to the Word of Christ as it was preached and expounded to them . . . and bowed to its authority. By this means Christ's rule would be exercised in their lives."[14] Scripture is never more like a script than when it directs disciples in their roles, enabling them to act out the story of Christ. Then we can say with Paul, "It is no longer I who live, but Christ who lives in me" (Gal 2:20).

Conclusion: Three Ways of Singing *Sola*

Practicing *sola Scriptura* means adopting the Bible, the written Word of God, as the church's principal rule for action, understanding and life. Scripture alone is above all earthly powers, for Scripture alone is the God-given means that lights our way, orients us to the truth and guides our common life in

---

[13]I explore the theatrical model in much more detail in *Faith Speaking Understanding: Performing the Drama of Doctrine* (Louisville, KY: Westminster John Knox Press, 2014).

[14]Peter O'Brien, *Colossians, Philemon*, Word Bible Commentary (Waco, TX: Word Books, 2000), 207.

Jesus Christ. We need to recover all three ways of singing *sola* if its divine wisdom is to be not simply taught but caught.

One final thought. *Sola Scriptura* does not exclude but rather calls for the ministry of the Holy Spirit, who typically works in conjunction with Scripture. As Christ is the sole content of Scripture, so spirituality is a matter of the Spirit's ministering Scripture's words to hearts and minds. God's Word holds the preeminent place in Christian worship, for worship is the crucible wherein Word and Spirit shape our souls as well as our theological systems. It is in worship that we are caught up in the rhythms of the Word, so that the way the biblical words go become the way our words go.

To let Scripture light your way, orient you to the truth and serve as your inner script means letting its triune Author have an authoritative say in everything you do. *Sola Scriptura* means that the Bible both describes and is itself an ingredient in God's making all things new in Christ through the Spirit. May we all learn to sing the Scriptures, remembering them in our heads, celebrating them in our hearts and enacting them with our bodies as living sacrifices, which is our daily worship (Rom 12:1).

PICTURES OF THE CHURCH'S WORSHIP

four

WORSHIP AT THE WELL

From Dogmatics to Doxology (and Back Again)

This essay began life as a chapel message at Trinity Evangelical Divinity School in September 2001, three years into my "second coming" (I had returned to Trinity from the University of Edinburgh in 1998). Trinity is located in Deerfield, Illinois, about thirty miles north of Chicago in Lake County (hence the reference in the opening line). I was invited to publish the message in the Trinity Journal, and did so in the Spring 2002 issue (after a little revising). In its final form, it is more a reflection on worship based on Jesus' conversation with the Samaritan woman in John 4:7-26. The challenge is to relate dogmatic theology to the doxology, typically sung in a church service immediately following the offering. This sequence is apt, and thoroughly theological: theology forms disciples who desire and know how to present their embodied daily life as their spiritual worship (Rom 12:1). Theology gives the church not marching but worshiping orders. Done rightly, theology is itself a way of serving God with our minds. Christians everywhere at all times—but especially in a seminary setting—must resist opposing doxology to dogmatics. On the contrary, we need to add a seventh thing theology is for to our list in chapter one. Theology is for leading the church in right worship: orthodoxology.

INTRODUCTION: WELLS, WOMEN AND WORSHIP

Lake County, as its name indicates, hardly resembles the arid lands of Palestine, where having access to water is a matter of life and death. No wonder water is such an important image in the Bible.[1] Long before Europeans or

---

[1]See "Water," in Leland Ryken, James C. Wilhoit and Tremper Longman, eds., *Dictionary of Biblical Imagery* (Downers Grove, IL: InterVarsity Press, 1998), 929-32.

Americans built cities on rivers, communities in Palestine formed around supplies of fresh water, such as wells. Wells became social centers—a place to meet your future wife, for example (Gen 24; Ex 2:15-22). Like everything else, the laws of supply and demand determine value of water—as a native of California, where water is in short supply and high demand, I am especially sensitive to this. There will always be a demand for water, since it is essential to life.

Imagine my surprise, then, when I received notice some years back from the Lake County Department of Public Works informing me that the contents of our drinking water came from a well! I never discovered where this well was, but I strongly suspect it was not the best place to meet girls. Today it is a moot point: we now get our water from Lake Michigan. I still receive regular notification of the contents of my drinking water, down to the last micron. I have learned that, in addition to a number of natural minerals, there are also a number of chemical contaminants and even a radioactive isotope or two, though all within what the EPA considers acceptable limits.

With this in mind, let us consider the last in the series of biblical stories of meetings at a well: the account of Jesus' conversation with the Samaritan woman in John 4. Water is a rich theological theme in the Fourth Gospel. Jesus mentions water in John 3:5 in connection with regeneration ("born of water and the Spirit"), but here in John 4 it is well water that is in view in a conversation that eventually leads to teaching about the nature of proper worship. While it may not be the *locus classicus* on the subject, in many respects John 4 does seem to represent the final word on right worship.

We get our English word *worship* from an Old English term that referred to a person of worth: your "worth-ship."[2] What do we do when we worship? We acknowledge and celebrate *God's worth*.[3] In worship we come together to remember and to respond to who God is and what God has done for us. In short, we come together to do theology, though in a form that is more informal, participatory and musical than it is scholastic or systematic.

---

[2] For discussion of this word, see James F. White, *Introduction to Christian Worship*, rev. ed. (Nashville, TN: Abingdon Press, 1990), 33.

[3] See N. T. Wright, *For All God's Worth: True Worship and the Calling of the Church* (Grand Rapids: Eerdmans, 1997).

Given the confusion that reigns in many churches over the nature and style of worship, it would be nice to know: *What would Jesus do* on Sunday morning? Where would Jesus go to worship? *How* would he worship? Would he prefer high-church liturgy or low-church choruses? Smells and bells or acoustic guitar and drums? Perhaps no passage gives us a better answer to these WWJD questions than John 4.[4] Augustine's comment about Jesus' discourse with the Samaritan woman is apt: "Great mysteries were stated there, and analogies of great matters."[5]

L'AFFAIRE SAMARITAN: LOCAL KNOWLEDGE

The larger historical context: worship wars. We begin by considering the broader historical context of John 4—"*l'affaire* Samaritan." The Samaritans were a mixed race descended from the remnant of Israelites who were not deported by Assyria after the fall of the northern kingdom in 722 BC, and from the foreign colonists brought in from Babylon and beyond by the Assyrian conquerors. We learn of the origin of the Samaritans in 2 Kings 17.

Worship War I: Where? Which place? The woman's claim that Jacob left the well to his descendants the Samaritans (Jn 4:12) is a tradition with no biblical support. The well itself, however, is "perhaps the most identifiable site in modern Israel connected with the ministry of Jesus."[6]

Some earlier commentators thought that the woman's five husbands stood for the five gods of the nations that formed ancient Samaria, since the Hebrew word for "husband" is *ba'al*, also the name for pagan deities. Josephus mentions "Five nations. . . . Each brought its own god to Samaria." The sixth—Yahweh—was not really a husband, that is, one to whom the people had an exclusive commitment. However, by the time of this episode—the first century—the Samaritans were confirmed monotheists.

When the woman begins to realize that Jesus is a prophet, she quickly turns to one of the most controversial theological questions of her day, namely, the location of the religious center of the world. There was a

---

[4] I explore the various ways John 4 has recently been interpreted in my "The Reader at the Well: Responding to John 4," in Kevin Vanhoozer, *First Theology: God, Scripture and Hermeneutics* (Downers Grove, IL: InterVarsity Press, 2002), 236-56.

[5] St. Augustine, *Tractates on the Gospel of John 11–27*, in *The Fathers of the Church*, trans. John W. Rettig (Baltimore: Catholic University of America Press, 2003), 78.

[6] George R. Beasley-Murray, *John*, Word Biblical Commentary (Dallas: Word, 1987), 58.

long-standing controversy between the Jews and Samaritans over the proper center of worship. According to Samaritan tradition, Mount Gerizim was the mountain where Abraham had climbed to sacrifice Isaac. Jacob's well was at the foot of Mount Gerizim.

Because the Samaritans recognized only the Pentateuch as authoritative, references later in the Old Testament stipulating worship at the Jerusalem temple were not considered binding. The Samaritans actually made the obligation to worship on Mount Gerizim part of the Decalogue.[7] Differences were accentuated after the Jews returned from the Babylonian exile, when the Samaritans put obstacles in the way of the restoration of Jerusalem and the temple. Finally, in the second century BC the Samaritans helped the Syrian monarchs in their wars against the Jews, a favor the Jews returned by destroying the Samaritan temple on Mount Gerizim in 128 BC. "Worship wars" indeed!

Worship War II: How? What style? If a prophet were to appear in Lake County today, I suspect that most of us would be inclined to ask not about locations but about *styles* of worship. The debate between the Jews and Samaritans over *where* to worship stands in a certain parallel to contemporary debates about *how* to worship. Instead of appreciating the fact that both sides worship the same God, there was and is great bitterness over the differences: over place (for them) and style (for us).

Jesus' teaching shows that in the ancient and the contemporary worship wars alike, all parties may be guilty of relying too heavily on what we might call (with the anthropologist Clifford Geertz) "local knowledge": that is, the influence of our place, time, history and tradition on what we think we know.[8] After all, North America is a locale too. How can we be sure we are not subscribing to local knowledge only—popular culture—in our worship?[9]

Does it really matter how we worship? Yes it does, because ultimately it is not only a question of *how* but also of *what*. Questions of style are not unrelated to questions of substance. This is the point of Jesus' teaching on worshiping the Father in Spirit and in truth.

---

[7]See Raymond E. Brown, *The Gospel According to John I-XII*, The Anchor Bible (Garden City, NY: Doubleday & Co., 1966), 172.

[8]Clifford Geertz, *Local Knowledge: Further Essays in Interpretive Anthropology*, 3rd ed. (New York: Basic Books, 1983).

[9]For an excellent treatment of this question, see Marva J. Dawn, *Reaching Out Without Dumbing Down: A Theology of Worship for the Turn-of-the-Century Culture* (Grand Rapids: Eerdmans, 1995).

The larger literary context: the water of life. Before we turn to Jesus'
teaching about worship at the well in verses 22-24, it may help to recall that
the broader context of Jesus' remarks pertain to knowing God and eternal
life. The imagery in John 4 runs deep. Verses 6-18 distinguish earthly water,
which offers only a provisional satisfaction, from the living water that Christ
offers, which satisfies eternally. While the conversation appears to shift to a
different topic altogether—the worship the Father seeks—I believe that there
is a connection between them, even if it is somewhat subterranean.

"Living water." Most commentators agree that "living water" is a common
expression for flowing or spring water, in contrast to still water. The qualifi-
cation is important. In the Old Testament, the presence or emergence of
springs became the sign of God's special help to a pilgrim people (Is 41:18).
Springs in the desert were literally life-giving. Springs also stand for a renewal of inner strength and joy, as in Isaiah 12:3: "With joy you will draw
water from the wells of salvation." Finally, the prophets associate living water
with an eschatological blessing. Take, for example, Zechariah's vision of the
restoration of Israel: "On that day living waters shall flow out from Jerusalem
. . . on that day the LORD will be one" (Zech 14:8-9). We see a similar use in
the New Testament in Revelation 22, where a river of life flows from the
throne of God in heaven (Rev 22:1).

There are two main possibilities as to what Jesus meant by "living water"
in his dialogue with the Samaritan woman. On the one hand, living water
might represent the revelation Jesus gives (or is), which leads to eternal life.
Proverbs 13:14 says "The teaching of the wise is a fountain of life." In rabbinic
Judaism, living water was associated particularly with the Torah. As one of
the rabbis wrote, "As water is life for the world, so are the words of the Torah
life for the world." On this reading, then, the living water that Jesus offers
the woman is a new and better revelation, which is perhaps why she says, "I
perceive that you are a prophet" (Jn 4:19). On the basis of this first interpretation, then, we may associate living water with truth.

On the other hand, Jesus may be referring to the Holy Spirit. In John 3
he told Nicodemus that those who would be born again must be born of
water and spirit (3:5). The connection between water and the Spirit is even
stronger in John 7:37-38: "If anyone thirsts, let him come to me and drink.
Whoever believes in me, as the Scripture has said, 'Out of his heart will flow

rivers of living water.'" The Evangelist then adds an extraordinarily helpful explanatory note: "Now this he said about the Spirit, whom those who believed in him were to receive" (Jn 7:39). The point is clear. Our receiving the living water is a consequence of faith in Jesus' death and exaltation. As we know from John 14–16, Jesus is the one who communicates the Spirit to his disciples, the same Spirit who is elsewhere called "the spirit of truth" (Jn 14:17; 15:26; 16:13) and "the giver of life" (Jn 6:63). This living water is likely a reference to the Holy Spirit. Calvin remarks that Jesus here depicts the Spirit as a constantly flowing well of eternal life. The Spirit springs forth from God—hence those who receive the Spirit have God's own life flowing through them.

The symbolism of the Fourth Gospel often achieves well-like depths. I see no reason why Jesus could not have intended "living water" to refer to both truth and the Spirit—the same two conditions he later invokes as necessary for right worship.

"The hour is coming." Up to this point, Jesus' discussion with the Samaritan woman has focused on water and place. But in verse 21 Jesus introduces a temporal dimension. An hour is coming when the Father will be worshiped neither on Mount Gerizim nor in Jerusalem. The hour, of course, is the hour of Jesus' death and resurrection: the eschatological event by which God creates a new, living temple. As we know from the upper room discourse in John 14–16, Jesus has to go away in order for the Spirit to come. Jesus' work becomes the means by which the Father gains "true worshipers." The hour that is coming, then, is nothing less than the event that makes worship possible.

WORSHIP IN SPIRIT AND TRUTH (John 4:22-24)

The first half of John 4 deals with knowing God and with eternal life. These two themes are not merely the backdrop for a new topic of discussion. On the contrary, they are what is primarily at issue in right worship. The two parts of Jesus' discourse with the Samaritan woman thus form an integral whole. What is the connecting link? Just this: Jesus too is looking for a bride at Jacob's well, one who will worship the Father in spirit and in truth. Jesus' description of true worshipers is a description of the true church: the assembly of those who know God because they have been born again of the Spirit.

The object of worship: "You worship what you do not know" (v. 22). Sincerity without knowledge is wrong worship. Sincerity alone is an insufficient condition of right worship. Jesus says in John 4:22, "You [Samaritans] worship what you do not know." The first Samaritans serve as prime examples of the danger of limited knowledge of God. According to 2 Kings 17, each national group the Assyrians used to colonize Samaria brought its own local deity too. 2 Kings 17:33 is especially striking: "So they feared the Lord but also served their own gods, after the manner of the nations from among whom they had been carried away."

Apparently Samaritan religion was as promiscuous as the Samaritan woman. What is written about the Samaritans thus serves as an example to us. Let it not be said of the church that we fear the Lord but also worship other gods—cultural idols such as money, career, fame, celebrity, healthy, beauty, efficiency—after the manner of the nations.

By Jesus' time the Samaritans had become monotheists, yet they still had only a partial knowledge of God. Their Bible consisted of the Torah—the Samaritan Pentateuch—alone. They lacked the riches of the Psalms and the prophets. The Samaritans were drawing from only certain parts of the biblical well. Because their canon went as far as the Pentateuch only, they did not know God as he revealed himself in the subsequent history of Israel. As to the Messiah, for example, the Samaritans expected a prophet-like figure, but not a king (hence the woman's comment to Jesus).

It is easy to empathize with the Samaritans. Who more than seminary students can appreciate the incomprehensibility of God? It is nevertheless sobering to note that this excuse did not sit well with Jesus. "You worship what you do not know." It is hard not to hear a rebuke in this statement. The Samaritans' knowledge of God was partial, hence their worship was defective. The problem was not that the Samaritans lacked *exhaustive* knowledge of God (don't we all?), but that they did not know enough to worship him correctly. Calvin comments: "For unless there is knowledge present, it is not God that we worship but a spectre or ghost."[10] All of our pious intentions are struck by this thunderbolt: we cannot help but worship falsely unless we are guided by God's Word.

---

[10]John Calvin, *John 1–10*, Calvin's New Testament Commentaries, vol. 4, trans. T. H. L. Parker (Grand Rapids: Eerdmans, 1995), 98.

The object of right worship: who God is and what God has done. Whereas the Samaritan woman appealed to "our fathers," Jesus directs her to the one who is Father of all. Calvin fixes on this distinction and uses it to chide Roman Catholics who attend more to human tradition (what the Fathers say) than to Scripture (what the Father says). His point is well taken. If right worship depends on knowing God, as Jesus here implies, then we would do well to remember that we know God only when and where God gives himself to be known. This is why Jesus says the Jews worship what they know: their faith was based on God's revelation in history. Consider Psalm 136. A first voice narrates all the things that God has done as Creator and Deliverer of Israel, while a second voice responds, twenty-six times, "For his steadfast love endures forever." Right worship proceeds from right knowledge of God.

Divine revelation accounts not only for the difference between Jews and Samaritans, but also for the difference between Christians and Jews. The Samaritans cut themselves off from the prophets, but the Jews failed to recognize Jesus as the Son of God. Calvin says that it is those "who forsake the Word fall [who] into idolatry."[11] This is because, as Jesus taught, those who do not know the Son cannot know the Father (Jn 14:7; cf. 8:19; 10:30; 14:9). Yes, God is incomprehensible (Ps 145:3), but the one whose greatness is unsearchable has made himself known in Jesus Christ. Knowing Jesus Christ—the locus of God's fullest self-revelation—is the preeminent condition for right worship.

Worship is simply a matter of acknowledging who God is and what God has done. There is precedent for worship directed to an unknown God (Acts 17:23) but, strictly speaking, "worship of what we do not know" is a contradiction in terms. The solution to the problem of ignorant worship is belief in Jesus Christ. Jesus uniquely reveals the Father, "exegeting" him as love, light and life (Jn 1:14). Who God is and what God has done has been made known in Jesus Christ.

Focusing on the right object is everything in worship. Ignorant worship fails to invigorate or to quench our spiritual thirst. Ignorant worship is a liturgy of death, not life. In Jeremiah God says: "My people have committed two sins: they have forsaken me, the spring of living water, and have dug

---

[11]Ibid., 99.

their own cisterns, broken cisterns that cannot hold water" (Jer 2:13). Through our own efforts we can attain neither a right knowledge nor a right worship of God.

The principle of worship: a brief transition. The transition from the object of worship to the manner of worship is short and direct: *The nature of worship should govern the way we worship.* We find this principle in Westcott's commentary, long before Karl Barth turned it into a key methodological principle for doing theology. Westcott wrote that "the object of worship determines its condition."[12] The manner of knowing and worshiping must be suited to the object. This is the principle that explains the connection between verses 22 and 23.

The manner of worship: "True worshipers will worship the Father in spirit and truth" (v. 23). Westcott simplifies only slightly when he says that Judaism was a worship of the letter rather than spirit, while Samaritanism was a worship of falsehood rather than truth.[13] The Father seeks real worshipers who know how to integrate propositional knowledge with pietistic devotion. These are the types of worshipers whom he begets by giving them living water, in both senses of the term that we examined earlier: truth (the revelation of God in Christ) and Spirit (the regenerating energy of God).

Worship in truth: the cognitive dimension. Worship involves a conception of the object—the person—to whom our feeling, singing and praying is directed. Worship should not require us to turn off our minds. The purpose of theology and worship alike is to cultivate the vision of who God is and what God has done, and to cultivate it so well that, when we perceive it, it stops us in our tracks and elicits our praise.

Perhaps the most important cognitive faculty in worship is the imagination. By *imagination* I do not mean that mental faculty that produces fictions (things that are not real) but rather the mental capacity that enables us to see more of reality than what we can perceive with our eyes or other physical senses. It is the imagination that helps us to conceive God in terms of rich biblical metaphors like "Father" and "Son." These metaphors communicate content, to be sure, but they are abundant in meaning. Further thought and interpretation spring forth as from living water.

---

[12]B. F. Westcott, *The Gospel According to St. John* (Grand Rapids: Baker, 1980), 157.
[13]Ibid., 159.

The cognitive dimension of Christian worship is essentially the story of Jesus Christ, together with its implications for the identity of God. Jesus is the truth; he is God's truth claim as well as God's claim on humanity. This Jesus truth—that God loves sinners so much that he becomes one of us so that we might be one with him—is explosive. "You shall know the truth," Jesus tells his disciples, "and the truth shall make you free" (Jn 8:32). Truth sets us free *from* idolatry—from false religion and false striving after meaning and happiness and righteousness. Consequently, truth also sets us free *for* right worship—for worship bent on ultimate reality.

Worship in Spirit: the experiential dimension. To this point, we have seen the importance of having the right objective knowledge. But worship also requires the right subjective attitude: "spirit." The truth of who God is and what God has done for us engages not merely our intellects, but our whole being: not only our minds, but our hearts, hands and imaginations too.

Sermons rarely invoke the name of the philosopher Immanuel Kant, especially on the topic of worship. Kant was infamous for his dislike of formal or ritualized religion, and would regularly duck out of academic processions just as they were about to enter the church. Like Kant, many today, in the context of modernity, with its emphasis on individualism, have appealed to Jesus' words as a justification for privatized religion. On this modern view, Jesus' call for worship "in spirit and truth" is a call for piety and sincerity: an inward, subjective quality of devotion. I disagree. Jesus is not contrasting external with internal worship. John 4 is not a Magna Carta for individuals who want to worship alone in private. The point is rather that the Father creates true worshipers by begetting them again in the Spirit. The Father is creating a house of worship, a new temple, in the form of a new people, the body of Christ.

As we have seen in verse 22, real worship depends on knowing who God is and what God has done. In our contemporary context it is all too easy to pit ideas of God (theology) against an experience of God (worship). This dichotomy is as fatal for the knowledge of God as it is for knowledge in general. Kant may not have been a churchman, but he knew a little bit about knowledge. He combined the insights of rationalists and empiricists to argue that knowledge necessarily involves both ideas and experience. Hence his dictum: "Concepts without percepts are empty; percepts without concepts are blind." Let me co-opt Kant's dictum to paraphrase what I think Jesus is saying about worshiping in spirit and truth: Ideas of God without a corresponding devotional experience are empty; devotional experience of God without ideas of God are blind. *Theology without worship is empty; worship without theology is blind.* Even this adaptation of Kant's dictum does not go far enough, insofar as it leaves us with the impression that theology provides the brainpower and worship the experience. This may happen, but it should not be the norm. We need to make worship more like theology and theology more like worship, since both theology and worship concern objective truth *and* a right relation to the truth.

Jesus' teaching about spirit and truth addresses the two endemic problems of worship: hypocrisy and idolatry. These two toxins poison the well, robbing it of its life-giving effects. *Worship in truth is the antidote to idolatry, and worship in spirit is the antidote to hypocrisy.* Real worshipers both know the truth and are rightly related to it, holding onto it for dear—that is, eternal—life.

The rationale of worship (and of theology): "God is spirit" (v. 24). Whereas verse 22 concerns the object of worship and verse 23 the manner of worship, verse 24 pertains to the rationale behind worship. We must worship in spirit and truth because God *is* spirit and truth. Recall the principle mentioned above: the object of worship dictates the manner of worship.

"God is spirit." As a piece of speculative metaphysics, this statement implies that God is free from all limitations associated with embodiment, including limitations of space (and hence place) and time (finitude, mortality). He is free from the limitations that accompany all other forms of physical existence too, such as depletion and decay. "The Father has life in himself" (Jn 5:26).

Jesus is not giving a lesson on metaphysics, however, but on right worship. We should probably hear in this identity statement a reference back to Jesus' earlier identification of the Spirit with living water: precisely as Spirit, God is the font of every blessing, the fount of eternal life. In context, Jesus' point is about God's activity, not his immateriality. As Spirit, God is the breath— not water, but living *air*—that animates the dust and mud, creating living creatures; he is the breath that bears the prophets and God's Word. God the Spirit springs from Christ's life, death and resurrection to make all things permanently new.

Note, too, that it is God who seeks true worshipers. In most religions, the worshipers seek God. The Bible, however, depicts God embarking on a mission to humanity: a Trinitarian mission that involves God's twofold pouring out of himself for others in Son and Spirit. Jesus laid down his life in order to bestow his life—his Spirit—to us. Accordingly, the Father does not simply seek but also *creates* those who worship in spirit and in truth. Jesus is the truth (Jn 14:6), and the Spirit is the one who relates us to the truth (Jn 14:17). God is Spirit because through the Spirit he begets true worshipers. God is thus not only the object of worship, but also its active subject.

Right worship thus corresponds to God in two ways. Right worshipers come with the right objectivity, oriented to reality ("truth"), and right worshipers come with the right subjectivity, receiving truth in humility and joy ("spirit"). Jesus is teaching what we might call the "correspondence theory" of worship. Real worship is in spirit and truth *because* God is spirit and truth.

From Doxology to Dogmatics (and Back Again)

How does Jesus' teaching apply to the relationship of theology to corporate worship? Let me make a general application, and then a more specific one.

The place of worship in theology and the place of theology in worship. On one hand, doxology is the cradle of dogmatics. There is no question which comes first chronologically: doxology precedes dogmatics. The prayers and praises of the people of God precede sustained reflection. The earliest theologians were concerned not only with the meaning of the Scriptures, but also with the theological implications of such Christian practices as baptism and the Lord's Supper. Why? Because the way we worship shapes the way we believe. *Lex orandi, lex credendi* (what we pray shapes what we believe). If our worship is shallow and superficial, our faith will be too. Trivial music and trivial words trivialize the divine. Scripture enjoins us not to remain immature in faith, but to attain the maturity that comes from faith seeking understanding, from chewing over the tough red meat of Scripture rather than being content with merely sipping its warm milk (Heb 5:12-14). This chewing on the content of revelation, its meaning and significance, is what it means to do theology. Theology yields deeper insights into Scripture, into the mystery of the faith (what God was doing in Christ) and hence into what God is like, and this deeper understanding should in turn result in deeper worship. As we grow in our knowledge of God, our worship becomes more profound: "In shaping worship, the question must always be, 'Are these materials worthy of a BIG God?'"[14]

Make no mistake. *Worship makes theological statements.* Geoffrey Wainwright says that through its worship, the church "can transmit a vision of reality which helps decisively in the interpretation of life and the world."[15] Worship puts all of life into its right—that is, its biblical-theological—perspective. Worship is the place where our theological vision and understanding should come into sharpest focus and result in its most powerful expression.

"You worship what you do not know." What a powerful provocation, and hence an excellent incentive for studying theology! No worshiper wants to hear that rebuke. Suppose we turn it around: "You know what you do not worship." No theologian wants to hear that rebuke. The only remedy is par-ticipation in corporate worship. We can now restate Jesus' point. We must know what we worship, *and* we must worship what we know. Here, then, is the challenge not for the Samaritan but for us. Is our worship adequate to our knowledge? Is our knowledge adequate to our worship? The quality of the one is a measure of the quality of the other. Tom Wright puts it this way: "If your idea of God, if your idea of salvation offered in Christ, is vague or remote, your idea of worship will be fuzzy and ill-formed."[16] The nature and quality of our worship is an index of our theological understanding and our spiritual life, a measure of our apprehension and appropriation of God's truth and God's Spirit.

Theology both emerges from and leads us back to worship. Conversely, worship must be theological: it must reflect faith's understanding of who God is and what God has done. Worship must also be corporate, for one of the great things that God has done is precisely to form a *people*. Worship involves not only cognition, as we saw earlier, but also the public *recog-nition*—in commemoration and celebration—of what Christians know about God.

---

[14]Ronald Byars, *Christian Worship: Glorifying and Enjoying God* (Louisville, KY: Geneva Press, 2000), 112.

[15]Geoffrey Wainwright, *Doxology: The Praise of God in Worship, Doctrine, and Life* (New York: Oxford University Press, 1980), 2.

[16]Wright, *For All God's Worth*, 10.

What kind of theological statement does contemporary worship make? It is time to move beyond the worship wars. The Father desires worshipers who worship in spirit and in truth. Whatever we think about musical styles, let us at least agree on this. Worship must be theological (God-centered) not anthropological (me-centered, we-centered). Worship is first and foremost about what God has done, not how we feel about it. And yet, without the affective dimension, our theology opens up onto a mere desert rather than a Promised Land flowing with milk and honey—and the water of the Spirit. Let us therefore resolve to let our worship improve our theology, and our theology improve our worship. Of all the ugly ditches to which seminary students are exposed—the ditch between biblical and theological studies, between theory and practice, between the seminary and the church—none is uglier than the ditch between theology and worship.

Worship at the Trinitarian well. This leads me to a specific application for our seminary community, one that concerns Trinitarian worship. I am thinking not simply of worship *at* Trinity Evangelical Divinity School—as we have seen, the place of worship is not what counts. Rather, I am thinking of worship *in* the Trinity.

Here is my central claim. Christian worship *is* thoroughly theological. It is first and foremost the result of a Trinitarian initiative in which the Father seeks worshipers precisely by drawing us toward him through his Son and his Spirit. Proper worship is enabled only by God's preliminary breathing and speaking in Spirit and Word. Our response to God is the effect of God's prior summons. Our worship is but the communicative effect of God's prior communicative acts.

"We worship what we know." The knowledge of God that funds real worship has nothing to do with abstract theory. Theory yields dry knowledge only. True worship and theology alike require something more: wet knowledge, knowledge soaked in truth and spirituality, the revelation of Jesus Christ and the incorporation of the Holy Spirit. To know or to worship God we need to drink from the divine well. The Father is the source of the wellspring, the one who has life in himself; the Son is the spring that comes forth from the source; and the Spirit is the living water that proceeds from the spring, the channel that leads to every spiritual blessing.

In worship, we confess and celebrate who God is and what he has done.

Yet who God is and what God has done really amount to the same thing. The triune God *is* the Father's sending of Son and Spirit, and the purpose for which God sends his truth and his Spirit is to give life. What we celebrate in worship, then, is our life in the triune God, the giver of life. We confess and celebrate God's self-giving above all when we confess and celebrate Jesus Christ, the one and only mediator between God and humanity (1 Tim 2:5).

The purpose of water is to sustain life. So too with worship at the Trinitarian well, where what gets circulated is the stream of living water given by Christ. In worship, it is never winter but always spring. Every season of the church calendar celebrates a season of new life. Christian worship must be thoroughly Trinitarian, by which I mean not merely the doctrine of the Trinity, but the personal knowledge arising from participating in the very life of the triune God. We worship the Father through the Son in the Spirit. We worship by participating in the triune God's own mission—the sending of Son and Spirit to the world that is the grace and generosity of God. Worshiping in spirit and in truth—and gratitude—thus enables us to correspond to God, and to reflect God's own life, light and love back to him, to God's glory.

CONCLUSION: WHAT TO GIVE THE GOD WHO HAS EVERYTHING

Let me pause to rehearse my main points in the form of seven theses.

First, it is Jesus' life, death and resurrection that makes possible the sending of the Spirit who, in uniting us to the Son, draws us into God's triune life and enables us to worship in spirit and in truth.

Second, we worship what we know. If our knowledge is not deep, our worship won't be either.

Third, worship has a cognitive dimension: what we are to know, and thus worship, is who God is and what he has done.

Fourth, what we come to understand in the classroom should be celebrated in the chapel. The meaning of the gospel and the Christian life comes to focus in worship as nowhere else.

Fifth, theology is not only the study of God, but also a means for improving our worship. Conversely, worship is not only the praise of God, but also a means for improving our theology.

Sixth, our worship is the index to how well we have understood our faith.

And seventh, the "worth-ship" of our worship is a function of how deeply we perceive God's worth.

Our worship, like the well water we drink in my house, inevitably contains certain impurities. At times our worship, like that of the Samaritans, betrays the cultural contaminants of our place and time. As theology leads to worship, so worship leads to further theologizing and reform, as we seek to correspond rightly to God's Word and Spirit rather than to the words and spirit of the age.

What exactly do we give to God in worship? My family tells me that I'm hard to shop for at Christmas. We all know people for whom it's hard to know what to get. Sometimes it's hard because we don't know their tastes and hobbies, their likes and dislikes. Sometimes it's hard because they already seem to have everything they need. If it's hard to know what to give the *man* who has everything, how much more difficult is it to know what to give the *God* who has everything, the God who has life in himself?

Perhaps not. Jesus tells us exactly what the Father wants. "The Father is seeking such people to worship him" (Jn 4:23). "Such people" refers to those who will worship him in spirit and truth. We should give the God who has everything the acknowledgment and recognition of who he is and what he has done. We give God back to himself, as it were. Worshipers can do this in spirit and in truth in both theology and church service. Both dogmatics and doxology are a fitting tribute, for done in spirit and truth, both are expressions of gratitude that acknowledge God's infinite worth.

Worship should spring forth wherever the people of God are sojourning, or whenever two or three are gathered in Christ's name. As a springing-forth of the Spirit of God back toward God, worship localizes the Trinitarian well. Chapel may be our last best hope for integrating what otherwise risks staying departmentalized in our seminary context. Like the well, corporate worship provides a gathering place to refresh pilgrims along their Christian way. Worship replenishes our supply not of water but of spirit and of truth. Corporate worship—drinking from the Trinitarian well—is precisely what we need to sustain us during our sojourn in the groves of academe. May we all learn to worship—and to learn—in spirit and truth.

five

PRAISING GOD IN SONG

Beauty and the Arts

The work of art is the object seen sub specie aeternitatis;
and the good life is the world seen sub specie aeternitatis.
This is the connection between art and ethics.

LUDWIG WITTGENSTEIN

This essay originally appeared in The Blackwell Companion to Christian
Ethics, *edited by Stanley Hauerwas and Sam Wells. I met Stanley at a Society*
of Biblical Literature session where I was a respondent to his recently published
commentary on the Gospel of Mathew. Sam was one of my students at the
University of Edinburgh. The premise of their edited volume was to approach
issues concerning the Christian life (ethics) through the lens of Christian
worship. The central insight is that worship has a formative influence on moral
and spiritual character ("You are what you worship"). Their book was ecu-
menical, with Anglicans, Roman Catholics, mainline Protestants and a
handful of Evangelicals all contributing. My task was to reflect on aesthetics
via the lens of music in worship. This essay follows the previous one, then, by
moving from a consideration of worship in general to music and the other arts
in particular. As an amateur pianist, I have had a longstanding interest in the
relationship between music and theology. Indeed, before I started seminary I
did a stint as a short-term missionary to France, charged with fusing classical
music with a presentation of the gospel. The connecting link between music,
theology and the gospel, in addition to beauty, is joy. The influence of that early
experience can be found here, at least by those with ears to hear!

DOXOLOGY: IN PRAISE OF BEAUTY?

It is a familiar sight: a congregation sings the Doxology as the deacons bring forward the collection plates, acknowledging that God has given far more to us—"all blessings"—than we can ever give back. Many churches also sing the *Gloria Patri* after the confession and absolution, acknowledging the greatest divine gift of all: forgiveness, and the new sharing in the Triune life that ensues.

These and other musical offerings enhance the quality of our worship. But how? Wittgenstein's insight into what connects aesthetics and ethics also forges a tie to worship. Praising God in song enables the church not simply to see things *sub specie aeternitatis* ("from the perspective of eternity") but to *feel* them so. Praising God in song allows us to enter the antechamber of heaven, to stand on eternity's very brink.

Augustine defines the hymn as praise to God with song.[1] We praise what we prize, just as we worship what we consider worthy. Praises may be said or sung, but singing accomplishes something that saying cannot. First, singing is social, uniting the whole assembly in a harmony that both manifests and constitutes a community. Second, singing is personal, engaging all our faculties. "Singing clearly demonstrates worship—and therefore the divine kingdom and human salvation—to be an affair of the whole person, mind, heart, voice, body."[2] Third, singing is sensational. We perceive both visual art and music through our senses. (The original meaning of the Greek term *aesthetics* was "perception.")

This essay is not about styles of music in the church; it seeks rather to investigate the role of beauty and aesthetics in the Christian life. Specifically, how does praising God in song form Christian character? We listen to Scripture readings to hear the Word of God, but what should we be trying to perceive when we listen to church music? Aaron Copland's question to would-be music lovers provides a helpful starting point. Are you hearing everything that is going on; are you genuinely perceiving all that is there?[3]

---

[1] In his exposition of Psalm 72:20, Augustine says, "He who sings praise, not only sings, but also loves him of whom he sings." Augustine, *Enarrationes in Psalmos LI-C*, E. Dekkers and J. Fraipont, eds., Corpus Christianorum Series Latina, vol. 39 (Turnhout, Belgium: Brepols, 1990), 986.

[2] Geoffrey Wainwright, *Doxology: The Praise of God in Worship, Doctrine, and Life* (New York: Oxford University Press, 1980), 200.

[3] Aaron Copland, *What to Listen for in Music* (New York: McGraw-Hill, 1957), vii.

What is "going on" in hymns? What should Christians listen for in church music? What does praise have to do with aesthetics? Why has the contemporary church so often neglected aesthetics, and what are the consequences of doing so?

Let us make a preliminary distinction between *aesthetics* and *aesthetic*. *Aesthetics* is a branch of philosophy that deals with judgments about works of art. *Aesthetic* is an aspect of human nature in which an experience of beauty leads to a self-transcending delight. Beauty is central to aesthetic, but not necessarily to aesthetics. It is one thing to study religious art (aesthetics), another to examine the role of beauty in the life of faith (an aesthetic).[4] This essay is primarily a consideration of the latter, and hence with a *theological* aesthetic.

There is something about praising God in song that goes beyond both doctrine and piety. My argument is that praising God in song—a staple practice of the Church—forms our imaginations and hence our sensibilities as to what is fitting in the created (and redeemed) order. The imagination, particularly in the arts, is a vital means for perceiving and commending the good, the true and the beautiful, hidden and revealed in Christ.

THE GOOD, THE TRUE AND THE BEAUTIFUL:
THE ANCIENT/MODERN QUARREL

The fate of beauty is tied to that of goodness and truth. What the ancients united, the moderns have differentiated and the postmoderns have deconstructed. Society—including the church—is still learning to live amid the ruins.

Old alliance; ancient quarrel. Ancient philosophers parsed being in terms of the good, the true and the beautiful—transcendental properties that may be predicated of everything that is: flowers, birdsong, sunsets, geometrical proofs and, as we shall see, human virtues and actions. According to Plato, all instances of worldly goodness, truth and beauty participate in ideal or eternal forms. For Christian thinkers, the application was obvious. God, as perfect being, is himself the source of the good, the true and the beautiful. The glory of God consists in the sublime conjunction of goodness, truth and beauty.

---

[4]Edward Farley, *Faith and Beauty: A Theological Aesthetic* (Aldershot, UK: Ashgate, 2001), 117.

Plato also spoke of an "ancient quarrel between philosophy and poetry" (and by extension the other arts as well).[5] For Plato, the arts, whether visual, literary or musical, are actually crafts (*techné*) that make images. These images may imitate their originals but, precisely because they are imitations of objects that are themselves imitations of eternal forms, they are two steps removed from the realm of reality. Plato did allow that poetry and music, at their best, can be means of character formation, capable of inculcating moral virtue, but beauty has still often been the Cinderella of philosophy, the poor stepsister of goodness and truth.

The modern quarrel. In modernity, beauty became dispensable for both metaphysics and ethics. Indeed, beauty has become the "beast": alternately seductive, elitist, trivial, subjective, "an ornament of the bourgeois past."[6] Discourse on beauty disappeared in the academy, and beauty itself largely disappeared from society and the church, at least as a priority.

Modernity names a process of rationalization and differentiation in which social forces and institutional forms—secularization, industrialization, bureaucratization—came to embody the Enlightenment ideals of rationality, individual autonomy and progress. Modernity is the triumph of instrumental rationality in the social domain. The result is an ever-increasing differentiation or fragmentation of life, where every aspect of human experience becomes a new field for the specialist. From another perspective, modernity is the turn to the subject: a turn away from the consideration of the world in itself to a consideration of the world as it appears in human experience and thought. The arts have thus come to be associated not with being, but with feeling. Objective beauty has given way to the study of subjective sensibility.

Kant's philosophy illustrates both of these trends. Kant fragments the old alliance between the good, the true and the beautiful by showing each to be a corollary of a separate realm of human experience, each with its own a priori principles and rationality. For Kant, aesthetic judgments are neither cognitive nor moral. They concern neither truth nor moral goodness. Of what value, then, is aesthetic sensibility? Kant's own answer was that art mediates the realms of nature (fact) and freedom (value) by enabling us to

---

[5]Plato, *The Republic* X.3, trans. Desmond Lee (New York: Penguin Books, 2003), 349.
[6]Farley, *Faith and Beauty*, 1.

view the world *as if* it had purpose, *as if* nature were a meaningful context for moral action.[7]

Modern thinkers responded to the fragmentation of the good, true and beautiful in two diametrically opposed ways. Some saw art and beauty as a dispensable luxury to the essentials of life; others saw art and beauty as essential, the very things that make life worth living. Matthew Arnold and Leo Tolstoy argued that art has social value only when it is morally useful, as an incentive toward virtue. Others, like Oscar Wilde, advocated aestheticism, the notion that art needs no justification or reference to anything outside the work itself. The artist's calling is to strive for formal perfection as a value in its own right: art for art's sake. A poem, painting or prelude need not "mean" but should simply "be." Everyone agreed that aesthetics named a discrete aspect of human experience and that art had become a specialization in its own right. The disagreement was over how central to the rest of society artists actually are. Is beauty necessary to the good life or not?

The postmodern quarrel. Where moderns differentiate, postmoderns deconstruct, exposing claims to absolute goodness, truth or beauty as expressions of the merely individual or cultural will to power. Yet the same two tendencies that characterize the modern quarrel are also apparent in postmodernity.

Postmodern aestheticisim has become a veritable "first philosophy." Yet the postmodern celebration of creative interpretation comes with a certain despair of the imagination. Postmoderns revel in stories and images even as they drain them of ultimate significance by insisting that we cannot really believe in them. This is the great irony of postmodernity: that ideology-criticism ultimately *devalues* the imagination. Metanarratives shrink to mere narratives; deep symbols give way to superficial spin.

Dorothy Sayers foresaw the malaise of our time: sloth, the inability to believe in or do anything.[8] Nineteenth-century Romantic passion has shriveled into twenty-first century anemic irony. A lack of beauty in the diet leads to malnutrition of the imagination, a deficiency of vital symbols and

---

[7]See Immanuel Kant, *The Critique of Judgment*, trans. J. H. Bernard (Mineola, NY: Dover Classics, 2005).
[8]See Dorothy Sayers, "The Other Six Deadly Sins," in *Letters to a Diminished Church: Passionate Arguments for the Relevance of Christian Doctrine* (Nashville, TN: Thomas Nelson, 2004), 103.

stories in the bloodstream of the soul that results in world-weariness. Post-moderns suffer not from oversensation, as is commonly thought, but from desensitization, an anesthesia of the spirit. One is hard pressed to identify anything for which postmodern men and women are willing to live, or die.

In contrast, Emmanuel Lévinas makes ethics his "first philosophy."[9] On his view, recognizing one's infinite obligations to the other clearly takes priority over aesthetic delight. Indeed, for many today, a preoccupation with beauty is politically incorrect because art, like religion, can act as the people's opiate, distracting them from situations that cry out for social justice. Elaine Scarry believes that such arguments for the irrelevance of beauty are misguided, however, because the same sensibilities that enable the perception of beauty also oppose injustice. As she notes, the word *fair* means both "beautiful" and "just."[10] To perceive beauty is to undergo a transformation of sorts from self-centeredness to other-centeredness. Experiencing beauty prompts us to give up our imaginary position at the center and forces us to recognize that we are in the presence of something larger than ourselves.

BEAUTY IN SCRIPTURE AND CHRISTIAN TRADITION: A (VERY) BRIEF SURVEY

Beauty in the Bible. Christians profess their faith through art and song, in canon and catacomb, in response to God's beauty reflected in creation and housed in the temple, but seen most vividly in the tortured and transfigured face of Jesus Christ.

Nature. The biblical authors ascribe beauty to various natural phenomena, such as flowers (Jas 1:11), olive trees (Hos 14:6) and sunrises (Ps 19:1). The Greek word *kalos* ("beautiful") expresses more than aesthetic value, however. "It is the right, the fitting, the good, that which is appropriate to a being."[11] The Septuagint uses *kalos* to translate the Hebrew *ṭôb* ("good, pleasing, agreeable") in the refrain in the first chapter of Genesis: "And God saw everything that he had made, and behold, it was very good" (Gen 1:31), perhaps with the sense "good form" (i.e., beautiful).

---

[9]See Lévinas's *Ethics and Infinity: Conversations with Philippe Nemo* (Pittsburgh: Duquesne University Press, 1985).

[10]Elaine Scarry, *On Beauty and Being Just* (Princeton, NJ: Princeton University Press, 1999).

[11]Hans Urs von Balthasar, *The Glory of the Lord* (Edinburgh: T&T Clark, 1982), 4:201.

Temple. Scripture also describes human-made objects like crowns (Is 28:5), garments (Is 52:1), clay vessels (Rom 9:21) and even cities (Lam 2:15) as beautiful. Above all these, however, stand the tabernacle and temple. There are detailed accounts of the materials and plans for their construction (Ex 25-30; 35-39; 1 Kings 6-7; 1 Chron 22-27; 2 Chron 2-4). God's own Spirit filled those, like Bezalel, responsible for making the temple with the requisite skills and designs (Ex 31:2-5; 35:30-36:1). The psalmist's exclamation attests to the success of the end product: "How lovely is your dwelling place!" (Ps 84:1).

Persons. Significantly, both men and women are called beautiful (Gen 12:11; Is 44:13; Song 1:15-16). Proverbs makes clear, however, that what truly matters is inner beauty: "Charm is deceitful, and beauty is vain, but a woman who fears the LORD is to be praised" (Prov 31:30). The biblical contrast between beauty and ugliness is less about external appearances than the inner character or spirit that either serves God's purpose or distorts it (1 Pet 3:4).

Jesus Christ. Scripture ultimately locates the glory of God—the visible display of God's greatness—in the life of a humble carpenter. Jesus is the icon of the invisible God (Col 1:15), the tabernacle and temple in whom God's glory dwells (Jn 1:14; Mk 14:58), the exact representation of the divine being (Heb 1:3).

The body of Christ. Christians are individual and corporate temples of the Holy Spirit who display the "beauty [Hebrew *hădārâ*] of holiness" (1 Chron 16:29 KJV; Ps 29:2). The "holy array" in which the priests of ancient Israel worshiped God (1 Chron 16:29, RSV) now becomes the righteousness of Christ (Gal 3:27), the humility (1 Pet 5:5) that clothes all believers. "God's glory is revealed in humble, self-effacing lives of faith and love."[12]

Beauty in East and West: splendor and harmony. The Orthodox East associated beauty with the light of God: splendor. The Catholic West focused on form and order: harmony.

Eastern Orthodoxy. In the Orthodox tradition, Christ is the icon of God, the epiphany of the transcendent God, the light of the world. "The Orthodox Church, without losing sight of the moral dimension or the necessity of spiritual discipline, puts before us a vision of the beauty of

---

[12]Richard Harries, *Art and the Beauty of God: A Christian Understanding* (London: Mowbray, 1993), 56.

God, radiant in Christ, shining in the saints and beginning to glimmer in us."[13] All the world is a stage for epiphanies of glory: "The beauty of the visible world lies not in the transitory splendor of its present state, but in the very meaning of its existence, in its coming transfiguration. . . . In other words, beauty is holiness, and its radiance a participation of the creature in Divine Beauty."[14]

The Son is the image of the Father and the Spirit is the image of the Son. Icons depict the saints not as they were on earth, but in their heavenly reality—"in Christ." As we keep company with the saints, the Orthodox believe, we will progressively be changed into their image. Thanks to the indwelling Spirit, Christians can function as icons of Christ. But it is Christ alone who is the very image of God's being and beauty. Orthodox icons typically depict Jesus, even when he is hanging on the cross, as a radiant emblem of the triumph of God's loving purpose.

Augustine. Pythagoras explained musical harmony in terms of numeric proportions and mathematical relations, but it was Augustine who defined music as "the science of measuring well" [*scientia bene modulandi*].[15] Even today musical scores are made up of "measures" with notes that denote relative lengths of time. Music is the well-measured motion of sonorous forms. Augustine thought of music as the expression of an eternal order in time: the heavenly ratios in the mind of God. The beauty of creation stands in analogical relation to the perfect beauty of the Creator.

Thomas Aquinas. Aquinas lists three criteria of beauty: wholeness /integrity, right proportion/harmony and clarity/radiance.[16] Another thirteenth-century thinker, Robert Grosseteste, writes that "beauty is a concordance and fittingness of a thing to itself and of all its individual parts to themselves and to each other and to the whole, and of that whole to all things."[17] Here, as throughout much of Christian tradition, the emphasis is on metaphysics—beauty as a function of the created order. Yet Aquinas is

---

[13]Ibid., 7.

[14]Leonid Ouspensky and Vladimir Lossky, *The Meaning of Icons* (New York: St. Vladimir's Seminary Press, 1982), 35.

[15]Augustine, *De Musica* I.2.

[16]Aquinas, *Summa Theologiae* I, q. 39, a. 8.

[17]Cited in Umberto Eco, *Art and Beauty in the Middle Ages* (New Haven, CT: Yale University Press, 1986), 48.

able to view the soul too as beautiful insofar as wisdom, like the other virtues, derives from "the harmony of energies and the ordering of powers."[18]

Jonathan Edwards. Jonathan Edwards combines the ancient/medieval emphasis on beauty as objective harmony with the modern emphasis on beauty as subjective sensibility. We experience as beautiful the pleasing "agreements"—the ratios, proportions and harmonies—of the world and of those artworks that display and express such agreements. Yet Edwards describes such beauty as secondary. Secondary beauty alone provides no guarantee of moral integrity or holiness. Primary beauty, by contrast, is not just a feeling of pleasure but, more importantly, a disposition of the heart. In particular, it is a consent to being that immediately results in the exercise of good will. In secondary beauty, there is a formal consent or agreement to the various parts that together comprise a harmony, but in primary beauty there must be an agreement of the mind, will and feelings alike.

For Edwards, beauty is best exhibited in creative spiritual relations of consent rather than in created material relations of proportion. Thus beauty is less a matter of sensation than relation—an *ethical* relation, to be precise. What is primarily beautiful is benevolence: the "cordial or heart-felt consent of being to being."[19] The paradigmatic instance of such benevolence is the loving generosity of God. Primary beauty is ultimately rooted in the "agreement" of the Trinity, in God's own loving self-consent: "He that sees the beauty of holiness . . . sees the greatest and most important thing in the world."[20]

BEAUTY IN CONTEMPORARY THEOLOGY

Hans Urs von Balthasar. Balthasar's five-volume *The Glory of the Lord: A Theological Aesthetics* is the first of a theological trilogy that works a neat twist on the traditional order of the good, the true and the beautiful.[21] Balthasar begins with beauty in order to recover the sense of the wholeness of things and the grandeur of God that moderns and postmoderns have lost.

---

[18]Cited in Patrick Sherry, *Spirit and Beauty: An Introduction to Theological Aesthetics*, 2nd ed. (London: SCM, 2002), 34.

[19]Roland A. Delattre, *Beauty and Sensibility in the Thought of Jonathan Edwards: An Essay in Aesthetics and Theological Ethics* (New Haven, CT: Yale University Press, 1968), 17.

[20]Edwards, *The Works of Jonathan Edwards*, vol. 2, *Religious Affections* (New Haven, CT: Yale University Press, 1959), 274.

[21]Hans Urs von Balthasar, *The Glory of the Lord: A Theological Aesthetics*, 5 vols. (San Francisco: Ignatius Press, 1984–1991).

Balthasar's theological aesthetics treats the human perception of divine revelation. God has revealed himself not in a concept, but in Christ, the human and historical form of glory. The incarnation is "God's greatest work of art," the "luminous form" of the transcendent God. The incarnation does not cancel aesthetic experience but elevates it by enabling worldly realities—in this case, human flesh—to contain something infinitely greater than themselves.

Jesus is the very form (*Gestalt*) of Trinitarian love. For God's glory is manifested above all in Jesus' self-emptying. His humiliation is at once his glorification, as the Fourth Gospel indicates when it speaks of his being "lifted up" on the cross (Jn 12:32). When this *Gestalt* captivates those who see it, they begin to be drawn out of themselves and into it. "The moral response inevitably provoked by the beautiful involves the self in a process of transformation in which it remakes itself according to the likeness of the beautiful form that inspires it."[22]

The Spirit's role is to enable Christians to discern God's glory in the form of the Son, and to impress this form upon us. A theological aesthetic thus involves both "a theory about the incarnation of God's glory and the consequent elevation of man to participate in that glory."[23] Sanctification is thus related to beautification. There is an ethical demand implicit in genuine encounters with beauty: God manifests himself to people in order to commission them. In the bleak midwinter of contemporary Western society, the perception of Christ's splendid form is a divine summons to reimagine, and hence transform, our lives.

Edward Farley. According to Edward Farley, the most direct route to beauty is not the analogy of being but the fact of redemption itself: "A theological aesthetic works to uncover the way faith—that is, individual and corporate existence transformed by redemption—is beautiful and gives rise to sensibilities to beauty."[24] Before we can make sense of debates concerning the role of art in the church, we need to develop an understanding of the aesthetic dimension of faith itself.

---

[22]Kevin Mongrain, *The Systematic Thought of Hans Urs von Balthasar: An Irenaean Retrieval* (New York: Crossroad, 2002), 66.

[23]Balthasar, *Glory of the Lord,* vol. 1, 125.

[24]Farley, *Faith and Beauty,* 119.

With Edwards, Farley contends that "primary beauty is an ethical, empathetic self-transcendence" and identifies primary beauty with the *imago Dei*.[25] Sin distorts the divine image by dulling our sensibility to beauty and by cultivating self-preoccupation—narcissism—rather than self-transcendence. The sinner does not consent to being but seeks to control it, thus choosing use over enjoyment. Through the process of redemptive transformation, however, the beauty of the *imago Dei* is restored: "If sheer attractiveness is the criterion of the beautiful, we are surely more attracted to self-transcending love than we are to sheer proportion or harmony."[26]

Given his theme—beautiful faith—Farley is keen to surmount the dichotomy of the ethical and the aesthetic. Like Lévinas, he proposes that the "fragile beauty" in the face of the other evokes one's sense of responsibility.[27] The face of the other does not display secondary beauty, for every face combines elements of disorder as well as harmony, the ultimate disorder being perishability—the entropy of mortality. No, what we see in the face of the other is a self-transcending acknowledgment of our own irreducibility. The look that does not objectify me is what prompts my sense of infinite obligation to the other. It is precisely as we regard the other—and especially in the other's acknowledgment of the worth of what is ultimately perishing—that we most clearly perceive beauty's peculiar pathos.

BEAUTY AND IMAGINATION IN THE CHRISTIAN LIFE: BEHOLDING AND BEHOLDEN TO

Christian ethics concerns our response to the gift of Christian freedom. It is about using or creating forms of freedom that participate appropriately in the form of Jesus Christ. Appropriate action, however, requires understanding, and for this we need the evangelical imagination: the ability to see what God is doing for the world in Jesus Christ. The beauty of what God is doing is not merely in the eye of the beholder. On the contrary, beholding is the ability to see everything that is happening in Christ. The imagination is the power of synoptic vision, the ability to understand complex wholes. As such, it is related to wisdom: the discernment of how

---

[25]Ibid., 118.
[26]Ibid., 89.
[27]Ibid., 95.

things fit together, and hence of what we should do in a given situation. To behold is to be beholden.

The ethos of the mythos. Every worldview or model of the cosmos conveys an ethos, a palpable sense of the way things are and the kind of environment in which human freedom lives and moves. Human existence involves being-in-space (spatiality, physicality) and being-in-time (temporality, mortality). Our attunement toward space and time will thus contribute much to the "feel" of life. An ethos creates a moral ecology, a context for reflection and action.

There is an important, though often overlooked, tie between a culture's ethos, imagination and ethics. The foundation stories of a given culture, its stock of narratives and metanarratives, create the stage on which human freedom lives and moves. Culture cultivates an ethos via works of the imagination.

The imagination cultivates an awareness of a dimension of things inaccessible to empirical science and shapes our sense of the meaning of the whole. Art, "that human activity that goes beyond the useful to embody in allusive color, shape or sound the joy or pain of being human,"[28] is one of the principal means of cultivation. Art, music and literature (not to mention dance, architecture and film) indirectly communicate views about human life and love, about the meaning of life in its cosmic setting. Cultures thus cultivate the human spirit, encouraging certain forms of life rather than others. The irony of our time is that, though we have more powerful image-making technologies than ever, we continue to be caught in what the poet Paul Claudel called "the tragedy of a starved imagination."[29]

We began with music—"sonorous forms in motion." What we encounter in all works of art are meaningful forms—visual, verbal or audible—that communicate some kind of promise, project or proposition (a "real presence," to use Steiner's term) that calls for our response and has the potential to affect us.[30] Readers, viewers and listeners have an ethical responsibility to be hospitable toward the work of art instead of merely using it for one's own purposes. Genuine encounters with a work of art are nonviolent. *I receive in order to understand.*

---

[28]Dyrness, *Visual Faith,* 99.
[29]Paul Claudel, *Positions and Propositions* (Paris: Gallimard, 1926), 175.
[30]George Steiner, *Real Presences* (Chicago: University of Chicago, 1989).

Music conveys our sense, conditioned but not determined by time and culture, of what it is to "be in the world." Being-in-the-world involves a grasp both of our environment and of ourselves: of our place in the world and of our possibilities. What music conveys, then, is not so much a message as it is a *mood*. Martin Heidegger prefers to speak of "mood" rather than ethos, but both terms refer to a person's sense of being-in-the-world.[31] The German term for "mood" (*Stimmung*) originally referred to the tuning of a musical instrument, which may be why Heidegger also speaks of the importance of people "being attuned" toward existence. Understood in this deep existential sense, "mood" involves our sense of self, our sense of the world and the relationship between them (the "tuning"). Because music always conveys some sense of being-in-the world, all music is "mood" music.

What is the ethos of contemporary music? Much popular music is more conducive to protesting than to praising. After all, how does one compose music after Auschwitz? How can one make sense of anything after the demise of the Enlightenment project, after the violent and absurd twentieth century? This is a problem for theologians, ethicists, artists, novelists and composers alike. The waltzes of Johann Strauss may be charming, but we cannot take them too seriously. They are apt evocations of the lightness of being that characterized nineteenth-century Viennese bourgeois society: carefree, but shallow. Strauss wrote music for dancing our cares away, not for helping us bear one another's burdens. His waltzes are neither true nor beautiful, merely charming. Brahms's music is more true to life, more in touch with human joys and sorrows, more "authentic," to use Heidegger's language. Brahms wrote music for mortals, music that conveys the inevitability of death, but also a certain refusal of that very finality.[32]

Insofar as culture acknowledges the negativities of existence, it may be true to a penultimate point, but it is not beautiful. Much of contemporary culture is based on the premise of God's absence, and this premise creates an ethos that is distinctly hostile to attempts to make experiences of joy, hope and love intelligible. One persuasive present-day story is that only the strongest survive. This Darwinian *mythos* generates an ethos of

---

[31]See Martin Heidegger, *Being in Time*, trans. John Macquarrie (Oxford: Basil Blackwell, 1962).
[32]See further my "What Has Vienna to Do with Jerusalem? Barth, Brahms, and Bernstein's Unanswered Question," *Westminster Theological Journal* 63 (2001): 123-50.

conflict and competition. It is a violent, ugly story that views the world *sub specie evolutionatis.*

What evolution is to nature, the market is to society. Many churches have been possessed by the spirit of the financial times, where success means numerical growth. The church growth movement, with its seeker-sensitive appeal to the lowest common denominator, is as ugly as the popular culture it mimics, and so is the result: the "McDonaldization" of worship.[33] It is a sad case of the bland leading the bland. Marva Dawn argues that such dumbing-down leads many to stop participating in worship because of boredom. Even more tragic than a starved imagination is an imagination that starves in church!

Against a background of cultural bleakness and despair, church hymns act as powerful catalysts for countercultural world-making. The stories and songs of the church are indispensable moments in ethical and spiritual pedagogy, arrows that point to a glorious, eschatological order. William Brown has convincingly shown how the biblical pictures of creation helped shape Israel's moral character.[34] Yet it is the *logos* made flesh that compels us to reimagine God's glory in terms of "the face of Christ" (2 Cor 4:6). The biblical imagination depicts the entry of the eternal into human time and thus generates an evangelical ethos: "God with us." There is nothing depressing or boring about that.

Wisdom as moral imagination: right attention, right action. Wisdom— the virtue that orders all other virtues—is intrinsically linked to the imagination and beauty via the theme of fittingness. The wise person perceives and participates fittingly in the ordered beauty of creation. Wisdom thus integrates the good, the true and the beautiful. Works of art and music provide the lighting on the stage of human existence. They also cultivate the ability to imaginatively discern certain features of our situations that cannot be perceived with the physical senses. Right perception—the capacity to discern—is thus the connecting link between aesthetics and ethics. "The capacity to see what is there . . . is integrally related to the capacity to love."[35]

---

[33]See George Ritzer, *The McDonaldization of Society* (Thousand Oaks, CA: Sage Publications, 2013).

[34]William P. Brown, *The Ethos of the Cosmos: The Genesis of Moral Imagination in the Bible* (Grand Rapids: Eerdmans, 1999).

[35]Harries, *Art and the Beauty of God*, 106.

Modern philosophers often spoke dismissively of the imagination as a faculty of fancy that produces unreal images. Scripture is aware of this pathology, acknowledging the possibility of "vain imaginings"—of Satan appearing as an angel of light. Our present problem, however, is not so much demonic as it is a downsized imagination that can neither grasp the whole nor appreciate the sublime. "Kitsch" is art without seriousness—art that takes pretty, fashionable or cute forms. Alas, the cute is rarely curative. "The failure of kitsch is a moral and spiritual failure as much as an aesthetic one."[36] We suffer today not from too much imagination, but too little.

The imagination is an essential ingredient in wisdom. Gerard Manley Hopkins once wrote that the touchstone of great art was seriousness: "Not gravity but the being in earnest with your subject—reality."[37] Imagination is the ability to grasp the way things fit together—the capacity for beholding wholes. "Imagination is the tool by which we perceive reality concretely."[38] John McIntyre, in a telling phrase, refers to the Holy Spirit as "God's imagination let loose . . . in the world."[39] The same Spirit of truth who ministers the Word also ministers reality by opening our minds and hearts to God.

Art demands what Simone Weil calls "attention": the ability to transcend ourselves in order to see things as they are. In the words of the novelist Henry James, "The effort really to see and really to represent is no idle business in face of the *constant* force that makes for muddlement."[40] According to Martha Nussbaum, perception—"The ability to discern, acutely and responsively, the salient features of one's particular situation"[41]—lies at the core of practical wisdom. Wisdom is the ability to see what is right and fitting in a particular situation given our understanding of the larger whole of which we are a part. To act only according to general rules easily generates into a kind of ethical Philistinism where we fail to appreciate the shape and nuances of our situation. It is to act without seeing what we are doing. The

---

[36]Ibid., p. 60.

[37]Cited in Harries, *Art and the Beauty of God*, 50.

[38]Brown, *The Ethos of the Cosmos*, 20.

[39]John McIntyre, *Faith, Theology and the Imagination* (Edinburgh: Handsel Press, 1987), 64.

[40]Henry James, *The Art of the Novel* (New York: C. Scribner's Sons, 1934), 149; emphasis original.

[41]Martha C. Nussbaum, *Love's Knowledge: Essays on Philosophy and Literature* (Oxford: Oxford University Press, 1990), 37.

wise person, by contrast, is imaginatively attentive, like James's novelist: "Finely aware and richly responsible."[42]

Great art can bring about what Edith Sitwell calls "heightened consciousness": an inner clarification and cleansing that refines our capacity for discernment and inclines us to respond more sensitively to the world and those around us.[43] Similarly, growing up into Christ and speaking the truth in love (Eph 4:15) involves learning to see what is fitting and appropriate—beautiful—in concrete situations. To see the glory of God in the form of Christ is to actively participate in—not simply intellectually apprehend—the drama of redemption. To be wise is to discern and to do what is fitting—what glorifies God—in each and every situation. To be wise is to discern and participate in evangelical goodness, truth and beauty: the way of Jesus Christ. The best ethics is therefore a good—which is to say gospel-centered—aesthetics.

The ends of beauty: the ethos of the eschaton. Christian worship fosters an eschatologically charged ethos—a sense of being-in-the-world, but not of it. Hymns make explicit what experiences of beauty implicitly suggest: namely, that there is a new world emerging out of the shed skin of the old. "Behold, the new has come" (2 Cor 5:17). The ethos of the eschaton—the new order in Christ announced in the gospel—gives rise to practices that do not compute according to the operating systems of this world. The Christian life is about more than survival or success. The *kalos* of Christian beauty includes the pathos of the cross. The cross is beautiful, not because of some numeric ratio that obtains between beam and crossbar, but because it radiates the splendid form of God's self-giving love. "He hung therefore on the cross deformed, but his deformity is our beauty" (Augustine).[44]

Experiences of beauty have eschatological significance insofar as they anticipate the transfiguration of the people of God and the cosmological *shalom*, when all will be well. Presently, however, humans inhabit a fallen world where "passing away" inexorably attends experiences of beauty. Beauty in its truth and fullness is seen only in the resurrection, the breaking in of the eschatological into human history.[45] In the meantime, the Spirit communicates

---

[42]James, *The Art of the Novel*, 149.

[43]Edith Sitwell, *Poetry and Criticism* (New York: H. Holt and Company, 1926), 22.

[44]Cited in Sherry, *Spirit and Beauty*, 74.

[45]See Eberhard Jüngel, "Even the Beautiful Must Die," *Theological Essays II* (Edinburgh: T&T Clark, 1995).

the first fruits of the beautiful end in Christ. "True beauty is the radiance of the Holy Spirit, the holiness and the participation in the life of the world to come."[46]

"Praise Without Ceasing": A Diet of Doxology

Praising God in song is an apt metaphor not only for worship but for the whole Christian life, including the arts. Like worship, great art embodies the pedagogy of eternity to the extent that it lifts our gaze to a real presence that transcends ourselves. Both great art and worship awaken our senses and imaginations to the contours of the created order. Yet, unlike art, worship engrafts us into the drama of redemption, into that Trinitarian design for life in which beauty is a loving consent toward another. Making melody (an intelligible sonorous form) to the Lord is one way to engage in the practice of self-transcending thanksgiving.

Doxological aesthetics. There is a precarious relationship between the arts and worship. Art is not an end in itself. We must not worship art. On the other hand, the aesthetic quality of our worship may well be an index of our appreciation of God's beauty, and of our wisdom. Those who lack aesthetic sensibility are tone-deaf to God's Word and colorblind to God's glory. The fool says in his heart, "There is no beauty," and thus refuses to see the fittingness of the gospel. Things fall apart; wisdom is no more. Where the capacity to see and appreciate beauty is absent, the true and the good are uncompelling.

Beauty is not simply a value-added extra to worship, or to life. On the contrary, we are made for beauty, as we are for truth and goodness. We are created for fellowship with God, the one in whom the the good, the true and the beautiful are ultimately grounded and find their unity. To discern the fittingness of the new order of things "in Christ" requires a robust imagination, nurtured on compelling and intelligible forms. Hymns help to discern and project the intelligible form of the new order in Christ. Because wisdom, too, is a matter of perceiving what is fitting, imaginative worship—the use of songs and stories to cultivate our sense of evangelical and eschatological fittingness—also makes us wise.

---

[46]Leonid Ouspensky, cited in Sherry, *Spirit and Beauty*, 142.

It is precisely through learning to worship that our aesthetic sensibilities themselves can be galvanized and restored. Still, the church is not a concert hall, nor are worshipers concertgoers whose primary focus is disinterested aesthetic experience. Those who worship in spirit and in truth must do more than appreciate music on a purely aesthetic level. We must *praise God*, in singing and in listening. Listening, in the words of the composer Roger Sessions, implies "a real participation, a real response, a real sharing in the work."[47] To experience beauty is to be drawn beyond ourselves into an experience of something greater than ourselves. Encountering a beautiful form provokes a moral response, even a desire to lead a changed life. Apart from such experiences, our worship and praise will be about us—"instances of natural egocentrism and even idolatrous self-securing"[48]—rather than God.

Worship, like experiences of beauty, solicits our attention and seeks to shape our character into the image of the one to whom we are attending in our prayers and praise: the triune benevolence. The shape of primary beauty is love. It follows that praise edifies the church insofar as it enables us to become like what we adore. The shape of Christian freedom is the shape of love. This essay is thus less about using the arts to enhance worship than it is about indwelling worship practices in order to enhance the arts. Specifically, participating in worship practices prepares the people of God to proclaim the good news of redemption in Christ in myriad forms of articulate action, including the creative activity of the arts.

Being-toward-resurrection: living hymns. Praising God in song shapes our sense of space and time, the conditions for all experience. Praising God in song helps us attend to the wonder and the wideness of the love of God, enabling us to perceive it, celebrate it, rehearse it and take comfort in it. Praising God in song creates a specific "mood," a sense of being-in-the-world-before-God. Specifically, praising the God who raised Jesus from the dead forms a sense of *being-toward-resurrection*. Doxology turns out to be much more than a moment in a worship service. It is the Christian's everyday mode of being-in-time. Christians glorify God in all that they do not simply as living letters (2 Cor 3:3), but as living hymns.

---

[47] Cited in Nicholas Wolterstorff, *Art in Action: Toward a Christian Aesthetic* (Grand Rapids: Eerdmans, 1980), 25.

[48] Farley, *Faith and Beauty*, 106.

Hymns that celebrate. A doxological aesthetics forms Christian character by helping us attend to the depths of the riches of the love of God. Hymns celebrate the resurrection and so make those who sing them celebrants. Hymns celebrate not the sparkle of Strauss's Vienna, but the joy of Jesus' Jerusalem—a joy that has been tested and refined by fire. Praise choruses with words and harmonies that are too trite trivialize their subject matter and minimize the cost of discipleship.

Genuine experiences of beauty do not simply entertain but transform. Even secular psychologists distinguish the pleasant from real joy. As Farley says, "Joy arises only when there is a transcending of egocentric pleasure into the life of the other."[49] Joy is the perception of, and the participation in, a larger fittingness that satisfies our longing for ultimate meaning. Joy is not a passing feeling, but an enduring mood or orientation to the whole of life. Christian joy is *being-toward-resurrection.*

Hymns that rehearse. One does not have to be a Christian to enjoy great music. But it is one thing to be a spectator and quite another to be a participant. The saints—living hymns—become part of the music, fitting into the created and redeemed order as witnesses to the new life made manifest in Jesus Christ. To worship well is to live well, and vice versa. Aesthetics and ethics alike cultivate sensibilities that enable us to make judgments concerning fittingness.

To praise God in all that we do is to join in the company of the redeemed who have been performing parables of the kingdom of God for centuries. To worship in spirit and truth is to bear witness to the evangelical and eschatological nature of reality, giving holy substance to what would otherwise be hollow shades. As living hymns, Christians create forms of life that are both meaningful and true because they participate in the drama of redemption. Worship is nothing less than the appropriate response to the reality of what God has done, is doing and will do in Jesus Christ.

Hymns that console. Music consoles. Yet the unanswered question posed by Brahms's music (and not only his) is whether music's power to console is rooted in reality or only in wishful thinking. Consolation that is not grounded in the way things are is only an effect of rhetoric. Indeed, whether

---

[49]Ibid., 106.

the power of music to console is grounded in rhetoric or in reality is perhaps the great question of all art. The gospel provides the answer: Immanuel, "God with us." The birth of Christ is the eucatastrophe of human history. Music has become fact. Yet, like all truth, it needs to be embodied in beautiful lives in order to be compelling. True religion—and this probably includes worship and ethics too—is "to visit orphans and widows in their affliction" (Jas 1:27). Christians must be living hymns of consolation.

Beauty consoles, not because it promises material blessings but because it enables us to see the larger whole of which our histories are a part. Being-toward-resurrection means living toward the joy of Easter without forgetting the sufferings of Good Friday. Christians have a responsibility to live lives of solemn joy, acknowledging both present pain and future hope. To be a living hymn means to live and love in ways that show forth joy, faith and hope: in other words, being-toward-resurrection.

CONCLUSION: LIVING BEAUTIFULLY

Wittgenstein was *almost* right. The beautiful conveys an ethos of eternity that cultivates the wisdom for living well in time, but only insofar as it anticipates the eschatological order inaugurated in Jesus Christ. Hymns are harbingers of the new creation, and "the beauty of holiness" is its dawn. Christian existence is not merely pretty. The beauty of holiness is not without pathos. Yet the wisdom implied in beauty sees that even suffering has a place, or rather a time, within the broader drama of redemption. The eschatological ethos conveyed in hymns and Christian worship, precisely by helping us see the radiance of God's eternal glory, equips us for our life in time. Praising God in song informs and energizes the whole of Christian life, ministering to the whole person—heart, mind and imagination.

To think aesthetics and ethics together leads us to consider art as an instance of responsible action, but also action as a work of art. Indeed, we might say that ethics is all about "designs for living," though such a notion can be understood in two very different ways, which we can abbreviate by asking: Nietzsche or Kierkegaard?

Friedrich Nietzsche preached (and to some extent personified) what we might call the Gospel of Art.[50] He believed that art reveals values beyond the

---

[50]See the essays in Daniel Carne, ed., *Nietzsche on Art and Life* (Oxford: Oxford University Press, 2014).

reach of reason and morality. Art is holy because it is the product of human creativity. Nietzsche's highest calling was to become the creator of his own life. He sought to "aestheticize" life, striving to become like God, not in the sense of imitating divine creativity but of challenging it. To make one's own life a work of art is a Promethean task that would only appear possible to someone like Nietzsche, who held a Romantic view of the imagination as the capacity for the infinite. But why believe in human creativity at all? Nietzsche was ultimately unable to avoid the conclusion that art is merely a beautiful lie humans tell themselves in order to make life bearable. Ironically, the products of the creative imagination, like truth claims and moral values, are for Nietzsche only masks for the will-to-power.

Søren Kierkegaard seems an exceedingly odd "or" to set against Nietzsche's "either." Didn't Kierkegaard distinguish the "aesthetic" from the "ethical" stage of existence? And didn't he distance both from the stages of religion and Christian faith? Indeed, both Balthasar and Farley fault Kierkegaard for bifurcating beauty and faith. While it is true that Kierkegaard held the aesthetic stage to be inimical to Christian faith, we have to understand what he meant by aesthetics. By aesthetics, Kierkegaard meant a way of life that is given over to the senses and to sensual pleasure.[51] Kierkegaard's focus on inwardness makes room for the notion of inner beauty, the beauty of holiness—not the self-made beauty like that of the creative genius, but the Spirit-made beauty of the faithful disciple.

Kierkegaard believed that our lives must conform to our message; our politics must follow our passion. The Christian's passion must be the Passion of Jesus. Accordingly, the Christian life acquires a beautiful shape when it takes on the shape of the cross. Inner beauty expresses itself outwardly through works of cruciform love, works of self-emptying humility and self-giving action (and passion).

According to Johann Sebastian Bach, the highest activity open to human beings is praise, and the only object worthy of praise is the triune God. Bach wrote all of his music, sacred and secular, for the glory of God alone. He thus exemplifies not Nietzsche's passion for the holiness of beauty but rather Kierkegaard's passion for the beauty of holiness. "The motif of Enlightenment

---

[51]See Sylvia Walsh, *Living Poetically: Kierkegaard's Existential Aesthetics* (University Park: Pennsylvania State University Press, 1994).

theology was the generally religious, the motif of Bach's theology was the specifically Christian."[52] The glory of the cross of Christ was for Bach the criterion of true beauty.

William Morris, the founder of the Arts and Crafts Movement, engaged in the secular equivalent of a "holy war" against the ugliness of nineteenth-century industrial culture and against the dehumanizing utilitarianism of factory labor. Along with other knights of beauty, Morris formed his own company of designers and decorators that sought to recapture the dignity, quality and sense of vocation that characterized the work of medieval craftsmen. Over the years, Morris and his partners designed furniture, wallpaper, tapestry, stained glass, books, tiles, homes and gardens, transforming the stuff of everyday life into myriad beautiful forms. If Morris, an agnostic, could transform the humdrum world about him, how much more should the Christian seek to transfigure the ordinary by being an icon of Christ—not by designing beautiful tapestries, but by creating a beautiful tapestry of life.

In a sermon on 1 John 4, Augustine remarks that it is by loving that we are made beautiful.[53] We have been given the dignity of glorification, a fitting dignity for creatures who have received the gift of freedom. A passage from the Gospels brilliantly illustrates the beautifying nature of right action. An anonymous woman approached Jesus in a house in Bethany and poured expensive ointment over his head while he sat at the table. Jesus' rebuke to his disciples' criticism of her act is swift and unequivocal: "She has done a beautiful thing to me" (Mt 26:10; Mk 14:6). Beauty is something to be done, a generous self-giving love for the other that anticipates the eschatological "and all things shall be well." Perhaps it is for this reason that "wherever this gospel is proclaimed in the whole world, what she has done will also be told in memory of her" (Mt 26:13).

The chief end of life is to glorify God and enjoy him forever, and the chief means for doing so is to achieve a beautiful body. This is the task of the Holy Spirit, who creates and perfects the church, the body of Christ. Primary beauty is best seen in persons who love as God loves. Praising God in song

---

[52]Jaroslav Pelikan, *Fools for Christ: Essays on the True, the Good and the Beautiful* (Philadelphia: Muhlenberg Press, 1955), 151.

[53]From *Homilies on the First Epistle of John*, Homily 9 (on 1 Jn 4:17-21).

is a vital part of the curriculum of worship, part of the pedagogy of the church as that beauty school that seeks to produce forms of individual and communal holiness. As the etymology of the term reminds us, persons are sounding boards (*per* + *sonare*, to sound through). The Christian life is itself a sonorous form in motion, a distinctive shape of being-in-time oriented to the risen Christ. Art and ethics thus converge in persons through whom the praise of God is shown and sounded in lives that display cruciform forms of holy wisdom. The church's highest calling is thus to be a beautiful body, a community of persons in and through whom the love of God—the way, the truth and the life of Christ—sounds through, a glorious sonorous form in active, loving, bodily motion.

six

MOSES' *MAGNIFICAT*

A Song for the Semester—and the Ages

A Sermon on Exodus 15:1-18

In light of our focus on the church as a holy nation, it is appropriate that our tour of Gallery One at a theological exhibition concludes with a portrait of the beginning of God's plan to form Israel into a set-apart people. This chapter was originally a sermon I preached in September 2014. It was the first message in a wonderful chapel series at Trinity Evangelical Divinity School on the theme "A Way in the Wilderness." I'm not sure whether or not the organizers intended to suggest that an academic semester is like a wilderness. At least that's not the message the Admissions Office leads with! Nevertheless I was glad to have this powerful metaphor to work with, since to take a merely academic approach to the study of the Bible and theology is to wander in the wilderness, with our eyes closed to the streams of living water that I discussed in chapter four. Moreover, I was glad to preach on such a central passage for understanding God's purpose not only for Israel, but also for the church. The church needs to learn what Israel needed to learn: how to be a set-apart people, and how to worship God rightly. Finally, I was intrigued to have been assigned a portion of Scripture in the form of (sung) poetry, not least because I knew it was the perfect companion piece to the previous chapter.

Introduction: The "Song of the Sea"

A systematic theologian who preaches on the Old Testament is a tightrope walker who must balance exegesis and history on one hand with a respect for canon and tradition on the other. It's a high wire act, and when the text is poetry it's like doing it on a unicycle, with a blindfold—which must be why the members of the Old Testament department are on the edge of their seats, gulping down popcorn. In all seriousness, I'm grateful for the opportunity to preach on a passage filled not only with theology, but also with music and drama. It's the story of my life—indeed, of all our lives, as I trust we shall see.

Singing—praising God by making melody—is a very theological activity. We would do well to ponder why this is so, especially at the beginning of an academic semester, where the privileged form of discourse is the lecture. Our passage, Exodus 15:1-18, is commonly known as "The Song of the Sea." It is the first hymn in the Eastern Orthodox canon, where it is known as "The Song of Moses" (not to be confused with Moses' other song, in Deut 32).

Why do I say that singing is a theological activity? Because, first, it involves praising God with the whole person: body (vocal cords and lungs), mind and spirit. I'm not sneaking in trichotomy through the back door—I'm only echoing Paul's distinction in 1 Corinthians 14:15: "I will sing praise with my spirit, but I will sing with my mind also." We may need to reverse Paul's thought for our context: "I will sing with my mind, but I will sing praise with my spirit also."

"I will sing with my mind." Augustine uses the example of a song to explain the difference between past, present and future in his famous analysis of time in his *Confessions*.[1] When we sing, he says, our souls are stretched: the present is the soul aware of the note it is now singing, the future is the soul in its expectation of the notes to come and the past is the soul's memory of what has already been sung. As we shall see, "The Song of the Sea" stretches Israel's mind in these three temporal directions as well.

"I will sing praise with my spirit." Singing praise *with my spirit* means that my religious affections are also involved. "Religious affection" is Jonathan Edwards's term for an emotion or disposition that is the fruit of the Spirit, the chief affection being love. To sing praise with the spirit is to do more than state propositions. It is to love and delight in the song's content. For Edwards, that heartfelt delight is evidence of true faith, and thus true religion. Which

---

[1]Augustine, *Confessions* 11.31.41.

raises the question: Can we truly know God *without* singing his praise? Is not theology without doxology a contradiction in terms?

What does Moses' "Song of the Sea" have to say to us today? Quite a bit, as it turns out. To be sure, we're on the verge not of the Promised Land but of an academic semester. Nevertheless, like Israel, we have a journey before us, one that may from time to time make us feel as if we too are wandering in the wilderness. God has brought us to this place, yes, but soon we will be grumbling to faculty about homework and murmuring against administrators about tuition, and some may rise up against their admission counselors and cry, "You have brought us out into this wilderness to kill us with grades and bills!" Will we still have a song of praise in our hearts come December?

BEHIND THE SONG: EVENT AND CONTEXT

Before examining the Song itself it may help to put it in its historical and canonical context.

The events (historical prelude). Exodus chapters 1–14 describe the way that God brought Israel out of Egypt. God tells Moses in Exodus 3 that he had heard his people's cry and that he will deliver them from their oppressor to a land flowing with milk and honey. It was not liberation for liberation's sake, by the way, but liberation for the sake of worship. Moses repeatedly relays God's Word to Pharaoh: "Let my people go, *so that they may worship me*" (Ex 8:1; cf. 4:23; 5:1; 7:16; 8:1, 20; 9:1, 13). Pharaoh can't let go, suffers the ten plagues, appears to relent, but at the last moment has another change of heart and pursues Israel with his army of chariots. When the people of Israel see the force amassed against them, they cry out to Moses, "It would have been better for us to serve the Egyptians than to die in the wilderness" (Ex 14:12), to which Moses replies, "The LORD will fight for you, and you have only to be silent" (Ex 14:14).

What happens next is enough, in the words of biblical commentator Terence Fretheim, "to make a movie mogul's mouth water."[2] And so it has! Ridley Scott's film *Exodus: Gods and Kings* is coming to a theater near you this fall, featuring the biggest wall of water seen on the big screen since *Step into Liquid*, the 2003 documentary about surfers. Fretheim thinks Exodus

---

[2]Terence E. Fretheim, *Exodus (Interpretation)* (Louisville, KY: John Knox, 1991), 148.

gives us only an impressionistic picture and is therefore unwilling to commit himself to the historicity of the event, acknowledging only that "tidal movements in the delta region might be a factor."[3]

The parting of the Red Sea, together with the drowning of the Egyptian army, is the most spectacular saving event in the Bible until Jesus' birth. It's so important that Moses tells it twice: first in prose (in chapter 14) and then in poetry (the Song of chapter 15). Whichever way you look at it, in narrative or verse, Israel's deliverance at the sea is the great gospel story of the Old Testament: the Lord God saves.

The text (canonical interlude). The first fourteen chapters of Exodus recount the process by which God called Israel out of Egypt in order to worship him in the desert. Exodus 15 marks the beginning of a major new section: Israel's journey to Sinai, where Yahweh gives the Ten Commandments and the rest of the law to help prepare the people to live rightly in his presence, a presence eventually located in the tabernacle. The final chapters of Exodus depict Israel's covenant breaking, God's covenant renewal, the completion of the Tabernacle and, climactically, the cloud of God's presence settling on the Tabernacle and filling it with the glory of the Lord. Exodus is ultimately about God polishing his treasured possession—his covenant people—so that they can practice the presence of God.[4] But before Israel gets there, the people must make a long journey through the wilderness.

"The Song of the Sea" therefore constitutes an important hinge text that takes us out of Egypt, through the Red Sea, into the wilderness and eventually to the foot of Mount Sinai. Israel has been delivered *from* Egypt but not quite yet delivered *to* the place God has promised them. As we'll see, the Song helps Israel to look both back and forward, to what has just happened and what is about to happen, as well as to what is happening in Israel's present.

THE SONG: FORM AND CONTENT

We turn now to the Song itself, looking first at verses 1-12 and then focusing on verses 13-18.

"The Lord is my song" (vv. 1-12). *"I will sing to the* LORD, *for he has triumphed gloriously" (Ex 15:1).* The prose account of chapter 14 ends by saying:

---

[3]Ibid., 158.
[4]See esp. J. Durham, *Exodus*, Word Biblical Commentary (Waco, TX: Word, 1987), xxi-xxiii.

"Israel saw the great power that the LORD used against the Egyptians, so the people feared the LORD, and they believed in the LORD" (Ex 14:31). The Song is a fitting response to God's mighty act. The Song is not really about the sea, or Moses, or victory over Egypt or even Israel's gratitude for deliverance. It is about God and what God has done. The Song is thoroughly theocentric rather than anthropocentric (composers of praise choruses, take note). The triumph is the Lord's, and what Yahweh has done sets him apart from the other supposed deities. "Who is like you, O LORD, among the gods?" (Ex 15:11).

"At the blast of your nostrils the waters piled up" (Ex 15:8). The second thing to notice in this first section is that the terms for both "deep" and "the waters" (Ex 15:5, 8) are also found in Genesis 1:2. God divides the waters of the Red Sea in the same way he divided the waters at creation, in both cases producing dry land (Gen 1:9; Ex 14:29). This is a subtle yet unmistakable way of identifying the Creator of all things with the Redeemer of Israel. Interestingly, the Hebrew term for "deep waters" (*təhōmōt*) sounds like Tiamat, the name of the Babylonian goddess of chaos. Listen to Ezekiel's allusion: "Thus says the Lord God: 'Behold, I am against you, Pharaoh king of Egypt, the great dragon that lies in the midst of his streams, that says "My Nile is my own; I made it for myself.""" (Ezek 29:3). Like Satan, Pharaoh's downfall was his pride. Pharaoh says "I will" six times in Exodus 15:9 alone, and then goes on to describe his plans to defeat Israel. There is deep irony here. God conquers Pharaoh's armies with the forces of chaos that God had already conquered (as it were) at creation.[5] This must have seemed the sweetest of victories in the eyes of Israel: their God, the Lord God, displayed his absolute sovereignty not only over Pharaoh but also over all the gods and symbols of chaos in the ancient Near East. There is cosmic significance in the waters of the Red Sea.

"You have led . . ." (vv. 13-18). The second section of the Song relates the Lord's victory at sea to his plans for Israel.

"The people . . . whom you have purchased" (v. 16). It is through the sea that God redeems, and in some sense creates, Israel as his treasured possession, a set apart people. Out of the chaos of the waters, God creates a holy nation.

---

[5]So Peter Enns: "The enemy God slays at the sea is Egypt, an act that clearly reflects the slaying of the primordial enemy sea" (*Exodus*, NIV Application Commentary [Grand Rapids: Zondervan, 2000], 298).

There are hints of a parallel between Moses' song and Mary's "Magnificat" in Luke 1:46-55. Like Moses, Mary sings a song of praise to the Lord who has shown mercy and done a great thing: "He has shown strength with his arm" (Lk 1:51) and "He has helped his servant Israel" (Lk 1:54). The verb used in Exodus 15:16, *qānâ*, can mean "purchased," "created" or even "begat." Moses' song celebrates God bringing forth a people through the watery chaos; Mary's song celebrates God's bringing forth a person through the waters of childbirth. Both the Exodus and the incarnation are miracles of salvation. Luke tells us later in his Gospel that the whole point of Jesus' coming to earth was to accomplish a "departure" (the Greek term in Luke 9:31 is *exodos*) from the earth: at Jerusalem, on a cross.

"You will bring them in and plant them on your mountain" (v. 13). Mary and Moses sing to the same God, the God of miracle-working strength and promise-keeping steadfast love. Indeed, God's steadfast love is so certain that verses 13-16 speak of the conquest of the Promised Land as if it had already happened. Some Bible translations put the verbs in these verses in the future tense, others in the past. This indecision reflects the verbs' "prophetic perfect" form, a way of referring to future events in the past tense: "*Now* are the chiefs of Edom dismayed . . . all the inhabitants of Canaan have melted away" (Ex 15:15).[6] In actual fact Israel is not there yet, but these words affirm that the victory is as good as theirs; such is the strength and faithfulness of the Lord.

Verse 17 states the purpose of God's redemption: "You will bring them in and plant them on your own mountain, the place . . . which you have made for your abode, the sanctuary . . . which your hands have established." Again, some translations employ the future and some the past, but the real focus is not when but *where*. Where is God leading Israel? Mountain, place or sanctuary? There are three main interpretive possibilities: Mount Sinai, the Promised Land of Canaan and the Jerusalem temple. We need not feel obliged to choose one: all three are true. God meets Israel spectacularly at Mount Sinai, then in Canaan via the tabernacle and eventually in his more permanent dwelling in the Jerusalem temple on Mount Zion: "God is bringing his people out of Egypt in order that he might be present with

---

[6]Douglas K. Stuart, *Exodus: An Exegetical and Theological Exposition of Holy Scripture*, New American Commentary (Nashville, TN: B&H Publishing, 2006), 357.

them, and that presence will be manifest in 'sacred space' that takes three forms."[7] That the final form is a temple is only fitting. As Greg Beale and others have shown, Yahweh reveals himself to be the great king by building temples that commemorate his victories over evil: the Garden of Eden marks his dividing the waters of chaos, and the temple in Jerusalem puts the exclamation point on his dividing the waters of the Red Sea.[8] God is leading Israel into the wilderness to his holy abode. Life with God is the ultimate covenant blessing.

The song concludes with verse 18: "The Lord will reign forever and ever." It's a fitting climax indeed, since the exodus is both a historical redemption for Israel and a cosmic victory for God—a means by which God further extends his reign. The exodus is conclusive proof of the infinite qualitative distinction between the one Creator God and the many creaturely powers. "Who is like you, O LORD?" The marvel is that it is precisely this God, Maker of heaven and earth, who enters into the most intimate of personal relationships with Israel: a marriage covenant. Moses' "Song of the Sea" celebrates the force and faithfulness of the Lord, not with "They lived happily ever after," but rather with "The Lord will reign forever and ever."

IN FRONT OF THE SONG: "ARE WE THERE YET?"

How can we, on the shores of Lake Michigan, sing with Moses "The Song of the Sea"? What is God saying to us today in Exodus 15 to encourage us in our own way through the wilderness? Are we there yet?

"Written for our instruction" (1 Cor 10:11). We need not strain our hermeneutical muscles reaching for abstract principles from Moses' Song to apply to our situation. These things that happened to Israel happened, says Paul, as an example, but "they were written down for our instruction, on whom the end of the ages has come" (1 Cor 10:11). Israel's history teaches us about the identity of God and his purpose for his people, and they are *us*. Christians too are a people delivered from bondage, called together to be a holy nation (1 Pet 2:9). Of all the historical books of the Bible, the forty chapters of Exodus "chronicle the formation of the core identity of the

---

[7]Enns, *Exodus*, 300.
[8]G. K. Beale, *The Temple and the Church's Mission: A Biblical Theology of the Dwelling Place of God* (Downers Grove, IL: IVP Academic, 2004).

people of God."[9] Our task therefore is not to apply abstract principles but to participate concretely in the same drama of redemption as Israel. In an important sense, Israel is playing our scene, and we are replaying Israel's.

How, then, does Moses' "Magnificat" instruct Christians to live as God's people? As the Lord's Prayer teaches us how to pray, the Song of Moses teaches us how to sing. The Song teaches us to walk—even in the wilderness—as the Lord's delivered people.[10] This is especially relevant to us, a community invested in theological education, at the beginning of an academic semester.

"Beyond the desert of criticism." The academic year is divided into two sixteen-week semesters. Our word *semester* comes from the Latin *semestris*: *sex* for "six" and *mensis* for "month," or half a year. Israel wandered in the wilderness for eighty semesters! Likening the beginning of an academic year to Israel's wilderness wanderings is probably not the most upbeat note on which to start the semester—or is it?

Israel's wilderness wandering began as soon as Moses' Song ended. Just three days after being saved from the Red Sea, they found themselves in the wilderness of Shur with no potable water. God told Moses how to sweeten the bitter water of Marah (Ex 15:22-25). Later, in the wilderness of Sin, they are again without water. So how exactly are we like Israel? After all, we live in Lake County. Lack of water is not the problem.

Here's the connection. God has brought us here, to TEDS, for a purpose, just as he brought Israel to the threshold of the Promised Land. We're being sent into the wilderness for the same purpose God sent Israel: to learn to become a people who can worship rightly, in spirit and in truth. But we will be tested: literally (think final exams!) and spiritually. I am more concerned about the latter kind of testing, which is ultimately a matter of trusting God for our salvation.

Lack of water is not our problem, but our journey this semester will nevertheless take us through a kind of desert. I'm thinking of Paul Ricoeur's description of the loss of meaning and truth in an age dominated by the hermeneutics of suspicion and an epistemology of doubt. Ricoeur says,

---

[9]James J. Bruckner, *Exodus* (Grand Rapids: Baker, 2008), 7.
[10]This coincides with what Bruckner says about the purpose of Exodus as a whole: "Exodus challenges us to learn to live as the Lord's delivered people" (*Exodus*, xiii).

"Beyond the desert of criticism, we wish to be called again."[11] The desert of criticism refers to ways of studying texts that create critical distance: the suspension of belief, a refusal to trust appearances or authority, a refusal to respond personally to what has been said. Criticism keeps textual demands at arm's length. Criticism promises knowledge (deliverance) but ultimately leaves us, like Moses, able only to glimpse, but not reach, the Promised Land.

The critic is adept at talking about texts (of the making of theories there is no end), always reading but never coming (at least through criticism) to a personal knowledge of the truth (cf. 2 Tim 3:7). Beyond the desert of criticism—the sum total of our own paltry efforts to understand Scripture and know God after the flesh—we would be called again, called by the living and active word that circumcises the heart and pierces to bone and marrow. Faith comes by *hearing* the Word, not by its criticism.

The academic semester can be a critical desert that starves our faith, and we will die in the desert if we do only criticism, examining the water that flows from the rock but never trusting it enough to drink it. I'm speaking to myself first, but you may want to listen in. Paul identifies the rock from which Israel drank in the desert as Christ (1 Cor 10:4). The water of life flows from Christ, but we receive no benefit if it remains outside us, held at a critical distance. It is one thing to know how to use the text critical apparatus, to know the background to Galatians, or the causes of the Reformation, or to know how various theologians use the Bible. It is quite another thing to trust Christ as one's Lord and Savior. It is not that criticism cannot be helpful; only that, by itself, it cannot give life or satisfy thirst. Academic excellence alone will not get us to the Promised Land, to life "in Christ."

CONCLUSION: "A SONG FOR THE AGES"

Exodus 15 is a poetic description of the Exodus event. Think of it as Moses' "Magnificat," which celebrates, like Mary's, God's merciful yet mighty acts in history. Miriam and the women of Israel repeat the song in verse 21, and we can surmise that it became instantly popular, taking over the number one spot in Israel's top ten singles chart and remaining there not just for weeks, but for the ages. Indeed, Revelation 15:3 depicts the saints in heaven singing Moses' Song. What better way to teach Israelite teenagers about their history,

---

[11]Paul Ricoeur, *The Symbolism of Evil* (Boston: Beacon Press, 1967), 349.

and the identity of God, than by singing "The Song of the Sea" as they wandered through the desert?[12]

Why include a song when the substance of the Exodus event had already been narrated in the previous chapter? This is an excellent question. The answer, I submit, is that the song is there to remind us not simply to study the Scriptures or merely confess our theology, but delight in God's Word and live out sound doctrine with every fiber of our being. The truth of the gospel must both stick in our minds and sing in our souls. Orthodoxy without doxology will not get us through the wilderness.

And that was Israel's problem. Their singing turned to whining; they exchanged praising for complaining. The same people who had witnessed God's faithfulness failed to go on living as God's faithful people. This is precisely the challenge of Exodus to us: to be alert and responsive to God's presence and activity even when it is not on conspicuous display, dividing the waters.[13] God is present with us on the journey, but we must be awake and alert in order to delight in his presence. It is one thing to write a term paper on the faithfulness of God, another to sing "Great Is Thy Faithfulness," and still another to live faithfully each day, delighting in the truth of God's faithfulness. As we begin this semester let us resolve, individually and corporately, not to keep our academic work separate from our discipleship, our faith from learning, as though we were critics only. Let us rather resolve both to study and sing together the glorious reality of our Savior God.[14]

A song, says Augustine, is "a thing of joy; more profoundly, it is a thing of love. Anyone, therefore, who has learned to love the new life has learned to sing a new song, and the new song reminds us of our new life." He then adds something we would do well to remember at the start of a semester—or really at any time: "But make sure that your life does not contradict your words. Sing with your voices, your hearts, your lips and your lives. . . . If you desire to praise him, then live what you express. Live good lives, and you yourselves will be his praise."[15]

Let us therefore sing to the Lord an old song, a new song—a song for the ages.

---

[12]Fretheim suggests that the women's repetition of the song is part of a more complex liturgical ritual "in which *the sea crossing is dramatically reactualized*" (*Exodus*, 162, his emphasis).

[13]"Exodus challenges us to learn to live as the Lord's delivered people" (Bruckner, *Exodus*, xiii).

[14]"Worshiping the Lord was Israel's transition to a new existence" (Bruckner, *Exodus*, 137).

[15]Augustine, *Sermon* 34:1-3 (on "Sing to the Lord a new song"); CCL 41, 424-26.

GALLERY TWO

PICTURES OF THE
CHURCH'S WITNESS

seven

THE DRAMA OF THE CHRIST

*The Gospel as Thing Done
and Word Made*

The genesis for this essay was an invitation to present a paper at an Evangelism Roundtable in April 2008, sponsored by the Billy Graham Center and the Marion E. Wade Center at Wheaton College. These two centers, devoted to the work of evangelism and the work of C. S. Lewis respectively, pooled their resources to put together a Roundtable discussion on the theme "Imagination and the Gospel: Harnessing the Imagination to Engage Contemporary Culture and Communicate the Life-Changing Gospel." I am grateful to Rick Richardson, Roundtable director, for an invitation so well suited to my interests in the gospel, the imagination and the work of C. S. Lewis. This essay allowed me to relate my work on the dramatic nature of doctrine to the pressing problem of communicating the gospel for the sake of making disciples in a world in which theoretical theology, though propositionally true, often fails to compel. Here I set forth my case for theatrical theology by arguing that the way we do our theology ought to correspond to its subject matter, which is the drama of the Christ: the announcement, embodied by the church, that Jesus Christ is Lord, and that those who respond to him in faith will be transferred into his kingdom of light and life. Here, too, I argue that the imagination is not simply a matter of visual images, but also of verbal action and bodily motions—in a word, drama. Drama is the fertile ground on which the gospel, theology, imagination and the church converge. Here I focus on the nature of the gospel itself; in the next chapter I examine the nature of the disciples' participation.

George Lindbeck, formerly professor of theology at Yale University, made a statement about our inability to read the Bible with imagination that is as striking today as when he wrote it in 1986: "This loss of intratextuality [the ability to use the biblical narrative as a framework for understanding our world] is perhaps a more serious part of the global crisis than are the social, economic, and political problems to which we more commonly advert."[1] Lindbeck is echoing a concern that Hans Frei drove home in his book *The Eclipse of Biblical Narrative*, about the "great reversal" in hermeneutics that took place in the eighteenth century.[2] No doubt many readers find Lindbeck's comparison overblown. Surely it is sheer hermeneutical hysteria to compare the loss of intratextuality to global crises like war, racism and poverty, not to mention global warming? To write off Lindbeck's concern is to underestimate the power of story to interpret and shape individual and corporate experience.

Once upon a time, Christians lived within the imaginative and linguistic world of the Bible. That is, they accepted the biblical narrative as the true story of the world and thus used Scripture to interpret their experience. Today, however, the interpretive polarities have been reversed. Modern men and women accept the story told by the various sciences, and this becomes the template through which we now interpret the Bible. Instead of taking the biblical stories as the story of reality, post-Enlightenment thinkers typically try to fit the biblical stories into the "real world" that is discovered independently of the biblical text. Whereas patristic, medieval and Reformation Christians fit their world into the world of the Bible, moderns consider the Bible's stories true only if they can be fit into our critically revised conception of reality. This is a stupendous development, comparable with Kant's Copernican Revolution. This great reversal in hermeneutics is nothing less than a revolution in the realm of the imagination, a conversion of its governing framework from supernaturalism and the Christ of faith to naturalism and the Jesus of history. Many of the stories that hold present-day imaginations captive are variations on a Darwinian (that is, naturalistic and evolutionary) theme. Christian thinking—theology, faith seeking under-

---

[1]George Lindbeck, "Barth and Textuality," *Theology Today* 43 (1986): 372.
[2]Hans Frei, *The Eclipse of Biblical Narrative: A Study in Eighteenth and Nineteenth Century Hermeneutics* (New Haven, CT: Yale University Press, 1974).

standing—goes wrong whenever it relies on "extratextual" control stories (metanarratives taken from elsewhere than the Bible) in its search for understanding, instead of on the biblical narrative.

THE GOSPEL ACCORDING TO RODDENBERRY: WORLDS THAT COLONIZE THE IMAGINATION

The great hermeneutical reversal took place before the advent of film, that powerful new means to re-enchant the imagination. Mel Gibson's 2004 film *The Passion of the Christ* was a cinematic phenomenon, which saw planet Hollywood align with the church to produce a cultural supernova (and the highest grossing non-English language film ever). The only question is whether it produced more heat than light.

Films provide instant worldviews—literal views of a world. At its best, cinema offers us a powerful new means of "faith showing understanding," a medium for telling stories that, in combining pictures, words and bodies in motion, give a sense of what the world is like and why we are here. Some films present nihilistic views of life; others, like Gibson's, tell the story of Jesus, and still others pander other gospels. An example of the latter category is the 2006 film *Pursuit of Happyness*, an uplifting rags-to-riches tale depicting success as a combination of opportunity, hard work and perseverance, which winsomely proclaims the gospel of the American Dream.

Anyone in the market for a metaphor to live by has plenty of choice these days. Each week the local cineplex offers numerous *movies* for to live by. The stories now in popular release in our electronic society may not take the form of three-point sermons, but they still preach, on screens large and small. Television commercials insert viewers into narratives too, whose message pertains to products and programs that will enhance our lives. Their goal is to capture our imaginations and thereby to form us into capitalist-consumers who are willing to literally buy into their vision of the good. Of course, what they hold out as good for *us* is really good—that is, lucrative—for *them*: manufacturers, stockholders, retailers and so on. This too is evangelism.

For several years now I have been showing my Cultural Hermeneutics class a Frontline PBS video called *The Persuaders*. The persuaders in question are marketing gurus who know how to tell a story through words and images so that they elicit the desired response (a purchase). Evangelists are persuaders too. In the words of the Fourth Gospel, "these [stories] are written so that you may believe that Jesus is the Christ" (Jn 20:31). Today's persuaders know that culture is a means of indoctrination (and, I would add, spiritual formation) and that success in marketing is less a matter of giving someone a convincing argument than it is of capturing the imagination with a compelling image or story. The persuaders are after hearts, not minds. They want to reach us at the very root of our desires. Thanks to ubiquitous advertising, we are now bombarded with mininarratives that say we can have the world and ourselves (or at least our burger) just the way we want it. Health and wealth are only a phone call (or prescription) away. Coca-Cola, for instance, has done a particularly good job of associating their product with world peace, and Christmas.

Another instructive film I routinely show my Cultural Hermeneutics class is *Trekkies*, a 1997 documentary about fans of the various *Star Trek* shows. The film contains amazing testimonies of enthusiasts who collect Trek paraphernalia, attend conventions, learn Klingon and otherwise express their devotion to the sci-fi myth. In their fanaticism, some believers inhabit the story too literally, like the man who asked the actor who played Dr. McCoy: "How does it feel to be beamed up?" Most Trekkies, however, are ordinary folk, but the level of their commitment to the primacy of the *Star Trek* narrative is striking. There are Trekkie clubs all over the world. I remember *Star Trek: The Exhibition* coming to Scotland in 1995, when I was teaching at the University of Edinburgh. The exhibit attracted 190,000 visitors in Edinburgh alone. Some aficionados dressed up like Trek characters—a visible sign of their desire to live as Trekkies, in the world but not of it!

What is behind such devotion? It begins with a comprehensive vision: the world of the Trek-text. In the future projected by the *Star Trek* narrative, science will solve our problems and there will be no need for money. Everyone will be treated equally regardless of gender, race or class. Many of the fans interviewed in the documentary made a special point of mentioning how they were attracted to the inclusiveness of the *Star Trek* narrative. Gene Roddenberry, the author-producer of the original series, was a humanist who believed that peace and enlightenment lie only four hundred years in the future. Roddenberry was an evangelist, colonizing the social imaginary one episode at a time. Trekkies today are continuing his aborted mission. As one subject of the documentary put it: "We're always recruiting. Wherever we are, whatever we're doing, we're Trekkies, 24/7." Would that Christians were as zealous about preaching their narrative—and enacting it—as Trekkies are about theirs!

BAD FAITH: THE IMAGINATION OF (VAIN)GLORY

That other stories effectively employ imaginative techniques is a cautionary reminder for evangelists and theologians alike. Rhetoric is the art of persuasion, and early Christians made good use of it. However, as Augustine rightly warns, we must be as concerned with the truth of the message as its means of presentation.[3]

Like other forms of storytelling, film is a powerful medium of communication, combining images and sounds that engage the mind and senses, the imagination and emotions. Film calls our whole person to attention, engaging us on a variety of levels. Film not only tells but shows stories: if a picture is worth a thousand words, a moving picture must be worth ten thousand. While all narrative texts invite us to inhabit the worlds they display, film literally displays the sights and sounds of its world. Whether this is good or bad for the imagination in an intriguing question, but a good case can be made that, in showing more, film leaves less work for the imagination than oral or written stories.

Our Roundtable topic is the role of the imagination in evangelism. Let's consider Mel Gibson's *The Passion of the Christ* again, in particular the film's tacit Christology. Who does Mel say that Christ is? One plausible response, especially in light of the extreme violence of the drawn out crucifixion scene, is "the suffering servant." In restoring the horror and sheer physical agony not only of the cross but of the scourging that preceded it, Gibson effectively de-sentimentalizes Christ's suffering.

In other respects, however, his film is an example of what we could call "bad faith," insofar as it conveys Gibson's interpretation of the narrative rather than the narrative itself. In this respect, we can compare *The Passion of the Christ* to what Luther called the "theology of glory." Even though the

---

[3]Additionally, the means of presentation must be consistent with the end for which the message is given. If Marshall McLuhan is right that "the medium is the message," what are the implications for evangelism?

subject matter of Gibson's film is the cross, it is as much about Gibson's creativity as it is biblical fidelity. Three features in Gibson's film incline me to associate his imagination with vainglory. (1) The film invents details and episodes that were not in the text. We call this "fancy": the bringing to mind things that are not real. (2) The film emphasizes pictures. For many, this is what the imagination is: the ability to create images (verbal, mental or celluloid) that represent scenes to which we have no empirical access. Ironically, in picturing Jesus and his passion in just this way, he shuts down the viewer's imagination. (3) The rhetorical purpose of Gibson's pictorial imagination of Jesus' passion is to affect our emotions. The prolonged scourging scene in particular is intended not to increase our understanding of the event, but to appeal to our pity.

The term *imagination* does not get a particularly good rap in the Bible— at least not in the King James Version, which has a tendency to link the imagination with the evil inclinations of the heart (Gen 6:5; Prov 6:18), with vain or futile thinking (Rom 1:21) and with conceiving mischief (Ps 140:2). Not particularly auspicious linguistic company!

There is no term in the biblical Hebrew or Greek for imagination. That alone is no excuse for jettisoning the concept, of course—we can say the same about the term *Trinity*. Though there is no one biblical term, the concept of the Trinity—and, I would argue, the imagination—is thoroughly biblical. Some people worry that the imagination, in the sense of the production of images, is a license for idolatry. It is true that there are false images of God—and of Jesus Christ. Ludwig Feuerbach is right to remind us of the danger of confusing our best thoughts about God, or Jesus, with the reality. The best way forward is to acknowledge the possibility of vain imaginings. I will argue in the next section that there can be a virtuous imagining, whereby biblical stories discipline us in ways of thinking in terms of a metanarrative and meaningful framework that gives pride of place to Jesus Christ. What follows is an attempt to set forth the contours of such a gospel-governed imagination: an *evangelical* imagination.

GOOD FAITH: THE EVANGELICAL IMAGINATION

Gibson's imagination is too pictorial, physical and "projective" (i.e., he projects his own feelings about Jesus' physical agony into Jesus' Passion). As such, it falls on the "theology of glory" side of Luther's ledger, which emphasizes human reason (and human feelings) in coming to know what God is like. The Gospels (the revealed source of what Luther calls the "theology of the cross") depict Jesus' Passion somewhat differently. To be sure, the imagination is still involved, but it functions not to picture physical suffering but to connect the canonical dots and to show us that Jesus' suffering and death on the cross is the wholly unexpected shape of God's power and love.

Recall the problem mentioned at the outset of this essay: namely, the loss of the ability to read our world through the interpretive biblical lens of God's Word. At some point in the eighteenth or nineteenth century, the educated American, under the influence of German higher criticism, lost confidence in the Bible: "The assumption that historical process is the bed of human perception, that knowledge is the product of a fluid process, had come to be the hallmark of the modern mind."[4] This mindset has more or less taken over modern biblical studies. Even evangelical biblical exegetes are often more comfortable analyzing the text into smaller and smaller bits than they are in tracing the longitudinal lines that hold the Old and New Testaments together. A lack of imagination complicates the project of discerning canonical coherence.

An inadequate picture of the imagination as the power of picturing the absent real, or of conjuring up the unreal, holds critics captive. As I argue elsewhere in this volume, the imagination is the power of "synoptic" vision: the ability to see things (e.g., Gospels, Testaments) together; to connect apparently unrelated elements into a meaningful canonical pattern that converges on Christ. The special intellectual talent of the imagination is that of discerning the relation between parts and whole. This ability to think synthetically, according to the logic of part/whole, is as much a form of reason as is the ability to think analytically, break things down into smaller parts, or in terms of cause and effect. Yes, Virginia, there are vain imaginings, but this no more disqualifies the imagination from serving theology than the existence of logical fallacies disqualifies reason. The task of theology—interpreting the world and human experience in light of Scripture—involves reason (analysis) and imagination (synthesis) alike.

---

[4]Grant Wacker, "The Demise of Biblical Civilization," in Nathan O. Hatch and Mark A. Noll, eds., *The Bible in America: Essays in Cultural History* (Oxford: Oxford University Press, 1982), 125.

The imagination also has a second function to play in theology: it enables us not only to synthesize but also to participate in the biblical text. Whereas analytic reason excels in "looking at," the imagination allows us to "look along" the grain of the text, indwelling it rather than remaining at a critical distance. Christians in all cultures need to develop this skill of textual indwelling, which is merely another name for what Lindbeck calls intratextuality. In order to take every thought captive (2 Cor 10:5), theology must also take every imagination captive to Christ as well.

The evangelical imagination involves more than re-creating pictures of Jesus' suffering. The imagination is more than a mental photocopier. The true power of the imagination resides not simply in its capacity to reproduce images but to relate and organize them into larger patterns. To have imagination is to have the capacity to make or perceive meaningful frameworks. If pictures are worth a thousand words and moving pictures ten thousand, frameworks are worth a hundred thousand words. The imagination is primarily about frameworks for understanding, and only secondarily about the pictures that are framed.

The large-scale interpretive frameworks (worldviews) that are the products of the imagination engage not only the emotions but the will and the mind—what Scripture calls the "heart."[5] The apostle Paul prays for God to give his readers a spirit of wisdom, "having the eyes of your hearts enlightened, that you may know what is the hope to which he has called you . . . and what is the immeasurable greatness of his power toward us who believe . . . that he worked in Christ when he raised him from the dead" (Eph 1:18-20). Paul prays for God to use his texts to open the eyes of his readers to theological truths in order to live together in unity and to fight together against the evil around them. The Scriptures, says Calvin, are our "spectacles" of faith: we don't merely look at but *through* them at God, the world and ourselves.[6] The Bible ultimately provides us with a set of corrective imaginative lenses that comprise a framework for living. And this brings us to my main contribution: a proposal about the gospel, imagination and drama.

---

[5]See Alison Searle, *"The Eyes of Your Heart": Literary and Theological Trajectories of Imagining Biblically* (Eugene, OR: Wipf & Stock, 2009).

[6]John Calvin, *Institutes of the Christian Religion*, trans. Ford Lewis Battles (Philadelphia: Westminster Press, 1960), I.vi.1.

THE DRAMA OF THE CHRIST: SPEAK-ACTING, STORY MADE FLESH

Storytelling is a powerful means of shaping a person's view of the world.[7] Storytelling is the imagination in its narrative mode: the ability to form a meaningful whole (or unified plot) out of what otherwise appears as an unrelated diversity of persons, incidents and events. Storytelling does not simply recite what is happening. It also provides evaluative insights into what is happening by the way the story is told. Some stories end, for example, with explicit morals. It's not merely that the story packages the moral better than a propositional statement might. Stories do not simply communicate information and teach morals; they affect us, not least by engaging our emotions. The best stories teach, move, delight and transform us, perhaps by helping us to resolve to become better persons.

If telling stories can do all this, how much more can acting stories out do, enfleshing them in bodily form? The gospel is *the story of God made flesh*. The gospel—that God has provided for the world's salvation by sending the Son and making his Lord—was enacted before it was proclaimed. We have something to proclaim because something has been done. God has become flesh, dwelt among us and given us a share in his life. The gospel is the good news that God has done something on the stage of world history. The gospel was a *thing done* before it was a *word made*.

The gospel as "thing done" and "word made." The gospel of Jesus Christ is essentially dramatic, involving word and deed, speech and action. In the first place, the gospel is a thing done (something seen and witnessed) with a human body: the Son of God has poured out his life on a cross (Acts 2:23), the Father has raised the Son to new life (Acts 2:24) and the Son has poured out this new life, in the form of the Spirit, to those who put their trust in him (Acts 2:33). This is the historical aspect of the gospel, the thing done: the reconciliation of the world to God in Christ (2 Cor 5:18). Yet the gospel is also a word made: a proclamation; a written Gospel. Something wonderful has happened, but it must be communicated in a way that bears true witness and persuades others of its truth.

Drama captures both aspects (thing done and word made). A drama is, first, a doing: a unified sequence of action (from the Greek word *draō*, "to do,

---

[7]N. T. Wright says that a story-shaped worldview provides "the grid through which humans perceive reality" (*The New Testament and the People of God*, vol. 1 of *Christian Origins and the Question of God* [Minneapolis: Fortress, 1992], 38).

to take action"). The drama of redemption refers to what God has done in the history of Israel and then, definitively, in the history of Jesus Christ. Drama involves doings. Not impersonal events, but actions, many of which involve language (speech-acts). A drama is a "word made" to the extent that monologues and dialogues often carry the action along. This is particularly true of the drama of redemption. The basic plot in the story of Israel concerns the "word of the Lord," and whether the Lord would deliver on his promises.

Drama also refers to a type of literature designed for stage representation. A script preserves the drama in writing until it can again be enacted in performance. Scripture is both a transcript of the "thing done" and a "word made" that solicits our performance (more on this below). To understand Scripture rightly we must appreciate both the "thing done" and the "word made." As to the latter, there are actually many types of "words made" (genres) within Scripture. Each of the Gospel narratives, for instance, has a literary integrity of its own. The same story of Jesus Christ is told in four different yet complementary narrative ways. There are other kinds of "words made" in Scripture besides narrative: songs, proverbs, prophecies, apocalyptic and so forth. It requires imagination to grasp the way the various parts relate to their respective wholes. What requires even more imagination, however, is discerning how so many different kinds of texts fit into the overarching drama of the Christ.

God's "thing done" and "word made": theodrama. The gospel is intrinsically *theodramatic*, a matter of what God (*theos*) has said and done (*draō*) in history. In particular, theodrama refers to what the triune God has said and done in the history of Jesus Christ. At the heart of Christianity is not merely an *idea* of God (or the Good) but God's self-communicating word and acts. There is good news because something has been done and someone has told us about it in words.

Theodrama is the substance that lies at the heart of Scripture. Taken together, these words and deeds serve as the interpretative framework (story) through which Christians think, make sense of their experience and decide what to do and how to do it. Theodrama is both a theoretical framework for understanding God and a theatrical framework for living the Christian life. The goal of the Christian life—to know and love God and our neighbor as ourselves—is essentially a matter of theodramatic understanding.

Faith's search for understanding begins by realizing that much of what God does in the drama of redemption is *speak*. Indeed, God's speech kicks off both the creational and covenantal action: "Let there be light" (Gen 1:3); "I will make of you a great nation, and I will bless you . . . and in you all the families of the earth shall be blessed" (Gen 12:2-3). The theodrama continues with God making good on his Abrahamic *promissio* thanks to the *missio* (sending) of Son and Spirit.

Unlike narrative stories, however, where the medium is words, or film, where the medium is celluloid images, the medium of drama is the living presence and activity of persons. Theater occurs when one or more persons "present" themselves to others.[8] Drama involves either audible speech or visible, bodily activity that makes known a person's inner life or spirit. This is precisely what happens in revelation. The living God presents himself to others through the medium of human words or, in the case of Jesus, through a particular embodied human life.

According to the Scriptures, human history is a God-driven drama with five acts. Each act of the play is set in motion by a mighty speech act of God, yet in each case there is human or satanic opposition to God's act (thing done/word made). The first act is creation (Gen 1–3), the setting for everything else that follows. The drama really begins when Satan tempts Adam and Eve to corrupt the created order. Act Two (beginning from Genesis 12 and running through the rest of the Old Testament) concerns God's election, rejection and restoration of Israel. It begins with his promise to make of Abraham a great nation and to bless all the families of the earth in him (Gen 12:2-3). The drama here is a function of whether or not Israel will believe and obey the Word of God. The pivotal and climactic Act Three is Jesus: God's Word made flesh. Here, too, what generates the drama is the question of how people will respond to Jesus. Act Four begins with a new creation: the risen Christ sends his Spirit to constitute the church. The fifth and final act is the Last Judgment, the eschatological consummation of all things, when all things will be rightly ordered under the ascended Christ.

This is the imaginative framework that ought to regulate Christian faith, thought and life. This is the story in which we live and move and have our

---

[8]Bernard Beckerman, *Dynamics of Drama: Theory and Method of Analysis* (New York: Alfred A. Knopf, 1970), 8.

being. The church today is living between the first and second comings of Jesus, in the closing scenes of Act Four, poised between memory and hope. Note that the climax of the drama has already happened: the risen Christ has ascended into heaven and now sits at the right hand of the Father.[9] The drama, however, continues. Christ has won the victory, but the mopping-up operation continues. The victory of the triune God is something to which the church bears witnesses and in which the church participates. The biblical story summons us to be participants "in something larger than our sin-defined needs."[10] It is the summons to turn away from other stories falsely called knowledge and to embrace the drama—the thing done and the word made—of the Christ.

The drama of the Christ is not one more narrative, the one the church happens to live by, but the true story of the world in which everyone is a participant, whether they acknowledge it or not. "The truth of Christianity is that it offers a story which is the story of the whole world. It is public truth."[11] Evangelism is the proclamation that something has been done not only for our good, but also for the good of the whole world.

THE THEODRAMATIC IMAGINATION: FOLLOWING THE WAY, DOING THE TRUTH, LIVING THE LIFE

The church, too, is something done and made by the triune God, a creature of word and Spirit: "For we are his workmanship [*poiēma*], created in Christ Jesus for good works" (Eph 2:10). The church does not make the gospel true but it should be evidence of its truth. Theology's task is to equip disciples who, in following the way of Jesus Christ, will also embody the truth claims of Christian theology. Theology is not simply a theoretical matter pertaining to propositions but a practical and *performative* matter pertaining to persons.

That Christians are participants in a drama rather than a narrative makes a significant difference. *Story* refers to what is told—for example, the plot of a person's life. *Narrative* and *drama* refer to how we tell/show the story—its mode of presentation. The same sequence of events can be narrated in

---

[9]For a further account of why I see this as the climax of the drama, see my *Faith Speaking Understanding: Performing the Drama of Doctrine* (Louisville, KY: Westminster John Knox, 2014), 209-14.

[10]Eugene H. Peterson, *Eat This Book: A Conversation in the Art of Spiritual Reading* (Grand Rapids: Eerdmans, 2006), 41.

[11]Wright, *The New Testament and People of God*, 41-42.

different ways (e.g., as comedy or as tragedy), but what narratives have in common is the way the stories are told, which is usually in the third person. Dramas, by contrast, show rather than tell, and are typically enacted with others. Story becomes drama when we enter into it in an embodied way. This is precisely what the gospel summons us to do. Disciples are not simply to listen to the story but to *believe* it, and not simply to believe the story but to *follow* it, entering into it with all our minds, hearts, souls and strength. We follow the gospel not as we would an argument, but as we would a dramatic script. Drama preserves the emphasis on story but does a better job integrating the interpreters into its play.

Thinking biblically, with imagination: cultivating canon sense. As we have seen, there is a cognitive aspect to the imagination. How do we let the story recounted in Scripture serve as our supreme interpretive framework? What does it mean to think biblically? Biblical exegetes and systematic theologians have in modern times tended to answer this question differently. The twin sets of methods, criteria and vocabulary, can be edifying, but when the two disciplines fail to speak one another's language, the result can often be unedifying disagreement. Systematic theology sometimes resembles what Aristotle called *epistemē*: theoretical knowledge, arranged systematically. Biblical exegesis, with its analytic tools and its arsenal of lexical aids, sometimes resembles what Aristotle called *technē*: technical knowledge about grammar and history.

Thinking about Scripture as the church's script and theodramatic transcript gets us beyond the impasse. The theatrical paradigm is more conducive to Aristotle's third model of rationality: *phronēsis. Phronēsis* is *practical* reasoning—deliberation about what to say or do in particular situations in order to realize some good. This is precisely what Scripture frequently brings to the fore too. The epistles, for example, are pastoral letters that address particular problems in particular situations. "All Scripture is . . . profitable . . . for training in righteousness" (2 Tim 3:16). The cultural scenery may have changed, but the basic plot has not. What is at stake for Christians in every situation is how to speak and act in ways that correspond to the good of the gospel. It is precisely by indwelling the biblical text that our minds are renewed and we are able to "discern what is the will of God, what is good" (Rom 12:2). Scripture does not offer a detailed blueprint for every particular question we may have, but it is filled with case studies on Christian *phronēsis*. What we learn from Scripture is how disciples are to act: namely, to act out the goodness—the light, life and love—that is in Jesus Christ.

Thinking biblically is a matter of developing not common sense but *canon sense*. The canon is more than a list of books. It is a measuring or divining rod that helps us discern what we should say and do today to continue and correspond to the way, truth and life made known in Jesus Christ. It is both source and norm of the church's corporate identity and witness, its authoritative script and transcript. Those with canon sense know how the two Testaments fit together. They also know how to locate themselves in relation to the overall creation-fall-redemption-consummation storyline of the Bible. To have canon sense is to know where you are in the drama and what scene you're playing. Canon sense requires imagination.

The drama of the Christ is both historical and eschatological. It is a matter of what God has already done, of what God is currently doing and of what God will do in the future. It is noteworthy that Jesus explained his own person and work, and the nature of the kingdom of God, in terms of parables. The kingdom of God is like a series of dramatic scenes where the ordinary and extraordinary rub shoulders. The parables cultivate what we might term the *eschatological imagination*: the ability to perceive the coming kingdom of God in the midst of the everyday, the capacity to discern the triune God at work in Christ through the Spirit making all things new. We need a biblically disciplined, eschatological imagination to see the coming kingdom because the presence and activity of God is neither immediately obvious nor empirically observable.

In order to follow the theodrama we need to see, judge and act according to what is already/not yet the case in Christ. The "whole" that the imagination discerns is a unified and complete action: the reconciliation of all things "in Christ." It takes imagination to grasp this theodrama. It also takes faith, which may be another way of describing what I am here calling the eschatological imagination: "Now faith is the assurance of things hoped for, the conviction of things not seen" (Heb 11:1).

Canon sense involves the training of our minds and imaginations to "read" the world in faith: to see our everyday life as participating in the drama of the Christ. Canon sense is more than a hermeneutical method.

Ultimately, it is a means of spiritual formation. Spiritual formation is simply the process by which the Spirit, ministering the Word, conforms us to Christ. To be conformed to Christ means acting out his mind with our bodies. This process of formation is tied to the literary forms of the Bible. Each of the Bible's literary forms contributes in its own way to the understanding of faith, our ability to imaginatively discern the thrust of the theodramatic action. Attending to biblical form and content is one of the primary means by which Scripture trains—or *disciples*—our perception, reason and imagination. As Hans Urs von Balthasar says, Scripture is a "vehicle that impresses the Christ-form in the hearts of men."[12] I would add only that Scripture impresses the Christ-*mind*—the *phronēsis* or practical reason of Jesus—upon our minds, wills, imaginations and hearts as well.

The drama of the Christ and Christian understanding. Evangelism involves a conversion of the imagination and understanding. Theology is a ministry of ultimate reality that deepens and develops understanding. These claims prompt at least the three following questions. (1) What *is* understanding? (2) Do we really believe that it's vital for people of faith to seek it? (3) What is the role of the imagination in getting understanding?

Understanding is the capacity to discern order and patterns and, in the case of textual interpretation, to perceive how a set of words works together to enact an author's communicative intent. Understanding is a somewhat mysterious and precious capacity (especially in spouses and book reviewers).

Paul Ricoeur demystifies things considerably when he speaks of a specifically *narrative* understanding. Narrative is a cognitive instrument for ordering a heterogeneous set of people, places and events, and provides a way to perceiving coherence amidst diversity. Ricoeur believes that both historians and novelists make sense of life through "emplotment": the process of putting events into an unfolding yet unified story.[13] The narrative understanding is thus the ability to follow a story, seeing how the beginning, middle and end fit together. Christians too must have narrative understanding in order to see how each part of the Bible relates to the canonical whole, the unified story of the Christ: "Every part of the Bible—each event,

---

[12]Hans Urs von Balthasar, *The Glory of the Lord: A Theological Aesthetics* (San Francisco: Ignatius Press, 1984–1991), 1:530.

[13]Paul Ricoeur, *Time and Narrative* (Chicago: University of Chicago Press, 1984), 1:31-51.

book, character, command, prophecy, and poem—must be understood in the context of the *one* story line."[14]

We can go further. Christian understanding, the kind that embodies the good news that lies at the heart of our faith, is neither simply theoretical nor even narrative but ultimately theodramatic. We ultimately fail to demonstrate understanding of the way, truth and life of Jesus Christ unless we are able to walk his way, exhibit his life and do his truth. We fail to demonstrate understanding if we remain spectators only: hearers, not doers of the word (Jas 1:22-25). Mere spectators are not yet witnesses. An onlooker is not necessarily involved in an action; the witness is an active participant.[15] We must not confuse being a bystander with understanding.

Understanding matters because it provides the primary framework for life. To understand where we are in the drama of redemption is to be oriented toward Christ. The primacy of the drama of the Christ must be both theoretical and practical, not only a lens but the concrete medium in which we live and move and have our daily being.

The imagination is a minister of understanding, a means and medium for gaining a sense of how the various parts of the Bible, or our lives, fit into a meaningful pattern—the whole in which Christ unifies the plot (see esp. Eph 1:10). It is thanks to the imagination that we can hold things together and achieve a sense of coherence. The natural tendency of things, as we know from the law of entropy, is to fall apart. To be sure, there will be moments and events that do not seem to fit nicely our worldviews (e.g., the problem of evil). At other times we lose sight of the big picture because there is too much information to process. When we are overwhelmed either by the amount of data or by recalcitrant data (events that seem not to fit into our sense of the whole), we are on the verge of losing understanding.

The gospel withstands even these difficult times. "In him all things hold together" (Col 1:17). The pattern of the theodrama is neither contrived nor coerced, but capacious. The drama of the Christ encompasses unthinkable evil and apparent absurdity. They, too, have a place in the meaningful pattern of the theodrama. They are surds that will be made null, nailed to the cross

---

[14]Craig G. Bartholomew and Michael W. Goheen, *The Drama of Scripture: Finding Our Place in the Biblical Story*, 2nd ed. (Grand Rapids: Baker Academic, 2014), 14.

[15]See Gabriel Marcel, *The Mystery of Being*, trans. René Hague (Chicago: H. Regnery, 1960), 1:121-24.

(Col 2:14). The drama of the Christ is a unified meaningful action that stretches from creation to consummation, and accounts for both the fall and redemption of the powers and principalities that perplex mere philosophy. Outside the drama of the Christ there is no ultimate explanation.

The drama of the Christ attunes us to the way things really are. This "attunement" is not only cognitive, however, but imaginative, affective and volitional as well. The drama of the Christ is the Christian touchstone by which we discern and do the truth. In order to grasp the drama of the Christ, we need the Word written, the holy script and transcript, and the illumination of the Holy Spirit that John McIntyre calls "God's imagination let loose . . . in the world."[16] Theology is ultimately a Word and Spirit-enabled ministry of theodramatic understanding.

The drama of the Christ and Christian community. The drama of the Christ ought to be the church's primary "social imaginary." Charles Taylor defines a social imaginary as "what enables, through making sense of, the practices of a society."[17] Whereas Taylor deploys the concept to come to a better understanding of modernity, I want to use it to come to a better understanding of Christianity, and the church.

The drama of the Christ is our social imaginary. This is just another way of speaking of a biblically generated and governed theodramatic understanding, and of the ecclesial imaginary that explains the practices of the society of Jesus. Whatever we do as Christians—whether we eat, drink, work or worship—we do to participate rightly in the triune action whereby the Father is making all things new in Christ through the Spirit. The challenge for evangelism, theology and preaching alike is to take every imagination captive by displaying the meaning and glory of life *sub specie theodramatis* (from the perspective of the theodrama).[18]

Perhaps the single most significant service that imagining the drama of the Christ gives theology is the ability to help disciples get beyond theoretical

---

[16]McIntyre, *Faith, Theology, and the Imagination* (Edinburgh: Handsel, 1987), 64. See also my "The Spirit of Light After the Age of Enlightenment: Renewing/Reforming Pneumatic Hermeneutics via the Economy of Illumination," in Jeffrey Barbeau and Beth Felker Jones, eds., *Spirit of God: Christian Renewal in the Community of Faith* (Downers Grove, IL: IVP Academic, 2015), 149-67.

[17]Charles Taylor, *Modern Social Imaginaries* (Durham, NC and London: Duke University Press, 2004), 2. See also above, pp. 36-39.

[18]For a further elaboration of this idea, see my *The Drama of Doctrine: A Canonical-Linguistic Approach to Christian Theology* (Louisville, KY: Westminster John Knox, 2005), 329-32.

knowledge to practical witness. In the final analysis, the real value of the theodramatic imagination lies in its ability to help us make right judgments: judgments about how to participate rightly in the drama of the Christ, and hence to speak and act in ways that glorify him. We know we are close to having theodramatic wisdom when we can employ canon sense to answer the following five questions:[19]

1. Where are we? What kind of scene are we playing?

2. Who are we? In what kind of plot are our lives entangled?

3. What time is it? What act and scene of the drama of redemption are we playing?

4. What's happening? What is God doing?

5. What should we say or do?

Together, these questions add up to a single, comprehensive question: What does discipleship look like and why are we (the church) here? The answer to this question is a mission statement. We are here to participate rightly in God's triune mission to the world. We are here to demonstrate our understanding of and bear witness to the drama of the Christ in words of wisdom and works of love.

THESES ON RADICAL EVANGELICALISM

To imagine God, church and world biblically is to become radically evangelical. Evangelicalism is radical, first, insofar as it retrieves the dramatic root (Latin *radix*, "root") of the gospel: what the triune God is doing in Christ. Evangelicalism is radical in a second, surgical sense when it renews the mind and restores the malnourished ecclesial imagination to health. And evangelicalism is radical, finally, when it participates in social, political and intellectual reform, not least of the evangelical tradition itself.[20]

---

[19]I am modifying these from Wright, *The New Testament and the People of God*, 122-23, who in turn takes them from J. Brian Walsh and Richard Middleton, *The Transforming Vision: Shaping a Christian World View* (Downers Grove, IL: InterVarsity Press, 1984).

[20]Cf. John Milbank's Radical Orthodoxy, which is orthodox in the sense of commitment to creedal Christianity, and radical in its rejection of secular reason's attempt to think about the world and humanity non-theologically (see John Milbank, Graham Ward and Catherine Pickstock, eds., *Radical Orthodoxy* [New York and London: Routledge, 1999]).

And now five summary theses:

1. Spiritual formation is happening all the time, as the media powers and market principalities colonize the popular imagination. There are many stories circulating in our society that clamor for our allegiance, each eager to script our lives for us. Many of the most powerful forces in contemporary Western culture seek to turn us into capitalist consumers who want only to maximize our own happiness, health and wealth. The drama continues: Will God's people hearken to his word and the gospel, or to other words and some other gospel (Gal 1:7)?

2. We don't need more pictures (i.e., more information, more knowledge, more data) to live by. We need a new frame(work). Theology must not be content to merely state truth. Most evangelicals know what they are supposed to believe. Our problem is not that we don't have the right information but that we don't know how to process it, or what to do with it. Too often the church exhibits a bipolar disorder. We profess Christ but follow secular scriptures. We accord authority to the biblical canon but abide by social codes. The task of evangelism, and theology, is to take every imagination captive to Scripture, nurture it and help it indwell the drama of the Christ. We must taste, discern and act in the world as it is—made new in Christ. For this we need a theodramatic framework and a biblically invigorated imagination.

3. The evangelical imagination, as a form of synoptic judgment that relates parts to a larger whole, is an organ of meaning that ministers theodramatic understanding. The imagination is particularly needed in biblical studies as a counter to the fragmenting analytic procedures that presently rule the academic roost. Congregations, too, need to read with imagination in order to gain canon sense: a sense of how the whole canon fits together and where the church fits into the action.

4. Evangelists and theologians need to communicate an alternative social imaginary: namely, the drama of the Christ: what God is doing to renew creation and restore his image in the human creature. Theology's special mandate is to understand God, world, self and community in light of the drama of redemption that is being accomplished in world history and authoritatively transcribed in God's written word. Theology ministers the understanding of Scripture in order to foster a vibrant evangelical imagination (faith), without which we will not be able to see, taste or do theodramatic truth: the truth of what the triune God is doing in Jesus Christ for us and our salvation.

5. Christians best bear witness when they understand themselves to be actors in the drama of the Christ, and when they exhibit that understanding in wise and loving words and deeds. The challenge of cultivating minds and hearts captive to the drama of the Christ is to convert and sanctify our imaginations. We need to see and *feel* ourselves as actors in the ongoing play of the world, initiated, kept in motion and directed by the triune God. The church exists in part to "make disciples of all nations" (Mt 28:19), and this means training men and women not only to understand the good news of what God has done, is doing and will do, but to demonstrate that understanding by participating rightly in the action. The church has no more important vocation than this: to be an embodied parable of the kingdom of God.

CONCLUSION: LOSE THE DREAM, LIVE THE DRAMA

The good life, according to the American Standard Version (the authorized version of the American Dream) includes 2.2 children, a single family home, an SUV, a 401k retirement plan and dinner out once a week (at least). There's room for God too. God is the giver of the good life, guarantor of the status quo, bestower of rewards for overtime. At least this is the caricature of God in which America's teenagers apparently believe: the god of Moralistic Therapeutic Deism, the God who wants you to be nice to others and feel good in the process.[21] This is the picture of God that currently has a lock on the popular American imagination.

Mel Gibson's *Passion of the Christ*, by contrast, is a plea for a different spirituality, marked more by sacrifice and suffering than material gain. In a pivotal scene, Christ says to Mary "See, mother, I make all things new" (a line taken not from the Gospels but from Rev 21:5-6).[22] Yet one reviewer complained that, when all is said and done, Gibson's Christ is as trapped by suffering, death and despair as contemporary non-Christians. Gibson's film

---

[21]The term "Moralistic Therapeutic Deism" figures prominently in Christian Smith's *Soul Searching: The Religious and Spiritual Lives of American Teenagers* (Oxford: Oxford University Press, 2005).

[22]Mark Wrathall, "Seeing the World Made New," in Jorge J. E. Gracia, ed., *Mel Gibson's Passion and Philosophy: The Cross, the Questions, the Controversy* (Peru, IL: Carus Publishing Company, 2004), 17.

helps us see the world in a new way, but this is not necessarily what it means to see the world made new.[23] In this respect, Gibson's *Passion of the Christ* falls short of Radical Evangelicalism.

What Jesus says and does according to the Scriptures—the *drama* of the Christ—really does make all things new (cf. 2 Cor 5:17). Jesus is the first radical evangelical: "The Spirit of the Lord is upon me because he has anointed me to proclaim good news to the poor. He has sent me to proclaim liberty to the captives . . . to set at liberty those who are oppressed" (Lk 4:18). The drama of the Christ is all about delivering sinners from the domain of darkness (Col 1:13) and setting the prisoners free—free to glorify God and enjoy him forever, and free to be themselves. When the church participates rightly in this drama, it becomes a revolutionary and reconciliatory theater.

To have one's imagination seized by the drama of the Christ is to accept the Lord's summons to follow him: to be an active participant, a player in the continuing action. This means adopting the pattern of seeing, judging and acting exemplified by Christ Jesus himself. Acting out what *is* in Christ—cruciform love—may make us appear as fools in the eyes of the world, but it is God's embodied wisdom and power (1 Cor 1:18). Indeed, the most potent form of evangelism is the church living out the drama, witnessing in all that it says and does to the manifold ways in which God has made all things new in Christ.

---

[23]Ibid., 22.

eight

THE DRAMA OF DISCIPLESHIP
A Vocation of Spiritual Formation

The following essay is heavily redacted from a number of talks I have given over the years to different audiences on more or less the same topic: the role of theology in the life of the disciple. The various iterations of this essay could be viewed as a set of variations on the theme of theological vocation. The disciple's vocation was also the subject of my March 2015 address to the Chicago chapter, ably led by KJ Johnson, of the C. S. Lewis Institute Fellows program. The purpose of the Institute is to further the cause of discipleship of heart and mind, thereby helping believers to become, in C. S. Lewis's words, "little Christs." If the ultimate purpose of doctrine is to make disciples and cultivate godliness (that is, Christlikeness), it follows that there is a properly spiritual dimension to learning theology. Christian witness involves both speaking the truth in love and loving the truth we speak. Theological knowledge without Christian love falls terribly short. As I have written elsewhere: "If I speak in the tongues of Reformers and of professional theologians, and have not personal faith in Christ, my theology is nothing but the noisy beating of a snare drum. And if I give myself to resolving the debate between supra- and infralapsarianism, and to defending inerrancy, and to learning the Westminster Catechism, yea, even the larger one, so as to recite it by heart backwards and forwards, and have not love, I have gained nothing."[1] We are answerable for what we know. Theology without spiritual formation is a recipe book from which we never cook. I care so much about doctrinal development and truth because they ultimately

---

[1]Kevin J. Vanhoozer, *First Theology: God, Scripture and Hermeneutics* (Downers Grove, IL: InterVarsity Press, 2002), 40.

serve the project of making disciples—in a word, dramatizing Christ. If the disciple's dramatization of Christ is to be genuine, the performance must be from the heart. We must act out only what is truly in us. The drama of discipleship concerns this inner preparation (spiritual formation) every bit as much as it does the public performance (witness). The structure of this essay corresponds to the four ways in which Jesus instructs us to love God—with all our heart, soul, mind and strength.

INTRODUCTION: DOCTRINE, DISCIPLESHIP AND THE GREAT COMMANDMENT

"'Teacher, which is the great commandment in the Law?' And [Jesus] said to him, 'You shall love the Lord your God with all your heart, and with all your soul and with all your mind'" (Mt 22:36-37). Mark and Luke add "and with all your strength" (Mk 12:30; Lk 10:27). Jesus' answer is no novelty. He is reminding his listeners of what they should already know from the Hebrew Scriptures. Loving and serving God "with all your heart and with all your soul" is a frequent theme throughout the Old Testament (Deut 6:5; 10:12; 11:13; 13:3; 26:16; 30:2; 30:6; 30:10; Josh 22:5; 1 Sam 12:20; 12:24; Prov 3:5). The moral is clear. It is not enough to know *about* God. We must know and love him as Lord—something that requires much more than intellectual assent.

There is a connection between Jesus' reformulation of the Great Commandment and his teaching about the importance of building one's house upon a rock: "Everyone then who hears these words of mine and does them will be like a wise man who built his house on the rock" (Mt 7:24). In contrast, everyone who hear Jesus' words but has only head knowledge of them will be like a foolish man who built his house on the sand (Mt 7:26). Jesus' words must be put into practice. We must practice the eloquence of God.

We find the same lesson in James. "For if anyone is a hearer of the word and not a doer, he is like a man who observes his natural face in a mirror. For he looks at himself and goes away and at once forgets what he was like" (Jas 1:23-24). Intellectual assent—theoretical knowledge—falls short of true faith if it is unaccompanied by action. "Even the demons believe" (Jas 2:19). The difference between a demon and a disciple, then, depends on God's Word taking root in human hearts and bearing fruit in the work of love.

The call to discipleship: vocation. Discipleship is a vocation, not a career.[2] Career involves a self-chosen trajectory: an occupation. By contrast, vocation begins with a call that originates from outside of us. Most radically, it begins with God *invoking* us into existence. That we are here at all is entirely by God's grace. Only God "calls into existence the things that do not exist" (Rom 4:17). Furthermore, God calls people to specific tasks and roles. God called Abraham to leave his country (Gen 12:1), making Abraham, in the words of one commentator, "the first man with a definite, explicit sense of vocation."[3] This is something of an exaggeration, of course, for Adam and Eve had a vocation too: realizing their purpose as human beings to be living images (icons) of God.

Our highest calling as men and women is not to some cause (e.g., medicine, motherhood or ministry), but to a person. Whatever our occupation, we are the Lord's. Hence "everything we are, everything we do, and everything we have is invested with a special devotion, dynamism, and direction."[4] The way we respond to God's call on our lives defines us and reveals who we are at our deepest core. The idea that our social class, gender or ethnicity defines us is only partially correct. Our most radical identity, the seat of our personhood, is rather a function of how we habitually respond to the call of God. Human beings are fundamentally dialogic rather than monologic creatures. The way we habitually respond to the call of God is the shape of our freedom and responsibility.

Our concern is not with God's general call on human beings to reflect his image but on the specific call Jesus lays on his disciples: "Follow me" (Mt 4:19; Mk 1:7; Lk 5:27; Jn 1:43). The call to discipleship is dramatic because (1) it requires a response and (2) the response involves action. There are no armchair disciples.

The implicit call to all human beings is to bear the image of God. The explicit call to Christian disciples is to follow Jesus, who *is* the image of God (2 Cor 4:4). It follows that being a disciple of Jesus is an intensification of the general human vocation. *The drama of discipleship is about how a person*

---

[2]For more on the contrast between vocation and career, see Eugene H. Peterson, *Under the Unpredictable Plant: An Exploration in Vocational Holiness* (Grand Rapids: Eerdmans, 1992).

[3]W. R. Forrester, *Christian Vocation* (New York: Scribner's, 1953), 23.

[4]Os Guinness, *The Call: Finding and Fulfilling the Central Purpose of Your Life* (Nashville, TN: Thomas Nelson, 2003), 29.

responds to the call to image God by following Christ. There is no vacation from this vocation. Bearing witness to Jesus as the image of God is a full-time prospect: "I therefore, a prisoner for the Lord, urge you to walk in a manner worthy of the calling to which you have been called" (Eph 4:1).

To walk worthily is to walk like Jesus. The vocation of the disciple is to become the kind of person who resembles Christ, the kind of person who can do God's will on earth as it is in heaven, and so represent a bit of heaven (God's reign) on earth. Jesus says this burden is light (Mt 11:30). I can think of at least two reasons for this bearable lightness of being a disciple. First, the risen Christ sends us his Spirit to empower us. Second, he is calling us to be what we fundamentally are, or were originally created to be—images of God. Disciples are called to be "little Christs."[5]

The challenge of discipleship: spiritual formation. The reality, of course, is that Christians too struggle with their fallen nature. Like the kings of ancient Israel, we fail to hearken to the word of the Lord and do what is evil in the Lord's sight. There is a debilitating disconnect between our original created design and our actual present corruption. Without this conflict, there would be no drama. The good news is that Jesus has fulfilled our covenant obligations for us, making possible a new covenant, a new pouring out of the Spirit (Joel 2:28; Acts 2:16-17) and a circumcision of the heart (Deut 30:6). These are the necessary conditions for the very possibility of Christian discipleship.

There are neither armchair nor automaton disciples. As believers we have been made new in Christ, yet we must make every effort to respond to our calling. The gospel involves indicatives and imperatives alike: we are in Christ, even as we must become more like Christ. This is the fundamental reason why theology and spiritual formation belong together. Both are vital ingredients in the making of disciples.

Discipleship is dramatic because it is possible to deny one's calling, at least on certain occasions (Peter did it three times). There are many obstacles and stumbling blocks along the Christian way. There are also other gospels and false doctrines to mislead the would-be disciple. Idolatry—an orientation to what is *not* God—is an ever-present danger.

---

[5]C. S. Lewis says, "Every Christian is to become a little Christ. The whole purpose of becoming a Christian is simply nothing else" (*Mere Christianity* [New York: Touchstone, 1996], 154).

"What do you want to *be* when you grow up?" Adults are increasingly asking this perennial children's question of themselves. Theology, I submit, is about "growing up" into Christ. This involves knowing who Jesus is, understanding our identity "in Christ" and realizing our call to become what we are "in Christ." It follows that the true end of theology is not only theoretical knowledge, but spirituality: a matter of the heart, a dispositional way of being.

Let us call "spirit" that unique manner of being, doing and relating that defines a person at his or her heart. The self is like a communications center, and our personal identity is a function of the characteristic style of our relationships with others—the pattern of our response to being called by others and by God. "Spirit" is the name for the self's characteristic pattern of response to the call of God and the cries of others.[6] To be a disciple is to have a habitual pattern of Christlike response to the call of God: it is to have the "spirit" (and the Spirit) of Christ.

We are now in a position to make explicit the connection between theology, discipleship and spiritual formation. Doctrine sets forth in speech the new state of affairs "in Christ." Discipleship is the project of bringing our lives into correspondence with this state of affairs. Spiritual formation is that part of the process whereby our spirits—our habitual way of responding to the call of God and others on our lives—are formed into a particular identity.

Spiritual formation does not take place in a vacuum. On the contrary, spiritual formation is happening always, everywhere and to everyone. There are cultural powers and principalities at work to shape our habits of seeing, thinking and doing. Culture constitutes the nurture side of the nature/nurture debate regarding what makes us who we are. What culture cultivates is the human spirit. Indeed, a culture is nothing less than a strategy for cultivating a particular shape of life, a means of spiritual formation.

Consider the idea of career. The headlong pursuit of career has become for many North Americans a golden calf to which we devote our lives and, at the limit, sacrifice our children. As such, it is perhaps the dominant symptom of our spiritual malformation. For many, career has become the chief means to the end of self-fulfillment. That we tend to regard personal

---

[6]See further Alistair I. McFayden, *The Call to Personhood: A Christian Theory of the Individual in Social Relationships* (Cambridge: Cambridge University Press, 1990).

worth in terms of net worth shows how distorted our consumerist spirits have become. What our media and market-saturated contemporary culture ultimately forms are mean-spirited individuals who care more for themselves than for others.

What has systematic theology to do with the process of spiritual formation? In the first place, systematic theology deprograms those who have been brainwashed by false doctrine. The best tonic for the toxins of contemporary culture is the reminder of what is ultimately real—the way things are in Christ. Systematic theology sets forth in speech the reality of what *is* in Christ. Spiritual formation "is our continuing response to the reality of God's grace shaping us into the likeness of Jesus Christ, through the work of the Holy Spirit, in the community of faith, for the sake of the world."[7]

At its best, systematic theology "seeks to inform, guide and nurture the whole person, since it equips the saints to obey the Great Commandment, loving God with all our being—heart, soul, mind and strength—and our neighbors as ourselves."[8] When it is at its best, theology "informs, guides and nurtures the church's fundamental vocation: to serve as God's representatives in the world, sharing in the mission of the triune God."[9] Recall Jesus' last words on earth, spoken to his disciples: "But you will receive power when the Holy Spirit has come upon you, and you will be my witnesses in Jerusalem and in all Judea and Samaria, and to the end of the earth" (Acts 1:8).

What kind of spirit should characterize disciples who are called to be Christlike? I answer: the spirit of one who loves and obeys God with all one's heart, soul, mind and strength, one whose spirit has been conformed to Christ by the Holy Spirit.

LOVING GOD "WITH ALL YOUR HEART": RIGHTLY ORDERED DESIRES

Spiritual formation involves, first, coming to desire the same things that Jesus desired: sharing his passions.

---

[7]Jeffrey P. Greenman, "Spiritual Formation in Theological Perspective: Classic Issues, Contemporary Challenges," in Greenman and George Kalantzis, eds., *Life in the Spirit: Spiritual Formation in Theological Perspective* (Downers Grove, IL: IVP Academic, 2010), 24.

[8]Ibid., 34.

[9]Ibid., 35.

Orienting the heart. Augustine once asked a question that pierces to the heart of the disciple's vocation: What do I love when I love my God? Augustine realized, to his credit, that discipleship is a matter not only of the head (right thoughts) and hands (right deeds) but especially of the heart (right desires). He realizes that our sin—the disease of our spirit—is more than a matter of what one does. Many of us avoid the really bad things—stealing, committing adultery and murder—yet our hearts are feckless until they find repose in desiring God. Augustine realized that the real site of the battle between the savior and Satan, and thus the drama of discipleship, is the human heart.

One of the most important means the Holy Spirit uses to form Christ in us is Scripture: the Word of God that presents Christ in many and various ways. We tend to think of the Bible's authority in terms of content: it is authoritative because it speaks the truth. Yes! But we need to say more. Scripture is more than informative. It is formative and transformative, not least when it is a means of reordering our desires.

Elsewhere in this book we have explored the power of biblical metaphors and stories in shaping our imaginations. Here we would do well to remember that Paul associates the imagination with the "eyes of your hearts" (Eph 1:18). We can only desire God if we understand something of who and what God is, and we need both Word (the stories of the Bible) and Spirit (to open the eyes of our heart) to do that. As C. S. Lewis knew, the imagination allows us to *taste* with the heart what reason only *sees* in the mind's eye.

Martha Nussbaum calls for the literary imagination in public life: we need poets and novelists because "in today's political life we lack the capacity to see one another as fully human."[10] How much more do we need the biblical imagination to help us see one another as men and women created in the image of God, persons with eternal destinies. Abraham Kuyper says that the reason the Bible contains so many literary forms is that they enable revelation to strike all the chords of the human soul, and not the intellect only.[11]

James K. A. Smith makes a similar connection between the heart and our humanity, arguing that the primary purpose of Christian education is not

---

[10]Martha C. Nussbaum, *Poetic Justice: The Literary Imagination and Public Life* (Boston: Beacon Press, 1995), xiii.

[11]Abraham Kuyper, *Principles of Sacred Theology*, trans. J. Hendrik De Vries (Grand Rapids: Eerdmans, 1954), 520.

to inform the mind but to transform the imagination and to form good habits. "Because our hearts are oriented primarily by desire, by what we love, and because those desires are shaped and molded by the habit-forming practices in which we participate, it is the ritual and practices of the mall—the liturgies of mall and market—that shape our imaginations and how we orient ourselves to the world."[12] What he calls "liturgies" are those everyday habits that shape our character and desires.

Scripture's diverse literary forms contribute to what is ultimately a building project: an edification or "repair" of the reader's soul through canonical practices that renew our knowledge and refresh our love of God. In the words of Hugh of St. Victor: "Scripture teaches that which delights to know and that which is expedient to imitate."[13] Taken together, the stories, songs, promises, prophecies and teachings of Scripture soften hearts, orient desires, sharpen tastes, form beliefs, shape imaginations and prompt actions. To let the Word of Christ dwell in us richly (Col 3:15) is to have one's heart habituated in the way of Jesus.

Vocation as worship. What do we love when we love our God? Perhaps the best diagnostic test for assessing the spirit of our hearts is to ask, "What is my passion?" It is a revealing question. If you aren't sure how to answer, ask yourself another question: "In what area of life am I a big spender? Where do I spend the most energy, the most time, the most thought, the most money?" These are usually good indicators of where our treasure is, and where the passions of our hearts lie.

The wonder of the gospel is that it discloses the heart of God: God's passion for humanity. While we were yet sinners, God gave himself for us—poured himself out in the person of the Son into the fragility of human flesh and blood, and suffered for us to the point of death. The truth is patently obvious: *we* are God's passion! Surely our vocation is to express our gratitude to God in ways that are no less passionate. Those who follow Jesus will share Jesus' passion for God, the kingdom of God, the poor and the ministry of reconciliation.

---

[12]James K. A. Smith, *Desiring the Kingdom: Worship, Worldview, and Cultural Formation* (Grand Rapids: Baker, 2009), 25.

[13]Cited in Boyd Taylor Coolman, *The Theology of Hugh of St. Victor: An Interpretation* (Cambridge: Cambridge University Press, 2013), 134.

The Holy Spirit gives us a "new sense of the heart" that enables us not only to see but also to taste the goodness of the gospel, thus arousing our holy affections and producing new habits of holy practices.[14] The drama of discipleship is nothing less than the story of how the Spirit grafts us into the new humanity in Christ and thus draws us into the very life of God. What Edwards calls "spiritual perception" I am calling the eschatological imagination: the ability to view our individual lives as caught up in this triune drama.

For the Christian, there is ultimately only one answer to the question "What should I do with my life?" Love. We are nothing if we have not love. The apostle Paul writes that even if we have the kind of faith that can move mountains, we are nothing if we have not love (1 Cor 13:2). To share Christ's passion is to share Christ's love for the world. I can think of no more demanding vocation than to pour oneself out for others as a way of witnessing to the prior outpouring of the triune God in the missions of the Son and Spirit.

Loving God "With All Your Soul": Cultivating Virtue

Spiritual formation involves, second, cultivating the same qualities of soul that characterized Jesus' life and ministry, sharing the *habits* of Jesus' heart: the virtues.

Aristotle distinguished the intellectual from the moral virtues. Like the other virtues, the intellectual virtues are acquired habits—excellences—that involve a motivation to produce a desired end and reliable success in bringing about that end. Recent virtue epistemologists—philosophers who have retrieved Aristotle's virtue theory for the sake of modern theories of knowledge—argue that knowledge is achieved not merely by following right procedures (method) but also by cultivating right intellectual habits (virtue).[15] Gaining knowledge is a matter of becoming a certain kind of person—a person who exhibits the intellectual virtues, like honesty, impartiality, patience, humility and so on.

---

[14]See Michael J. McClymond and Gerald R. McDermott, *The Theology of Jonathan Edwards* (Oxford: Oxford University Press, 2012), 316.

[15]See Linda Trinkhaus Zagzebski, *Virtues of the Mind: An Inquiry into the Nature of Virtue and the Ethical Foundations of Knowledge* (Cambridge: Cambridge University Press, 1996); Robert C. Roberts, *Intellectual Virtues: An Essay in Regulative Epistemology*, 4th ed. (Oxford: Oxford University Press, 2010); W. Jay Wood, *Epistemology: Becoming Intellectually Virtuous* (Downers Grove, IL: IVP Academic, 1998).

Clearly Jesus was a person of intellectual virtue. But saying this does not go nearly far enough. As the wisdom of God made flesh, Jesus was the perfect embodiment of all the virtues, intellectual, moral and spiritual. If intellectual virtues are habits that lead a person to knowledge of the truth, and if moral virtues are habits that dispose a person to do the right thing, how might we define spiritual virtues? Here we can recall what we said earlier about "spirit" being the distinct style or pattern of a person's relationship to others. Think, for example, of the difference between a meek and a mean-spirited person. A spiritual virtue is a habit of communicative activity that is conducive to right relatedness to other persons, especially God. Jesus is the exemplar of the spiritual virtues, not least in his single-minded commitment to love, please and obey his heavenly Father (Jn 4:34). Jesus manifests the spiritual virtues by relating to God in ways that express his filial relationship, as well as the cardinal theological virtues: faith, hope and love.

Learning Christian judgment. According to William Ames, theology is "the teaching of living to God."[16] On this definition, Jesus is theology incarnate, for we best learn how to live to God by imitating him.[17] Doctrine sets forth in speech what *is* in Christ. Even the doctrine of the incarnation helps disciples to learn to live to God insofar as it teaches us about the self-abnegating humility of the eternal Son who was willing to make himself nothing in order to save sinners (Phil 2:5-11). The example of Jesus is all the curriculum disciples need.

Where do we learn Christ? From Scripture. Scripture is composed of a variety of kinds of discourse, all of which are profitable for *training* (Greek *paideia*; cf. 2 Tim 3:16) in Christlikeness. The Bible is authoritative not least in serving as a canonical pedagogue that instructs us in the mind of Christ. God gives us his Word and Spirit not simply to inform but to form and transform, to cultivate not only new thoughts but also *habits* of thought, a way of thinking in accordance with the gospel. The canon trains us to think evangelically. In Kuyperian terms, the canon *tunes* each string in our soul so that we vibrate in sympathy (in harmony) with what God is doing in Christ.[18]

---

[16]William Ames, *The Marrow of Theology* (Grand Rapids: Baker, 1997), 77.

[17]See further Jason B. Hood, *Imitating God in Christ: Recapturing a Biblical Pattern* (Downers Grove, IL: IVP Academic, 2013).

[18]Sympathetic vibration occurs when a passive string responds to external vibrations from another source.

In earlier chapters we compared Scripture to a transcript of what God has done (theodrama) and as a script that helps disciples understand how they can participate in what God is doing to renew all things. I argued that drama is a better way of thinking about the *form* of the story of God's doings precisely because we do not simply read about God but, through Scripture, God addresses us and thus draws us into the action. What we need to add here is that the *content* of the drama is an interpersonal action and relation.

Both Scripture and Christian doctrine give theatrical direction to disciples. We learn what the play is about and what our role is. We learn what has already been done (by God) and what remains to be done (by us). We also learn how a person's soul gets "played out" by the way a person responds to the call of God on his or her life. In particular, we learn about the consequences of making judgments about what to say and do in particular situations.

"Judgment" is the most basic level of thinking when we make our mind up about the most elementary things: "this is x"; "this is not x." The content of an act of judging is a proposition, something proposed for some kind of consideration, and perhaps action. We can agree or disagree with it, commend or condemn it, and so forth. We make judgments about truth, purpose, the good, the beautiful, the right—logical, teleological, moral, aesthetic, judicial decisions.

Training in right judgment gets even closer to what it means to have the mind of Christ. The apostle Paul exhorts those who are mature to "think this way" (his way, Christ's way) and, by implication, to "act this way" as well. In Philippians, Paul employs the term *phroneō* ("to think, judge, or give one's mind to") and its cognates ten out of the twenty-three times it occurs in his letters (1:7; 2:2 [twice]; 2:5; 3:15 [twice]; 3:19; 4:2; 4:10 [twice]). *Phronēsis* refers to reason in its practical rather than theoretical mode, but it doesn't follow that *phronēsis* has nothing to do with systematic theology. Insofar as it must deliberate on what to say and do to be faithful to the word of God in the face of intellectual and cultural problems, *phronēsis* is a form of practical reasoning too.

The culturally conditioned language or concepts need not be preserved, but the apostolic judgment that comes to light through these servant forms must be. In biblical discourse we have exemplary theological judgments rendered in a variety of particular ways. We learn a lesson about the nature of Christian freedom, for example, from Paul's epistle to Philemon. There Paul uses a very particular incident to communicate what being "in Christ" means in practice. The judgment Paul wants Philemon to make about his slave is but one concrete expression of his overall understanding of the new reality in Christ. This understanding is what lies behind and gets expressed in judgments about what to say and do as disciples. The patterns of judgments (e.g., the way Matthew reads the Old Testament that enables him to identify Jesus as the Messiah the prophets foretold) as well as the actual judgments themselves (e.g., the way Paul views everything "in Christ" as a new creation in 2 Cor 5:17) are paradigmatic in Scripture. What we learn from Scripture are *canonical universals*: embodiments of divinely authorized judgments in particular textual forms.

Vocation as witness. This is not the place to treat the nature of the human constitution as physical (body) and immaterial (soul). By *soul* I simply mean that animating principle that is the source of our activity, the core that lies beneath the surface of our bodies whose bodily and mental expressions have a distinct identity or signature. The soul is the spirit of our personhood. Human persons are ensouled bodies or embodied souls. If I speak of vocation as witness under the rubric of soul, then please, banish all thoughts of otherworldliness. The soul may be immaterial, but human persons are not: everything we say and do discloses the state of our soul. A person's words and deeds are witnesses that give eloquent testimony to their soul.

The disciple's calling is to imitate Christ's love for God with all of his or her soul. To love God with all your soul is to commit your whole life to a life of God-glorifying witness. Indeed, Hans Urs von Balthasar believes that it is possible to view a saint's entire life as an attempt to live out just one verse of Scripture. Talk about the drama of discipleship! In fact, the disciple's remit is even more ambitious: we are to do witness to the whole counsel of God (Acts 20:27).

Disciples are able to imitate Christ only as they learn how to act and react as he did to the call of God and others, only as they learn the characteristic reflexes of his soul. As I have suggested, these characteristic reflexes include filial obedience, as well as the theological virtues of faith, hope and love.[19]

N. T. Wright has written a helpful book on how Christians become virtuous. The most important thing that happens after disciples believe is the transformation of their character.[20] Central to Wright's account is his insistence that Jesus came not simply to provide an example but to inaugurate God's new creation. The transformation we're aiming for—Paul calls it "new humanity" (Eph 4:24; Col 3:10)—has already begun in Jesus, with his resurrection. The virtuous human life—putting on the mind of Christ—is a life shaped "by God's promised future" and lived "within the ongoing story of God's people."[21] After all, this is God's missionary purpose, the point of the whole drama: to bring heaven—the place where God's will is freely and joyfully performed—down to earth. Christian living in the present "consists of anticipating this ultimate reality through the Spirit-led, habit-forming, truly human practice of faith, hope, and love."[22] To put on virtue—to put on Christ—is to live in ways that anticipate the life in the age to come.

Wright invokes the concept of "eschatological authenticity," that is, rehearsing now what we will only fully become in the future. Wright calls it a God-given "second nature": "The authenticity that really matters is living in accordance with the genuine human being God is calling you to become."[23] Christian character formation is a matter of becoming what one *already is* in Christ. Wright argues that Paul has thoroughly Christianized the ancient pagan (Aristotelian) theory of virtue, not just because it features humility but also because it locates us in the story of Jesus Christ.[24] One of the most important habits Christians need to cultivate is reading the Bible: "The more you do it the more it will form the habits of mind and heart, soul and body, which will slowly but surely form your character into the likeness of Christ Jesus."[25]

---

[19]For a study of Jesus' exemplification of one of these theological virtues, see R. Michael Allen, *The Christ's Faith: A Dogmatic Account* (London and New York: T&T Clark, 2008).

[20]N. T. Wright, *After You Believe: Why Christian Character Matters* (New York: HarperOne, 2010), 26.

[21]Ibid., 57.

[22]Ibid., 67.

[23]Ibid., 108.

[24]Ibid., 261.

[25]Ibid., 262.

LOVING GOD "WITH ALL YOUR MIND":
TAKING CAPTIVE EVERY THOUGHT

Spiritual formation involves, third, the renewal of the mind to imagine the world as Scripture imagines it.

Becoming scripturally sapient. Many creatures great and small have *sentience*: the ability to have sensations and thus to have at least minimal awareness of the world. Only human creatures have the biological classification of *sapience* (*homo sapiens*) indicating not simply sensation and feeling but also deliberation and wisdom. According to Scripture, however, God has made foolish the sapience of this world (1 Cor 1:20). The "foolishness" of God—the cross of Christ—is "wiser than men" (1 Cor 1:25). Moreover, *homo sapiens* have rejected the knowledge of God available through nature and reason because of their rebellious hearts ("I don't *want* to know"), thus exchanging the truth about God for lies: "Claiming to be wise, they became fools" (Rom. 1:22).

To love God with all our minds—to achieve the wisdom of God embodied in Christ—thus requires radical remedial education. Thankfully God has given disciples a radical curriculum of Word and Spirit. Scripture is a scalpel and the Holy Spirit is the surgeon in whose hands the Word of God pierces to the division of soul and spirit (Heb 4:12). Scripture is one of the gifts of God for the people of God, a gift that does not merely inform but transforms us, precisely by forming Christ in us. We become wise when by the renewing of our minds we begin to think biblically.

To think biblically requires a revolution of our worldview. Consider the case of the apostle Paul. Acts 9 recounts Saul's enlightenment and apostolic commissioning on the road to Damascus, where a blinding light from heaven flashed, spoke and identified itself as Jesus (Acts 9:3-8). After three days without sight, Saul meets Ananias, regains his sight, is filled with the Holy Spirit and immediately begins proclaiming Jesus. Indeed, Saul does advanced theology, penetrating to the heart of the christological matter: "He is the Son of God" (Acts 9:20). He "confounded the Jews who lived in Damascus by proving that Jesus was the Christ" (Acts 9:22). The Greek verb for "prove" is *symbibazō*, which elsewhere means unite, knit together or put together in one's mind (as in gathering one's thoughts). Luke does not say how Saul made his case, but in the epistles he would later write the pattern of his reasoning is evident. In particular, Paul's "proof" to the Jews at Damascus that Jesus was the Christ involved reading the Jewish Scriptures in light of their fulfillment in the history of Jesus (and vice versa).

It is one thing to have the facts, quite another to know how they fit together. Thinking biblically about God, the world, Jesus Christ and ourselves requires more than information. Paul's preconversion style of thinking ("Saul") *knew* about the crucifixion of Jesus, but it was simply an item of knowledge in his overall ethnocentric narrative. It was only meeting the risen Christ that allowed Paul to come to his right mind and to see the cross for what it really was: "The power and the wisdom of God" (1 Cor 1:23-24). Paul is involved in remedial education too, helping others see how the Old Testament makes sense of Jesus (and vice versa).

The drama of discipleship involves becoming wise in Christ. This means coming to understand God and ourselves with the symbolic resources of Scripture (types and figures), especially as these come to a head in the history of Jesus Christ: "These symbols . . . show us who we are."[26] The drama of discipleship is less about identifying key propositional truths than inhabiting the Bible's symbolic universe. It involves our ability to indwell the richly patterned story-world of the canon, to imagine the world that Scripture imagines and to mirror in our lives the reality that Scripture mirrors—what I have previously called *canon-sense*.[27]

To learn canon sense is to cultivate what St. Athanasius referred to as the "mind of Scripture." No one has the mind of Scripture more than Jesus himself, of course. And this is largely because Jesus was able to answer the key questions that defined his life—Who am I? What is my mission?—because he knew in which drama he was acting. Jesus tried to help his disciples to imagine the world Scripture imagines too, not least by teaching them in parables about the kingdom of God.

Vocation as wisdom. Spiritual formation involves remedial education, what Paul calls "the renewal of your mind" (Rom 12:2). The biblical Word and the Holy Spirit work together both to renew and to illumine minds.

---

[26]James M. Hamilton Jr., *What Is Biblical Theology? A Guide to the Bible's Story, Symbolism, and Patterns* (Wheaton, IL: Crossway, 2014), 90.

[27]See Luke Timothy Johnson, "Imagining the World Scripture Imagines," in L. Gregory Jones and James J. Buckley, eds., *Theology and Scriptural Imagination* (Oxford: Blackwell, 1998), 3-18.

Christian doctrine can help too. Ellen Charry's book *By the Renewing of Your Minds: The Pastoral Function of Christian Doctrine* argues that doctrine is good for our spiritual health—and, I would add, for our discipleship. Charry also speaks of sapience: "Sapience includes correct information about God but emphasizes attachment to that knowledge. Sapience is engaged knowledge that emotionally connects the knower to the known."[28] We love God and come to grow like him in part by coming to know him and to behave in ways that befit what we know. When we know what God is like and what God has done, we learn to trust God in life and death. Learning that trust is what the drama of discipleship is all about: it is the story of becoming a holy nation, a God-ward people.

Every disciple is called to exhibit the wisdom of Jesus Christ. This involves practicing what we know about God, the gospel and ourselves. And it all begins with a conversion of our minds—our thoughts and imaginations—when we come to see, accept and trust the goodness of God as it has been revealed in Christ and the cross. Wisdom is the ability to see how Christ is the center of both the created and the renewed order, and thus to see the place of disciples in the grand scheme of things. Being wise unto Christ involves not merely assenting to but practicing what we know. It is a matter of practicing the premise, presence and promise of God.

The vocation of the disciple is to wake up to what is real—the meaning of the whole of history revealed in Christ—and to stay awake. Interestingly, Jesus' disciples were most apt to fall asleep when they were supposed to be praying. Both prayer and theology helps us remain awake and aware of the truth of our being in Christ, the reality of our adoption into God's family, with all the rights and responsibilities that entails: "Now the moment of prayer," says Lewis, "is for me . . . the awareness, the re-awakened awareness that this 'real world' and 'real self' are very far from being rock-bottom realities."[29]

"But we have the mind [*nous*] of Christ" (1 Cor 2:16). Paul is not saying that we have the same beliefs—much less brainwaves—as the historical Jesus did. We are neither carbon nor cerebral copies of Jesus Christ. In context, Paul is explaining why the wise of this age do not understand the

---

[28]Ellen T. Charry, *By the Renewing of Your Minds: The Pastoral Function of Christian Doctrine* (Oxford: Oxford University Press, 1997), 4.

[29]C. S. Lewis, *Letters to Malcolm: Chiefly on Prayer* (New York: Harcourt, Brace & World, 1964), 81.

wisdom of God. They cannot accept, or even comprehend, the thoughts of God because they do not have the Spirit of God, or the big biblical picture. By "mind of Christ" Paul means not simply to our information-processing faculty but our faculty of judgment: that orientation of heart vis-à-vis the drama of redemption out of which proceeds decisions about the issues of life. The drama of discipleship is simply the process of the Spirit using God's Word to form the mind of Christ in us one day, and one decision, at a time.

LOVING GOD "WITH ALL YOUR STRENGTH": CONFORMING ONE'S LIFE TO CHRIST

Spiritual formation involves, finally, the continual strengthening of the heart, soul and mind by constantly practicing the presence (and activity) of Christ in the power of the Spirit.

Growing stronger. Strength pertains to the very real human energy needed to bring about changes or to get things moving. To love God with all one's strength means to do the will of God in action and deed rather than in theory only. Is it possible that our work can be an aspect of our larger Christian vocation? Can we be disciples even as we do our household chores? That will indeed be my suggestion.

"I can do all things through him who strengthens me" (Phil 4:13). This is crucial. We do not grow as disciples through our own efforts. It requires grace. Yet Scripture, like Christ himself, is full of grace as well as truth. It is thanks to Christ's Spirit's ministering the Word of Christ to our minds, hearts and souls that we have the strength through Christ to follow Christ. And, as in weightlifting, we become stronger by carrying one another's burdens—doing "reps" of love.

Everyday life affords plenty of opportunities to practice the way of Jesus Christ. For example, Scripture trains us never to treat anything that is not God as if it were God. Non-Christians typically lack this skill: they treat things that are not God as God. We call this idolatry. You don't have to worship images carved in wood to be an idolater—Paul mentions some whose god is their stomach. Others worship money, sex or some kind of power. Disciples grow stronger in the faith as they learn to respect the Creator/creature distinction on a daily basis.

Scripture is profitable for "training in righteousness" (2 Tim 3:16). Scripture trains us to see things rightly and act as followers of Christ—and citizens of the gospel—by presenting us with both good and bad examples of discipleship. The chief example, of course, is Jesus himself (Jn 13:15; 1 Tim 1:16; 1 Pet 2:21). By attending to Scripture and in particular to Christ, disciples learn righteousness, or what we might call *right theodramatic judgment*: namely, the ability to speak and act in every situation in ways that advance the drama of redemption, further the mission of the church and increase the knowledge and love of God (cf. 2 Cor 10:15; Phil 4:17; Col 1:6, 10; 1 Thess 3:12; 2 Thess 1:3).

Discipleship as vocation. The special calling of the disciple is to follow Jesus and thus to love God with all our heart, mind, soul and strength. The calling is to love God *in* and *as* we go about our daily life and work. All baptized members of Christ's body are by definition full-time disciples, but they are not "professionals." There is no such thing as either part-time or professional disciples.

We have already mentioned the role of informing, forming and transforming the hearts, minds and souls of disciples. In conclusion, I want to talk about the peculiar strength required for *conforming* spirits to Christ. The Latin *conformare* means "to make of the same form." This is precisely the vocation of the church: to make disciples, people who have the same "form" as Jesus Christ: that is, the form of a servant, the form of a son—not to mention the form of prophets, priests and kings, the offices that make up the holy nation. In the final analysis, God is not shaping individuals only, but a people. It's a long-term building project. Israel had to spend forty years wandering in the wilderness in order to be formed into a people who knew how to obey and worship rightly. Paul says their story was written for our instruction (1 Cor 10:11). Let's not repeat their mistake!

Disciples cannot conform themselves to Christ through the flesh alone. In acting out the life of Christ, disciples rely not on moral strivings but on what is eschatologically already the case: that we are "his workmanship, created in Christ Jesus for good works" (Eph 2:10). As Herman Ridderbos rightly observes, the change of costume—the putting off of the old humanity and the putting on of the new—is not something we do (a step in our personal *ordo salutis*) but something Christ has accomplished (an event in the *historia salutis*): "If anyone is in Christ, he is a new creation" (2 Cor 5:17).[30] It is the special role of the Holy Spirit to make us Christlike. The Spirit ministers Christ, the new man in Christ and nothing but Christ. To put on the new man is not to pretend to be something we're not; rather, it is to participate in the new humanity that is in Christ. In putting on the new self, we are but corresponding to the way things are "in Christ." It takes eschatological imagination to see what is already/not yet in Christ.

Holy Scripture is written in ordinary language but communicates an extraordinary culture: a set of belief, values and practices that correspond to the new created order "in Christ." God gives us Scripture to help us understand what is in Christ, and to render us right-minded and right-hearted readers, able to play our parts in the drama of redemption as witnesses to this reality with both scriptural fidelity and improvisational freedom. Scripture's role in the economy of revelation and redemption is that of finishing school. It is the Spirit's curriculum for imparting habits of right thinking and desiring, for cultivating the mind of Christ in his disciples.

CONCLUSION: HABITS OF THE DISCIPLE'S HEART

To fulfill our vocation as disciples of Jesus Christ, we must attend to theology not only for the sake of intellectual information but also of spiritual formation. Disciples do not act out Christ from a propositional template that lists his qualities. Rather they act from the inside out, from the heart where the Word of Christ dwells richly, to the external world where the form of Christ takes concrete shape in the disciples' speech and actions. *The drama of discipleship is a matter of acting out what is in Christ, and doing it from the inside out.*

What defines us as disciples is who we are in Christ, something we learn by looking intently into the mirror of Scripture. The gospel involves indicatives: statements about what is the case ("You have been crucified and raised with Christ"). Inside those indicatives we hear the whisper of an imperative: become what you are in Christ. There are two things that help us do this.

Reading and studying Scripture. "Let the word of Christ dwell in you richly" (Col 3:16). When the Spirit impresses the words of Scripture on our

---

[30]Herman Ridderbos, *Paul: An Outline of His Theology* (Grand Rapids: Eerdmans, 1997), 63.

hearts, we have a better grasp of who we are in Christ.[31] The Spirit renews our minds by rehearsing what was happened in the theodrama, thereby enabling us to see and savor its beauty and excellency.[32]

Corporate worship. A second means of spiritual formation is shared worship. Scripture may be the soul of theology, but doxology is the soul's embodiment: "Present your bodies as a living sacrifice" (Rom 12:1). There is no more theodramatic act than sharing the Lord's Supper. The central actions—breaking and taking the bread, pouring and passing the wine—not only recapitulates what Christ has done but, as we do it in remembrance of him, *performs* it. Communicants enact the communion they have with one another in Christ: "Such worship is the central performance that trains and rehearses us for the rest of our lives."[33]

While doctrine sets forth in speech the goodness, truth and beauty of what is in Christ, worship sets forth in the church's corporate life, and discipleship sets forth in the life of individual Christians. Each day affords us plenty of opportunities to act out what is in Christ by presenting our bodies as living sacrifices. Through reading Scripture, learning doctrine and doing church, disciples sharpen the sense of their hearts to embody the mind of Christ by second (spiritual) nature. We have the mind/spirit of Christ because we have the Spirit of Christ dwelling in us.

---

[31]N. T. Wright puts reading Scripture at the top of his circle of virtue because "soaking oneself in Scripture . . . has been seen from the earliest days of Christianity as central to the formation of Christian character" (*After You Believe*, 261).

[32]McClymond and McDermott, *Theology of Jonathan Edwards*, 378.

[33]Shannon Craiggo-Snell, *The Empty Church: Theater, Theology, and Bodily Hope* (Oxford: Oxford University Press, 2014), 5.

nine

THE STRANGE NEW STATUS
SYMBOL OF THE CROSS

A SERMON ON PHILIPPIANS 2:5-11

*In view of the focus of this second gallery of pictures on the church's witness
to the drama of the Christ, it seems appropriate to include this piece on the
significance of the climax of the drama of redemption: Jesus' crucifixion. I
preached this sermon in a Wheaton College chapel service in March 2008, two
days before Good Friday, a date that influenced my choice of biblical text. The
title is a play on Karl Barth's 1916 address to the church in Lentwil, "The
Strange New World Within the Bible." The cross turns everything upside down,
including social expectations about a person's status or worth. Somewhere
about this time I came across Alain de Botton's eye-opening book* Status
Anxiety. *My sermon brings the liberating message of the cross to bear on the
world of undergraduates, which I know from experience (my own and my
daughters') to be pockmarked by status anxiety. During my research for* The
Drama of Doctrine, *I discovered to my surprise that status is an important
concept in theatrical improvisation. Theater is one person presenting herself
to another, and every such personal interaction also involves a status trans-
action to the extent that every encounter affects a person's sense of worth. The
following sermon thus draws from three tributaries: status anxiety, status
transactions and the "wonderful exchange" of status (justification) that is the
result of the cross of Christ. This too is part of the drama of discipleship:
bearing witness in every personal encounter to the strange new status logic of
the Christian faith.*

INTRODUCTION: STATUS SYMBOLISM AND REALITY

It is a truth universally acknowledged, that a single man (or woman), whether in possession of a fortune or not, must be in want of a status symbol. All of us, single or married of whatever age, rely on various ways of signaling our place in the social pecking order.

Status means standing (from Latin *stare* "to stand"), and refers to one's social, professional or legal position in the world: royal or commoner, white collar or blue collar, master or slave, innocent or guilty, winner or loser. There are ways of assessing a person's status wherever two or more are gathered: every class, tribe or culture has its own ways of determining an individual's standing in a group. The spectrum ranges from "at the top of the pile" to "at the bottom of the heap." We recognize our superiors and inferiors and treat them accordingly. We defer to people of high status and expect those who have less status than we do to defer to us. Status colors almost all our interactions with other people. Status isn't static, however. Rather, like the money in your bank account, your status capital goes up and down depending on your performance—in the classroom, on the athletic field and on the stage of life.

Three types of status in particular go a long way toward informing our sense of who we are. In the academy, we are tempted to define ourselves by our scholastic status (intelligence or, failing that, education). In society, we tend to define ourselves by our social status (rank, salary, fame). And in Christian communities, we often define ourselves by our spirituality. It is important to most of us to maintain a certain standing in the eyes of our family, friends, teachers, neighbors and colleagues. Status-hunger—the desire to increase our status—motivates much, if not most, of what we do: the way we dress, converse and generally present ourselves to others. For some, status is a function of GPA; for others, of one's MBA; for still others (specifically baseball players), of RBIs.

Neither self-perception nor self-conception is an accurate indicator of our real worth. Nor is popular opinion. If status were simply a function of how other people perceive us, a function of popular opinion, then it would be wholly subjective. Society may indeed determine value that way, but Christian disciples are citizens of a different status kingdom. Disciples need to take periodic status reality checks, and to do that we need to come to the foot of the cross. For there is a fourth kind of status—our theological status—that trumps all the others. Theological status reveals our standing in the eyes of God. With the apostle Paul, we must get into the habit of asking ourselves the critical question, "Are we now seeking the approval of men, or of God?" (Gal 1:10).

Status symbols. A status symbol is an external sign that alerts others to one's standing in the group. They are meant to be fairly obvious: the number of stripes on a uniform or feathers in a war bonnet, the degrees before and after a person's name, one's ranking in the Forbes 100. I'm wearing two status symbols now: the ring on my fourth finger indicates my marital status (married, hence unavailable), and my tie indicates my alma mater (Cambridge University). Many status symbols are less formal: the Porsche, the designer clothes or watch, the bling. My mother used to judge a person's status by his or her shoes.

Too many people believe their own status publicity. They think, "I must be bright—I get straight As"; or "I must be popular—look at how many friends I have on Facebook." Or: "I must be spiritual—they made me an elder." Yet these external appearances often hide a very different internal reality. We are often unsure of where we stand with others. This uncertainty generates status anxiety: the crippling worry that we may not be good enough, that we don't live up to the standards by which the world measures us or simply that for some reason people don't like us. Status anxiety is the penetrating dread that underneath the glittering image we project lies an abject failure. In those moments of quiet desperation we think, "I'm a fraud. I don't really belong here. I don't deserve this goodwill. Don't they know how ignorant I am, how relationally inept, how little I love God?"

Status anxiety: an old/new social epidemic. Status anxiety can strike anytime, anywhere and with anyone. Whenever we're with others the conditions are ripe. When it happens, it feels as though we are besieged. It's not simply an anxiety attack—it's a *status anxiety* attack: a panicky feeling that others may regard us with contempt. Status anxiety attacks are psychological earthquakes whose fault line runs right through our core sense of self worth. I am not aware that anyone has ever died from a status anxiety attack—only that they wished they had died.

Alain de Botton has written a fascinating book on the subject called *Status Anxiety*.[1] The first five chapters treat the causes (e.g., expectation, meritocracy, snobbery), the last five the solutions (e.g., philosophy, art, politics, religion). According to de Botton, status anxiety afflicts as many people as the common cold. Everyone is vulnerable because our self-assessment of our looks, intelligence and even spirituality depends so much on how others view us. Other people's attention matters to us "because we labor under a congenital uncertainty as to our own value."[2] Life, says Botton, is defined by two great love stories: the quest for romantic love and the lesser known quest for love from the world. What better way to relieve one's status anxiety than to be worshiped and adored? Karl Marx got it wrong: the kind of capital we most desire is not monetary but social.

I can relate to what de Botton is talking about. I had a particularly acute status anxiety attack in 1985. I had successfully defended my doctoral dissertation but had to jump one last hurdle before I could graduate. I had to purchase an academic gown from the university outfitters (that's British English for "clothing store"). Here I need to provide a bit of back story in order to give you the full context of my ordeal. The term "snobbery" originated in the 1820s in Oxbridge (that's snobbish for "Oxford and Cambridge"). The term derives from the Latin *sine nobilitate* ("without nobility") and was used to distinguish "ordinary" students from their aristocratic peers. So there I was, a newly minted PhD. But in that outfitter's shop, amidst the specialist salesclerks, I felt like the commoner I really was: a Californian Yankee in Sir Isaac Newton's court, who had neither the right accent nor the technical terms to place his order. I must have sounded like a Starbucks customer: "I'd like a tall skim robé with doctoral drizzle down the front, no zip." The salesclerk, an immaculately dressed and manicured man, my senior in every respect, gave me a withering look that confirmed what I already knew: I was a person of little social worth, of a certain academic status, to be sure, but entirely without nobility, and ultimately an impostor who did not deserve to graduate from Cambridge!

Status anxiety attacks both individuals and whole epochs. Modernity was afraid of the dark. We can view the Enlightenment as an acute knee jerk

---

[1] Alain de Botton, *Status Anxiety* (New York: Pantheon, 2004).
[2] Ibid., 8.

status reflex that positioned itself against the "Dark" ages. Similarly, post-modernity resembles a prolonged anxiety over the status of modernity itself, especially as concerns the latter's trust in reason and the scientific method—the status quo. No wonder we're suffering from status insecurity: How can we stand firm when the foundations themselves are shaking? Who will wake us from this Narnian nightmare where it is always Lent, but never Easter?

What is the proper Christian response to status anxiety? The events of Holy Week two thousand years ago have a direct bearing on this question. The apostle Paul plots the whole career of the Word made flesh—from heavenly pre-existence to incarnate earthly existence to risen new existence—in a single paragraph (Phil 2:5-11). This passage gets us to the heart of what happened on Good Friday and Easter Sunday, and thus to the sacred head and heart of Jesus. It is there, in Christ, that we will ultimately find the answer to our status anxiety.

Status anxiety in the church: yesterday and today. The church at Philippi, to whom Paul wrote his epistle, knew all about status anxiety. In particular they had to worry about their socio-political standing as Christians in the Roman Empire. Philippi was a Roman colony and thus the Philippians enjoyed citizenship, but Christians did not take part in pagan festivals, especially those that honored the Emperor. To complicate matters more, their leader, the apostle Paul, was imprisoned by the Praetorian Guard. Paul was on the wrong side of the Empire.

Churches in twenty-first century North America have challenges too, though at least we do not have to worry about our status in the empire. Or do we? The political philosophers Michael Hardt and Antonio Negri have recently argued that empire is alive and well, though it is now disguised as something other than a nation-state. "Our basic hypothesis," they write, "is that sovereignty has taken a new form."[3] Globalization has created a new worldwide order of production and marketing that effectively regulates the exchange of money, people and goods that make up modern life. Unlike Roman imperialism, which had fixed boundaries, this new empire is decentered, yet precisely for that reason it encompasses the entire globe.

How does empire rule this new global economy? Hardt and Negri's

---

[3]Michael Hardt and Antonio Negri, *Empire* (Cambridge, MA: Harvard University Press, 2000), xii.

answer is instructive: "The creation of wealth tends ever more towards what we call biopolitical production, the production of social life itself, in which the economic, the political, and the cultural increasingly overlap and invest one another."[4] This subterranean empire rules social life in its entirety. The sovereignty of ancient Rome was a function of its hardware: legions, columns, arches, Senate—and instruments of capital punishment, like crucifixion. By contrast, the new empire rules by software: sociocultural programming and the various rhetorical strategies the new media employs to market not only goods but lifestyles. We don't have to agree with the details of their theory to see what the authors are getting at. Even the most powerful nations can no longer simply impose their wills on the world. The real superpower today is the global communications-marketing technocracy. Ancient Rome is small potatoes compared to today's postindustrial-business-entertainment complex.

As in ancient Philippi, so our present-day Western churches struggle with status anxiety in the face of the new empire of popular culture. Like status-anxious individuals, we are tempted to employ the tools of empire—mass marketing, music videos and other tools from the merchants of cool—in order to achieve larger numbers of adherents, more money and more programs in order to be reckoned successful in the eyes of the world. In the present-day empire of popular culture, success and high status are ultimately a matter of what sells. Popularity is next to godliness. The community of the faithful must beware its own empire-building temptation, for our Lord marches to the beat of a different drama.

PAUL'S CONCERN: LIVING AS MINDFUL CITIZENS OF THE GOSPEL

Paul's christological hymn in Philippians 2:6-11 is as relevant to us today as it was for the church at Philippi two thousand years ago. Ralph Martin notes that "Christian hymns expose the nerve ends of the gospel itself."[5] As mentioned earlier, this brief passage also exposes the bookends of the Son's life, from his self-emptying journey into the far country (humiliation) to his

---

[4]Ibid., xiii.

[5]Ralph Martin, "Hymns in the New Testament," in Geoffrey Bromiley, ed., *International Standard Bible Encyclopedia*, vol. 2 (Grand Rapids: Eerdmans, 1982), 789. See also Ralph P. Martin, *A Hymn of Christ: Philippians 2:5-11 in Recent Interpretation and in the Setting of Early Christian Worship* (Downers Grove, IL: InterVarsity Press, 1997).

homecoming and divine coronation (exaltation). Indeed, looking at the bookends, we find that the whole story of the Son can be told as a series of status transactions.

"*. . . worthy of the gospel . . .*" *(1:27)*. The Christ hymn is part of a series of exhortations that begins in Philippians 1:27: "Only let the manner of your life be worthy of the gospel of Christ." The presence of the word *only* acts as a raised index finger emphasizing the speaker's point: "just one thing . . ." Well, what is it? What's so important as to elicit this rhetorical highlighting? The answer is in the verb Paul uses, and it's an unusual one: *politeuomai*. It derives from the Greek term *polis* ("city-state"), from which we get our word *politics*, and means "to live as a citizen." Christians are not earthly citizens but citizens of the gospel of Jesus Christ. Furthermore, he adds that we are to live as becomes citizens of the gospel—*worthily* [*axiōs*]. Later in the epistle he tells the Philippians "our citizenship is in heaven" (3:20). We may paraphrase Paul's thought as follows: "As citizens of heaven conduct yourselves in your day-to-day life in a manner that reflects the gospel." Citizenship in the city of God evidently requires a manner of life to which citizens of Rome were not accustomed. It is one thing to serve Caesar, another to serve Christ. Christian citizenship was a threat to the glory of Rome, which presumably is why Paul encourages his readers not to be "frightened in anything by your opponents" (Phil 1:28).

In addition to the external opposition of the Roman Empire, the church at Philippi faced an internal threat: disunity and factionalism. Paul urges the Philippians to "stand firm in one spirit, with one mind striving side by side for the faith of the gospel" (1:27). He makes a special point of encouraging the Philippians to be united, especially in their thinking. In 2:2 he asks them to complete his joy "by being of the same mind, having the same love, being in full accord and of one mind." Note that this implies not seeking to improve our own social status: "Do nothing from selfish ambition or conceit, but in humility count others more significant than yourselves" (Phil 2:3).

"*Have this mind . . .*" *(2:5)*. "Mindfulness" is all the rage these days. Especially when associated with yoga classes, it refers to the quiet, accepting awareness of everything you are experiencing in the present moment—especially our breathing. We're told that practicing mindfulness even a few minutes a day can relieve stress and prolong our lives. Accordingly, mindfulness is now part of many school programs and corporate cultures. If mindfulness is the opposite of thoughtlessness, what's not to like—especially if it frees us from anxiety?[6]

At first glance, it appears that the apostle Paul is getting in on the act too. Philippians is filled with references to *minds* and *minding*. *Phroneō* is the key verb in the epistle and pertains to thinking. It is also the term Aristotle uses for "practical reason"—reasoning about what to do in a particular situation. Paul uses the term in 2:2, where he exhorts his readers to be "of the same mind." Paul mentions it twice in the same verse, so it must be important. What does it mean to be "of the same mind"? Is Paul advocating mindfulness? Does he want the church to be a collection of Stepford wives and husbands who in the words of one commentator "all have to wear grey and eat gruel at every meal"?[7]

Paul is not asking members of the church at Philippi to become robots marching in lockstep. Neither is he asking them to empty their minds of everything. On the contrary, he's asking them to adopt the same perspective—a gospel-centered perspective—so that together they will understand their situation rightly and act accordingly. By "their situation" I mean their status as citizens not only of Philippi but, more importantly, of the gospel. Paul is asking the Philippians to adopt a common pattern of thinking and acting that focuses not on ingratiating themselves with the Roman Empire but rather on living in a way that befits the kingdom of God. It takes *phronēsis* (practical reasoning) to be a disciple.

And so at last to our main text: "Have this mind among yourselves, which is yours in Christ Jesus" (Phil 2:5). There's that word again, *phroneō*, this time as a verb in the imperative: "Have this mind" or "your attitude should be" (NIV).[8] The mind indeed holds a special place for Paul in the Christian life. How does Pauline mindfulness differ from its Buddhist or secular counterparts? It's an excellent question. Paul is asking his readers neither to empty

---

[6]As many books promise it does. See John P. Forsyth and George H. Eifert, *The Mindfulness and Acceptance Workbook for Anxiety: A Guide to Breaking Free from Anxiety, Phobias and Worry Using Acceptance and Commitment Therapy* (Oakland, CA: New Harbinger Publications, 2008).

[7]Stephen E. Fowl, *Philippians*, The Two Horizons New Testament Commentary (Grand Rapids: Eerdmans, 2005), 83.

[8]The NIV translation of Philippians 2:5 reads "Your attitude should be the same as that of Christ Jesus."

their minds of belief nor to add one more belief to faith's inventory. Having
the same mind involves more than entertaining a particular set of ideas. It
has nothing to do with brainwashing. Paul is after bigger game than ideology.
Paul wants to change the software that governs his readers' thinking. He
wants to convert our imaginations. "Have this mind among yourselves"
means something like "adopt this pattern of thinking, acting and feeling."
Which pattern? The pattern that Christ displays (embodies) in the hymn of
Philippians 2:6-11: the drama of the Son coming to earth as a lowly servant
and returning to heaven as an exalted Lord.

THE TEMPLATE FOR GOSPEL CITIZENSHIP: THE MIND OF CHRIST (PHILIPPIANS 2:6-8)

It's all laid out in poetic form in verses 6-8. Christ Jesus was in the form of
God (a status greater than which cannot be conceived), but made himself
nothing, taking the form of a servant, that is, a human being. Then, as a
human, he humbled himself even further, becoming obedient to the point
of death—indeed, the lowest kind of death, death on a cross. This is a striking
summary of the gospel that rehearses in short compass the main action of
the drama of the Christ—from Christmas to the cross—in a scant three
verses. Let's examine them more closely, keeping in mind Paul's exhortation:
"Have *this* mind"—the mind of Christ.

"In the form of God . . ." (2:6). Verse 6 says that Christ was originally in
the "form of God." It is not altogether clear what "form" amounts to, but
minimally we could say that the visible form of God is his glory, the external
manifestation of what God is (cf. Jn 17:5).[9] God is invisible, but his glory is
not. The eternal Son is "the radiance of the glory of God and the exact imprint of his nature" (Heb 1:3). To share in the glory of God is to enjoy the
highest possible status. Indeed, the Son enjoyed "equality" (some commentators explain this as "pre-existence") with God. Yet, though he was clothed
with the majesty of God, he did not think to use this equality to further his
own cause. The Son did not consider his high status or glorious form as

---

[9]I cannot possibly hope to do justice to all the exegetical issues raised by this marvelous hymn to
Christ. Readers looking for sustained exegetical attention are advised to consult the commentaries, in particular Peter T. O'Brien, *The Epistle to the Philippians*, New International Greek Testament Commentary (Grand Rapids: Eerdmans, 1991), 186-270.

something to exploit. Here's how Eugene Peterson translates verse 6 in *The Message*: "He had equal *status* with God but didn't think so much of himself that he had to cling to the advantages of that status no matter what."[10]

"Emptied himself" (2:7). While verse 6 tells us what the Son did *not* do, verse 7 tells us what he *did*: he "emptied himself." We should not take this overly literally, as if the Son poured out his divine being as we might pour out the contents of a bucket. Paul is referring to the incarnation of the Son, his becoming flesh (while *remaining* God). The point is that the Son gave up his divine prerogatives (e.g., his glory) in order to become one of us. He took the form of a slave, a person with a distinct lack of glory, lacking even the most basic civil rights. Out of obedience to the Father and love for the world, the Son emptied himself of all status privileges: "for your sake he became poor" (2 Cor 8:9). It is vital to understand that the Son did not give up his divinity. It is not that he "*exchanged* the form of God for the form of a slave, but that he *manifested* the form of God in the form of a slave."[11] Already we see that Paul is out to demolish the status systems of the world (cf. 2 Cor 10:4-5).

"Humbled himself" (2:8). The Son did something else: "He humbled himself" (2:8). Note that Paul does not say, "He was humiliated." The Son is not a passive victim but a willing agent of his humbling.[12] Moreover, the "humbling" in question involves descending to the very lowest of estates: a criminal's death by crucifixion—"he humbled himself and became obedience to the point of death—even death on a cross."

Instead of insisting on the honor he deserved, Jesus relinquished what most people desperately want to hold onto: the world's good opinion. In the course of humbling himself, Jesus had to stand before representatives of imperial Rome. From a human perspective, this is surely a status anxiety–generating prospect:

---

[10]Larry Hurtado also makes use of the status concept in his comment on this passage: "'Being in the form of God' is surely best taken to represent a different and prior status or mode of being much higher than being human, which he chose not to exploit for his own advantage" ("A 'Case Study' in Early Christian Devotion to Jesus: Philippians 2:6-11," in *How on Earth Did Jesus Become a God? Historical Questions About Earliest Christian Devotion to Jesus* [Grand Rapids: Eerdmans, 2005], 102).

[11]F. F. Bruce, "St. Paul in Macedonia: The Philippian Correspondence, Pt. 3," in *Bulletin of the John Rylands Library* 63 (1980–1981): 270 (emphasis added).

[12]A point recognized by both Søren Kierkegaard and Karl Barth, as evidenced by the latter's citing the former: "Christ humbled himself—not, he was humbled" (Karl Barth, *The Epistle to the Philippians*, trans. J. W. Leitch [London: 1962], 64; emphasis original).

to stand as a solitary individual before the greatest power the world had ever known. In the eyes of that Empire, Jesus was regarded as no better than a common criminal. Moreover, the Empire sentenced him to die as only those of the lowest status did: on a cross. Humbling here becomes humiliation. Yet, strictly speaking, Rome did not take his life: "No one takes my life from me" (Jn 10:18). Even his dying was his own doing, part and parcel of his self-humbling.

Far from negating his divinity, then, Jesus' incarnate life and death *defines* it. In refusing to hold on to his elevated status and making himself nothing, Christ does not stop being God but displays God's true form. The Son's self-emptying was not a quirky, isolated out-of-character act but a demonstration of God's true character. Our sovereign God is a self-giving God. On the cross, the Roman Empire met the kingdom of God, but did not prevail against it.

THE "WONDROUS (STATUS) EXCHANGE": FROM LORD TO LOWEST (AND BACK AGAIN) (PHILIPPIANS 2:9-11)

We've now discovered the pattern of thinking and acting that Paul wants us to adopt. But that's not the end of the story, or of Paul's hymn.

"Therefore God has highly exalted him" (2:9). The sun comes out over the second half of the Christ hymn. Or rather, the Son comes out, and returns home. Commentators cannot help but call attention to the decidedly different tone and content of verses 9-11 compared to the three preceding verses. There is a dramatic change of subject: God the Father is now the subject of the verbs. It is a startling reversal. Instead of the Son lowering himself, the Father exalts him, giving the Son a name above all others names that acknowledges his true status: *kyrios* ("Lord")—the very name used in the Greek translation of the Hebrew Scriptures for Yahweh. To whom else should every knee in heaven and on earth bow if not to the one true God, maker of heaven and earth?

What accounts for this dramatic reversal of the Son's status? The "therefore" in verse 9 provides a clue. The Father's exaltation is a response to the Son's self-humiliation. It is not a reward for obedience as much as a validation of who Jesus is and what he does. In exalting Jesus, the Father puts his stamp of approval on the "mind" (that is, the attitude) of Christ.[13] God vindicates Christ's willingness to make himself nothing by giving him everything back,

---

[13] So J. A. Motyer, who says that the Father's response is "to the sort of person Jesus is, the way he looks at things . . . his 'mind'" (*The Message of Philippians* [Leicester, UK: Inter-Varsity Press, 1984], 122).

and more. Indeed, the climax of the drama is the universal recognition of who Jesus really is, such that every tongue should confess that Jesus Christ is Lord (2:11). Jesus is Lord because he does what only the Lord *can* do: he loves the world to the uttermost. "In his marvelous stoop we behold his glory. Greatness is never so glorious as when it takes the place of lowliness . . . . Sovereignty is never so winsome as when it is seen in the place of service."[14]

There we have it. Paul compresses the whole drama of redemption, from the implied pre-existence of the Son to his incarnation, death, resurrection and ascension, all in a scant six verses. Note how the plot of this minidrama centers on the Son's change in status. God vindicates Christ's willingness to make himself nothing by giving him everything, including the good opinion of the world—glory. Jesus' death is thus the linchpin for a wondrous status exchange. Through the cross and its proclamation in the gospel, God makes foolish the status wisdom of the world.

" . . . but in humility count others more significant than yourselves . . ." *(2:3).* What does this have to do with Paul's exhortation to the church at Philippi to lead lives worthy of citizens of the gospel—or, for that matter, with the problem of status anxiety? Let's recall where we started, with Paul's injunction to "Have this mind" (2:5).

Paul's epistle provides the Philippians with an exemplar of good gospel citizenship: the mind of Christ. The hymn displays Christ's mind by rehearsing what the Son has done. We come to understand that the Son's fundamental disposition is humility. If the Son, with his exalted status (equal to God), is willing to lower himself for us, can we do any less for one another, or for him? Paul's overriding concern, and the summit of his joy, has everything to do with the church at Philippi displaying union and communion by embodying the mind of Christ.

The events of Holy Week provide the grounds for Paul's plea: "Do nothing from selfish ambition or conceit, but in humility count others more significant than yourselves" (2:3). We have our answer. *Humility* is the manner of life worthy of the gospel, the key feature of Christian citizenship, the way a disciple enacts the mind of Christ. But what does humility—our Lord's pattern of practical reasoning—look like in contemporary practice?

---

[14]Arthur W. Pink, *Exposition of the Gospel of John* (Grand Rapids: Zondervan, 1975), 41.

Paul urges us to imitate first and foremost the attitude that gave rise to Jesus' actions, not the exact actions themselves. We don't necessarily have to die on wooden crosses as criminals—though we will have to suffer in other ways. Rather, we are to display the *pattern* of a life that fundamentally looks not to its own interests but to the interests of others. This may come as a particular challenge in a society that encourages self-promotion, not least through detailed (and sometimes exaggerated) résumés, as ours does.

Paul specifically singles out "selfish ambition" and "vainglory" (*kenodoxia*) as symptoms of a mind that is the polar opposite of Christ's. As we have seen, Christ's mind is bent not on self-interest but on the interests of others (2:4). This is the hallmark of humility. It's worth noting that neither Greek literature nor Roman citizens had much regard for humility. The ancients considered humility a weakness, not a virtue. For them, humility connoted the kind of servility associated with Uriah Heep, that character in *David Copperfield* whose annoying and exaggerated self-deprecations are actually a ploy to ingratiate himself with others: "I am well aware that I am the 'umblest person going. . . . My mother is likewise a very 'umble person. We live in an 'umble abode."[15] Heep is actually using humility strategically to gain status. His "'umbleness" is a mask for the vain conceit that Paul explicitly prohibits in verse 3. Heep's inflated sense of self gives rise to a manner of living that is unworthy of the gospel. Heep is an example of someone who so craves social status that he uses humility as a means to a social end. The problem with such self-glorification is that it is self-defeating.

Paul's insistence in verse 3 that we should count others better than ourselves goes against conventional political wisdom in Greco-Roman and contemporary culture alike. In the world, we maintain social stability by treating people according to their status. We cater to people of influence and command those who lack it. In the present world-order, humility—treating those lower than you as if they were higher—is socially subversive. So is the gospel.

What does discipleship—gospel citizenship—look like in a status-conscious empire like ours, where a person's net social worth is a function of spin and perception rather than reality? In order to respond rightly to Paul's main exhortation ("Have *this* mind"), we must learn to view things in

---

[15]Charles Dickens, *The Personal History of David Copperfield* (London: Penguin Classics, 1996), 244.

a new way. We must learn to see one another as citizens of a different kind of city, one that belongs neither to the Roman nor to the new media Empire. We must learn to view God, the world and ourselves according to the strange new status symbol of the cross.

CONCLUSION: STATUS PEACE

What about status anxiety? If we habitually think of others as better than ourselves, won't that exacerbate rather than solve the problem? Let me offer three final thoughts by way of conclusion.

In the first place, adopting a life pattern of thinking and acting in humility is not at all the same thing as deciding to be a passive doormat. As we have seen, the Romans didn't walk all over Jesus. They didn't take his life, he *gave* it. The Son humbled himself, yet it took boldness to set his face toward Jerusalem. The cross is our humility principle, but the empty tomb is our boldness principle. In the Christian life, boldness and humility do not cancel one another out. On the contrary, to have Jesus' mind—to adopt his pattern of thinking and acting—requires *the boldness of humility*, the power of worldly weakness. It takes strength to consider others better than yourself. Most of all, it takes boldness not to care what the world thinks of you. Status anxiety is debilitating, but there is strength in humility. We can do all things—even make ourselves nothing—through Christ who strengthens us (Phil 4:13).

Second, and more importantly, the gospel responds to the problem of status anxiety with *status peace*. The gospel is the good news that, because of Jesus' status exchange, our status before God is secure. By not exploiting his own divine status, Christ established ours. When God looks at us, he does not see our sinfulness but Christ's righteousness. I am referring, of course, to the doctrine of justification by faith. Those who enjoy union with Christ through faith are "in" him, and because they are in him they are declared righteous. Paul cared not a whit for social status, but he staked everything on his status in Christ as an innocent and adopted child of God.[16]

---

[16]For more on the question of justification and our status before God, see my "Wrighting the Wrongs of the Reformation? The State of the Union with Christ in St. Paul and Protestant Soteriology," in Richard Hays and Nicholas Perrin, eds., *Jesus, Paul, and the People of God; A Theological Dialogue with N. T. Wright* (Downers Grove, IL: IVP Academic, 2011), 235-58.

Nothing can separate those who are in Christ from the love of God (Rom 8:38-39). There is therefore now no status anxiety for those who are in Christ Jesus (Rom 8:1)!

Finally, the way God sees us—as incorporated into Christ and thus made new—is the way we truly are. Worldly status is a game of smoke and mirrors. It's about appearances, not reality. In asking us to live lives worthy of the gospel, Paul is not asking us to pretend to be what we are not. Rather, he is asking us to live in a way that corresponds to the way things really are, to act out who we really are "in Christ."

To be sure, what we really are cannot be perceived by the senses or established scientifically with experiments. We have no papers proving our God-declared status as his adopted children. That is because our being in Christ is eschatological, a matter of God's invisible kingdom entering into our present space and time. As Paul says: "You have died, and your life is hidden with Christ in God" (Col 3:3). Our status is hidden but nevertheless secure, for "we know that when he appears we shall be like him" (1 Jn 3:2).

The church—the company of saints—is where we go to experience the reality of our citizenship of the gospel. Outside the church, there is only play-acting and wish fulfillment. Disciples know the ultimate truth about ultimate reality—"he is risen!"—and this truth sets them free to think boldly about everything else.

Socrates said that the unexamined life is not worth living. True enough. But the life we need to examine is not our own but Jesus Christ's. His life is ours: broken and poured out, humbled unto death for us. Moreover, his *mind* is ours, and having Christ's mind—embodying the pattern of his cruciform life—is the key to genuine human flourishing. Therefore, be status-anxious for nothing. Rather, adopt this attitude—the humility of Jesus' life and death, and the boldness of his resurrection—and put on the strange new status symbol of the cross.

PICTURES OF THE
CHURCH'S WISDOM

ten

SAPIENTIAL APOLOGETICS

The Dramatic Demonstration of Gospel Truth

The occasion for this essay was an invitation to deliver two keynote addresses at the 2014 Philosophy Conference at California Baptist University on the theme "Embodied Reason: Wisdom, Tradition, and Contemporary Apologetics." I am grateful to Todd Bates for the invitation, to Chris Morgan for his hospitality and to the other presenters whose papers made for a stimulating conference. Apologetics was my first intellectual love. Kierkegaard's image of the Knight of Faith, combined with Paul's imagery of the shield of faith and sword of the Spirit (Eph 6:11-17), greatly appealed to me. I never had to draw my sword until my freshman year at Amherst College, where I did my best to fend off various attacks, metaphorical and literal, in defense of my Christian faith (I have a vivid memory of being chased down a dormitory hall by an inebriated undergrad wielding his fencing sword and shouting "Kill the Christian"—all in good fun, of course). All I had to defend myself with was the dagger of Stott: John Stott's little book Your Mind Matters. *Years later, while teaching a philosophy of religion class at the University of Edinburgh, the tables were turned when a student accused me of oppressing her with my truth claims. It was the high noon of postmodernity, when truth was routinely explained away as an ideological tool of the will to power. It was about this time that I participated in a international multiyear study program on epistemology, under the auspices of Wilbert Shenk's "Toward a Missiology of Western Culture" project. It was with this group that I first formulated what I called the "Epistemology of the Cross," which drew on distinctly Christian virtues for staking*

truth claims.[1] *It wasn't until a few years later, however, that I made the connection between martyrological and theatrical ways of bearing witness to Christian wisdom. The following essay is the result: a wisdom-oriented theodramatic apologetics that focuses on practical rather than theoretical demonstrations—doing, and being, the truth.*

INTRODUCING THEODRAMATIC APOLOGETICS

If apologetics has a proof text, it's usually 1 Peter 3:15: "In your hearts honor Christ the Lord as holy, always being prepared to make a defense to anyone who asks you for a reason for the hope that is in you." What strikes me about this is the "always ready," for this refers to a dispositional quality in persons—readiness—that may be as important as the defense itself. Indeed, that will be my suggestion: that members of the church are not only living "letters of recommendation" (2 Cor 3:1-2) but also *living proofs.* Note too that Peter's focus is not on what to say but on how to say it: "Yet do it [make a defense] with gentleness and respect, having a good conscience, so that, when you are slandered, those who revile your good behavior in Christ may be put to shame" (1 Pet 3:15-16).

Another biblical text that similarly stresses the *how* of apologetics is Ephesians 4:11-16.

> And he gave the apostles, the prophets, the evangelists, the shepherds and teachers, [and I think we could add, the apologists] to equip the saints for the work of ministry, for building up the body of Christ, until we all attain to the unity of the faith and of the knowledge of the Son of God, to mature manhood, to the measure of the stature of the fullness of Christ, so that we may no longer be children, tossed to and fro by the waves and carried about by every wind of doctrine, by human cunning, by craftiness in deceitful schemes. Rather, speaking the truth in love, we are to grow up in every way into him who is the head, into Christ, from whom the whole body, joined and held together by every joint with which it is equipped, when each part is working properly, makes the body grow so that it builds itself up in love.

Did you notice? The truth is not to be hammered into recalcitrant heads but spoken "in love." Paul also warns his readers against being distracted by

---

[1] J. Andrew Kirk and Kevin J. Vanhoozer, eds., *To Stake a Claim: Mission and the Western Crisis of Knowledge* (Maryknoll, NY: Orbis, 1999).

various ideas or taken captive by various ideologies and instead to focus on remaining a healthy body. The church is the body of Christ, the embodied reason and wisdom of God. That's dramatic. But I'm getting ahead of myself.

My task is to set out a new vision for Christian apologetics, and to say why I think it's time to rethink the way we defend the faith. Three convictions undergird my project: (1) Christian apologists should defend distinctly Christian claims, (2) there is a distinctly Christian way to do that, which lets the matter of Christian faith—the gospel—shape the way in which it is communicated, and (3) a theatrical framework best orients apologetics to the work of defending Christian truth, using practical demonstrations of Christian wisdom through the shapes of community life, which effectively make the church an embodied rational argument. But why should anyone think that? Do we really need to rewrite the apologetics playbook?

In what follows I first provide a sketch of where we are in cultural and intellectual history and examine what our options are. I'll suggest that we're stuck somewhere between modernity and postmodernity, between what I'll call "epic" and "lyric" mentalities. Next I'll examine what I call the "turn to drama" in philosophy and culture, and suggest that there are reasons intrinsic to the Christian faith for turning to drama. Next comes my constructive proposal itself: that we reorient apologetics toward wisdom, specifically the wisdom of God incarnate in Jesus Christ. The vocation of the Christian apologist is not to defend theism in general, but the gospel, and not only with ideas but with lives that witness to the wisdom of the cross. I'll conclude by showing why it takes a city—the church community—to demonstrate the truth of Jesus Christ adequately.

APOLOGETICS TODAY: BETWEEN EPIC AND LYRIC

Some view the theologian as a mere interloper in longstanding discussions of apologetics. I'm only an amateur epistemologist, not an expert witness. My testimony, like anyone else's, reflects my particular perspective, location and set of interests. That in and of itself, of course, is no reason to discount what I say. One should no more dismiss a person's testimony *merely* because he or she is culturally situated than you should Newton's Second Law of Motion just because he was a seventeenth-century Englishman. The discovery of truth may be local, but the truth itself is not.

If I belabor the point, it's because I'm about to stake some big claims. I want to bear true witness, but I have to admit the fallibility of my perceptions and thoughts. I take some encouragement, however, from the knowledge that other people are seeing similar things.[2] I begin by examining the styles of philosophizing in modernity and postmodernity under the rubrics of "epic" and "lyric" and by inquiring whether our broader intellectual and cultural ethos has affected (or infected) the theory and practice of apologetics.[3] In each case I'll offer a general description of the mindset, show how it gets worked out in philosophy and then relate it to apologetics.

The epic mindset. An epic is a story told "from above," usually in the voice of an omniscient narrator who stands nowhere in particular, located as they are above the action. Epic poetry strives to attain a kind of impersonal objectivity. It states what has happened and how things are, and does so without intruding a personal point of view or, indeed, any form of subjectivity whatsoever. The epic mindset "likes clarity, completeness, and objectivity, systems, overviews, and comprehensive structures."[4]

Modern philosophy is epic in its ambition. Hegel's philosophy is perhaps the preeminent case in point. Hegel tells the story of *Geist*—Reason itself—as it dialectically develops with a kind of foreordained necessity. This was precisely Kierkegaard's complaint about Hegel's philosophy: it is an epic "System" and, precisely for this reason, cannot do justice to the messiness—the freedom and contingency—of life. This is also the typical complaint about those most epic of philosophical and theological forms, metaphysics and systematics, respectively. Each is epic to the extent that it appears to be the product of impersonal or omniscient narrators who stand nowhere in particular (we know now, of course, that the Wizard of Oz is really a white Euro-American male). We can chart the history of modern

---

[2]I am particularly encouraged by two new books, each of which argue in their own ways for the rationality of believing biblical testimony. Mats Wahlberg, *Revelation as Testimony: A Philosophical-Theological Study* (Grand Rapids: Eerdmans, 2014) and Kevin Diller, *Theology's Epistemological Dilemma: How Karl Barth and Alvin Plantinga Provide a Unified Response* (Downers Grove, IL: IVP Academic, 2014).

[3]I draw my two descriptive categories, "epic" and "lyric," from Hans Urs von Balthasar's appropriation of Hegel's discussion of three forms of poetry: epic, lyric and dramatic. Like Balthasar, my choice is designed in part to highlight the contrast of the epic and lyric with the dramatic, the style I will propose for Christian apologetics.

[4]David F. Ford, *The Future of Christian Theology* (Oxford: Wiley-Blackwell, 2011), 25.

philosophy (and theology) in terms of the competition between various "epic" accounts—rival systems and conceptual *-isms*, like existentialism, feminism, Marxism and so forth. The epic voice is the one that assumes the universal truth and applicability of its perspective. The major difficulty with the epic mentality is its assumption that reason affords an external, spectator's perspective on reality. If *theoria* ("to behold") means to see with the mind's eye, then the epic mentality is quintessentially *theoretical*. And this, indeed, is the measure of epic's ambition: to see everything, from a God's eye point of view.

A great number of our apologetic efforts have similarly been epic in their approach. Take, for example, Descartes's proof for the existence of God, his ontological argument. It involves no particular point of view, nor does it dirty its hands with evidence. Rather, it is a "from above," a purely theoretical affair. It asks us only to form a "clear and distinct idea" of a supremely perfect being.[5] We can no more think of God as *not* existing than we can think of a mountain without a valley. Then, in response to the objection that we can form the idea of things that do not actually exist (e.g., a winged horse), Descartes argues that if we're conceiving God rightly, we will simply "see" (with reason, the mind's eye) that a perfect being will necessarily exist: "But from the fact that I cannot think of God except as existing, it follows that existence is inseparable from God, and that for this reason he really exists."[6] That is, if we conceive of God correctly we will see that he must exist in all possible worlds, including the one we happen to inhabit. Therefore, God actually exists—and necessarily so. Now that's what I call an epic proof!

Athens, we have a problem. The problem is not simply that some people find Descartes unpersuasive. The real problem lies elsewhere. It is a twofold problem. First, I'm not convinced that Descartes's ontological proof defends a distinctly *Christian* truth. Second, even if it does, it is not a truth that requires anything in particular in response from us. It is purely theoretical: epic, but sterile.

The lyric mindset. Whereas epic leaves little scope for personal participation in what is represented objectively, lyric swings to the other extreme

---

[5]The argument is found in Descartes's fifth meditation in *Meditations on First Philosophy*, 3rd. ed., trans. Donald A. Cress (Indianapolis, IN: Hackett, 1993), 42-46.
[6]Ibid., 44.

and revels in the experience of the individual. Subjectivity rules. Lyric poetry is concerned with expressing inwardness. Where epic is impersonal, lyric is intimately personal. Think of Walt Whitman, in his poem "Song of Myself": "I celebrate myself, and sing myself"—of me I sing! Hegel says lyric is "the self-expression of the subjective life."[7]

In lyric, one's bodily situation is central to one's experience. Indeed, postmodern thinkers criticize the modern epic mentality precisely for trying to hide the situatedness of the knowing subject, his or her bodily place in race, gender, class and culture. If epic focuses on reason to the exclusion of the body, lyric does the opposite. One's particular locatedness takes the place of the God's eye point of view, and becomes the site from which to do philosophy. Some postmoderns make consistently critical gestures, deconstructing all truth claims by showing how they originate in particular political situations and benefit those who wield the power. Other postmodern thinkers make a virtue out of necessity (situatedness), arguing that there are still criteria for rationality, although they are located and only function properly within particular traditions.[8]

To what kind of apologetics does the lyric mentality correspond? I'm tempted to mention Van Til's presuppositionalism, because the primary thing that matters is subjectivity, that is, whether or not one's heart is regenerate. Presuppositionalism also emphasizes the importance of being in the right tradition in order to think rightly. However, given lyric's emphasis on expressing particularity and subjectivity, I am also inclined to posit a connection between the lyric mentality and cultural apologetics. In an increasingly secular age, some Christian apologists are looking not to arguments but to images in popular culture as "the most profound provocative, exciting expressions of legitimate spiritual yearning in at least one hundred years."[9] This is a postmodern lyrical apologetics that works with evidence of spiritual desire.

---

[7] *Aesthetics: Lectures on Fine Art*, 2 vols. (Oxford: Oxford University Press, 1975), 1038.
[8] See, for example, Alasdair MacIntyre's *After Virtue: A Study in Moral Theory*, 3rd ed. (Notre Dame, IN: Notre Dame University Press, 2007) and *Three Rival Versions of Moral Enquiry: Encyclopedia, Genealogy, and Tradition* (Notre Dame, IN: Notre Dame University Press, 1991). Note that MacIntyre's "encyclopedia" and "genealogy" correspond to what I have called "epic" and "lyric," respectively.
[9] Craig Detweiler and Barry Taylor, *A Matrix of Meanings: Finding God in Pop Culture* (Grand Rapids: Baker, 2003), 9.

The Turn to Drama: Philosophy (and Culture)

If *epic* and *lyric* are the thesis and antithesis of my brief history of recent apologetics, it will come as no surprise that *drama* is the synthesis, transcending the objective/subjective dichotomy with intersubjectivity. In drama, embodied human beings are themselves the medium of aesthetic expression, not as solitary individuals but in interaction with others. "At its best, drama is able to embrace the objective and the subjective, to maintain a sense of plot and purpose without suppressing the individuality, diversity, and the complexity of levels, perspectives, motivations, and ideas."[10] Drama balances order and anarchy, coherence and cacophony, the suprapersonal meaning of a purposeful plot (directed by God, as we shall see) with the freedom of embodied personal agents.

Whatever one thinks of Hegel's comparison of epic, lyric and drama, it is hard to deny the extent to which contemporary philosophy and culture in general have become "theatrical." I have elsewhere described the present moment as a "turn to drama."[11] A "turn" is a radical reorientation, a paradigm shift that alters the way people across a range of disciplines view themselves and the world. Take Kant's "Copernican revolution," for example. As Copernicus showed that the earth revolves around the sun rather than the sun the earth, so Kant showed knowledge to be a matter of the world's conformity to the mind rather than the mind to the world.

Three preliminary turns. The turn to drama is the culmination of three prior turns.

The turn to language. Probably the biggest event in twentieth-century philosophy was the turn to language. Thinkers in both the analytic and continental traditions came to see language as the medium of both thought and existence. The turn to language acknowledges something prior to and deeper than the knowing subject, something—a structure, a system of conceptual differences—that serves as a framework for human reason and experience.[12] Analytic thinkers thought about language in order to make concepts clearer

---

[10]Ford, *Future of Christian Theology*, 26.

[11]See my "Once More into the Borderlands: The Way of Wisdom in Philosophy and Theology After the 'Turn to Drama,'" in Vanhoozer and Martin Warner, eds., *Transcending Boundaries in Philosophy and Theology* (Aldershot, UK: Ashgate, 2007), 31-54.

[12]See Richard Rorty, *The Linguistic Turn: Essays in Philosophical Method* (Chicago: University of Chicago Press, 1967).

(analysis). Continental thinkers thought about language in order to understand human existence (hermeneutics).

The turn to narrative. Of all the uses of language, perhaps none is more intimately connected to questions of human self-understanding than narrative. Because we are beings-in-time, with pasts and futures as well as presents, our lives have an irreducible narrative quality.[13] Indeed, the philosopher Paul Ricoeur thinks that narrative is the only way to articulate human identity over time.[14] Narratives are also indispensable for shaping community identity. The traditions that shape us, religious and nonreligious alike, have narrative foundations. Even analytic philosophers have recourse to narrative in explaining historical events: to explain an event is to "emplot" it in a story.

The turn to traditioned practice. The turn to narrative is a rejection of the requirement that in order to be rational we have to "extricate ourselves from our particular traditions and frameworks of convictions so as to conduct ourselves as generic human beings."[15] Rationality after the turn to narrative is tied not to a universally shared human nature but to a historically shared tradition. A living tradition, says Alasdair MacIntyre, is a "historically extended, socially embodied argument."[16] Narratives beget traditions that in turn beget certain practices: a cluster of activities shared by a social group and oriented to a social goal. Those who make the turn to traditioned practice typically relocate the standards for speech, thought and action from universal rational criteria to the logic implicit in their local institutional practices. Even analytic philosophy is a shared practice whose members share certain goals, including striving for clarity and precision. Note that on this view the human person is no longer a disembodied mind (contra Descartes) but an agent who acts, with others, in a cultural-linguistic world.[17]

---

[13]For more on the interdisciplinary significance of narrative, see Stanley Hauerwas and L. Gregory Jones, eds., *Why Narrative? Readings in Narrative Theology* (Grand Rapids: Eerdmans, 1989).

[14]See my *Biblical Narrative in the Philosophy of Paul Ricoeur: A Study in Hermeneutics and Theology* (Cambridge: Cambridge University Press, 1990).

[15]Nicholas Wolterstorff, "Analytic Philosophy of Religion: Retrospect and Prospect," in T. Lehonten and T. Koistene, eds., *Perspectives in Contemporary Philosophy of Religion* (Helsinki: Luther-Agricola-Society, 2000) 167.

[16]MacIntyre, *After Virtue*, 222.

[17]In the realm of theology, perhaps the clearest example of the turn to traditioned practice is George Lindbeck's cultural-linguistic approach, the centerpiece of his *The Nature of Doctrine: Religion and Theology in a Postliberal Age* (Philadelphia: Westminster Press, 1984).

The dramatic turn. Philosophy is "a series of footnotes to Plato."[18] Did you know that Plato, according to his first biographer, Diogenes Laertius, was an erstwhile dramatist?[19] The plot thickens!

Many philosophers have written about the theater (e.g., Aristotle's *Poetics*), and several philosophers have also been notable playwrights (e.g., Gotthold Ephraim Lessing, Jean-Paul Sartre, Iris Murdoch, Alain Badiou). This is not what I mean by the dramatic turn, however. I mean to call attention to the way in which several disciplines have appropriated the theatrical model of exploring many of philosophy's perennial concerns: truth, reality and the good life. Socrates said that "the unexamined life is not worth living," but I say unto you, the theater is a powerful tool for examining life! And not only life, but ideas too.

Plato himself wrote in dramatic form—the Socratic dialogue. He paid attention to character, setting and plot in his dialogues, combining ideas, actions and arguments: "By writing dramatically, Plato presented us with constant reminders of the tangible, the personal, and the concrete."[20] And let's not forget that four of Plato's most important early dialogues (*Euthyphro*, *Apology*, *Crito* and *Phaedo*) had the trial and execution of Socrates as their central theme. Plato here anticipates another collection of dramatic dialogues that have another trial and execution as their main theme: the Fourth Gospel.

There is also an interesting etymological link between philosophy and theater. The Greek term *theoria*, from which we get our word *theory*, means "to see" or "to behold." Theories are beheld in the mind's eye. A theater is a physical place in which to behold some kind of spectacle. The apostle Paul uses the term *theatron* in 1 Corinthians 4:9: "For I think that God has exhibited us apostles as last of all, like men sentenced to death, because we have become a spectacle [*theatron*] to the world, to angels, and to men."[21]

The medium of theater is not physical but personal: human action and interaction. Theater happens whenever one or more persons present

---

[18]Alfred North Whitehead, *Process and Reality*, rev. ed. (New York: Free Press, 1978), 39.

[19]"[H]e applied himself to painting and wrote poems . . . and tragedies." Diogenes Laertius, *Lives of the Eminent Philosophers* 1.3, Loeb Classical Library, vol. 184, trans. R. D. Hicks (Cambridge, MA: Harvard University Press, 1925).

[20]Martin Puchner, *The Drama of Ideas: Platonic Provocations in Theater and Philosophy* (Oxford: Oxford University Press, 2010), 173.

[21]See further Andrea Wilson Nightingale, *Spectacles of Truth in Classical Greek Philosophy: Theoria in Its Cultural Context* (Cambridge: Cambridge University Press, 2004).

themselves to others in space and time. Theater, then, is the place where the unexamined life is examined, not least by watching how actors live out (or embody) ideas, emotions and sometimes madness. We may not be consciously acting out scripts, yet we are unconsciously enacting social scripts day in and day out. And underneath these social scripts lurk *metaphysical* scripts: metanarratives. Rowan Williams defines metaphysics as the underlying convictions about the way things are that are implied by our most important practices.[22] Our daily lives are thus replete with "metaphysical performances"—enactments of our fundamental convictions about the nature of reality.

We are now in a position to see how the turns to language, narrative and practice have led to the dramatic turn. First, language is often the primary medium of dramatic interaction, hence theater reminds us that *saying* is a kind of *doing*. Many plays consist largely if not solely of dialogical action. Second, dramas have plots. Theater speaks the language of action: dramas *show* rather than tell. Drama is story made flesh. Third, the turn to drama gives a practical twist to the notion of *theoria*, returning it to its original home in physical theater. Everyday life is a play of embodied ideas, and the audience is not abstracted from but caught up in the action.

Phronesis: theatrical rationality. Drama involves speech, story and practice alike, and it happens whenever we speak or act with others with whom we share a particular situation. Drama, in other words, is practical *theoria*. A number of contemporary thinkers have come to realize that philosophy that is always theoretical and abstract is not particularly useful for human flourishing. For example, Martha Nussbaum thinks ethicists ought to pay more attention to novels because of their ability to help us make sense of particular situations. She finds epistemological significance in the novels of Henry James, for instance, where wisdom is largely a function of the characters' noticing the morally relevant details of a situation.[23] I want to say something similar about theology and apologetics. *Drama is a form of understanding that fosters and facilitates concrete rather than abstract reflections about key Christian truth claims.*

---

[22]Rowan Williams, "Beyond Politics and Metaphysics," *Modern Theology* 11 (1995): 3-22.
[23]See Martha C. Nussbaum, *Love's Knowledge: Essays on Philosophy and Literature* (Oxford: Oxford University Press, 1990).

The theater "should function like a laboratory, serving the purposes of knowledge and analysis."[24] Aristotle said that poetry is more philosophical than history, because it magnifies the essential traits of the human condition. So too with drama. By examining the actions of representative individuals in particular circumstances, playwrights explore humanity and experiment with the conditions under which humans flourish (or not). Like narrative, drama is a cognitive instrument, a vehicle for thought to examine the meaning of life, and the metaphysical assumptions that undergird various conceptions of the good life.

To determine what is right to say or do in a particular situation requires not simply information, or even theoretical principles, but also a dramatic framework, a sense of how things hang together and of how your action fits into the big picture. The turn to drama involves the working out and testing of our most important convictions in the crucible of everyday life. We might say, paraphrasing Shakespeare, that all the world's a metaphysical stage. Drama blends concepts and existence together, as well as language, narrative and traditioned practice, as ingredients in our judgments about what to do and say. Judgment is the operative dramatic term, and the kind of judgment I have in mind involves not speculative or instrumental rationality (what Aristotle calls *epistemē* and *technē* respectively) but rather *phronesis*: practical rationality.

This, at least, is my thesis. The turn to drama brings to the fore the importance of practical reason, the process of deliberating well about what to say and do in order to realize some good in a particular situation. The turn to drama injects new life into old apologetic questions by reframing the discussion not in theoretical terms (e.g., faith vs. reason) but rather in terms of rival forms of *phronesis*. The task of Christian apologetics ought to include a defense of Christian *phronesis*.

What the turn to drama adds to Aristotle's notion of *phronesis* is the idea that understanding is a kind of *performance*. We demonstrate that we have understood something (e.g., how to use an espresso machine) by right action (making lattes). Similarly, we demonstrate our understanding of Christian faith by, *inter alia*, making disciples and loving one another. The point is that

---

[24]Puchner, *The Drama of Ideas*, 108 (commenting on the drama theory of Bertholt Brecht).

practical reasoning embodies our implicit understanding of why we are here and what we are to do—our grasp of the meaning of the whole. The turn to drama is thus a turn to embodied reason and enacted wisdom, toward concrete displays of our ability to grasp meaningful patterns, solve practical problems and live well in the world. Wisdom is lived knowledge, and thus integrates theory and practice. The wise person sees what to do in particular situations—and does it.

THE TURN TO DRAMA: THEOLOGY (AND DISCIPLESHIP)

Christians ought not adopt a policy of monkey see, monkey do—even if the doing in question is dramatic *phronesis*. The fact that something is fashionable is no reason to follow it. However, I believe there are reasons intrinsic to the Christian faith that commend the dramatic turn to theologians and apologists.

The nature of the gospel: beyond generic theism. First and foremost, Christianity is neither a philosophy nor a system of morality. These are only the by-products of what is central: the gospel, an announcement of the good news that God has acted in the history of Jesus, making good on his word and proving himself to be righteous, a God of steadfast love and faithfulness. Christianity is essentially a theodrama: a divine doing. In the words of the late Cambridge theologian Donald MacKinnon: "At the foundation of the faith there lies a deed done."[25] The gospel of Jesus Christ—the story of his crucifixion, resurrection, ascension and second coming—is intrinsically dramatic.

Second, because at its heart Christianity is a divine act, we must let God's own saying and doing define his being, not our abstract thoughts about what passes for divine perfection. Christian apologists are not defending generic theism but faith in the God who acted to bring Israel out of Egypt and Jesus Christ from the dead. The truth we defend concerns the God who embodied his wisdom in the person and history of Jesus Christ. God does not simply reveal truth theoretically. Rather, he becomes incarnate, revealing his mind and heart in everything that Jesus says and does. This is divine theater on a cosmic scale, for the words and deeds of this particular man dramatically

---

[25]Donald MacKinnon, *Explorations in Theology 5* (London: SCM, 1979), 21.

change the nature of the relationship between Creator and creation. The triune God, then, is essentially dramatic, for his being is a being-in-missionary-activity, a self-giving in Son and Spirit to and for the world.[26]

The nature of theology: doctrine for disciples. The nature of theology provides a third reason for making the dramatic turn. According to Anselm's celebrated definition, theology is "faith seeking understanding."[27] Disciples require not merely theoretical but *theodramatic* understanding: a grasp not only of what God has said and done, but also of what we must say and do in response in order to participate rightly in his action. It is only by our right participation that we can show that we have understood. The demonstration of Christian understanding is itself necessarily dramatic. This is a contentious point that deserves further consideration.

Whenever theology is defined as a science, whether science is understood in medieval or modern terms, it is tempting to think about doctrine as knowledge and knowledge as information: true content. There is nothing wrong with this, unless it becomes the exclusive picture of what it is to know. To think of knowledge as packets of information, however, is to encourage the idea that we can somehow "complete" our educations. Esther Meek identifies two problems with reducing knowledge to information. (1) It compartmentalizes information, putting it in the head and leaving the body and heart untouched, thus depersonalizing (and I would add dedramatizing) knowledge. (2) It also exacerbates the theory/practice dichotomy. "We think that knowledge is information or theory, and that application and action is something else—and thus, not knowledge."[28] Even the demons *know* the right things (Jas 2:19). However, knowledge that simply idles in the mind falls short of *phronesis*.

What the Christian apologist wants to defend—the existence of God, the true and trustworthy sayings of Scripture, sound doctrine—are not simply packets of information but an understanding that comprehends, and gives instructions for participating in, the theodrama. The truth claims we make and defend as theologians and apologists have to do with the triune God

---

[26]For a fuller account of the doctrine of God presupposed by this rubric, see my *Remythologizing Theology: Divine Action, Passion, and Authorship* (Cambridge: Cambridge University Press, 2010).

[27]Anselm of Canterbury, *Proslogion*, trans. M. J. Charlesworth in *The Major Works*, ed. Brian Davies and G. R. Evans (New York: Oxford University Press, 1998), 83.

[28]Esther Lightcap Meek, *A Little Manual for Knowing* (Eugene, OR: Cascade, 2014), 3.

and the gospel—theodrama. Faith seeks and defends its understanding not because it cares about theoretical systems of truth but because it aims at directing disciples in the way of truth and life. Doctrinal truth is a means of grace by which we fulfill the Great Commission to make disciples: men and women able to display the lived knowledge—the *phronesis*—of the gospel.

Toward a Sapiential Apologetics: Embodied Demonstrations of Salutary Truth

We can now draw some preliminary morals for what I am calling sapiential apologetics: the defense not of isolated truth claims (at least not primarily) but of the wisdom of the gospel. So far I have claimed that doctrine provides disciples with theatrical direction for Christian *phronesis*, or practical understanding: that is, direction for fitting rightly into the ongoing drama of redemption. Doctrine is sound not simply because it conveys true information but because it is healthy and life-giving, cultivating goodness and godliness. The primary truth Christian apologists defend is not theoretical but practical—in a word, *salutary*. Truth is salutary because it corresponds to what is. It is the fool who seeks to live against the metaphysical grain. Furthermore, the nature of this truth affects the apologist's task: we want to demonstrate not simply the truth of the gospel, but its goodness and beauty too.

Beliefs and dispositions. We misconstrue the truth of Christianity when we present it as a system of theoretical belief. Indeed, when doctrine fails to relate to life, it becomes an argument *against* the truth of Christianity. Thus we do well to begin with the notion of Christian belief itself. H. H. Price sets out a dispositional account of belief: to say *we believe x* is to make a dispositional statement. It is to say that we are disposed to act as if x were true.[29] When a Christian says "I believe in God the Father Almighty," she is not simply reporting on the content of her consciousness. Rather, she is implying that she stands behind what she says and will act in ways appropriate to her belief. "Belief, then, is *action-orientated, situation-related*, and embedded in the *particularities and contingencies* of everyday living."[30] To put

---

[29]H. H. Price, *Belief* (London: Allen & Unwin, 1969), 20.
[30]Anthony C. Thiselton, *The Hermeneutics of Doctrine* (Grand Rapids: Eerdmans, 2007), 21; emphasis original.

it in the terms of this chapter, believing involves *theoria* and *phronesis*. It follows that belief in doctrine is intrinsically dramatic, a matter not only of what we say, but also of what we are disposed to do: "Christian doctrine is the communal endorsement and transmission of such belief, as expressed in life, worship, and action."[31]

The apologist as witness to wisdom. The turn to drama suggests that what Christian apologists should be defending is not this or that truth claim—isolated bits of information—but rather the coherence and truth of the entire theodramatic framework. It is less a matter of proving that the resurrection actually happened, for example, than of understanding the resurrection in its broader theodramatic context, and ultimately of living in such a way that demonstrates what that belief entails. What needs defense is the Christian way, Jesus' way of cruciform wisdom. My working hypothesis is that the best defense of the wisdom of the gospel is its practical demonstration in everyday speech and action. The apologist is an active witness to Christian wisdom.

Wisdom is first cousin to understanding. Faith gets understanding, and wisdom, when it grasps how things fit together into a larger whole—that is, in Christ—and then lives in that light. To "learn Christ" (Eph 4:20) is not merely to learn *about* him. It is rather the ability to demonstrate how Christ unites all things, including oneself, to him (Eph 1:10). Faith aids, abets and enables learning by pointing us toward right participation in the whole, apart from which there can be only information. To defend Christian wisdom is to defend the Christian interpretation of reality as theodramatic.

The problem, of course, is that contemporary universities are not really set up for getting wisdom. To quote Stanley Hauerwas, "Too often university curriculums make it impossible for anyone . . . to make sense of the world in which we find ourselves."[32] Dallas Willard agrees: "There are no *knowledge* universities now in the Western world. . . . But everywhere there are 'research universities'. . . . The proof? You can't get a grant for knowledge or truth, but you can for research."[33] T. S. Eliot phrased it best: "Where is the wisdom we

---

[31]Ibid., 34.

[32]Stanley Hauerwas, *The State of the University: Academic Knowledges and the Knowledge of God* (Oxford: Wiley-Blackwell, 2007), 2.

[33]Dallas Willard, "Introduction," in Willard, ed., *A Place for Truth: Leading Thinkers Explore Life's Hardest Questions* (Downers Grove, IL: InterVarsity Press, 2010), 17-18.

have lost in knowledge? Where is the knowledge we have lost in information?"[34] Christian apologists would do well to ponder these questions. I want to underline three aspects of wisdom that are part and parcel of Christian knowledge: it is good, true and beautiful. The turn to drama allows us to defend all three.

Active (the good). Wisdom is lived knowledge. It is matter of knowing what to do to respond to the good news. Doctrine is a form of practical wisdom that aims at certain theodramatic goods: the *salus* of the individual, the *shalom* of the community and the glorification of the *shema* or name of God. We need to demonstrate, in theory and practice, the goodness of the Christian way.

Imaginative (the beautiful). The turn to drama involves the imagination because understanding drama means grasping the overarching story. We can only act rightly in the middle if we have some idea of the beginning and the end. The imagination is the organ for discerning meaningful patterns, especially patterns that make what would otherwise be a series of unrelated persons and events into a unified story with a beginning, middle and end. It takes imagination to see this world as caught up in an age-old conflict of heaven and hell, where these refer not so much to literal places as to opposing powers and principalities. We're familiar with the role of imagination in stories. What makes dramas different is that they are stories in which we participate. Each new day is a new scene in the drama that is your discipleship. Effective apologetics requires a theodramatic imagination.

I associate the imaginative with the beautiful because the part-whole patterns the imagination invents and discovers are aesthetically pleasing. We have a name for this pleasing fittingness: harmony. Human beings harbor a deep desire for fittingness, which is why we are drawn to happy endings. This is precisely what theodrama promises: the marriage of the Lamb and his bride, a divine comedy. Accordingly, theodramatic apologetics should appeal to head and heart alike.

Authentic (the true). In our age of irony and cynicism, market-savvy millennials are not buying "they lived happily ever after." It is not that they are rejecting our arguments. Rather, they do not perceive our claims as

---

[34]T. S. Eliot, *Choruses from the Rock* (1934).

being authentic. Ideas (and theoretical arguments) are cheap. Show me a changed life.

This is indeed the challenge of sapiential apologetics: to demonstrate the truth of Christianity (the theodrama, not a theoretical system) with our whole being: intellect, will and emotion. To live out our knowledge of the gospel is to integrate what we say we believe with what we desire and do. Any hint of a theory/practice dichotomy, any suspicion that we do not practice what we profess, and it's "Good night, Christian apologetics." The sapiential apologist is not only a sooth-sayer but a truth doer, an actor in dramatic dialogical scenes where what is at stake everywhere, with everyone, at all times is the challenge of embodying the truth, goodness and beauty of the gospel of Jesus Christ.

James Davison Hunter argues that what ultimately makes the decisive difference in changing the world are not simply great men with great ideas, but ideas embedded in culture-producing institutions.[35] Sadly, the church in North America no longer figures on that list. According to Hunter, the church should be less concerned with seizing social power through the ballot box than with being *faithfully present*. "The vocation of the church is to bear witness to and to be the embodiment of the coming Kingdom of God."[36] The church's apologetic vocation is to bear authentic witness—to get real.

Embodying the wisdom of God. Both the "what" and the "how" of Christian apologetics are intrinsically dramatic. The what—the content of what we're trying to defend—is a matter of what God has done, especially in Jesus Christ. The "how" pertains to what we must say and do in response. Embodied dialogical interaction is the essence of drama. There is drama when the Word of the Lord comes to Israel through the words of prophets and, ultimately, through the incarnate Christ.

What exactly is the relationship of apologetics to theology? Theology exists to make the faith comprehensible; apologetics to make it plausible. Maintaining a faithful and credible witness to the gospel should be a vital concern of all Christians. It is probably unhelpful, then, to draw too sharp

---

[35]James Davison Hunter, *To Change the World: The Irony, Tragedy, and Possibility of Christianity in the Late Modern World* (Oxford: Oxford University Press, 2010).
[36]Ibid., 95.

a distinction between theology and apologetics. Each seeks to preserve and promote the integrity of Christian faith in its own way. Theology and apologetics are not two separate specializations but two moments or stages in the lifelong witness of the Christian disciple. The mission of the church, likewise, is to bear witness to the gospel's meaning *and* truth.

Today we badly need an enlarged vision of what apologetics involves that integrates logical arguments, the narrative imagination and faithful practices all for the sake of bearing witness in word and deed to the wisdom of God embodied in Jesus Christ. That is what a theodramatic, sapiential apologetics provides.

What Is in Christ: The Faith for Which We Contend

Christian apologists are charged with defending the truth not of some generic deity but of the triune God: Father, Son and Spirit. What the apologists defend is the announcement that the good, the true and the beautiful have been realized in Jesus Christ. There is nothing more authentic than Jesus Christ, the Real Man and Real God. Theology helps disciples display everywhere, to everyone and at all times the *lived* knowledge of the gospel: that is, the mind of Christ embodied in persons embedded in particular situations. The best apologetic is an embodiment of Christ's *phronesis*.

The unifying theme is embodied reason: from the wisdom of the eternal Son to its embodiment in Jesus Christ to the church as the embodiment of the mind of Christ. I am assuming, once again, that the manner of our apologetic must correspond to its subject matter. We turn, then, to examine more carefully what exactly the apologist defends in defending the faith.

Elsewhere I have presented Christian doctrine as a primary means by which the church makes disciples and so fulfills the Great Commission by teaching them to perceive, name and act in ways that demonstrate the reality of the gospel: *what is* "in Christ."[37] Doctrine exists to form disciples, not to withdraw from the world into their own enclave, but rather to *get real*. Sapiential apologetics is the art and science of enacting the mind of Christ, the embodied reason of God.

---

[37]This is the main thrust of my book *Faith Speaking Understanding: Performing the Drama of Doctrine* (Louisville, KY: Westminster John Knox, 2014).

"L'être, c'est moi": messianic metaphysics. Metaphysics is the study of reality: what *is*. Here we may recall Aristotle's definition of truth: "To say of what is that it is, and of what is not that it is not, is true."[38] The primary task of Christian apologetics, I submit, is to defend the truth of what *is* in Christ. While the task of theology is to set forth in speech what is in Christ, the task of apologetics is to bear witness to the goodness, truth and beauty of what is in Christ. It will help to pause and consider the content of this claim.

What is "in Christ"? First, there is *true deity*. Christ is the "image of the invisible God" (Col 1:15), the "exact representation of God's being" (Heb 1:3 NIV). In Christ is true knowledge of God, including things we might not have expected if we had only the concept of "most perfect being" to go by.[39]

The second thing there is in Christ is *true humanity*. Christ is the second Adam, the Son of Man, the true Israel, the exemplary covenant servant of the Lord, the loving Son who resists temptation and displays filial obedience, thereby showing us the purpose for which God created human beings in the first place.

The third thing there is in Christ is a preview—a taste—of *the end of creation*. We know what God has done in Christ, the *logos* by whom all things in heaven and on earth, visible and invisible were created (Col 1:15): "All things were created through him and for him" (Col 1:16), and "in him all things hold together" (Col 1:17). We also know what God is now doing in Christ as well as what will be in Christ: "In Christ God was reconciling the world to himself" (2 Cor 5:19), so that "if anyone is in Christ, he is a new creation" (2 Cor 5:17). In addition, there is *telos* in this *logos*, a final purpose in this person. In Christ is the true destiny of creation: "When all things are subjected to him, then the Son himself will also be subjected to him who put all things in subjection under him, that God may be all in all" (1 Cor 15:28). What there is in Christ is thus nothing less than the sum total of the whole (Eph 1:10). To think theologically is to understand persons, events and things (the parts) in relation to what is in Christ (the whole).

The fourth and final thing there is in Christ is *us*! The great doctrines of the Reformation all derive from our union with Christ: justification (we are

---

[38] Aristotle, *Metaphysics* 1011b25.

[39] Obviously much more could be said about the Son as the Word of God and revelation of the Father. Karl Barth took this christological concentration and ran with it, producing about two million words of testimony to the nature of God on the basis of examining God's Word: the revelation of *what is* in Christ.

in Christ) and sanctification (Christ is in us). Union with Christ is at the heart of the gospel: the good news that, in Christ and through the Spirit, God is on the move, actively renewing and restoring his fallen creation.

What is in Christ is "all the treasures of wisdom and knowledge" (Col 2:3), treasures beyond anything unaided reason could have imagined. This is the primary content of the faith for which we are to contend (Jude 3), the good deposit that Knights of Faith, to borrow Kierkegaard's phrase, are to guard with their lives, and their publications (1 Tim 6:20; 2 Tim 1:14).[40]

What is ultimately at stake in defending Christian belief, preserving the integrity of Christian witness and demonstrating the meaning and truth of the gospel, is not simply God's existence but God's wisdom. The best way to defend God's wisdom is to demonstrate Christ's "salutariness": his perfect truth/reliability, goodness/soundness and beauty/excellence.

The eschatological "is." Given that the way we defend gospel truth must correspond to what that truth is, I need to say one more thing about what is in Christ. *Is* is the operative term, and it's an elusive one.

It's one thing to say that the fullness of God was pleased to dwell in Jesus (Col 1:19). That is difficult enough to comprehend, but at least it's clear that we are making an indicative statement: Jesus is *homoousios*—"of the same being" as the Father. It is harder to defend claims like "It is no longer I who live, but Christ who lives in me" (Gal 2:20) or the claim that we have been transferred from the kingdom of darkness to the kingdom of light (Col 1:13). Neither of these are empirically verifiable claims. That's because the *is* in what is in Christ is not a straightforward present indicative. No—it takes faith, and a sanctified imagination, to appreciate the truth of "I have been crucified with Christ" (Gal 2:20).

By now it should be clear that when I say *imagination* I am not referring to fiction. It is of the utmost importance not to confuse the *is* in what is in Christ with *as if*. That would be a case of bad pretending—even hypocrisy—and has nothing to do with the theodramatic apologetics I am setting forth here. The apostle Paul is indeed a man *in* Christ, but not in the same way a shoe is *in* a shoebox.

---

[40]For Kierkegaard Abraham is the paradigmatic knight of faith: a person who is free to act for no other purpose than to please God (see espeically *Fear and Trembling*, Kierkegaard's Writings, vol. VI, eds. Howard V. Hong and Edna H. Hong [Princeton, NJ: Princeton University Press, 1983], 38-41, 46-50). While I use the phrase and affirm what Kierkegaard means by it, I am adding an apologetic nuance (using words and deeds to "demonstrate" the truth of Christian faith).

The way forward is to interpret the *is* of what is in Christ as having eschatological force. The eschatological *is* describes an already/not yet truth. Disciples enjoy union with Christ *already*, thanks to the indwelling Holy Spirit,
but they have *not yet* attained to the full measure of Christlikeness. Doctrine
that sets forth what is in Christ requires a robust eschatological imagining,
a faith-based seeing that perceives what is *not yet* complete—our salvation—
as *already* finished, because of our union with Christ. It is a matter of seeing
what is present-partial as future-perfect.

Much in apologetics depends on getting this point right. Wisdom leads
to human flourishing only because it lives out a knowledge that corresponds
to the way things are *eschatologically* (not empirically). We won't get far in
defending truth if reality is not on our side. The eschatological *is* highlights
the importance of the question of the nature of reality. Indicative statements
in the past and present refer to what was and is. That works well for most
kinds of ordinary things and events (though I'm not sure about quantum
physics). But the gospel concerns not *ousia* (being in general) but *parousia*
(the new reality that is coming into being in the person of Christ). Demonstrating what is in Christ involves more than laboratory experimentation or
empirical verification.

The economy of truth. To think Christianly about God is to view everything that God does in terms of the work of three persons: Father, Son and
Spirit. The theological term for this work is *economy*, from two Greek terms,
oikos (house) and *nomos* (law), pertaining to household management. The
economy refers to how the three persons manage, or work out, the "plan"
(*oikonomia*) of salvation that is summed up in Christ (Eph 1:10): the union
and communion of all things "in him."

To think about creation and redemption in the context of the economy is
to give a properly dogmatic description of these things. "Properly dogmatic"
means "in terms of God's triune work" or "in the context of the triune
economy." Incidentally, it is God's triune work that both initiates the theodrama and propels it forward. The first act of the divine drama was a speech
act ("Let there be light," Gen 1:3) and the drama picks up speed with further
divine speech acts (e.g., the promise to Abraham, the covenant with Moses
and Israel). The heart of the drama concerns the word of God and how God's
people will respond to it, the interplay of divine and human freedom.

Let me now introduce the notion of an "economy" of truth. In order to appreciate the distinctly Christian nature of the apologetic task, we need to give a dogmatic description not only of what the truth is but also of how truth is communicated from God to us. We need to think theologically—which is to say, in the context of the triune economy—about truth. First, the triune God is the source and norm of all truth because he is faithful to (that is, he corresponds to) himself. God is the only thing in heaven and on earth on which we may ultimately rely. Second, God's Word is true because it is similarly reliable: what God says corresponds to who he is and what he plans to do. It is for this reason that God's Word is the measure of reality. After all, it was God's Word that ordered creation, and decided the nature of every entity. No wonder, then, that God's Word corresponds to reality: it created reality! Third, Jesus Christ is truth incarnate, God's embodied truth claim. Fourth, the Holy Spirit speaks only Christ and, precisely for this reason, guides the church into all truth (Jn 16:13), not least by helping saints to understand Scripture, the true words of commissioned human witnesses to God and the gospel.

Apologists today need to understand their vocation in light of this economy of truth. The role of the apologist in the drama of redemption is not to establish truth—only God can do that—but to bear compelling witness to it. Only God's Spirit can change human hearts. Thus the apologist's task cannot be to change people's minds. Yet there is something urgent that needs to be done concerning the truth of the gospel: God has given to every person the dignity of communicative agency. We all have a part to play in God's drama of redemption, whether it is speaking, doing or, as we shall see, suffering the truth. Thinking about apologetics in the context of the economy of truth reminds us that the purpose in truth-speaking is to convict, to liberate and to edify. The triune God has a *plan* for truth. The Spirit of truth convicts the world of the error of its ways (Jn 16:8-9). Jesus says "the truth [about him] will set you free" (Jn 8:32).

The divinely sanctioned and supervised economy of truth requires apologists not merely to push propositions around in theoretical arguments but to embody them in concrete forms of practical reasoning, and to do so not least for the purpose of building up the faithful into Christ. The economy of truth terminates not in conclusions but in us. We realize Scripture's truth the way a musician realizes a score, or an actor a script.

The Knight of Faith: Genius, Apostle or Witness/Martyr?

We turn now to consider the vocation of the apologist: the Knight of Faith. Given what we're trying to defend, how should we do it? What kind of persons do we need to be?

The role of the apologist.

Genius. Plato's *Apology* is his dramatic rendition of the speech given by Socrates in defense of the charge that he did not believe in the gods and thereby corrupted the young. The Athenian religious establishment persecuted Socrates, as the Jerusalem establishment would persecute Jesus. And, like Paul at Corinth, Socrates assures his listeners that he will not use fancy language or rhetorical tricks. The gist of Socrates's defense is that he is a sincere seeker of wisdom, and that he is aware of how much he does not know. At stake in both Jesus' and Socrates's trials, then, is a way of wisdom. But there the resemblances end.

Jacques-Louis David's painting *The Death of Socrates* is instructive, especially if we view it as a portrait of embodied reason. Socrates is pointing upwards. Martin Puchner calls that pointing "Platonism's most fundamental gesture."[41] Unlike the famous Isenheim altarpiece where John the Baptist points to the crucified Jesus, Socrates is pointing into the air. It is a symbolic gesture, indicating that the truth lies beyond the realm of material things, in the realm of ideal Platonic Forms. For Plato, the truths that matter exist in a realm accessible to theoretical reason. In the context of Greek philosophy, apologetics has everything to do with universal truth, accessible to reason alone.

Søren Kierkegaard reflects a Pauline concern in contrasting the genius and the apostle (and, I would add, apologist).[42] In the first place, the wisdom of the genius is negative by nature. Socrates is wise because he knows his reasoning is limited. The oracle at Delphi pronounced Socrates the wisest of men because he was an agnostic! Within the limits of reason, however, Socrates was a quick study. He knew what reason gives us sooner and faster than everybody else.

One problem with making the genius the role model for the Christian apologist is that it suggests that only a few intellectual elite are up to the

---

[41]Puchner, *The Drama of Ideas*, 198.
[42]Søren Kierkegaard, *Addendum II* in *Kierkegaard's Writings, XXIV: The Book on Adler*, ed. Howard V. Hong and Edna H. Hong (Princeton, NJ: Princeton University Press, 1998), 173-88.

task—as if defending the truth depended on marshaling complex intellectual arguments. To identify the Knight of Faith with the genius is to relieve laypersons of the privilege and responsibility of contending for the faith. It is simply not the case that only very intelligent people can demonstrate Christian truth, or that demonstrating intellectual superiority—reasonableness—is the ultimate apologetic aim.[43]

Apostle. An apostle is simply "one sent" (Greek *apo* + *stello* = "to send out"). An apostle is a delegate on a mission from the risen Christ. This was Paul's personal experience (Acts 9:1-22; 1 Cor 15:8-9), and apostles figure along with evangelists and teachers as gifts from the risen Christ for building up the Christ's body (Eph 4:11-12). To be an apostle is to be assigned a role in what we have called the "economy of truth." The genius is born (or self-appointed), but the apostle is called and sent. But the "whence" is not the only difference. The apostolic "what" and "how" also differ from their genius counterparts.

As to the *content* of what Paul defends (the apologetic "what"), Paul clearly states that he speaks a word of wisdom, though it is not the wisdom of the genius, or a philosopher: "For the word of the cross is folly to those who are perishing, but to us who are being saved it is the power of God" (1 Cor 1:18). The word of the cross is not something that Paul discovered on his own, working in the Jerusalem Public Library. Nor is it something he arrived at by rational speculation. Paul knows about the cross only because he was told. Moreover, Paul recognizes that the message of the cross is foolishness by the standards of worldly wisdom. No matter. The apostle's authority stems not from speculative reason but from special revelation. Paul says that he was "put here for the defense of the gospel" (Phil 1:16).

As to the *manner* in which Paul contends for the faith (the apologetic "how"), it is largely a matter of testifying, in word and deed. Recall that Paul is not defending isolated pieces of information but the wisdom of God poured out on the cross. It is precisely because wisdom is lived knowledge that Paul needs to do more than lay out theoretical arguments. He has to testify to the truth of the gospel in language and life. There is therefore an *economy of testimony* that stands in parallel with the *economy of truth.* This is particularly clear in the Fourth Gospel, where the miracles that Jesus does

---

[43]See further Myron Penner, *The End of Apologetics: Christian Witness in a Postmodern Context* (Grand Rapids: Baker, 2013), 49-58.

are "signs" that testify to him. Indeed, everything and everyone in the Fourth Gospel testifies to Jesus as the Christ: John the Baptist (Jn 1:19), the Samaritan woman (Jn 4:39), God the Father (Jn 5:37), the Spirit of God (Jn 15:26) and of course the author of the Fourth Gospel himself (Jn 21:24).

Testifying is a way of putting others in a position of coming to know something. A number of philosophers, including Thomas Reid, have made the case that it is rational to believe something someone tells you: "Our trust in the word of others is fundamental to the very idea of serious cognitive activity."[44] To testify is to assert *that p*, and a person's having asserted *that p* is good grounds for accepting *p* (at least in a cognitively clean environment). H. H. Price's "principle A" states "Believe what you are told by others unless or until you have reason for doubting it."[45] The knowledge we gain from others through testimony is not inferential but is properly basic: hearing testimony is as sufficient a warrant for belief, and reliable a source of knowledge, as believing what you see (perception) or remember (memory).[46]

Witness/martyr. Most of us are neither geniuses nor apostles. This is no impediment to discipleship, or to contending for the faith, because the next role model for the Knight of Faith is one with which we can all identify: the witness. *Witness* is perhaps the best term for the apologist's characteristic activity: testifying, giving evidence and in general arguing a case so that a jury (our interlocutor) can reach a verdict. All disciples are called to be witnesses, and thus to play an active role in the economy of truth.

The first witness in the early church to die for his testimony was Stephen (Acts 6–7). We can learn something about Christian apologetics by studying his example. Luke introduces Stephen as "a man full of faith and of the Holy Spirit" (Acts 6:5) whose wisdom was intimidating to the Jews (Acts 6:10). Stephen's lengthy speech (Acts 7:2-53) is essentially a summary of the theodrama: he is putting his listeners in a position to know Jesus as the Christ by narrating his story. Stephen participates in Jesus' story in another sense too when, like his Lord, he stands trial for his faith. It is thanks to Stephen's precedent (and others) that the Greek term for witness, *martys*, has taken on the additional connotation of "one who suffers for his beliefs" (i.e., a martyr).

---

[44]C. A. J. Coady, *Testimony: A Philosophical Study* (Oxford: Clarendon, 1992), vii.
[45]Price, *Belief*, ch. 5.
[46]See also Wahlberg, *Revelation as Testimony*, and Diller, *Theology's Epistemological Dilemma*.

Sometimes, suffering is the form testimony to the truth must take. This is a far cry from the romantic picture of the Knight of Faith I entertained in my youth. Where is the triumph in suffering? Aren't battles meant to be won?

We could ask the same question of Jesus' death, and the answer would be that the triumph is in the suffering. This is precisely the "foolishness" of the wisdom of God, and it brings us back to the importance of demonstrating in practice our understanding of the drama of redemption. The willingness of people of faith to suffer for it, and their ability to endure their suffering, is precisely the form the demonstration of God's wisdom often takes (1 Cor 4:9).

What we are defending must dictate the *manner* of our defense. To think otherwise is to risk mounting a defense that collapses into performative contradiction. If our defense includes our whole-person witness, we must take care not to refute our words by our deeds. The true martyr/witness testifies in word and deed, life and death. This is the cost of apologetics. Cheap apologetics is the defense of Christian truth without martyrdom.

The way a witness gives testimony must cohere with that to which testimony is given: "A witness's life expresses the message and embodied the truth the witness proclaims."[47] There is an everyday martyrdom of life, as well as the extraordinary martyrdom of death. The apologetic task is not simply to recite but to embody one's argument, not simply to proclaim but to become the truth. Martyrdom—living (and if necessary dying) in ways that testify to what is in Christ—is a powerful form of truth-disclosing action. Christian martyrs bear witness to the wisdom of the cross and the lordship of Jesus Christ. Lest this sound too abstract, let's return to the example of Stephen.

The witness of Stephen went beyond recounting past events. "I see the heavens opened, and the Son of Man standing at the right hand of God" (Acts 7:56). Whether or not we should understand a literal seeing here is beside the point. What we have here is a portrait of faith: Stephen gets the eschatological *is*. Calvin points out that it was by his looking up into heaven and beholding Christ that Stephen gathered the courage to endure, so that "by dying he may triumph gloriously, having overcome death."[48]

---

[47]Penner, *The End of Apologetics*, 106.
[48]John Calvin, *Commentary on Acts of the Apostles*, ed. Henry Beveridge (Edinburgh: Calvin Translation Society, 1844), 313.

Endurance is indicative truth to the extent that it displays what can be ultimately relied upon.

Stephen's martyrdom was a consequence of his willingness to live on earth as Jesus is in heaven. He submits to no other lord than Jesus Christ. Is this not the gospel to which believers today also bear witness, the good news that Jesus has overcome the world (Jn 16:33) with all its injustice, violence and pain? I find 1 John 5:4 most encouraging: "For everyone who has been born of God overcomes the world. And this is the victory that has overcome the world—our faith." Christian faith "proves" true when it submits to every kind of critical test, intellectual and existential, and endures to the end. The author of Hebrews asks his readers to remember their previous endurance of sufferings, which included "being publicly exposed [this Greek word stems from *theatrizo*—"to make a show of"] to reproach and affliction" (Heb 10:32-33). What is shown in the theater of faith is truth that endures critical testing, suffering, ridicule and death. This is the martyrdom of Christian life: a show of faith and embodied rationality alike. Such is the cost when the *how* corresponds to the *what* of apologetics. The passion of Jesus Christ is a model for how we ought to stake our truth claims today. Cruciform wisdom is both *what* and *how*.

Theodramatic fittingness: everyday apologetics. I hope that you will not have to pay the ultimate price for your Christian witness. Yet there is a real sense in which we, like the apostle Paul, are to die daily as we exhibit our faith (1 Cor 15:31), since everyday situations give us plenty of opportunities to offer compelling demonstrations of the truth that is "in Christ."

The key concept here is *fittingness*. Apologies for the cross where the *what* coincides with the *how* will display fittingness, which is more than logical coherence. Fittingness involves *theodramatic* coherence: a way of speaking and acting that coheres the pattern of Jesus Christ, the concrete embodiment of the wisdom of God. It may be a mouthful, but *theodramatic fittingness* ought to be the disciple's daily watchword. Each new day brings new opportunities to bear true and faithful witness to the gospel.

The apologetic virtues. Here we do well to pause and consider the moral and intellectual virtues. A virtue is not a process, an objective means of doing something, but an inclination, attitude or habit. Virtues are learned character traits, acquired excellences. For example, a moral virtue inclines

us to desire and will the good. Similarly, an intellectual virtue is a habit of
the mind conducive to attaining truth. For example, honesty, openness
and humility are intellectual virtues because they are truth-conducive,
whereas their counterpart vices are more likely to lead us away from the
truth. Whereas method names an impersonal process, moral and intellectual virtues are qualities of our character and thus define who we are:
"We need not rule-books, but a *training* that nurtures *people* in the right
intellectual *dispositions*."[49]

Moral and intellectual virtues we know, but what is an apologetic virtue?
An apologetic virtue is a way of living that is conducive to demonstrating
and persuading people of the truth. Paul may have had something similar
in mind when he speaks of being "transformed by the renewal of your mind,
that you may prove [Greek *dokimazō*, "discern, put to the test"] what is the
will of God, what is good" (Rom 12:2, RSV). Kierkegaard put it this way:
"Christianity is *praxis*, a character-task."[50]

The list of apologetic virtues will largely overlap with what we could call
the sapiential virtues: habits of heart and mind, like the "fear of the Lord,"
which are conducive to enacting godly wisdom.[51] Sapiential apologetics is
simply the acknowledgment that defending the Christian faith is intrinsic
to the disciples' witness to the wisdom of God, and that the shape of this
witness involves actions that display the sapiential virtues. The Knight of
Faith is a person of sapiential virtue, a worker in theodramatic *fittingness*
who know how to speak and act in ways that not only bear witness to but
also advance the evangelical action.

Perhaps the prime apologetic virtue is theodramatic *readiness*. Here we
may recall our starting point: "Always being prepared to make a defense
[*apologian*] to anyone who asks you for a reason [*logos*] for the hope that is
in you" (1 Pet 3:15). Readiness is the willing capacity to say and do what is
Christianly appropriate in and for a particular situation—appropriate, that
is, in the sense of fitting with both the particular situation and the broader

---

[49]W. Jay Wood and Robert C. Roberts, *Intellectual Virtues: An Essay in Regulative Epistemology*
(Oxford: Oxford University Press, 2007), 22; emphasis original.
[50]Søren Kierkegaard, *Søren Kierkegaard's Journals and Papers*, vol. 2, ed. and trans. Howard V. Hong
and Edna H. Hong (Bloomington: Indiana University Press, 1967–1979), 20.
[51]Because wisdom is lived knowledge, the sapiential virtues embrace the moral and intellectual
virtues alike.

drama of the Christ.[52] I have written elsewhere about improvisation, arguing that the purpose of doctrine is to form disciples into wise improvisers, who both understand and are prepared to act out what is in Christ whenever and wherever two or three are gathered in his name. And this brings us to the role of the performing community.

A PERFORMING COMPANY OF WISE FOOLS: TRIALS OF TRUTH, THEATER OF LIFE

It takes a church, not a village, to make a well-rounded and compelling apologetic. In Stanley Hauerwas's provocative words: "If the Holy Spirit does not witness to the Father and Son through the witnesses of Christians, then Christians have no arguments to make."[53] While truth itself is not relative to the Christian community, its contemporary demonstration may be. Arguments alone are not enough; we need a biblically informed imagination and biblically shaped community life to see, and to taste, the wisdom of God in a plausible and persuasive manner. We turn, then, to the church: the body of Christ, the embodied rationality of the gospel.

Indwelling and displaying plausibility structures and fiduciary frameworks. One of the biggest obstacles to apologetics today is the secular picture that holds our imaginations captive. The picture I have in mind is a plausibility structure, a social structure of assumptions that conditions what those who inhabit that structure take to be meaningful and true. The term *plausibility structure* comes from Peter Berger, a sociologist of knowledge, who used the concept to explain how what we believe, or consider believable, depends on what other people believe. A plausibility structure refers to the sociocultural conditions that make a worldview plausible (or render it implausible). Plausibility structures come and go. The social conditions make Marxism seem very plausible to millions of people—for a while. The problem today in our globalized context is that we are more aware than ever of many competing plausibility structures, undermining our confidence that any one plausibility structure could be absolutely true.

---

[52]See further Wesley Vander Lugt, who treats what I am calling theodramatic readiness in terms of *disponibility*. See his *Living Theodrama: Reimagining Theological Ethics* (Farnham, UK: Ashgate, 2014), 33-47. See also Jonathan R. Wilson, *Gospel Virtues: Practicing Faith, Hope, and Love* (Downers Grove, IL: InterVarsity Press, 1998).

[53]Stanley Hauerwas, *With the Grain of the Universe: The Church's Witness and Natural Theology* (Grand Rapids: Brazos, 2001), 210.

Perhaps the dominant plausibility structure in the Western world is scientific materialism. Because of the way we now think not only about natural phenomena but, in particular, about the human person, it is harder for committed evangelical Christians to read the Bible the way Christians did in the past. For example, the Bible says that God created human beings "male and female" (Gen 1:27), but the contemporary plausibility structure, drawing on biology, brain studies and psychology, suggests that these do not exhaust the options. The phenomenon of intersex and gender dysphoria make a certain reading of Genesis 1 less plausible than it used to be, even for those who subscribe to biblical authority.[54] When a secular plausibility structure takes hold, it can lead to a debilitating disconnect between what we profess and what we can imagine.

I'm an Augustinian: I believe in order to understand.[55] While faith opens the door to the halls of learning, reason explores them. All knowing thus begins with what Michael Polanyi calls "fiduciary frameworks": interpretive frameworks that we take initially on faith until they prove themselves by yielding a harvest of understanding (or not).[56] I believe in order to understand, and I act in order to demonstrate understanding.

The theodrama is the Christian's fiduciary framework. It is not simply what we look at; it is what we look *through*.[57] Theodrama is the fiduciary framework believers indwell. When the church acts out the theodrama, it becomes a lived plausibility structure. It is not that consensus makes something true, or that Christianity would not be true if people were not living it out. I am a staunch realist. The truth of the faith is independent of what we say, think or do about it. However, what I am saying here concerns not the truth of the faith but its *demonstration*. God has created the church to become a plausibility structure that makes the theodrama intelligible by acting out what is in Christ. Jesus prays for this lived demonstration when

---

[54]For a discussion of these issues, see Megan K. DeFranza, *Sex Difference and Christian Theology: Male, Female, and Intersex in the Image of God* (Grand Rapids: Eerdmans, 2015).

[55]Augustine says "believe so that you may understand" [*crede, ut intelligas*] in his *Tractates on the Gospel of John* 29.6 (on Jn 7:14-18).

[56]On fiduciary frameworks, see Michael Polanyi, *Personal Knowledge: Towards a Post-Critical Philosophy* (Chicago: University of Chicago, 1962), 266.

[57]Cf. C. S. Lewis's famous statement: "I believe in Christianity as I believe that the sun has risen: not only because I see it, but because by it I see everything else" ("They Asked for a Paper," in *Is Theology Poetry?* [London: Geoffrey Bles, 1962], 165).

he asks the Father "that [my disciples] may all be one . . . so that the world may believe that you have sent me" (Jn 17:21).

Signs and wonders, truth and reconciliation. The early church confirmed the gospel with signs and wonders. But isn't the church in itself a sign and wonder, and thus an embodied argument for the truth of the gospel? The church is "a demonstration of the Spirit and power" (1 Cor 2:4). This is a matter not of performing miracles but of displaying the reality of the strange new world of the gospel: *what is in Christ.* Apologetics today requires the church's being a *lived* plausibility framework.

The most telling objection to God's existence is the problem of evil. Theism's critics maintain that the existence of an all-powerful, all-loving being is incompatible with the reality of evil. The implicit assumption seems to be that, if *I* were the supreme being, I would not tolerate evil. This assumption refuses to recognize the identity of God as described in Scripture. Instead, it projects our best ideas about what qualities a perfect being should have onto God.[58] Interestingly enough, the "answer" that God gives Job when he raises the problem of evil is not a proposition that Job needs to believe but rather an appeal to the greatness—the beauty—of the created order. How much more are the cross and resurrection—the twin events that reconcile and renew this same created order—a matter of the wisdom of God? The Christ event, together with the broader drama of redemption of which it is the climax, is the biblical answer to the problem of evil, and everything else. My contention is that Christian apologetics ought to reorient itself away from proving the existence of a supreme being and concentrate instead on demonstrating the wisdom—the goodness, truth and beauty—of the cross.

The cross remains as scandalous today as it was in Jesus' time. What does the God who is love have to do with the violence associated with the shedding of blood? How can we justify the death of an innocent man? Again, the way forward is to display theodramatic understanding. When the church displays its understanding of the cross—when the people of God act out the cross of Christ—it becomes a compelling theater of racial and social reconciliation.

---

[58]Ludwig Feuerbach argued that all theology is merely a projection of human ideals onto a heavenly figure. My argument is that we must let God's self-revelation tell us what God is like, and when we do that we find that God's power is something altogether different than we might have expected. I have yet to come across a speculative concept of a perfect being that includes suffering on a cross!

What the world needs now is reconciliation, as everything from dysfunctional family dynamics to dysfunctional geopolitics sadly attests.

To act out the cross of Christ is to engage in everyday practices that exhibit and foster reconciliation, especially in the church. To date, society has been unable to break down the dividing walls of hostility (Eph 2:14) that separate one racial or social group from another. Forming multiethnic congregations may seem like folly to a pragmatic world, yet it is just such communities of holy folly that constitute the hope of the world. It is difficult to argue with a reconciled community.

Doing church, demonstrating communion. The church is part of the economy of truth, charged with communicating the truth of the gospel. As Jonathan Edwards says: "There is a difference between having a rational judgment that honey is sweet, and having a sense of its sweetness."[59] It is possible that natural reason will not be able to sense the "divine excellence" of the thing displayed in the life of the believing community, but the same could be said of any other evidence or argument we use. Ultimately it is the Spirit's role to illumine hearts and minds so that they will feel the force of our arguments and demonstrations.[60] Still, we must do all we can as a community to communicate both the sense, and the sweetness, of what is in Christ.

One of the most precious things we have in Christ is communion with one another. Dietrich Bonhoeffer says, "Christian community is not an ideal we have to realize, but rather a reality created by God in Christ in which we may participate."[61] We participate in this reality—and do so dramatically—every time we celebrate the Lord's Supper.

The celebration of the Lord's Supper is an untapped apologetic resource. It is a theatrical presentation, in a highly concentrated and mysterious form, of the redemption won by Christ. When we celebrate the Lord's Supper, we enact the climax of the drama of redemption—the creation of a new, unified body of Christ, in which there are no racial or social or economic divisions. The

---

[59]"A Divine and Supernatural Light," in *The Sermons of Jonathan Edwards: A Reader* (New Haven, CT: Yale University Press, 1999), 126.

[60]See my essay "The Spirit of Light After the Age of Enlightenment: Reforming/Renewing Pneumatic Hermeneutics via the Economy of Illumination," in Jeffrey W. Barbeau and Beth Felker Jones, eds., *Spirit of God: Christian Renewal in the Community of Faith* (Downers Grove, IL: IVP Academic, 2015), 149-67.

[61]Dietrich Bonhoeffer, *Life Together and Prayerbook of the Bible, Dietrich Bonhoeffer Works*, vol. 5 (Minneapolis: Augsburg Fortress, 1996), 38.

Lord's Supper is thus a *summa* of the gospel. In celebrating communion, the church not only proclaims but also enacts its unity in an embodied way that recognizes the truth of what we confess in the Creed: "I believe in the holy catholic church; the communion of saints; the forgiveness of sins." Whenever he spoke of the forgiveness of sins, Jacques Derrida always added a qualifier: "if such a thing exists." When Christians celebrate the Lord's Supper, they dramatically demonstrate the forgiveness of sins, the reality of what is in Christ.

Conclusion: The Church as Embodied
Reason and Theater of the Gospel

As the body of Christ, the church is the embodiment of evangelical reason. Each person is a member of the company of performers charged with acting out what is in Christ. At the end of the day, however, the Knight of Faith is not a crusader, wielding force, but a knight of the Lord's Table, one who knows how to live out union and communion in Christ. Knights of the Lord's Table are grateful realists who joyfully affirm their faith in Christ, and are ready to put their faith to all sorts of critical tests, intellectual, existential and social. Knights of Faith are ready to demonstrate the gospel at all times and, when necessary, to use words.

Lesslie Newbigin once referred to the church as a "hermeneutic of the gospel."[62] This is probably a better way of communicating how the church functions as a framework of plausibility for the story of Jesus. In its corporate life, we come to understand the love of God, the peace of Christ and the fellowship of the Spirit. Building on Newbigin, then, I suggest that we think of the church as an "apologetic of the gospel," a lived demonstration of the truth.

I am certainly not the first to call for a theodramatic apologetic. Jesus says in John 13:35, "By this all people will know that you are my disciples, if you have love for one another." Tertullian, probably recalling Jesus' words, wrote in his *Apology*, "'Look,' they say, 'how they love one another' (for themselves hate one another); 'and how they are ready to die for each other' (for themselves will be readier to kill each other)."[63] Perhaps the most famous appeal

---

[62]Lesslie Newbigin, *The Gospel in a Pluralist Society* (Grand Rapids: Eerdmans, 1989), 234.
[63]Tertullian, *Apology and De Spectaculis*. Loeb Classical Library (Cambridge, MA: Harvard University Press, 1931), 177.

to the life of Christians as an argument for the truth of the gospel is the following excerpt from the second-century work *Epistle to Diognetus*:

> Christians are not distinguished from the rest of mankind by either country, speech, or customs. . . . Certainly, this creed of theirs is no discovery due to some fancy or speculation of inquisitive men. . . . Yet while they dwell in both Greek and non-Greek cities . . . and conform to the customs of the country in dress, food, and mode of life in general, the whole tenor of their way of living stamps it as worthy of admiration and admittedly extraordinary. They reside in their respective countries, but only as aliens. . . . Every foreign land is their home, and every home a foreign land. They marry like all others and beget children; but they do not expose their offspring. Their board they spread for all, but not their bed. They find themselves in the flesh, but do not live according to the flesh. They spend their days on earth, but hold citizenship in heaven.[64]

Jesus spoke in parables: subversive stories that overturned the assumptions of the worldly-wise. More to the dramatic point, Jesus *was* a parable. Similarly, the church is a living parable, a revolutionary and subversive theater with the potential to "turn the world upside down" (Acts 17:6), exposing false plausibility structures and putting the fiduciary structures of the theodrama in their place.

The best Christian apologetic is the church speaking and acting as a reconciled community of faithful disciples of Jesus Christ: arguing, living and, if necessary, dying as wise witnesses to his way, truth and life. This kind of argument, a socially embodied dramatic *phronesis* that demonstrates faith, hope and love, is hard to make fun of and even more difficult to refute. It may be easy in our postmodern world to dismiss Descartes's ontological argument; it is much harder to ignore scenes that enact, through racial reconciliation, familial forgiveness, social justice and ecclesial communion, the reality of God's coming kingdom in Christ. This is apologetics. May we all be ready to do our part in this most serious business: performing the gospel to the glory of God.

---

[64]*Ancient Christian Writers: The Works of the Fathers in Translation*, Book 6, Johannes Quasten and Joseph C. Plumpe, eds. (Mahwah, NJ: Paulist Press, 1948), 138-39.

eleven

ENHANCEMENT IN THE CATHEDRAL

Power, Knowledge and Smart Pills

Temporal power, to build a good world,
To keep order, as the world knows order.
Those who put their faith in worldly order
Not controlled by the order of God,
In confident ignorance, but arrest disorder,
Make it fast, breed fatal disease,
Degrade what they exalt.

T. S. ELIOT, *MURDER IN THE CATHEDRAL*

When humans abdicate their proper place, either by pride or
self-debasement, they blaspheme God and brutalize nature.

WENDELL BERRY, *STANDING BY WORDS*

For what does it profit a man if he gains the
whole world and loses or forfeits himself?

LUKE 9:25

A briefer version of this essay originally appeared in a volume titled Why the Church Needs Bioethics. *I am grateful to John Kilner both for the invitation and for his editorial help. The premise behind that volume was that new medical technologies confront the church with a number of challenging ethical issues. The book consisted of three case studies and of contributions from a variety of academic disciplines. I was part of a case study called "Gaining Every Advantage" in which a physics professor ("Dr. Bright") encourages his graduate assistants to use an illegal cognitive enhancing drug, a "smart pill" dubbed Epiginosko (from the Greek—"to know thoroughly") so that they can push forward more quickly with their research. The question: should Christians follow suit? Steroids are forbidden in baseball, but why couldn't an apologist be justified in taking a smart pill in order to defend the faith? This is only one of the many pressing questions that are presently trying the church's wisdom. For our case study we had contributors in medicine, law and intercultural studies. I represented the discipline of theology. If the previous chapter dealt with sapiential apologetics, this one is an exercise in sapiential theology. I devote the first part of the essay to describing the contemporary situation, not least because wisdom means paying attention to particulars before making judgments. The main task, however, is to help disciples work out what participation in the drama of redemption—the way of Jesus Christ—looks like when the cultural scenery is no longer that of first-century Palestine but the strange new technological world of the twenty-first century.*

"POWER-KNOWLEDGE": AN OLD/NEW TEMPTATION NARRATIVE

As Francis Bacon observed centuries ago, *"Ipsa scientia potestas est"* ("Knowledge itself is power").[1] So it is not surprising that the quest for cognitive enhancement (power-knowledge) is as old as Adam. The primal fall resulted when Eve desired the forbidden fruit, which Satan says would make her "like God, knowing good and evil" (Gen 3:5). Eve's act was sinful primarily because of its means and motivation—not necessarily the knowledge itself, but the manner in which she sought it. It is a familiar story, the first in a long line of temptation narratives.[2]

---

[1]From *Religious Meditations*, cited in *The Oxford Dictionary of Quotations*, 3rd ed. (Oxford: Oxford University Press, 1979), 28.

[2]The 2011 film *Limitless*, starring Bradley Cooper and Robert De Niro, is one of the more recent examples. It is based on Alan Glynn's novel *The Dark Fields* (2001).

Our case study brings the Edenic lust for knowledge up to date. Dr. Bright cuts a compelling Satan figure, offering the pharmaceutical fruit of scientific knowledge and urging his students to become, if not quite like God, then the next best thing: Nobel prize-winning physicists.

Well, why not? Especially when it's all for a good cause (solving the energy crisis, or maybe even proving the existence of God). And doesn't Proverbs urge people to "get wisdom; get insight" (Prov 4:5)? If God has created human beings with the ingenuity to subdue the chemical world, might this not constitute permission, if not a mandate, for Christians to take drugs in order to memorize more Bible verses, focus their attention in prayer or gain the stamina to minister even longer hours?

Clearly we need more than isolated biblical proof texts to discern God's Word to the church on this issue. On careful reflection, our case study challenges Christian thinkers to explain why the use of cognitive enhancement drugs by healthy persons counts as foolishness rather than wisdom. Specifically, it challenges theologians to draw the line between a right and a wrong way to improve our minds, and to say why transgressing this line is not only an infraction of state law but a fracturing of our sense of self and, at the limit, a refusal of both God's gift of life and the way of Jesus Christ. Make no mistake: though it may initially be difficult to see how, this temptation, like every other, ultimately concerns the human creature's denial of the Creator and the created order. Like Eve in her ur-temptation in the garden, the graduate students in our case study are on the verge of idolatry, desiring to be like God and thus willing to exchange God's glory for something less worthy of their devotion: power-knowledge.

To recognize what is at stake in pharmaceutical cognitive enhancement requires a discerning description of what is happening and a thick (i.e., theological) interpretation of what it means. What theology provides is not an abstract rule (e.g., "Thou shalt not injure thyself or another") but a large-scale interpretative framework with which to discuss the meaning of things in relation to God. Theology helps people to distinguish the true story—the way the world really is—from its several counterfeit narrations. What then is the true story of this quest for power-knowledge? It is but one chapter of a much broader temptation narrative whose recurring theme is people's desire to achieve mastery of the world, the future and hence their own fate.

The paradigmatic template of this broader temptation narrative is the story of Faust, the man who struck a deal with the devil in exchange for knowledge. Faust's willingness to trade his soul to satisfy his lust for knowledge is the stuff of literary and musical legend. The Latin *Faustus* originally meant "lucky," but thanks to the story the adjective "Faustian" now describes a person whose stubborn pursuit of self-fulfillment leads to diabolical destruction.

Christopher Marlowe's 1604 play *The Tragical History of Doctor Faustus* popularized the story in English. R. M. Dawkins famously remarked that Marlowe's *Doctor Faustus* tells "the story of a Renaissance man who had to pay the medieval price for being one."[3] While slightly simplistic, this quotation does get at the heart of one of the play's central themes: the clash between the medieval world (and theology) and early modernity (and science). It was during the Renaissance that (1) nature began to be studied through science and represented in art for its own sake, and (2) the doctrine of progress took hold of the Western imagination. This sea change in Western consciousness eventually led to a bloodless coup in the universities, where theology was deposed from its role as the queen of the sciences.

There is something Faustian about the notion that human reasoning is autonomous and omnicompetent, as implied by Dr. Bright. To the extent that the modern university is predicated on this assumption, Christians should beware. Consider, for example, the so-called Cathedral of Learning (which at forty-two stories and 535 feet is not only the second tallest education building in the world but also the geographic center and traditional heart of the University of Pittsburg) and its more than passing resemblance to Pieter Breugel the Elder's painting *The Tower of Babel*. That ancient work of engineering hubris resulted in the confusion of tongues (Gen 11). Who knows what kind of confusion will result from newer attempts to engineer humanity itself in the laboratory-nave of the Cathedral of Learning?

What makes cognitive enhancement such a temptation is its intimation that by accepting its offer we will achieve something desirable, something *good*—for instance, the ability to help the human race. Thomas Becket, the twelfth-century Archbishop of Canterbury in T. S. Eliot's play *Murder in the*

---

[3]Cited by Sylvan Barnet in the introduction to Christopher Marlowe, *Dr. Faustus* (New York: Signet Classics, 2001), xiii.

Cathedral provides another pertinent example. In the play, he has just returned from exile in France to Canterbury, where he is considered an enemy of the state. The play treats his inner struggle to remain true to his vocation, as well as the relationship of religion (the knowledge of faith) and politics (the power of the state). Thomas must resist four tempters if he is to bear true witness to his vocation.[4] The second tempter holds out the prospect of the Archbishop collaborating with the king in order to protect the poor, serve justice and rule for the good: "Power is present. Holiness hereafter." Who has time for ethics (or theology) when there is so much good to do now? This is precisely the temptation in the Cathedral of Learning today: to wield power-knowledge or, in Eliot's words, to use technology "to build a good world."

On one level, there is nothing objectionable about seeking to improve our world, others, or ourselves. But the devil is in the definitions: to *improve* is to make or become better. Who decides what criteria we use to distinguish "better" from "worse"? And even if people can agree on the goal—human flourishing—does it follow that Christians should use any means to arrive at this end? Those who regard cognitive-enhancement technology as inappropriate will have to work hard to say what is immoral or satanic about it. This new temptation to become a little bit more like God, then, is a courtroom drama: the temptation narrative is in effect a trial of Christian wisdom—the ability to say and do what glorifies God in particular situations. Thus the goal of this essay is to achieve a measure of theodramatic wisdom: the ability to make right theological judgments about what to say and do in order to display the mind of Christ in this particular case.

"To Build a Good World": The State
of the Enhancement Art

While Epiginosko belongs more to science fiction than to fact, the scenario of pharmaceutical cognitive enhancement is by no means farfetched. To some degree, it is already here.

Cognitive enhancement. The scientific will-to-power is alive and well, and in many cases people have reason to be grateful for the strides researchers

---

[4]Eliot clearly intends a reference to the temptations of Christ (Mt 4:1-11).

have made in coming to understand—and to manipulate, and sometimes to heal—the body and its biochemistry. The goal of medicine is health: the wholeness of body (and spirit). Medicine affects the body when it intervenes to make it better, to restore health and make us whole and well. The urgent question, however, is whether medicine should aim to make us "better than well," to cite the title of Carl Elliott's penetrating book.[5]

One of the most important contentious points concerns the meaning and scope of cognitive enhancement. Cognitive enhancement is the augmentation of basic mental capacities through improving internal or external information processing systems: "To enhance cognition is to increase an individual's analytical ability in scale and speed."[6] The proponents of pharmaceutical cognitive enhancement suggest that taking smart pills like Epiginosko is akin to drinking coffee. Both provide a boost to the brain, improving the ability to focus attention. Both improve the executive function of the brain—the part responsible for sorting and making choices. On this view we should no more hesitate to pop a smart pill than we would to sip an espresso. Call it the "analogy of enhancement": *this* (Epiginosko) is like *that* (coffee). The implication is that if the one is not objectionable, neither is the other. Everything depends, then, on whether the analogy holds.

There are two morally relevant (and related) distinctions that detractors of enhancement technologies regularly invoke and that its supporters just as regularly debunk: (1) "healing" vs. "enhancing" and (2) "natural" vs. "unnatural." The first distinction serves the practical end of ensuring that medical practitioners stick to the program (and to the Hippocratic Oath), and concentrate their energies on curing and preventing disease rather than improving the already healthy. To *heal* is to intervene therapeutically by aiming to correct a biological or biochemical defect. In contrast, to *enhance* is to improve normal function, to go beyond the natural. Defenders of enhancement technologies blur the distinction: Does restoring mild

---

[5]Carl Elliott, *Better Than Well: American Medicine Meets the American Dream* (New York: W. W. Norton & Company, 2003).

[6]"Boosting Your Brainpower: Ethical Aspects of Cognitive Enhancements," a discussion paper from the British Medical Association, November 2007, enhancingresponsibility.com/wp-content /uploads/2014/01/Boosting_brainpower_tcm41-147266.pdf. See also Thomas H. Murray, "Enhancement," in Bonnie Steinbock, ed., *Oxford Handbook to Bioethics* (Oxford: Oxford University Press, 2009), 491-515.

forgetfulness in a fifty-year-old count as therapy or enhancement? The answer depends on one's ability to pin down what has become a moving target in contemporary debate: the idea of the "natural."[7]

The validity of this first conceptual distinction is thus tied to the second. The aim of medicine is to restore or preserve "proper" physical functioning. An intervention counts as healing if it ultimately goes *with* rather than *against* the grain of nature. Advocates of enhancement technology contend that this distinction too lacks conceptual precision, laboring under the difficulty of defining the "natural." In this regard, Brent Waters rightly calls attention to an unholy alliance between postmodern ideology and enhancement technology: the technology that liberates us from the constraints of nature is but the flip side of the postmodern ideology that what passes for "nature" is actually an arbitrary social constriction ("culture").[8]

The pro-enhancement party is quick to deconstruct the Book of Nature, and with it every concept of the natural as an arbitrary and artificial cultural construct. They are also quick to point out that not everything natural is necessarily good (e.g., the Black Plague) nor is everything unnatural necessarily bad (e.g., the printing press). To their supporters, cognitive-enhancing drugs "seem morally equivalent to other, more familiar, enhancements."[9] The analogy of enhancement is riding the cultural tide that has washed over and reduced our sand castle concepts of the natural. Still, there does seem to be a significant difference—a *disanalogy*—between cognitive enhancement through sleep, study, nutrition and exercise on the one hand and pharmaceutical enhancements like Epiginosko on the other. The challenge is to articulate that difference and unpack its significance.[10]

Our case study focuses on a drug that enhances the intellectual abilities of normal, healthy people. These join the pantheon of other pharmaceutical

---

[7] I take this example from William P. Cheshire Jr., "Drugs for Enhancing Cognition and Their Ethical Implications: A Hot New Cup of Tea," *Expert Review of Neurotherapeutics* vol. 6 no. 3 (March 2006): 263-66.

[8] Brent Waters, *From Human to Posthuman: Christian Theology and Technology in a Postmodern World* (Aldershot, UK: Ashgate, 2006).

[9] Henry Greely et al., "Towards Responsible Use of Cognitive-Enhancing Drugs by the Healthy," *Nature* (December 2008): 703.

[10] One way to do it would be to invoke a distinction between conservative and radical enhancement, where the latter "involves improving significant human attributes and abilities to levels that greatly exceed what is currently possible for human beings" (Nicholas Agar, *Humanity's End: Why We Should Reject Radical Enhancement* [Cambridge, MA: MIT Press, 2012], 1).

enhancers that improve our strength, endurance, looks, mood and sex life. What conclusions we reach concerning the cognitive enhancement that features in our case study will likely be relevant in these other cases too. Yet our principal aim is Christian practical wisdom: knowing how to make good judgments about what the "renewing of our minds" (Rom 12:2) means in an age of biological enhancement.

Biotechnology. Biotechnology refers to processes and products that offer the potential "to alter and, to a degree, to control the phenomena of life."[11] As such, it is the latest and brightest installment of power-knowledge. Never mind what the natural sciences say about the survival of the fittest: the real issue is the survival of the *best-fitted* (i.e., the biotechnologically outfitted). Indeed, in one sense "*all* technology can be viewed as an enhancement of our native human capacities, enabling us to achieve certain effects that would otherwise require more effort or be altogether beyond our power."[12] Today there are pills to enhance muscles, enhance moods and enhance the mind—all readily supplied by the pharmaceutical industrial complex.

Its champions insist that cognitive enhancement will be "increasingly useful for improved quality of life and extended work productivity" and will thus "benefit both the individual and society."[13] That broad swathes of society are more willing to partake of the fruit of biomedical enhancement products should not, however, distract us from their revolutionary significance. While human beings have always used tools to cultivate the earth, neuroscience has discovered tools that tinker with the biological foundations of humanity in an unprecedented manner. Human tool-users today risk being retooled by the very tools they have made. What is unique about the new technology is its potential to move beyond repairing to *rewiring* nature: "If the modern project is to make humans better then the postmodern goal is to make creatures that are better than human."[14]

Martha J. Farah, director of the Center for Cognitive Neuroscience at the University of Pennsylvania, is one of the leading apologists for cognitive

---

[11]*Beyond Therapy: Biotechnology and the Pursuit of Happiness*, A Report of the President's Council on Bioethics (New York: Dana Press, 2003), 2.

[12]Nick Bostrom and Julian Savulescu, "Human Enhancement Ethics: The State of the Debate," in Savulescu and Bostrom, eds., *Human Enhancement* (Oxford: Oxford University Press, 2009), 2.

[13]Greely et al., "Towards Responsible Use of Cognitive-Enhancing Drugs," 705.

[14]Waters, *From Human to Posthuman*, 50.

enhancement. Her mantra is "better brains through biochemistry." She believes that a thought process is ultimately a matter of electrical and chemical events: "Pharmacological influences on these brains also remind us of the physical bases of human personality."[15] Advances in our ability to alter brain function have not only healed those with pathological conditions but enhanced the mental processes of normal individuals, prompting some to predict that the twenty-first century will be "the century of neuroscience."[16] These same prognosticators believe that our ability to alter our own brain function "might well shape history as powerfully as . . . mechanization in the Industrial Revolution."[17] Psychopharmacology is the cutting edge of this latest scientific revolution: "Our ability to achieve specific psychological changes by targeted neurochemical interventions . . . is evolving into the science of rational drug design."[18]

Even before the advent of neuroscience, however, Jacques Ellul cautioned against making *technique* the ultimate concept with which to understand human existence: "Here man himself becomes the object of technique."[19] Technology tends to form its users in the image of the tools they wield: to someone with a hammer, everything is a nail; to someone with neuroscience, everything is biochemical engineering. For champions of enhancement technologies, Epiginosko and its kin represent supporting proof of the claim that "Bioengineers will likely control the future of humans as a species."[20] The tacit promise—we will eventually be like God (Gen 2:5).

"In Confident Ignorance": Is Enhancement Without Theological Presuppositions Possible?

It remains to be seen how society will conduct a rational debate over the merits and demerits of cognitive enhancement techniques. The prevailing public discourse assumes a this-worldly framework, in which happiness in this life is the supreme good—a good that is ever nearer humanity's grasp.

---

[15]Martha J. Farah, "Neuroethics: The Practical and the Philosophical," in *Trends in Cognitive Sciences* vol. 9 no. 1 (January 2005): 34-40.

[16]Martha J. Farah et al., "Neurocognitive Enhancement: What Can We Do and What Should We Do?" *Nature Reviews—Neuroscience* vol. 5 (May 2004): 421.

[17]Ibid.

[18]Ibid.

[19]Jacques Ellul, *The Technological Society* (New York: Vintage, 1964), 22.

[20]Jane Bosveld, "Evolution by Intelligent Design," *Discover Magazine* (March 2009).

Ethical questions are part of the discussion, to be sure. But they tend to be the more obvious ones, such as safety, coercion and fairness.

But from the perspective of theology, the situation calls for a "thicker" description of what is happening and what is at stake. How, then, might we describe the project of cognitive enhancement in theological terms? What further concerns might Christians have in light of a theological interpretation of this and similar enhancement technologies? Before offering the view from theology, we should expose the counter-theology, as it were, that undergirds the case for enhancement.

The social imagination. The underlying social imagination[21] of modernity goes a long way toward explaining the appeal of biotechnology, its claim to legitimacy and its sense of entitlement. Thus it's important to clarify the presuppositions underlying the modern belief that cognitive enhancement is indeed a human good.

The presumption of physicalism. The presumption of physicalism—that the world can ultimately be explained in terms of physical matter and energy—has seeped into modern human self-understanding too.[22] This secular "disenchanted" understanding of the world as bereft of all but material entities and forces makes the culture of enhancement possible. If the processes and products of both mind (cognition) and heart (emotion) are ultimately a matter of brain chemistry, it is no surprise that neuroscience and psychopharmacology are increasingly the methods of choice of many psychologists. A physicalist understanding of the human condition makes possible biotechnological practices and a widely shared sense of their legitimacy. Conversely, the new biotechnological practices lend further weight to the presumption of physicalism. The enhancement of the body is the disenchantment of the soul. Is it really the case, however, that "soul care" is a misnomer—that the real problem can be reduced to something merely physical?

---

[21]The social imagination envisaged here is similar to the *social imaginary*, Charles Taylor's term for that basic conception of the order of things (transmitted by stories and images) that generates and makes sense of the practices of a society. See Taylor's *Modern Social Imaginaries* (Durham, NC: Duke University Press, 2004).

[22]One could equally refer to materialism or naturalism here. Each is a different way of describing what is essentially a kind of ontological monism: the idea that reality is ultimately material or physical, not supernatural.

The authority of scientism. If physicalism is the preferred modern metaphysic, then scientism—the belief that all properly grounded knowledge claims should use the scientific method—is the authoritative modern epistemology.[23] There is no room for an immaterial soul in the modern social imagination. However, if scientism is true it is far from clear where authority regarding value claims comes from: "Because the notion of purpose or end in relation to nature was abandoned in modern science, there is no basis in science or in technology for judging the value of the ends to be served by technologies and therefore no basis for judging that changes to natural entities are improvements. This isolation of ends from means creates an ethical gulf between technical knowledge and its applications."[24] Those who profess biblical authority, however, have recourse to another source and norm for discerning the end of things and for making value judgments.

The premise of consumerism. Modernity's Western inhabitants typically value individual freedom. Many Americans believe that such freedom includes the right to buy whatever they like, or can afford. Enhancement technologies have a vested interest in marketing their wares to eager consumers. The President's Council on Bioethics rightly notes that biotechnology "is now intimately bound up with industry and commerce" and goes on (again rightly) to observe that desires (e.g., to be young again) can be manufactured (and marketed) "almost as effectively as pills."[25] Proponents of a free market economy argue that individuals have as much right to purchase cognitive enhancement technologies as anything else. The market is all-knowing, all-powerful, omnipresent and brooks no argument.

The promise of medicalization. Cognitive enhancement technology, then, assumes that the good for humans will be physical, will be approved by science and will be something that people can buy. If life's fundamental problems can be reduced to (and solved by) science, then there is less need to trust in or pray to God. In the modern social imagination, even hope has become this-worldly. "Medicalization" is nothing less than the secularization of salvation. It is a way of conceiving life in medical terms, and hence in

---

[23]See Michael Stenmark, *Scientism: Science, Ethics and Religion* (Burlington, VT: Ashgate, 2001).
[24]Steven Goldman, "Progress," in Carl Mitcham, ed., *Encyclopedia of Science, Technology, and Ethics*, 4 vols. (New York: Macmillan, 2005), 3:1519.
[25]*Beyond Therapy*, 342-44.

terms of phenomena that are susceptible to various kinds of technical interventions. A picture of human good as something essentially biological beguiles the modern imagination, making us willing captives.

Eschatology and technology: What can people hope for? The social imagination of modernity comes complete with eschatology: a doctrine of last things and a vision of a possible future for which we can work and hope. Perhaps the greatest biotechnological breakthrough in recent times has been the mapping of the human genome. The tower we are building to reach the heavens—to lay hold of godlike power—is made up of strands of DNA. The spire of our Cathedral of Learning is shaped like the double helix.

"The unenhanced life is not worth living." This biotechnological revision of the wisdom of Socrates calls for careful examination. Specifically, what are the criteria for technological progress? What counts as improvement and success for the proponents of cognitive enhancement technologies? The prevailing social imagination encourages the McDonaldization of knowledge, so to speak—where the primary values are the fast-food values of convenience, quantification, efficiency and control—and the authenticity of the self.[26] It is not enough to know *how* to do things, though. We must also know *what for*. What should people make of themselves with the newfound biotechnology? Power-knowledge disconnected from right ends is not only blind but dangerous.

Carl Elliott: a good that is better than well? To speak of "enhancement" is to presuppose a certain conception of the human good, a desired end that justifies the chosen means. Can we improve the human condition by technology? Researchers typically bypass this question; no particular understanding of what a person is or is meant to be or do is involved. More commonly, cognitive enhancement technologies do not presuppose an end that justifies means, but a means that justifies ends.[27] The subtitle of Carl Elliott's book *Better than Well* says it all: "American medicine meets the American dream." Elliott worries that enhancement technologies cater to the consumerist temptation to reach fulfillment through acquisition of property or, in this case, personal properties: properties that can, moreover, be bought like

---

[26]See George Ritzer, *The McDonaldization of Society* (Los Angeles: Pine Forge Press, 2008).
[27]I am indebted to Oliver O'Donovan for this way of putting the matter (personal correspondence).

other commodities (e.g., new car, new wrinkle-free face, new mental power). The new American dream is less about owning one's home than of "honing one's ownness," achieving authenticity through technological means. Yet is it really the case that the attainment of these superbiological ends (even if they are achievable) will be truly fulfilling? Is it possible that in wanting to enhance themselves people risk despising who and what they are? In the modern social imagination, human existence is less a mystery to be pondered than a problem to be solved. The unanswered question is whether or not the cognitively (or cosmetically) enhanced person is the true self.

Wendell Berry: farms and the man. In a series of seminal and trenchant essays, Wendell Berry tackles the modern social imagination head-on, offering an agrarian counter-cultural alternative to the dominant technological paradigm. "The question of human limits, of the proper definition and place of human beings within the order of Creation, finally rests upon our attitude toward our biological existence, the life of the body in this world. What value and respect do we give to our bodies? What uses do we have for them?"[28] Because human bodies are "earthly," Berry notes that it is hardly surprising that there are "profound resemblances between our treatment of our bodies and our treatment of the earth."[29] The modern social imagination romanticizes the wilderness as something wild that humans need to tame. In doing so, we forget that it is the land that sustains us, that our health depends on the health of the land, and that health is a matter of wholeness. Modern people do the same thing to their bodies as we do to the land: we "murder to dissect" as Wordsworth put it. We exploit to enhance.

Berry warns against the ignorant use of knowledge to promote human flourishing: "Without formal restraints, power necessarily becomes inordinate and destructive."[30] The real danger of technological progress is the tendency to look down on the body and the natural world as millstones weighing down the self, combined with the arrogance that, in league with greed, sponsors "better living through biochemistry."

Faith in progress is a hallmark of the modern social imagination: "The

---

[28]Wendell Berry, *The Art of the Commonplace: The Agrarian Essays of Wendell Berry*, ed. Norman Wirzba (Washington, DC: Showmaker & Hoard, 2002), 93.
[29]Ibid.
[30]Wendell Berry, *The Way of Ignorance and Other Essays* (Berkeley, CA: Counterpoint, 2005), 62.

'idea of progress,' the most characteristic and firmly held article in the *credo* of modern man, is the inevitable philosophy of history emerging from the Renaissance."[31] The fundamental problem is pride. People's arrogant belief that they have the technical means of self-improvement—the power to reshape human nature, the ability to lift themselves up by their DNA strands, and the wisdom to use technology for good rather than ill. Human history makes only ambiguous progress. After all, like the story of Faust, world history ends in judgment. There is no intrinsic necessity that *more* is always *better*. It is misguided to equate advances in technology with genuine progress. To assume that all technological innovations are genuine enhancements is to hold a naive optimism concerning the human tendency to do evil.

WHAT ARE PERSONS (AND THEIR COGNITIVE FACULTIES) FOR?

We now turn from the medicalized reduction of eschatology ("in pharmacology we trust") to anthropology. The meaning of what it is to be human is the ultimate issue in our case study.

Being. Oliver O'Donovan's *Begotten or Made? Human Procreation and Medical Technique*[32] rightly identifies what is ultimately at stake in the enhancement habit of mind: the concept, and dignity, of human personhood. Enhancement technologies are revolutionary—different in kind and not merely degree—inasmuch as their aim is not to restore but to *transcend* human health or wholeness. When "making" becomes the key category in society's interpretive framework, so that everything is fair game for technological makeovers, then there is no reason to let things "be." However, what we make is fundamentally unlike us—artificial—and is at our disposal, a thing to be used rather than loved. "When a bioengineer intervenes for non-therapeutic ends, he stands not as nature's servant but as her aspiring master, guided by nothing but his own will and serving ends of his own devising."[33] Cognitive enhancement techniques resemble eugenics in at least one respect: "The problem with eugenics and genetic engineering is that

[31]Reinhold Niebuhr, *The Nature and Destiny of Man*, vol. 2 (New York: Charles Scribner's Sons, 1941), 154.

[32](Oxford: Oxford University Press, 1984).

[33]*Beyond Therapy*, 324.

they represent the one-sided triumph of willfulness over giftedness, of dominion over reverence, of molding over beholding."[34] By contrast, what people beget comes into the world as a gift to be received, respected and loved, for it is, amazingly, like them: not a thing to be manipulated, but a person, with all the rights and privileges pertaining thereto.

Christians confess that God has created everything that is or has being, including humans. God is the unauthored Author. To speak of creation is to acknowledge a divinely given and authoritative order of things: "The order of things that God has made is *there*. . . . Christian ethics, therefore, has an objective reference because it is concerned with man's life in accordance with this order."[35] Christians must therefore not participate in technologies that aim to revise or rewrite the created order. It is one thing to *restore* human beings to their proper form (that is the task of medicine), but quite another to *better* it.

Doing. Enhancement technologies have an adverse affect on a person's sense of personal agency: my sense of being myself, a *doing* being. My agency is a function of my embodiment, and I experience both as a given. I experience myself as free to act according to my nature. Indeed, to be human is to act according to my nature. Everything I do communicates my being. However, to suggest that I am a patient—a genetically programmed or biochemically enhanced person who merely responds to stimuli rather than an agent who initiates action—ultimately deprives me of the freedom that characterizes divine and human persons alike. The Scriptures depict humans as free and responsible actors in a divinely authored drama of creation and redemption. Where other beings have a natural tendency to "share" themselves through actions appropriate to their natures, human persons have a special capacity to engage in meaningful dialogue and so engage in properly communicative action (action oriented to understanding). To the extent that cognitive enhancement technologies call into question the conviction that "this is *me* acting," they undermine our personhood.[36]

---

[34]Michael J. Sandel, *The Case Against Perfection: Ethics in the Age of Genetic Engineering* (Cambridge, MA: Harvard University Press, 2007), 85.

[35]Oliver O'Donovan, *Resurrection and Moral Order: An Outline for Evangelical Ethics* (Leicester, UK: Inter-Varsity Press, 1986), 17.

[36]Paul Ricoeur views the self as a person to whom actions can be ascribed, responsibility imputed, and stories told (*Oneself as Another*, trans. Kathleen Blamey [Chicago: University of Chicago Press, 1992], 22).

Whereas O'Donovan worries about losing the notion of begetting, Jürgen Habermas finds disturbing the ways in which an enhancement mindset affects our self-understanding as responsible agents. Specifically, biotechnology blurs the line between being an object and being a person (i.e., a communicative agent in covenantal relationship): "The boundary between the nature that we 'are' and organic endowments we 'give' to ourselves disappears."[37] Viewing bodily enhancements as commodities and persons as things that can be improved, however, makes people more likely to treat others strategically—that is, as things to manipulate rather than as persons with whom to communicate. Freedom and justice alike require people to engage one another communicatively, as persons, not strategically, like things.

Relating. For people to understand their place in the created order is to understand their place in relation to everything else, to one another and especially to God. Elsewhere I have argued that the Bible depicts God as a triune communicative agent who in love and freedom shares his life with human creatures in Jesus Christ through the Holy Spirit.[38] Human persons are communicative agents in God's image, able to respond to the call of God and others. What are persons for? With the persons of the Trinity in mind, we can answer *to know and love others.* Human cognitive faculties allow persons to relate to God and others communicatively rather than merely strategically: "Come now, let us reason together" (Is 1:18). To be a human person is to be a begotten communicative agent in covenantal relationship with God and others, especially those human others who bear God's image (family members, fellow saints, neighbors, enemies). What are persons (and their cognitive faculties) for? In a word, *communion.*

"FOR WHAT DOES IT PROFIT . . . ?": WHICH GOOD, WHAT MEANS, WHOSE GOSPEL?

The graduate students in our case study face essentially the same challenge that confronts Christians of every age and place: to embody the mind of

---

[37]Jürgen Habermas, *The Future of Human Nature* (Malden, MA: Polity Press, 2003), 12. Whereas O'Donovan draws on Trinitarian theology in his "begotten not made" contrast, Habermas distinguishes between the "grown" and the "made" (44).

[38]Kevin J. Vanhoozer, *Remythologizing Theology: Divine Action, Passion, and Authorship* (Cambridge: Cambridge University Press, 2010), especially chapter 4.

Christ in new cultural and intellectual situations. The church's mission, and hence the preeminent equipping task of theology, is to demonstrate understanding (theodramatic fittingness) by exhibiting the good news of Jesus Christ in terms that are both faithful to Scripture and appropriate to the situation: to embody in concrete forms of life our theoretical and practical grasp of the drama of redemption.

The modern social imagination and newer enhancement technologies work together to support what is ultimately a different gospel: the "good news" that biochemistry gives humanity the means and mechanisms for self-improvement and self-transformation. The theology behind this gospel of enhancement comes complete with an alternative eschatology, anthropology and doctrine of salvation. The best way to detect these deficient doctrines is, of course, to have a sure feel for the real thing. We turn, then, to consider the performance-enhancing advantage, so to speak, of union with Christ. Christology is far from being tangential to our topic for the simple reason that Jesus Christ is the paradigm of true humanity. Those who seek salvation would thus do well to attend to his words: "For what does it profit a man if he gains the whole world and loses or forfeits himself?" (Lk 9:25). This is precisely the issue underlying the decision to employ enhancement technologies.

To approach our case study from the perspective of the biblical imagination is to see that true progress in humanity is a matter not of mastering one's biochemistry but of growing up in every way—truth, goodness and love—into Christ (Eph 4:15). There is a natural order of things, but it is centered on and discerned in Jesus Christ, for "all things were created through him and for him" (Col 1:16). In raising Jesus from the dead to a new bodily existence, God vindicates and completes his original intention for the created order. Jesus is thus both means and end of the good life that God has prepared for human creatures.[39] What followers of Jesus should most want to improve is not their cognitive, muscular or sexual functions but their Christlikeness. Accordingly, in this section we will reconsider (1) the use of the Bible in bioethics, (2) the *good of nature* in terms of the created order and (3) the *nature of the good* in terms of the ways the triune God restores the created order and human nature to humanity's great advantage.

---

[39]See Eugene H. Peterson, "Introduction: The Purification of Means," in *The Jesus Way: A Conversation on the Ways that Jesus Is the Way* (Grand Rapids: Eerdmans, 2007), 1-18.

Theodramatic theology: the use of Scripture in bioethics. There are surprisingly few explicit treatments of the use of Scripture in bioethics. Suffice it to say that the way forward is to think not so much in terms of inserting isolated biblical verses into contemporary debates—though some texts do rise like mountain peaks out of the fog of conceptual confusion—as putting the whole debate into biblical perspective, that is, into the drama of redemption for which the Bible is the authoritative script. Being biblical requires more (but not less) than appealing to Scripture here and there in the course of argumentation. It requires being apprenticed to the whole pattern of life that comprises Christian identity—the new creation already/ not yet inaugurated in Christ (2 Cor 5:17). This is how people learn how to make judgments about what to say and do today that accord with the reality of what the Father has done and will do in the Son through the Spirit. The goal is to enter into the story of the Bible so that it becomes possible to indwell its dramatic plot, its ethos and ultimately the divine *dramatis personae* themselves.[40]

Theology's aim is to direct the church to participate rightly in what God is doing—the *theodrama* (Greek *theos* + *drao,* "God doing")—so that it can both speak and do the truth. Christians must indwell the strange new world of the biblical text to the point that they can almost spontaneously contextualize the main theodramatic action—the Father's making all things new in Christ through the Spirit—as they proclaim and practice the gospel in new cultural scenes. The understanding of faith, theology and ethics, are thus interrelated: each in its own way is concerned with humanity's fitting participation in the redeemed order of creation.

Thanks to biblical revelation, the church knows what is most important: that God created and ordered everything in the world through his Word, and that God is redeeming the world from the disorder into which it has fallen because of sin through this same Word. The church, as the "society of Jesus," thus has a distinct social imagination. Being biblical in bioethics means making wise decisions about what actions and practices befit the theodrama. It is a matter of engaging in practical reasoning in light of the

---

[40]This way of putting it draws on my *The Drama of Doctrine: A Canonical-Linguistic Approach to Christian Theology* (Louisville, KY: Westminster John Knox, 2005) as well as Brian Brock's *Singing the Ethos of God: On the Place of Christian Ethics in Scripture* (Grand Rapids: Eerdmans, 2007).

truth and *telos* of the gospel: namely, the great story of what God has done, is doing and will do to renew—not enhance!—all things.[41]

Theology serves the church by setting forth God's design plan (see below) for his creatures and by providing instructions for proper functioning—directions for "doing the works of God" (Jn 6:28). The challenge for the company of Jesus Christ is to perform new life in the midst of the old, to put on scenes of God's kingdom in the public square. What is required is not simply a high view of Scripture but the wisdom to glean its rendering of reality and to conform to this reality in our speech and life, even in unprecedented situations. Scripture is the God-given resource with which the people of God confront the indeterminacy of practical decision and learn the wisdom of Christ.

Our case study is ultimately a test of what we might call the church's "performance knowledge." Obedience is a way of acting, and the church must study its script thoroughly in order to realize its true end. The decision whether or not to use cognitive-enhancement technologies requires biblical reasoning: careful thought that does not simply repeat old formulations but devises courses of action that display a sound practical understanding of the gospel and its implications. The church's wisdom is a measure of its ability to stage the new self and its practices (Col 3:9-10) by following the holy script into uncharted scenes.

Pharmacological cognitive enhancement and the doctrine of creation: toward whose shalom? The doctrine of creation addresses two closely related issues concerning enhancement technologies that have proved to be among the most intractable: (1) whether one can distinguish the "natural" from the "unnatural" with respect to human beings in order to respect the natural as God-given, and (2) whether and how far we ought to improve what we find in human nature if we are able to do so.

Nature: to let be or not to let be? Those in favor of cognitive enhancement remind us that not everything that is natural is good. No one is complaining about pharmacological technologies that combat infectious diseases, or about technological advances like jet propulsion, even though flying is hardly a natural form of human travel. In what sense is a cup of coffee more natural

---

[41]Practical reasoning is reasoning about action: what to say or do.

than a capsule of Epiginosko? If one is unobjectionable, so is the other (so goes the "analogy of enhancement"). This is the core of the present-day temptation to partake of this new form of power-knowledge: "In one sense, *all* technology can be viewed as an enhancement of our native human capacities."[42]

The core claim of the analogy of enhancement—that there is no significant difference between restoring/correcting and revising/improving nature—is fiendishly subtle. On one level, it suggests that the natural order of things is corrupt, tending to disorder and thus requiring technological intervention to put right. But this is to elide the distinction between creation and the fall. The natural—and this includes embodied human existence—is not simply what is there to be overcome through technological means. The body is more than an obstacle course for the mind. It is the divinely intended enabling condition of human communicative action, knowing and love. There is a divine design plan for human brains and bodies that enables people to identify a normative concept of health: *salus*, in the sense of proper physical (and mental) functioning.[43] "A thing's design plan is the way the thing in question is 'supposed' to work."[44]

Technological interventions in the human body are *natural* (i.e., they go with rather than against the grain of nature) only when they intervene in ways that respect and defer to the divine design plan. To *restore* proper function is one thing (by therapy or healing), but to *revise* proper function (by enhancement in the strict sense of going beyond nature) is quite another. Technologies that aim to redraw the boundaries that define the created order are unnatural inasmuch as they refuse to align with the divine design plan. The analogy of enhancement ultimately breaks down, then, since there is a qualitative and not merely quantitative difference between restoring proper function and rewiring it. It is one thing to articulate this conceptual distinction, and another to deploy it properly—hence the need to say more about the end for which humans were created.

My bodily limitations both partially define me and make possible a "proper" human existence. The givens of my existence (my height, IQ, gender,

---

[42]Bostrom and Savulescu, "Human Enhancement Ethics," 2.
[43]I am borrowing the concept of a divine design plan—"a set of specifications for a well-formed, properly functioning human being." Alvin Plantinga, *Warrant and Proper Function* (Oxford: Oxford University Press, 1993), 14.
[44]Ibid., 21.

date of birth, ethnicity and so on) do not constrain my freedom but are rather the condition of its possibility. Any attempt to transcend or transform these givens, except to restore health, is to reject my God-givenness. How much more tragic and self-defeating it is, then, to attempt to transcend the human condition itself. Martha Nussbaum illustrates this with the story from Homer's *Odyssey,* of Odysseus's decision to refuse the gift of immortality. Odysseus saw that divine existence would deprive him of the very opportunities he needed in order to accomplish the peculiar excellences of being human. As Nussbaum puts it, "Human limits structure the human excellences, and give excellent action its significance."[45] To remove certain limits is to remove the whole point of certain activities. There would be no meaningful concept of athletic excellence, for example, "in the life of a being that is, by nature, capable of anything."[46] Why praise people for jumping high hurdles if they are not subject to the laws of gravity?

Time is doubtless the most challenging limitation on human beings: hence the concerted efforts to extend the human lifespan. Yet the prospect of time running out (death) is also an aid to character and spiritual formation. While death may be a consequence of sin, finitude per se is not. God declared everything he created "good"—indeed, "very good" (Gen 1:31). The space-time world is the proper context for interpersonal interaction and covenantal relations. People can only become who God wants them to be through bodily temporal existence. The good news is not that God saves people from their created existence but rather that, in Christ, he realizes their original design plan through it. The resurrection of Jesus Christ anticipates the future realization of God's design plan for creation.

It is vital that we expose the lie behind the ancient Gnostic heresy that people's bodies are the fundamental problem. It is not physical existence but sin—rebellion against the creation and the created order (including the limitations of human finitude)—that is the problem. Nature as designed by the Creator is constitutionally open to transformation by grace. In Dietrich Bonhoeffer's words, "The natural is that which, after the Fall, is directed towards the coming of Christ. The unnatural is that which, after the Fall,

---

[45]Martha C. Nussbaum, *Love's Knowledge: Essays on Philosophy and Literature* (Oxford: Oxford University Press, 1990), 378.
[46]Ibid., 372.

closes its doors against the coming of Christ."[47] All things in nature were "created through him and for him" (Col 1:16). The final proof that bodily limitations are a matter of finitude rather than fallenness, and hence something to be received as a gift rather than rejected as an evil, is Jesus' own incarnation. Even Jesus "learned obedience" through his communicative action (prayer) to God during the "days of his flesh" (Heb 5:7-8).

Playing God? On enhancing the created order. As bearers of God's image, men and women enjoy the dignity of communicative agency. We are the actors, not producers (cocreators) of the drama of salvation history. Everything depends on playing our part rightly—and on playing the right part.

Critics of enhancement technologies would be right to urge the four students in our case study not to "play God." The prospect of being "like God, knowing" (Gen 3:5) is at the heart of the temptation to power-knowledge. Yet the Word of God clearly designates human creatures as stewards, not sovereigns, of the world. The meaning of stewardship is very much one of the key issues in the debate. How far should humanity seek to subdue the earth, to master its physical and biochemical processes? More pointedly: Do people have dominion over their own being?

Many who subscribe to the analogy of enhancement opt for a third possibility, between the extremes of actively dominating nature (sovereignty) and passively preserving it (stewardship). Humans have already improved upon the natural order, they say, by inventing things like aspirin and airplanes. The intent of the former is to restore health, but the intent of the latter is to enhance human existence. Why do people view antibiotics and airplanes as legitimate responses to the creation mandate rather than as rebellions against the created order? According to some advocates of enhancement, it is because aspirin and airplanes, together with Epiginosko, are examples neither of dominion nor stewardship, but cocreation. The idea is that God invites humans into a creative partnership in the ongoing task of forming and transforming the world.[48]

Accordingly, some would say the criticism that pharmaceutical enhancement is playing God is ambiguous. Is it playing God to expose a

---

[47]Dietrich Bonhoeffer, *Ethics* (New York: Macmillan, 1955), 143.
[48]See Ted Peters, *Playing God? Genetic Discrimination and Human Freedom*, 2nd ed. (New York: Routledge, 2002), 197.

pregnant mother to Bach's *Brandenburg Concertos* in hopes of enhancing the intellectual and artistic capacities of her child?[49] Is it playing God to insist that a child practice the piano even when he or she does not appear to be musically gifted? The pro-enhancement party would have people believe that cases like these soften the edge of the therapy/enhancement distinction. The analogy of enhancement suggests that there is no way to distinguish between the legitimate technological subduing of nature and supposedly illegitimate examples of enhancement. Who is in a position to judge which technological developments are acceptable offerings and which are unacceptable offerings, which usurp God's authorial rights by attempting to rewrite nature?

The way forward, I submit, is to recover the Creator/creature distinction together with the concept of the divine design plan.[50] The Genesis creation account or *mythos* ("plot") gives rise to a certain "ethos of the cosmos," which in turn suggests a certain way of dwelling responsibly in the world.[51] The Bible depicts God's Word as world-shaping and creation as God's good speech-act. Hence the key insights of the biblical imagination: that all things, including human beings, have been spoken into being, that God's Word sets the boundaries for human existence, and that human beings were created to hear and respond to God in faith and obedience. To see God, people and the rest of the world in light of the creation account is to grasp the significance of the fear of the Lord for bioethics, and for everything else. By contrast, to fail to respect the created order is to do violence to nature and ultimately to wreak havoc, if not chaos.

Humans are not cocreators ("authors") but stewards of creation, appointed as vice-regents to align creation, and themselves, to the Creator's design plan. It is one thing to use technology to cultivate the potential of the created order within its natural limits, and quite another to use technology to transcend (transgress) the boundaries of human nature. Epiginosko is in

---

[49]For a development of this point, see C. A. J. Coady, "Playing God," in Bostrom and Savulescu, eds., *Human Enhancement*, 155-80.

[50]Some authors who hold to evolutionary rather than creation control stories contend that the human species has "design flaws." See Allen Buchanan, *Better than Human: The Promise and Perils of Enhancing Ourselves* (Oxford: Oxford University Press, 2011), 30-31.

[51]I am indebted for this way of putting it to William P. Brown, *The Ethos of the Cosmos: The Genesis of Moral Imagination in the Bible* (Grand Rapids: Eerdmans, 1999), esp. 10-19.

very significant respects *not* like coffee, crutches or computers. These things do not set their users up as cocreators of humanity in the same way that Epiginosko does. Drinking coffee may keep you awake (whether you wish it or not), but even if you willfully engage in caffeine substance abuse, there is a significant difference between a morning jolt of joe and technological interventions in the brain's biochemistry. The intent of Epiginosko is to achieve a state of mental functioning that goes beyond the human species' natural limits and which aims at an end or *telos* other than the new humanity anticipated by the risen Christ.

Supporters of enhancement technologies argue that human beings come into their own precisely by using their God-given potential to develop the resources of creation, including knowledge about people's genetic and bio-chemical makeup. Epiginosko is not a threat to authentic selfhood but a tool that allows humanity to bring one more part of nature under human do-minion. By contrast, critics of enhancement technology worry that such attempts are ultimately self-defeating, to the extent that they deny the kind of existence that God has given to humanity. In trying to gain an advantage in life, people may lose it altogether by exchanging the created form of the human creature for a manufactured lie.

God has designed human beings to grow physically, morally and intel-lectually in certain natural ways. These have more to do with self-discipline than with self-mastery through biotechnology: "There is no mandate to ex-ercise dominion over *oneself*."[52] Epiginosko may increase intellectual ability and help people to arrive at the answer more quickly, but it cannot cultivate intellectual virtue. A drug that improves memory does not a scholar make. Human beings have the dignity of agency. They are able to take initiative, to *do* rather than, as patients, merely be biochemically *done to*. Ironically, the net result of enhancement technologies is the *diminished* agency of the person whose achievement is artificially enhanced.[53]

Radical cognitive enhancement technology is an insult to the Creator to the extent that it implies ungratefulness for one's divine design plan and impatience at the rate of its realization. It is a deeply poignant form of

---

[52]Waters, *From Human to Posthuman*, 144.
[53]Michael J. Sandel, *The Case Against Perfection: Ethics in the Age of Genetic Engineering* (Cambridge, MA: Belknap Press of Harvard University Press, 2007).

grumbling against God for not doing more than enabling proper cognitive functioning. To think of the good life in terms of maximal functioning only is to neglect the importance of another aspect of the created order: our *salus* is ultimately a matter not of justification by work—even Nobel-prize winning work—but of entering into God's Sabbath rest (Heb 4:9).

"To work and to keep": biblical reasoning, wise stewardship and the creation mandate. The second creation account includes a lesser-known variation on the creation mandate. Whereas Genesis 1:28 speaks of "filling," "subduing," and "having dominion" over the things in creation Genesis 2:15 depicts God putting Adam in the garden "to work it and keep it." To work something is to develop it, perhaps into a city. To keep something is to preserve it. Which action better leads to flourishing and *shalom*?

"To work and to keep." Is it possible that Genesis does not provide a single interpretive framework through which to reason biblically about technology, but two? Both perspectives are on display in Genesis 30. In response to Rachel's complaint that she is barren—"Give me children!" (Gen 30:1)—Jacob retorts "Am I in the place of God?" (Gen 30:2). Jacob here rightly expresses the "gratitude perspective" for the mysterious gift of begotten life.[54] Later in the chapter, however, Jacob adopts an innovative selective breeding technique in order to obtain his rightful share of sheep and goats from Laban (Gen 30:37-42). This act of Jacob expresses a "responsibility perspective," acknowledging that life sometimes puts people in situations where they must do or invent something to rectify or ameliorate their situation. There is no ultimate contradiction between the two perspectives, any more than there is between our covenantal privileges and our covenant obligations. To work the earth is a privilege, and to give thanks for it is a permanent responsibility.

Advocates of cognitive enhancement, however, prefer to speak of *creativity* rather than responsibility: "As one side emphasizes our obligation to remember that life is a gift and that we need to learn to let things be, the other emphasizes our obligation to transform that gift and to exhibit our creativity."[55] There is a time to intervene in nature with technology, they say,

---

[54]I owe this phrase, and the idea in this paragraph, to Erik Parens, "Toward a More Fruitful Debate About Enhancement," in Bostrom and Savulescu, eds., *Human Enhancement*, 181-97.
[55]Parens, "Toward a More Fruitful Debate," 189.

and a time not to intervene; a time to enhance, and a time not to enhance. However, without a sure grasp of the design plan and final purpose for human beings, advocates of enhancement technology have no means of telling time rightly—the default assumption is "can implies ought."[56] This way leads to madness and monsters.

Some readers at this point may find themselves still prone to lingering doubts. Is it any more monstrous to want our children to have keener memories or attention spans through pharmaceutical intervention than it is to want them to have straight teeth through orthodontic intervention? The analogy of enhancement is a slippery slope that lacks an obvious ledge or toehold. It invites people to accept a principle and to participate in a practice, a cooperative social activity ordered to certain goods that are really, in the light of the gospel, not goods. The problem with straightening teeth for purely cosmetic as opposed to health reasons is not that people violate a clear-cut moral rule, but rather that they get caught up in a search for what are ultimately false goods and false gods. For the goods that radical enhancement technologies promise are culturally relative: they conform to society's arbitrary ideal, not to God's design plan. Moreover, once one accedes in principle to serving this god—the all-knowing, all-powerful voice of social fashion—where do we stop? What if breast augmentation were to become as common as straightening teeth? Acts of enhancement participate in enhancement practices that ultimately (though inadvertently) encourage spiritual vices, not virtues. Such practices seem to be just another way to lay up treasure on earth (Mt 6:19-21).

The legitimate response to the creation mandate—the imperative to "work and keep" the garden—is to tend one's biochemical garden with reverence and respect for the Creator and the created order. Distinguishing between wise and foolish stewardship may be harder in some cases than others. Accordingly, Wendell Berry's words offer wise counsel: "It is plain to me that the line ought to be drawn without fail wherever it can be drawn easily."[57] What the company of the redeemed must always keep in mind is whether

---

[56]Contrast this with O'Donovan's claim that morality and wisdom pertain to our willing participation in a created order that precedes us, such that "*is* implies *ought*" (*Resurrection and Moral Order*, 17).

[57]Berry, *Art of the Commonplace*, 79.

what we say and do advances the main idea, and action, of the drama of redemption. Does it go with or against the grain of a creation groaning for transformation? Does it promote the practices of the kingdom of God? The line between grateful/responsible stewardship and irresponsible enhancement will be clearer if people keep in mind the reason for our being here in the first place: the point of the whole play of creation. It is to this that we now turn.

Radical pharmacological cognitive enhancement and the gospel: toward whose advantage? Toward which **salus***?* Science, medicine and theology each has an interest in saving lives, in *salus* ("health" or "salvation"). Dr. Bright claims that using Epiginosko is instrumental in solving the world's energy crisis. The soteriological end justifies the pharmaceutical means. Increasingly, however, *salus* in a medicalized society means performing "better than well" for as long as possible. Berry puts the lie to this functional understanding of success: "The standard of performance tends to be set by the capacity of the technology rather than the individual nature of places and creatures."[58] We need to move the notion of "doing well" from the realm of psychopharmacology to theodrama. To *perform well* is to play our part—to respond to our vocation—in a way that pleases God: "Well done, good and faithful servant." The question thus becomes: What are people trying to do in the world, and what can they use to improve their performance?

The goal: embodying the mind of Christ. God's purpose in creating the world was to form persons with whom he can have fellowship and share his life—persons in his image, fully human (but not transhuman) persons who, like Jesus, know how to love God and others.[59] The aim of God's communicative action is ultimately self-communication: union and communion. This is *salus*: eternal life with, in and through the triune God.

To see Jesus as the definition of true divinity and true humanity requires a reorientation of one's chief aim in life and a renovation of our imagination. To view the world in light of the gospel is to see that the purpose of life is not merely to expand people's minds but to conform them, together with their whole lives, to the mind of Christ: to Jesus' way of thinking and acting.

---

[58]Berry, *Way of Ignorance*, 87.

[59]So C. Ben Mitchell et al., *Biotechnology and the Human Good* (Washington, DC: Georgetown University Press, 2007), 150.

Jesus is "the way"; he is both means and end of truth and life (Jn 14:6). The problem is that too many of us adopt "the very ways and means that Jesus rejected" in order to pursue *salus* in a worldly fashion.[60] The aim must be to participate fittingly in what God is doing in Christ to renew all things: "For freedom Christ has set us free" (Gal 5:1). The freedom to fit rightly into the created order is not achieved through enhancement. It is a gift of grace.

The means of grace: Word and Spirit as means of salus. If the end for human beings is to love God and our neighbors as ourselves—to live as people who are free (1 Pet 2:16)—how do we get there? What are the appropriate means by which our natures may be redeemed, transformed and perfected? What are the performance-enhancing means that enable people to realize their divine design plan? The question of means concerns the process by which something occurs, the mechanism that brings about change. The Bible does indeed speak of an "advantage" that people need, but it is hardly biochemical.

Many have searched, like Faust, for that extra edge to give them an advantage over others. Some in the early church thought that Jews had a special advantage and that Christians had to avail themselves of this Jewish "technology," namely, circumcision (as symbolic stand-in for the whole law). The apostle Paul exposes this teaching: "Look: I, Paul, say to you that if you accept circumcision, Christ will be of no advantage to you" (Gal 5:2). There is no other way to be right before God than the way of Jesus Christ.

Others in the church looked to "Greek" advantages. Certain Gentile Christians in the church at Colossae were apparently following a syncretistic philosophy that promised an ascetic way to gain power-knowledge over the body and spirit world alike (Col 2:16-23). Here, too, Paul responds that there is no other truly effective power-knowledge than the way and wisdom of the risen Christ. Once again, the key resides in the biblical imagination—the ability to see all things not only as created through and for Christ, but as held together and reconciled *in* and *through* Christ (Col 1:17-20).

To be sure, Jews and Christians have advantages: cognitive, moral and spiritual. "Then what advantage has the Jew?" asks Paul in Romans 3:1. He answers himself that "the Jews were entrusted with the oracles of God" (Rom

---

[60]Peterson, *The Jesus Way*, 10.

3:2). To have special access to the Word of God is no little thing. And there is an additional advantage for the people of God. Jesus says to his disciples "It is to your advantage that I go away," referring to his death on the cross. Jesus' departure makes possible the performance-enhancing arrival of the Holy Spirit, as he goes on: "If I do not go away, the Helper will not come to you. But if I go, I will send him to you" (Jn 16:7).

In an era of biotechnological temptation, Christians must avail themselves of the distinctly Christian "advantage" of Jesus Christ, that is, the "technology," as it were, of Word and Spirit. The Holy Spirit conforms disciples to the image of Jesus Christ by illumining and ministering the divine commands, promises, warnings, consolations, narratives and so on that make up the canon. The Spirit uses the Scriptures to reprove, correct and train his saints in righteousness (2 Tim 3:16), to form in them the mind (including dispositions and desires) of Christ. What Christians need is not artificial enhancement but the "solid food" that improves their "powers of discernment" (Heb 5:14). The Word of Christ dwells in his followers richly (Col 3:16), renewing their minds (Rom 12:2). The peculiar advantage of Word and Spirit is nothing less than understanding and obedience. What Word and Spirit ultimately communicate is not merely information but a pattern of thinking and acting—the ability to participate rightly in the ongoing life of Christ through the Spirit.

Pharmaceutical cognitive enhancements are powerless to form the mind of Christ. How short-sighted are our four graduate students to think that a drug can offer them an opportunity for "gaining every advantage." Epiginosko and other products of that ilk are no substitute for the bread and the wine that effect not enhancement but communion with the body of the risen Christ. In the final analysis, Christians must subscribe to the disanalogy of enhancement: *this* (technological fittedness) is *not that* (theodramatic fittingness).

MARTYR IN THE CATHEDRAL? THE WAY OF RADICAL ENHANCEMENT VERSUS THE WAY OF TRUTH AND LIFE

The understanding that faith seeks is dramatic. The Christian actor-disciple must constantly improvise things to say and do that "fit" with the holy script and the theodrama that defines his or her identity as one whose life is "hidden with Christ" (Col 3:3). And this brings us back to our opening temptation narrative, and to the cathedral of modern learning, the university lab. What should the four students say and do—or, as we shall soon suggest, *suffer*—concerning radical enhancement technologies? How should Christians bear witness in the cathedral of learning?

Enhancement technology is first and foremost not a biochemical phenomenon but a philosophical and cultural ideal that is a peculiar yet distinctive byproduct of modernity. The idea that technological advances will save humanity is a false hope proceeding from a false diagnosis. While some technologies (e.g., eyeglasses and aspirin) may be appropriate instances of wise stewardship (because they aim to restore rather than revise proper functioning), the *way* of pharmaceutical cognitive enhancement is mistaken, both as to end and means. To pursue these advantages is to preach a different *salus*, to march to the beat of a different gospel, to play scenes from some other drama than that of Jesus Christ.

The challenge for disciples of Jesus Christ is to speak and act in ways that bear witness to their faith in *God's* power-knowledge—the wisdom of the cross and resurrection—rather than their own. The church is the community whose vocation and mission is to communicate Christ, bearing witness by participating in the history of his covenantal effects. Soldiers are trained to snap to attention at the command "Present arms!" The call to discipleship is even more urgent, and demanding: "Present your *bodies* as living sacrifices" (Rom 12:1). Discipleship begins with one person at a time leaving the advantages they enjoy in the world to take advantage of the way of Jesus Christ.

The underlying issue of radical enhancement is not simply moral, but martyrological. A martyr is one who suffers because of his or her witness. All Christians are called to bear witness to their identity in Christ, and this often means rejecting alternative ways of realizing our identity or securing social status. In the face of temptations that promise a different kind of *salus*, martyrdom is a way of affirming the created order and of offering ourselves up to the providence of God.[61] Specifically, it is a way of living that bears testimony to our identification with the story of Jesus Christ by participating in practices whose ultimate aim is the power-in-weakness of the kingdom of God rather than the power-knowledge of earthly kingdoms.

---

[61]I am indebted to Michael P. Jensen for this way of putting it. See his *Martyrdom and Identity: The Self on Trial* (London: T&T Clark International, 2010), 145, 179-82.

Martyrdom is a communicative act, a costly counter-cultural expression of our commitment to the truth of the gospel. Again, the issue is more than moral: what is ultimately at stake is the shape of the self, the very pattern of our being as people who hearken above all to God's Word. Christians have been elected—cast in the divine drama—to be God's servants, not his masters: "Thy will be done" (Mt 26:42). It may be that the graduate students will suffer for their choice not to take Epiginosko. But it is in resisting this temptation to ill-gained power-knowledge that they can discover their proper roles in the drama of redemption. To surrender to Dr. Bright's temptation would mean compromising their true identity—the end for which they were created—and mistaking the true means of character and spiritual formation. It would be to aspire to some *salus* other than the one provided by Jesus Christ.

The test of the church today as in every age is whether it can bear true witness to the way of Jesus Christ. As Christian disciples we stand at a fateful crossroads. What we do next concerning biotechnology will chart a course that cannot but leave a mark on our souls. Like the apostle Paul, Christians must be willing to suffer loss of status, and perhaps scorn, for living a theological life that understands its means and end in the light of the drama of creation and redemption. Those who are willing to do so will be in good company. For surely the apostle would count cognitive enhancement technology too as loss in view of the surpassing worth of another kind of cognition: "The surpassing worth of knowing Christ Jesus my Lord" (Phil 3:8).[62]

---

[62]My sincere thanks to Oliver O'Donovan for his incisive comments on an earlier draft of this essay, and for his willingness to guide a theological explorer through the strange new world of contemporary bioethics.

twelve

THE WISDOM OF ANGELS

*Brokenness and Wholeness in
the Academy and Church*

A Sermon on 1 Corinthians 1:18-25

The occasion of the following sermon, delivered in May 1998, was the last Communion service of the academic year at New College, the School of Divinity of the University of Edinburgh, located on "The Mound," an artificial hill in the middle of Edinburgh. The sermon was also my swan song, as I was on my way back to Trinity Evangelical Divinity School after teaching in Scotland for eight years. It had been a trying year, both individually and institutionally. Institutionally, because the Faculty had to revise the BD curriculum (the equivalent of the North American MDiv) to achieve greater "integration" and because the Faculty of Divinity lost its independent status and, for the sake of greater managerial efficiency, was grouped with the Faculties of Music and the Humanities. Individually, because I was in transition. I had just finished a major research project (Is There a Meaning in This Text?) in which I had to grapple with postmodern challenges to meaning and truth. Accordingly, the relevant context for the sermon was not simply ancient Corinth, but the late twentieth-century University of Edinburgh. This presented unique challenges. Though it is part of a secular university, the New College School of Divinity is also one of the three training colleges for candidates for the Church of Scotland (there are no seminaries). This broader context is important for understanding the balancing act that preaching a Communion service in the midst of curriculum upheaval in a post/modern intellectual context with both evangelical and nonevangelical students and faculty. I mention this to explain why this sermon is less expository than I ordinarily prefer. Still, the challenge of preaching in a secular university is in one sense no different from any other setting: always, everywhere and to everyone to present and promote Christ.

THE KNOWLEDGE OF ANGELS—AND ACADEMICS: A SERMON ON THE MOUND

The modern university promises wholeness, and therefore wisdom of a certain kind. It's a tacit promise, contained in the Latin prefix *uni-* ("one"). The term *university* is nephew to the term *universe* (from *uni-* "one," and *versus* "turned toward"). So what turns the different departmental pursuits into a unified whole? In the medieval university, the revelation of God was the unifying principle. Scripture provided the light by which to read the Book of Nature and thus to gain an understanding of the whole. Reason has largely supplanted revelation in this role in the modern university, casting its own light upon the world. The French revolution disposed of two queens: one (Marie Antoinette) lost her head, the other (Dame Theology) lost her throne as Queen of the Sciences. In place of a hierarchy of faith and reason, the modern university enshrined a monarchy of reason. In practice, of course, the modern university has begat fragmentation: even in the Faculty of Divinity we are now split into discrete areas of specialization—departments (or compartments), each with its own methods, aims, objectives and technical vocabulary. "What think ye of Christ?" Well, that depends on the particular departmental perspective from which we hazard a response. Integration—putting the diverse departmental answers into a meaningful whole—is left largely up to the student, a migrant worker who drifts from one academic field to another.

The knowledge of angels. It is worth pausing to consider our incredible privilege. We are an academic community intent on examining things that neither Old Testament prophets nor angels fully understand. Yes, life is filled with trials, but the subject matter of Christian theology is the living hope grounded in the resurrection of Christ. This salvation was the focus of critical analysis long before the university. According to 1 Peter 1:10, the prophets who spoke about the grace that is ours in Christ "enquired and searched diligently" (KJV)—"inquired carefully" (ESV)—"researched avidly"[1]—concerning the suffering and subsequent glory of the Christ. What they discovered (because it was revealed to them) was that it was not for them to know: "They were serving not themselves but you" (1 Pet 1:12). We have access to the gospel through the Scriptures. And yet Peter says that even the angels do not fully understand what God has accomplished in Christ. The grace of Christ's cross and resurrection are "things into which angels long to look" (1 Pet 1:12). These "things" include the good news that wholeness (meaning, integrity, soundness) is available in Christ, and that Christ is the one in whom the whole is being brought together (Eph 1:10).

Unlike the angels, we are part of a Faculty of Divinity dedicated to looking into precisely these things. Again, Latin proves instructive: the term *faculty* derives from the Latin *facultus*, meaning "power," "ability" or "capability." The term "Faculty of Divinity" thus tantalizes with its promise of the knowledge of God. So does the title of Jill Paton Walsh's 1994 novel, *The Knowledge of Angels*.[2] The story is set on an imaginary Mediterranean island in the fifteenth century. The book opens with shepherds coming across a wild young girl who, it turns out, has been raised by wolves, and with fishermen finding an exhausted swimmer, a foreigner named Palinor who has just survived a shipwreck. The child cannot speak; the foreigner is an atheist. Each becomes the subject of an experiment concerning the knowledge of God conducted by Severo, a cardinal of the church and prince of the island. Severo likes Palinor, but he asks, "Can one be an atheist in good faith?" If what can be known of God is available to everyone, then Palinor has rejected the truth and must be condemned to die the death of a heretic. On the other hand, if people come into the world with a blank slate, can the truth of God's existence be demonstrated?

The issue, then, is whether knowledge of God is innate and, if not, whether it is demonstrable. To answer the first question, Severo sends the child to live with a group of nuns. They are to teach the child to talk, but they are under strict orders never to mention anything about God in her hearing. If the girl eventually mentions God, that will constitute proof that the knowledge of God is innate. Meanwhile, Beneditx, a scholar-priest, sets out

---

[1]Translation by Robert H. Gundry, in his *Commentary on the New Testament: Verse-by-Verse Explanations with a Literal Translation* (Peabody, MA: Hendrickson, 2010), 938.
[2]Jill Paton Walsh, *The Knowledge of Angels* (London: Black Swan, 1995).

to persuade Palinor of God's existence. The book thus treats twin issues—whether knowledge of God is innate, and whether the existence of God can be rationally demonstrated.

We first meet Beneditx hard at work on a treatise concerning the knowledge of angels. Angels have both "morning knowledge" (of things as they were created, things as they are meant to be) and "evening knowledge" (of things as they really are in the world). Beneditx is a man who has "faith in reason"[3] and who aspires to the knowledge of angels. Alas, Palinor the atheist refutes Anselm's ontological argument, exposes flaws in Thomas Aquinas's five arguments for God's existence and ex-Humes the deficiencies of the teleological argument. Beneditx acknowledges the weaknesses in his arguments, laments the fact that God had given him "blunt tools," and ends up losing his faith, which was founded on reason alone. Walsh's final word on Beneditx serves as an indictment of modernity too. "Like an angel, he had sought a knowledge without shadows, holding up to creation a very bright mirror. And now the mirror of his soul was so fouled and darkened that neither morning nor evening could be distinguished from the black onrush of night."[4]

Palinor converts Beneditx as it were to the wisdom of Socrates. Socrates's mission, you may recall, was to make people wise by helping them to acknowledge their ignorance, the limits of reason. Humility and open-mindedness clearly figure among the intellectual virtues. Yet the knowledge of our limitations yields a negative wisdom only. It curtails our pride, but it does not tell us how to live well. To be sure, Socrates was also a genius. Like many Greeks, he had worldly wisdom—the knowledge of *angles*. Yet, as Kierkegaard poignantly notes, this makes Socrates an ironic figure. The genius arrives at truth before anyone else, but the truths the genius discovers all fall within the limits of reason alone. Reason never takes us beyond ourselves. But, Kierkegaard asks, what if self-understanding demands something beyond ourselves, beyond immanence? What if self-knowledge demands knowledge of transcendence? Socrates's wisdom is ultimately the wisdom of the agnostic, the wisdom of the limits of reason.

The knowledge of academics. What about the knowledge of academics? What did we learn of God during the experiments—the various forms of

---

[3]Ibid., 132.
[4]Ibid., 262.

careful departmental inquiry—we conducted this semester? Can we find God by research? My neighbor resents having even a fraction of his taxes go to funding theology as a university discipline. He thinks the idea that we can gain *knowledge* of God in a classroom to be a ludicrous pretense. He is not alone. Lesslie Newbigin's observation is astute: "We are living in a time when the ideal of knowledge is a knowledge of the physical world which can in principle be reduced to mathematical formulae which can be, if necessary, stored in an electronic computer."[5] Furthermore, there is so much data now available about the world that many of us suffer from information anxiety, the fear of either not having enough information or of not knowing how to process it.

Process is the operative term. Since Descartes's *Meditations on First Philosophy*, rationality has come to be seen as a method for obtaining certain knowledge. Descartes waved the green flag that started the race to find reliable methods or procedures for obtaining certain, or at least highly probable knowledge. As with Descartes's own method of doubt, the critical approach, no matter what the academic field, tends to privilege various kinds of suspicion in order to separate the chaff of appearance from the wheat of reality.

Is knowing God a matter of following certain procedures more than a matter of becoming a certain kind of person? Ellen Charry rightly points out one of the byproducts of the modern preoccupation with finding right methods: "Knowing the truth no longer implies loving it, wanting it, and being transformed by it, because the truth no longer brings the knower to God but to use information to subdue nature."[6] The other problem with methods inspired by scientific procedures is that they tend to yield more and more information about narrower and narrower slices of reality. There is no academic department that specializes in human flourishing.

Integration, wisdom and wholeness are even harder to achieve after the postmodern protest that objective methods are merely masks for the interpretations of a particular community. Francis Bacon's "idols of the mind"—bad intellectual habits like oversimplification—have become the idols of the modern lab (a too-elevated view of experimental methods) and now the idols

---

[5]Lesslie Newbigin, *Christ Our Eternal Contemporary* (Madras: The Christian Literature Society, 1968), 13.
[6]Ellen T. Charry, *By the Renewing of Your Minds: The Pastoral Function of Christian Doctrine* (Oxford: Oxford University Press, 1999), 236.

of the postmodern labyrinth. According to the radical postmodern prophets, academic methods are simply disguises for the institutional will to power. Reason is always/already situated, they say, and we are all caught in a web of language and social conventions from which there is no exit to "the way things are." The radical postmoderns deny the basic premise of the modern university: namely, that reason allows us to rise above our situatedness in gender, race, and class and attain a universal point of view. Whereas the modern university sought to build a cathedral of learning, the postmodern condition is the confusion of tongues that turns the ivory tower into a tower of Babel.

What is left is learning amid the ruins, a place to share a multiplicity of versions, none of which is authorized. In the absence of any overarching point of view, the *uni-* of the university is shaken. What is left after the shaking is one or another version of *-versity*: *diversity* or *adversity*. What becomes of wholeness now? What becomes of wisdom? Whereas in modernity the wise person was the one who lived according to universal reason, in postmodernity the wise person is a connoisseur of the varieties of local knowledge, a purveyor of many different ways.

Ronald Barnett, formerly Professor of Higher Education at the University of London, spent years asking, "What is a university?" He answers his own question by proposing a new role for the university. In a world where everything has become contestable, the university should not be a place where knowledge is handed on, but a place for learning to handle *ignorance*: "The task that the university performs supremely well is to enable individuals to live in a world where everything is infinitely contestable."[7] Inquiry that aims at knowledge and truth, he says, should be abandoned. "In generating uncertainty in its teaching and its research, the university can enable us to live in just that kind of world that the modern world has become." What is universal in today's university is *contestability*, the notion that everything that can be said can also be challenged.[8]

---

[7]Ronald Barnett, "What Role for University?" *The Independent*, June 26, 1997. www.independent .co.uk/news/education/education-news/what-role-for-university-1257935.html.

[8]Since I preached this sermon Professor Barnett has sought to recover the universal dimension of a university in a more hopeful vein, under the auspices of the "ecological university." He is now thinking of the university as a social institution that focuses on a variety of practical problems and aims at "emancipatory empiricism." In a world dominated by ideologies, he hopes the university can become a "feasible utopia." See Ronald Barnett, *Thinking and Rethinking the University: The Selected Works of Ronald Barnett* (New York: Routledge, 2015).

Unlike Cardinal Newman, who believed that theology had a crucial role to play in the university (namely, making sure that every other academic disciple did not exaggerate its own significance, thereby falling prey to reductionism), Professor Barnett is silent about the role of theology in today's university.[9] And yet, here we are. What counts as success in a Faculty of Divinity? If the knowledge of God is "infinitely contestable," do we have any means of knowing whether or not we are making progress?

THE KNOWLEDGE OF APOSTLES: WISDOM AND DISCIPLESHIP

Contrast the wisdom of Socrates with that of Solomon. "Let the wise hear and increase in learning" (Prov 1:5). The Hebrew term for "learning" [*leqaḥ*] derives from a root that can mean either "take" or "receive" (as in take or receive instruction). These two senses will structure the rest of what I say. First, then, learning as receiving.

The wisdom of the apostle. The apostle Paul mentions not the knowledge but the preaching of angels: "But even if . . . an angel from heaven should preach to you a gospel contrary to the one we preached to you, let him be accursed" (Gal 1:8). Paul is not boasting in his own genius, though he is defending his apostolic authority. What authority he has is based not on his own powers of ratiocination, or the intellectual discoveries of any other human being. Here is how Paul explains his knowledge of the gospel of God: "For I did not receive it from any man, nor was I taught it, but I received it through a revelation of Jesus Christ" (Gal 1:12).

Kierkegaard's essay "On the Difference Between a Genius and an Apostle" (1847) highlights the importance of receiving.[10] Apostles are those sent with a message that is not of their own devising. Apostolic truth—truth about the meaning of the whole summed up in Christ—eludes the grasp of genius. It is inaccessible to reason alone. The authoritative status of the apostle's knowledge is one of the key issues in the Corinthian correspondence. It does not take long for Paul to set out one of his main themes: namely, the "war of

---

[9] See John Henry Newman, *The Idea of a University* (Notre Dame, IN: Notre Dame University Press, 1982).

[10] Søren Kierkegaard, "On the Difference Between a Genius and an Apostle," *Addendum II in Kierkegaard's Writings, XXIV: The Book on Adler*, ed. Howard V. Hong and Edna H. Hong (Princeton, NJ: Princeton University Press, 1998), 173-88.

the wisdoms" between the wisdom of the wise (what a genius knows) and the wisdom of the cross (what an apostle knows).

Paul insists to the Corinthians that the gospel is not a new *sophia*, the latest theory, but rather something that contradicts all once and future human notions. Paul quotes God from Isaiah, "I will destroy the wisdom of the wise" (1 Cor 1:19, from Is 29:14). This should not surprise us. God has always been in the business of exposing idolatry for the sham it is. There is a sharp apostolic edge here, especially to us, people who allegedly have a special competence in the knowledge of God—what else is a Faculty of Divinity? What Paul asks of the Corinthians ought to give us pause too, whether or not we have tenure: "Where is the one who is wise?" (1 Cor 1:20). Paul's point is that what God has done in Christ confutes all manmade theologies, all human speculation as to the nature of divinity. "The judgment on the [world] is passed . . . not by reasoning, but by asserting an act of God."[11]

At this point the theologian might protest. To be sure, we couldn't know in advance what God would *do*, but reason alone can discover truths about God's *being*. To say this, however, is to place knowledge of God in the province of the genius, something accessible to reason alone. This is precisely what Paul contradicts: "The world did not know God through its wisdom" (1 Cor 1:21). God cannot be known merely by thinking about "a being than which nothing greater can be conceived." According to Scripture, we know God only because he has revealed himself in word and deed. God is a *who*, not a *what*, and we know God primarily because of what he has done. God is the one who brought Israel out of Egypt, the one who raised Jesus from the dead. Not even a genius could have anticipated that God would do these things. Paul goes further: God confutes the wisdom of the wise. Christ crucified is not simply unexpected, but foolishness. To the Jews who look for signs of the Messiah and Greeks who seek wisdom, the message that God is made known in Christ crucified is a virtual contradiction in terms, of the same category, says Gordon Fee, as "fried ice."[12]

Perhaps no theologian has put Paul's contrast between two kinds of

---

[11]Hans Conzelmann, *1 Corinthians*, Hermeneia (Philadelphia: Fortress, 1988), 43.

[12]Gordon D. Fee, *The First Epistle to the Corinthians* (Grand Rapids: Eerdmans, 1987), 75. Cf. C. K. Barrett: "What God has done in Christ crucified is a direct contradiction of human ideas of wisdom and power, yet it achieved what human wisdom and power fail to achieve." From *A Commentary on the First Epistle to the Corinthians* (New York: Harper & Row, 1968), 56.

wisdom to greater effect than Martin Luther in the theses of his 1518 *Heidelberg Disputation*. Instead of genius/apostle, Luther contrasts the "theology of glory" and the "theology of the cross." These are two ways of being a theologian: one that relies on the self's native capacities and one that proclaims the necessity of dying with Christ. The theology of glory refers to a wisdom that sees the invisible things of God through earthly things. Thomas Aquinas's analogy of being would be an example inasmuch as it extrapolates from creaturely goods to what God must be like as infinitely good. But Luther says a person deserves to be called a theologian only if they comprehend the visible things of God (e.g., glory and majesty) through the cross (e.g., humility and shame). The cross cancels out what we think we know about God through reason. "It [this worldly wisdom] is finished." And this is the scandal. The message of the cross means that people are unable to know God, speak of God or make themselves acceptable to God through their own resources. "Without the theology of the cross we will of necessity take credit for works ourselves and place trust in them."[13]

The wisdom of the apostle is thus of a wholly different order than Socratic wisdom. Formally, it is a matter of believing what we are told, first by Christ, and subsequently by those who impart his gospel. Materially, it is a matter of what God has done to set the world right through the cross and resurrection of Jesus. The wisdom of the apostle is the wisdom that comes in receiving (learning and believing) the gospel that salvation is the result not of what we do but of what the triune God has done for us in Christ.

The wisdom of the scholar-saint. Earlier I mentioned *faculty* as an ability or capacity for something. In the context of the university, it connotes an ability in knowledge. Yet the term also designates a particular group of people: a body of persons who have been deemed proficient to teach others, the members of a learned profession. I submit that a faculty of divinity is a community "set apart" for the knowledge of God. To study divinity is to embark on a sacred vocation. But what kind of wisdom is appropriate to the study of theology? Can we be theologians of the cross, in Luther's sense, in the university? Or does being a theologian of the cross require us to depart the groves of academe?

---

[13]Gerhard O. Forde, *On Being a Theologian of the Cross: Reflections on Luther's Heidelberg Disputation, 1518* (Grand Rapids: Eerdmans, 1997), 98.

Let me begin by calling your attention to Luther's focus on ways of being a theologian. His goal is not to commend a method of theology, but to encourage people to become theologians of the cross who call the thing what it actually is.[14] His concern is for persons, not procedures—call it Solomonic rather than Socratic wisdom. "The fear of the LORD is the beginning of knowledge" (Prov 1:7). A theologian of the cross sees things, including God, for what they are precisely by receiving the message of the cross. There are at least two ways to relate this to being a theologian in the context of the academy.

First, we need to retrieve the idea that it is rational to believe things on testimony. This is how we learn the wisdom of the apostles—by receiving what they say in the Scriptures. Interestingly enough a number of philosophers contend that testimony is as reliable a belief-forming faculty as memory or perception.[15] Those who fear the Lord carefully attend to and revere his Word. The fear of the Lord refers to an attitude of the heart that trusts the prophetic and apostolic testimony more than any other words.

Second, we need to appreciate the way the fear of the Lord and the theology of the cross together underline the importance of theologians becoming persons of intellectual and spiritual virtue. Luther refuses to acknowledge a theologian of glory as a true theologian because such a person relies on his or her own capacities (or genius). The theologian of glory is a person who succumbs to pride, the ultimate intellectual vice. Pride is a vice because a person who is proud is less likely to arrive at the truth. By contrast, intellectual virtues are habits of the mind that are conducive to the truth, that lead to "cognitive contact with reality."[16] Paul elsewhere encourages his readers to have the mind of Christ, which turns out to involve self-humbling obedience to the point of death—the theology of the cross (Phil 2:5-11). We deserve to be called theologians if we understand God, the world and others "through the cross." The theologian of the cross is a person of intellectual and spiritual virtue—in a word, a person of humility.

---

[14]Martin Luther, *Heidelberg Disputation*, thesis 21.

[15]See, for example, C. A. J. Coady, *Testimony: A Philosophical Study* (Oxford: Clarendon Press, 1995), and Jennifer Lackey and Ernest Sosa, eds., *The Epistemology of Testimony* (Oxford: Oxford University Press, 2006). The seminal figure in this discussion is Thomas Reid (1710–1796).

[16]Linda Trinkhaus Zagzebski, *Virtues of the Mind: An Inquiry Into the Nature of Virtue and the Ethical Foundations of Knowledge* (Cambridge: Cambridge University Press, 1996), 168.

Theology is unlike other fields of study because knowing God is not the same as knowing creatures. No other subject matter needs to be approached via the cross. But, just as important, no other knowledge results in the knower becoming like the known. To know God is to know the suffering of the cross, that is, the death of the old self. When we know God in Christ, we do not make mere cognitive contact; no, we who know God make covenantal contact with God—or rather, we make covenantal contact as we are covenantally contacted, for the initiative in the knowledge of God lies with God. God reaches out to us by his Son and Spirit. Moreover, to be in covenantal contact with God requires more than intellectual apprehension. To know *this* truth is to participate in it. To know God through the cross is to know the wisdom and power of God.

To make covenantal contact with God is to have personal knowledge. The light of knowledge of God is not the light of reason but "the light of the knowledge of glory of God in the face of Christ" (2 Cor 4:6). A face is not a fact to be proved or disproved by scientific procedures. A face, like a voice, calls forth a response from our whole person. We make contact with what is ultimately real in the face of Christ, and before this face disinterested objectivity is not possible. To make covenantal contact with the reality of the divine is not simply to cogitate a proposition but to commune with a person.

True knowledge of God leads to godliness. This means that we must conform to God rather than make God conform to our best thoughts about him. Can we be saints and scholars? Theology requires not a *sacrifice* of the intellect—turning off our minds, abandoning any criteria of truth and rationality and giving ourselves to sloppy thinking—but rather its *sanctification*. The way forward is not to evacuate but to evangelize the faculty of divinity: that is, to orient our knowledge of God to the theology of the cross.

WISDOM BROKEN FOR YOU: CRUCIFORM WHOLENESS

What about the wholeness or coherence that is the tacit promise of the university? Does the theology of the cross complete the deliverances of academic reason or subvert them? If wisdom is a matter of grasping the whole and fitting into it properly, to what extent does our academic work contribute to wisdom and wholeness? The term wholeness also connotes health. Wholeness pertains to wisdom inasmuch as wisdom is the ability to fit into the whole in a way that is conducive to human flourishing.

Wisdom and wholeness. Socratic wisdom involves knowing that you do not know. Other philosophers, such as Immanuel Kant, have also sought to determine the limits of reason. According to David Tracy, religious language and religious experience yield "limit experiences" (e.g., wonder, anxiety, joy) and "limit language" that call for "limit concepts," including the limit-concept of God.[17] Revelation concerns the disclosure of the whole (of reality) by the power of the whole (God). For Tracy, Jesus Christ is the revelation of God because he enacts his self-understanding (i.e., his relation to the whole) and thus communicates the meaning of the whole—of human life. The Gospels, in Tracy's words, are about "the disclosure of a certain limit-mode-of-being-in-the-world."[18] Say what?

Tracy's circumlocution is a function of the difficulty of his project: he is trying to give an account of Jesus Christ within the limits of phenomenological reason alone. Who does Tracy say that Christ is? Jesus is the symbolic representation of a human possibility (a way of being in the world) that is universal (i.e., essential). Jesus is the wisdom of God because he represents a permanent human possibility: namely, a trust in "the power of the whole"—faith. Tracy discovers at the heart of Christianity a fundamental trust in existence. Theology thus yields "a proper understanding of explicitly Christian faith [that] can render intellectually coherent and symbolically powerful that common secular faith which we share."[19]

Tracy is able to say what is universally true about Jesus, and to do so in an academically respectable way (that is, if one finds phenomenology respectable), but it is not clear that he has done justice to Paul's gospel. In what sense does the gospel proclaim what God has made new if the human possibility that Jesus represents has always/already been there? And what does the actual life of Jesus accomplish that his story does not, or for that matter the story of John the Baptist or of the martyrs of the faith?[20] Even poetic geniuses know what they know without having to be told.

---

[17]David Tracy, *Blessed Rage for Order: The New Pluralism in Theology* (New York: Seabury Press, 1975), 148.

[18]Ibid., 221.

[19]Ibid., 9.

[20]For a further critical analysis of Tracy's proposal, see my *Biblical Narrative in the Philosophy of Paul Ricoeur: A Study in Hermeneutics and Theology* (Cambridge: Cambridge University Press, 1990), 234-37.

By the way, the experiments with the child raised by wolves and the atheist washed up on shore in Walsh's novel, *The Knowledge of Angels*, do not end well. The priest charged with persuading the atheist of God's existence loses his faith, the atheist is executed for refusing to convert to Christianity and, while the girl does learn to speak, she ends up leaving the nuns and returning to the wolves. So much for the innate knowledge of God!

Brokenness and wholeness. "Let the wise hear and increase in learning, and the one who understands obtain guidance" (Prov 1:5). The second way we add to our learning, after *receiving* testimony, is by *taking*, as in "Take, eat."

The Lord's Table presents us with an object lesson, a visible enactment of what Christians have been told: the gospel. It is the mystery of salvation, the wisdom of God laid out on table in bread and wine. The Lord's Supper is a complex three-dimensional picture of Christ's Passion in the past, peace in the present and promise for the future: "For as often as you eat this bread and drink the cup, you proclaim the Lord's death until he comes" (1 Cor 11:26). There is holy wisdom in the breaking of Christ's body, and in the breaking of bread. There is fearsome wisdom in the shedding of blood, and in the sharing of wine. Wisdom and wholeness are bought at the cost of Christ's broken body. No genius could have predicted that God would make all things new through Jesus' obedient assumption of our sinful condition.

It is not enough to have the knowledge of angels—observation from a theoretical distance. Wisdom does more than register facts or admire from afar. To be wise is to know how to live out the knowledge of the cross of Christ, what Paul calls "the power of God" (1 Cor 1:24). The wisdom of an apostle involves personal participation, an active walking in Jesus' way, including taking up our cross daily ("I die every day!" 1 Cor 15:31). To live like Jesus is to love like him, and that means pouring ourselves out for others. A theological education without following or fellowship is incomplete: broken rather than whole, foolish rather than wise.

When we participate in the Lord's Supper, we live out what we know ("He is risen") and become practical demonstrations of Christian wisdom. Indeed, the Lord's Supper contains more wisdom than we can say. In breaking bread together in memory, celebration and hope, we know more than we can tell. For when we fellowship together around Christ's table, we are participating in wholeness: in the reconciliation in Christ. The Lord's Supper is a parable of the kingdom of God.

Christian witness to the way of Christ is summed up here, in our table fellowship. In the Lord's Supper we are living out the wisdom and power of God: namely, communion with God and others. To celebrate the Lord's Supper is to celebrate the person, work and living presence of Christ, and to begin to embody this knowledge in forms of corporate life. Here is the wisdom that makes the broken creature whole, and that makes of many one. This, I believe, is the ultimate goal of theological education: not the knowledge of angels or geniuses but the wisdom of apostles and disciples who receive with understanding what they are told in the gospel and who know how to live out what it proclaims: reconciliation in Christ and the fellowship of the Spirit.

THE MAN WITH THE X-RHO EYES

The following sermon is well travelled, but the story on which it comments has legs that are even longer. I preached versions of this sermon in three different places, to three different ethnicities over three decades: at a Trinity Evangelical Divinity School chapel in the 1980s, in my local Church of Scotland in Edinburgh in the 1990s and in a Chinese church in Illinois in 2009. It is a fitting conclusion for the present collection of essays for several reasons. First, it reminds us that the sermon is a quintessentially theological act: to preach the Word of God is to set forth in speech what is true in the light of Jesus Christ. Second, it reminds us that theology exists to serve the church by contributing to its edification, especially by helping people of faith come to a more mature understanding of what it means to live to God and live in Christ through the Spirit. Third, it treats the theme of faith coming to understanding "seeing" the presence and activity of the invisible God in the midst of the everyday and trusting in the truth of God for us. Fourth, it underlines the importance of having imaginations formed and disciplined by the Word of God. Fifth and finally, it reminds us that God's Word—especially its stories and metaphors— opens the eyes of our hearts (our imaginations), freeing us from the prevailing pictures of God and the good life in our cultures that too often hold God's people captive to fear and anxiety.

Once when my two daughters were younger they proposed playing a rather macabre game. "Which of the five senses would you be most willing to give up?" they asked. I have since learned that this is a popular game among college students (and others with too much time on their hands), and you can find a number of conversation threads on the topic online.

In almost all the surveys, people were most likely to give up the sense of smell, though many were probably not aware how closely smell and taste are connected. A bigger proportion than I would have guessed chose hearing, largely because they either knew or felt that they could learn sign language and lip reading and therefore compensate. As the surveys show, however, for most people vision is the most precious of the five senses.

TECHNOLOGIES FOR IMPROVING EYESIGHT: X-RAY VISION

We worry about failing eyesight, or about the insidious disease of glaucoma, which happens to run in my family. I can sympathize with the character of Sam Weller in Dickens's *The Pickwick Papers*, when he was cross-examined as a witness during a trial. The attorney is unhappy with his testimony and asks sarcastically, "Have you a pair of eyes, Mr. Weller?" to which the Cockney manservant answers: "Yes, I have a pair of eyes, and that's just it. If they wos a pair o' patent double million magnifyin' gas microscopes of hextra power, p'raps I might be able to see through a flight o' stairs and a deal door; but bein' only eyes, you see my wision's limited."[1]

Spectacles of science. Scientists have worked for centuries to expand Sam Weller's vision, and ours. Thanks to new technologies we can see in the dark and deep into space. Science is pushing back the boundaries of the invisible. Today we have more instruments for seeing better than ever before—yet we may also be blinder than ever. We have telescopes and microscopes for seeing things far away and very small, but we are still unable to put life's meaning in proper context. We have otoscopes for looking into the ear, but they don't facilitate our hearing of God's Word. We have devices for magnetic resonance imaging that allow us to visualize the structure of the body in any plane, but we are still unable to locate the soul. We can look again and again at the odd things people do on YouTube, yet we still have trouble

---

[1]Charles Dickens, *The Pickwick Papers* (London: The Amalgamated Press, 1905), 462.

understanding our children, parents, neighbors and those even stranger "others" who neither look nor talk like us. Where is the moral vision we have lost in video, the spiritual vision we have lost in fiber optics?

In technology we trust—at least until it gets out of hand, as it does in Roger Corman's 1963 film *The Man with the X-ray Eyes*. Although the film was made in just three weeks, it won the Best Film Award at the First International Festival of Science Fiction Films (where the trophies are not Oscars but Silver Spaceships). Like most science fiction films, *The Man with the X-ray Eyes* is not just out to entertain but to address our deepest anxieties. Science fiction films are always ultimately about our present fears: in this case, about where science and technology are taking us. Corman's film is an early example of a now common genre that poses the question: Will we still be human if we make use of enhancement technologies?

The film tells the story of a scientist, Dr. Xavier, played by Ray Milland, who loses government funding for his research but decides to press on with his experiment anyway, using himself as a guinea pig. He develops eye drops that he hopes will enhance his sight to the point of giving him x-ray vision, but his newfound abilities prove disastrous. At first, the drops seem harmless: Dr. Xavier amazes his friends by telling them what's in their pockets or behind closed doors. He finds he is able to do what Sam Weller could only joke about—see through doors. The experiment quickly becomes no laughing matter, however. X-ray vision turns out to be not particularly desirable. Think about it—if you're always seeing through the surface of things, you miss out on colors, clothes, even smiles. That's the worst of it: with x-ray vision you can't see people's faces, just the skeletal movements of their skulls. X-ray vision drains the brightness from things, leaving one with a bare-bones, monochrome view of the world.

This is the moral of Corman's film. The man with the x-ray eyes eventually loses the ability to see the world in human terms (the way God designed us to see, we might add). The drops do not expand but *reduce* his vision. This indeed is the besetting temptation of the scientist: to reduce reality to the basic elements that are the special focus of their own discipline or method. Dr. Xavier suffers from tunnel vision. He sees through a magnifying glass darkly. Unable to see the world the way humans were meant to, he begins to go mad (perhaps because he never found his special niche in society—in airport security, of course). The film ends as Dr. Xavier wanders aimlessly into, of all things, a revival tent meeting. The preacher asks if he would like to be saved, to which Dr. Xavier replies, "Saved? No, I came to tell you what I see."

Spectacles of Scripture. We live in a culture that privileges both technology and sight. More and more Americans come from Missouri, metaphorically speaking: they have to see things before they can believe them. *The Man with the X-ray Eyes* is a cinematic parable, a celluloid prophetic word to the wise. It asks, what are the tools or technology we trust to give us the right view of things? For many, reality is a function of what, and how far, we can see. Despite advances in optical technologies, our culture is suffering from an insidious disease: glaucoma of the spirit. This-worldly pressures distort our spiritual vision. We see through tunnels, perceiving only wealth, health, fame and so forth. In stark contrast, Christian faith is about perceiving what lies beyond the empirical, past what we observe with our physical eyes. More than sight we need "hindsight, "insight" and "foresight"—the ability to understand the past, present and future respectively—and we get these, as we shall see, by turning our eyes on the biblical Jesus.

Calvin considers an optical technology at the other end of the spectrum from Dr. Xavier's. Calvin describes the Bible as the "spectacles of faith," in two senses. First, the Bible recounts the great things God has done (the exodus is the great spectacle of the Old Testament, and the resurrection of the New Testament). Second (and more to Calvin's point), the Bible functions like a pair of eyeglasses—corrective lenses—that enable us to see the world in a new way, as it truly is before God. Without Scripture, we are like "old or bleary-eyed men and those with weak vision," who can scarcely construe two words of a beautiful volume like the Book of Nature.[2] Thanks to Scripture, however, we can "see" what God has done for us and what God is like. Just as importantly, because knowledge of God and knowledge of ourselves are a package deal, we ourselves come into focus only when we come to see God as Creator and Redeemer. No scientific instrument or eye drop can do that. The Bible is therefore the Christian's most important tool for correcting faulty (i.e., fallen) vision.

---

[2]John Calvin, *Institutes of the Christian Religion*, trans. Ford Lewis Battles (Philadelphia: Westminster Press, 1960), I.vi.1.

ELISHA AND THE PROPHETIC WORD: TOWARD X-RHO VISION

When our daughters were young we routinely encouraged them to "put on the spectacles of the future," a colorful (Reformed) metaphor about the importance of being mindful of the consequences of their actions. The books of Kings and Chronicles make a similar point about the importance of the kings of Israel putting on their spectacles (the Word of the Lord) and the consequences of not doing so. Those who remembered God's covenant and obeyed God's law, like David, "did what was right in the eyes of the LORD" (1 Kings 15:5). By way of contrast, those who forgot the covenant and disobeyed the law "did what was evil in the sight of the LORD" (2 Kings 8:27). God sent his prophets to the kings of Israel to be talking spectacles: the prophets typically describe the future before God brings it about.[3]

Elisha as "seer" and "sayer." One of the main themes in the book of Kings is God's sovereign reign over Israel. Israel's request for a human king stemmed largely from their desire to be like the other nations (1 Sam 8:5, 20). The whole point of being a "holy nation," however, was that Israelites were *not* supposed to be like everybody else. Instead, they were to be set apart, devoted to God's service, not some human monarch's. Israel was to be a light to the nations in her dedication to doing God's Word. The church, too, is a "holy nation" (1 Pet 2:9), a people set apart for the sake of following God's living Word, Jesus Christ. The real threat to Israel, and to us, was less the temptation to mistake human kings for God than to go chasing other gods—idols that are nothing more than empty illusions. One of the subplots of the books of Kings is that when the times get tough, the weak get idols.

The real heroes of 1 and 2 Kings are not the kings but the prophets, also called "seers" because they received visions from God. Prophetic seeing was theological, not technological. It had everything to do with perceiving, and then setting forth in speech, the depth-dimension of things, the meaning events have in relation to God. Prophets don't get private screenings. What the prophets saw they had to publicly proclaim. Prophets were therefore "sayers" too, who ministered God's Word both by reporting what they saw and by serving as God's mouthpiece. Prophecy involves a speaking forth, a forthtelling, as well as, sometimes, a foretelling. The prophets had a burning

---

[3] Iain Provan, "Kings," in T. D. Alexander and Brian S. Rosner, eds., *New Dictionary of Biblical Theology* (Downers Grove, IL: InterVarsity Press, 2000), 184.

obligation to proclaim to others what God showed them: "Thus saith the Lord!" Often the prophetic message was unpopular—people prefer their own way of looking at the world to what God has to say about it. Isaiah has a harsh indictment for such close-minded, hardhearted people:

> For they are a rebellious people,
>   lying children,
> children unwilling to hear
>   the instruction of the LORD;
> who say to the seers, "Do not see,"
>   and to the prophets, "Do not prophesy to us what is right;
> speak to us smooth things,
>   prophesy illusions." (Is 30:9-10)

The false prophet sees and says what is not true: that way lies emptiness and death. By contrast, true prophets minister God's Word, whose consequence is truth and life.

On one level, 2 Kings 6:8-23 concerns military strategy and the wars of nations. The situation has a strangely contemporary feel, not least because Israel and Syria are still eyeing one another warily today, just as they were in Elisha's time. Now I'm far-sighted, but not nearly as much as Elisha. He used his abilities as a "seer" to inform Israel's king of Syria's troop movements, allowing him to elude the Syrian army. At first the king of Syria wonders whether there is a spy in his war cabinet. Then he learns that it is Elisha who is serving as a one-man spy satellite, a kind of prophetic bugging device: "Elisha . . . tells the king of Israel the words that you speak in your bedroom" (6:12). The frustrated king sends horses, chariots and a great army to a small village to capture one man: "Go and *see* where he is" (6:13). Seeing, of course, is the operative term, and the source of the story's irony—for seeing is the one thing they do *not* do. Instead, they not only fail to recognize Elisha but follow him into enemy territory. This is about as close to slapstick as we get in the Bible: Keystone Cops, meet the Syrian cavalry!

Horses and fires and chariots, oh my! The focus of our passage, however, is Elisha and his unnamed helper, the "servant of the man of God" (6:15). The servant is the easiest to identify with. It is the servant who first spots the horses and chariots of the Syrian army that the king had sent to Dothan in search of Elisha. It must have been an intimidating experience to wake up and find yourself surrounded by a hostile force. Elisha's servant cries, "Alas, my master! What shall we do?" (6:15). This is the cry of one who sees all too well that, humanly speaking, the odds are stacked against him. It's the cry of Peter who can no longer hear his master's voice or walk on water because he sees only the wind and the waves (Mt 14:30). Like Peter, Elisha's servant sinks into despair, utterly overwhelmed.

We don't need an army surrounding us to feel that life is overwhelming. We only have to look and see what is happening in our world: crime, war, injustice, poverty, racism, unemployment—the list goes on. Many of us often feel over-whelmed on a personal level too. We struggle with insecurity, the fear of failure and the sense that we will never be able to escape from ourselves: our bad habits, disintegrating relationships and physical suffering. We cannot sleep; we lose our appetite; we are depressed. To feel overwhelmed is to feel overpowered: outwitted, outplayed and outlasted. We can identify with Elisha's servant.

What Elisha does next is a model of pastoral care. He tells his servant, "Do not be afraid, for those who are with us are more than those who are with them" (6:16). I wonder whether the servant found this altogether reassuring. In context, Elisha's reply must have sounded rather dubious. Next to Elisha's visionary Don Quixote, the servant resembles the pragmatic realist Sancho Panza. Despite Elisha's composure, all the servant can see is a hostile force ready to crush them. As the story progresses, however, we see that the servant is suffering from limited vision: secular nearsightedness, a kind of spiritual astigmatism. So Elisha prays to the Lord, "O LORD, please open his eyes that he may see" (6:17).

As many commentators observe, sight plays a crucial role throughout this story.[4] The episode begins with the king of Syria sending his men to "see" where Elisha is so that he can capture him (6:13). Elisha serves as a catalyst both for sight and blindness. In the verse immediately following his prayer to open his servant's eyes, Elisha prays that the Syrian army be struck with blindness. They are able to follow Elisha, but he leads them to Samaria and into the clutches of Israel's king. So the Syrian army that had been sent to "see" Elisha ends up not seeing anything at all until Elisha prays for their eyes to be opened. Then they see that they are themselves surrounded.

The Lord answers Elisha's prayer, opening the servant's eyes (6:17): "And he saw, and behold, the mountain was full of horses and chariots of fire all around

---

[4]See, for example, Peter Leithart, *1 & 2 Kings* (Grand Rapids: Brazos, 2006), 201.

Elisha" (6:17). In the space of just two verses, then, there is a sight/blindness reversal. The man who was blind now sees, and the army that had come to see is now blind. Sound familiar? It should, because Jesus works a similar reversal in John 9. He opens the eyes of the man who was born blind, showing that the Pharisees are actually the blind ones who cannot see who Jesus is. Jesus says, "For judgment I came into this world, that those who do not see may see, and those who see may become blind" (Jn 9:39). Jesus is the light of the world.

Elisha's name means "God saves" or "God is salvation." This is significant, for what Elisha sees and enables his servant to see is nothing less than the saving power of God. Jesus' name too means "God saves."[5]

What Elisha's servant sees is the mountain "full of horses and chariots of fire all around Elisha" (6:17). Excuse me: flaming go-carts? Talk about hot rods! What were these fiery, flying chariots? Some commentators—not the ones who teach in seminaries but the kind who have their own websites—suggest that what Elisha's servant really saw were UFOs! Our text itself is less interested in the technical specifications of this army than in confessing the presence of God, the great king. Chariots are, after all, symbols of royal power, and fire represents God's presence.

Some commentators argue that verses 15-17 are a later addition to the story because they contribute nothing to the plot. But on the contrary, the horses and chariots of fire play an indispensable role, materially regarding the theme of sight, and formally regarding the literary technique of ironic reversal.[6] This is not the first time horses and chariots of fire have appeared in the Elisha narrative. They are the means by which Elijah was taken up into heaven, and are thus tied to Elisha's role as Elijah's successor—not least because Elisha sees them, perhaps an indication of Elisha's special prophetic insight (2 Kings 2:9-13).[7] It is also possible that the horses and chariots of fire are associated with the blinding light that confuses the Syrian army into following Elisha into a trap.[8]

---

[5]Elijah is identified in the Gospels with John the Baptist, just one of many details, in addition to the etymology of their names, that establishes a link between Jesus and Elisha (see Iain Provan, "Elisha," in *New Dictionary of Biblical Theology*, 457).

[6]In this I follow Rachelle Gilmour, "A Note on the Horses and Chariots of Fire at Dothan," *Zeitschrift für die alttestamentlich Wissenschaft* 125 no. 2 (2013): 308-13.

[7]So Gilmour, "A Note on the Horses and Chariots of Fire at Dothan," 312.

[8]Leithart says that the horses and chariots of fire are the Lord's glory, and that the prophet, as one who speaks God's powerful word, is the true power and defense of Israel (*1 & 2 Kings*, 176).

The horses and chariots of fire belong to a heavenly host: not choirs (cf. Lk 2:13) but legions of angels—a "salvation army." Remember that Elisha first *says* "those who are with us are more than those who are with them" (6:16) but it is not until the man *sees* the horses and chariots that he understands how reliable the prophetic word is.

It is prayer that opens the servant's eyes. This too is a ministry of the prophetic word. The result of Elisha's words is a new kind of sight: the servant sees the world as Elisha sees it, with depth of vision, filled with the presence and provision of God. To speak of seer-sayer vision is not to contrast what we see with what we hear. Rather, it is to say that we see certain aspects of reality only by first hearing and believing the Word of God. This prophetic word—which as we know from the New Testament is ultimately about Jesus Christ, God's gracious provision for the world (Lk 24:27; 2 Pet 1:19)—opens our eyes to dimensions of reality unperceived by physicists and undreamt by philosophers.

Faith, Christ and X-Rho Vision

Elisha's servant is overwhelmed. Elisha prays, the eyes of his servant are opened and he sees the salvation of God. He too becomes a man with X-Rho eyes. The more accurate term is not "X-Rho" but "Chi-Rho" eyes. These are the first two capital letters of the Greek spelling of the name *Christos* (X, "ch" and P, "r"). Early Christians superimposed these letters to stand for Christ and his cross, since that is what the letters resemble when put together.

The Chi Rho sign, one of the earliest christograms, was used as early as the third century. Variations of the sign are often found in catacombs. It is also indirectly connected to the story of 2 Kings 6. According to the church historian Eusebius, the Roman emperor Constantine reportedly saw a vision in the sky of the Chi Rho sign on the eve of the Battle of the Milvian Bridge in AD 312, complete with a Latin caption: *in hoc signes vinces* ("in this sign conquer"). Constantine ordered the Chi Rho to be emblazoned on his soldier's shields. After the battle was won Constantine adopted the Chi Rho as the official imperial insignia. We do well to remember that our battle as Christians is not with flesh and blood but with powers and principalities, and this includes ideas and ideologies—evil empires that attack not our homeland security (at least not directly) but our heads and hearts. That is where the real battle is being waged between the kingdoms of light and darkness (Col 1:13).

Today there are more sophisticated technologies for expanding our vision than ever before, including retinal implants that, like cochlear implants, take over the function of damaged organs. Despite these new and powerful tools, people continue to live in darkness, blind to the reality of God's gracious provision in Jesus Christ. X-ray vision and its progeny focus on what science can help us to observe empirically and dominate our age, to the detriment of Elisha's Chi Rho vision. But science is not the problem—for, as our text makes clear, Elisha's servant initially trusted only what he could physically see. In this respect he was like T. E. Lawrence, who famously said that by "reality" he meant "shops like Selfridges, and motor buses, and the Daily Express."[9] The irony is that we risk falling prey to the same vision/blindness reversal as the Syrian army. They were sent to see and were blinded. We are a visual culture with a vision problem: "Where there is no vision, the people perish" (Prov 29:18, KJV).[10]

What is Chi-Rho vision and how can we get it? Chi-Rho vision is simply the faith that perceives and lays hold of Christ, the saving presence and power of God, and it comes "from hearing, and hearing through the word of Christ" (Rom 10:17). The prophetic word is the tool that enables the vision. The vision need not be literal: Chi-Rho vision, unlike an x-ray, is not a function of something physical, like electromagnetic radiation. Rather, faith is "the conviction of things not seen" (Heb 11:1). Elisha was a sayer, a minister of a reassuring word: "those who are with us are more than those who are with them" (2 Kings 6:16). Faith's seeing requires more than verbal instruction, however. Elisha also had to pray that the Spirit would open his servant's eyes. Word and Spirit together bring about Chi-Rho vision.

The ministry of word and Spirit is eye opening, but not in the same way that LASIK surgery is. What kind of eyes are we talking about? Paul's prayer for the Ephesians provides the crucial clue. Like Elisha before him, Paul

---

[9]Letter to W. Hurley, April 1, 1929, cited in J. M. and M. J. Cohen, eds., *The Penguin Dictionary of Modern Quotations*, 2nd ed. (New York: Penguin, 1980), 198.
[10]The ESV translation reads, "Where there is no prophetic vision the people lack restraint [let loose]."

prays that his words (i.e., his letter) will open the eyes of his readers to the great truths of the faith, fueling hope and spurring love. In particular, Paul prays that God will enlighten "the eyes of your heart" (Eph 1:18). When the eyes of our hearts are opened, we are able to know (see!) the hope to which God has called us, the riches of the glorious inheritance of the saints and the immeasurable greatness of God's power (Eph 1:19)—and, why not? the horses and chariots of fire too.

Chi-Rho vision refers to what we can see with the eyes of our hearts when prayer opens us to the truth of the prophetic word. What is the truth of the prophetic word? In a word, *Christ*. Christ is God's gracious provision for Israel and the world's salvation. All the stories about Israel written by the prophets were ultimately written for the instruction of the church (1 Cor 10:11; 1 Pet 1:10-12). We also know that everything in Moses and the prophets ultimately (typologically) refers to Christ (Lk 24:27). As Richard Hays says, "The Gospels teach us how to read the Old Testament, and—at the same time—the Old Testament teaches us how to read the Gospels."[11] This is true of our passage too, which is perhaps best read in conjunction with the story of Jesus' healing of the man born blind in John 9.

What are the "eyes of the heart"? In Scripture, the heart concerns the thinking, feeling and willing center at the core of our personhood. Paul is clearly thinking about the understanding of faith, but he may also be referring indirectly to what I describe as *imagination*: the ability to see patterns in things, the ability to see how all things fit together. To see with the eyes of the heart is to see the world through the spectacles of faith, that is, the sum total of the Bible stories to which Christ is the key. Faith is not physical sight, but it is a way of seeing—a biblically shaped imaginative viewing that sees that everything ultimately fits together in Christ.[12] Chi-Rho vision is the ability to see Christ as the one through whom and for whom everything was made (Col 1:16) and in whom everything coheres (Col 1:17). To see with Chi-Rho eyes is to have more than peripheral theological vision: it is to have a focal awareness of the presence and activity of Jesus Christ in all situations.

---

[11]Richard B. Hays, *Reading Backwards: Figural Christology and the Fourfold Gospel Witness* (Waco, TX: Baylor University Press, 2014), 4.

[12]Cf. Hays's comment about the disciples on the way to Emmaus who were discussing what happened to Jesus at Jerusalem: "The puzzled Emmaus disciples have all the facts but lack the pattern that makes them meaningful" (*Reading Backwards*, 14).

Don't wait to be surrounded by enemies before you use your Chi-Rho vision. It is as necessary for daily life as it is for crisis situations. The Christian life is more like a series of minor skirmishes than Armageddon. We all need to learn how to see everyday, ordinary life in the extraordinary light of God's Word: "For we walk by faith, not by [physical] sight" (2 Cor 5:7).

Faith is the ability to see with the eyes of the heart in the light of Scripture's testimony to God's gracious provision in Jesus Christ. Faith sees and understands everything that happens by viewing it in gospel perspective. *Perspective* is the key term.[13] To put something into perspective is to see what truly matters in a particular situation. To have perspective is to see that what is most visible or immediate may not be what counts most. It takes imagination to put things into the broadest perspective, to see things from the perspective of eternity. Yet it is only from this perspective that we begin to appreciate what is ultimately real and truly reliable. Jesus says, "Heaven and earth will pass away, but my words will not pass away" (Mt 24:35). This saying puts things in perspective, as do the rest of the Scriptures.

The person with Chi-Rho eyes sees the world as it truly is, as something God is with and for. Chi-Rho vision means viewing the world in gospel perspective. Chi-Rho vision is faith's imagining the world the Scripture imagines, and this means seeing our own situation, particularly in moments when we are tempted to feel overwhelmed, as full of horses and chariots of fire: namely, the gracious power and provision of God in Christ through the Spirit. After all, Jesus was a divine warrior too. On the cross, he defeated the power of sin, death and evil. Those are the same forces we struggle with today.

Philip Bliss's nineteenth-century hymn "Dare to Be a Daniel" celebrates the steadfastness of the Christian. I dare you to be an Elisha: a man or woman with Chi-Rho vision who grasps the reality of Jesus Christ through faith's prayerful hearing of the prophetic and apostolic word. Let the Word of God dwell in you richly, shaping your worldview and your life, the eyes and the desires of your heart. Dare to be an Elisha. Discern the divine depth-dimension of the everyday world. Read the Bible, both Old and New Testaments, with eyes open to seeing Christ. And, like Elisha, become the kind of person who is able to expand other people's vision too, opening up the

---

[13]I discuss perspective as a "sapiential virtue" in *The Drama of Doctrine: A Canonical-Linguistic Approach to Christian Theology* (Louisville, KY: Westminster John Knox, 2005), 334-35.

eyes of their hearts and encouraging them to see the greater power of Christ in midst of overwhelming situations. In a world filled with the spiritually nearsighted and sightless, let us have the courage to live as men and women with Chi-Rho eyes, sharing our vision with others: "One thing I do know, that though I was blind, now I see!" (Jn 9:25). Dare to be an Elisha—a person who looks at the world, and God's Word, with the X-Rho eyes of the heart.

NAME INDEX

SUBJECT INDEX

SCRIPTURE INDEX

ALSO BY KEVIN J. VANHOOZER

**First Theology: God,
Scripture and Hermeneutics**
978-0-8308-2681-0

and (with Daniel Treier)

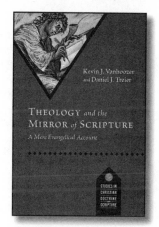

**Theology and the Mirror
of Scripture: A Mere
Evangelical Account**
978-0-8308-4076-2

Finding the Textbook You Need

The IVP Academic Textbook Selector
is an online tool for instantly finding the IVP books
suitable for over 250 courses across 24 disciplines.

---

ivpacademic.com